ALTERNATIVES *to* ECONOMIC GLOBALIZATION

SECOND EDITION / UPDATED AND EXPANDED

# ALTERNATIVES *to* ECONOMIC GLOBALIZATION

## ⟦ *A Better World Is Possible* ⟧

~

A REPORT OF THE
INTERNATIONAL FORUM ON GLOBALIZATION

JOHN CAVANAGH AND JERRY MANDER, EDITORS

### *Contributors:*

Sarah Anderson
Debi Barker
Maude Barlow
Walden Bello
Robin Broad
John Cavanagh
Tony Clarke
Edward Goldsmith
Randall Hayes
Colin Hines
Antonia Juhasz

Andrew Kimbrell
David Korten
Sara Larrain
Jerry Mander
Victor Menotti
Helena Norberg-
Hodge
Simon Retallack
Vandana Shiva
Victoria Tauli-Corpuz
Lori Wallach

BK

BERRETT-KOEHLER PUBLISHERS, INC.
San Francisco

schroth

**Berrett-Koehler Publishers, Inc.**
235 Montgomery Street, Suite 650
San Francisco, CA 94104-2916
Tel: (415) 288-0260   Fax: (415) 362-2512
www.bkconnection.com

### Ordering Information

**Quantity sales.** Special discounts are available on quantity purchases by corporations, associations, and others. For details, contact the "Special Sales Department" at the Berrett-Koehler address above.
**Individual sales.** Berrett-Koehler publications are available through most bookstores. They can also be ordered direct from Berrett-Koehler: Tel: (800) 929-2929; Fax: (802) 864-7626; www.bkconnection.com
**Orders for college textbook/course adoption use.** Please contact Berrett-Koehler: Tel: (800) 929-2929; Fax: (802) 864-7626.
**Orders by U.S. trade bookstores and wholesalers.** Please contact Publishers Group West, 1700 Fourth Street, Berkeley, CA 94710. Tel: (510) 528-1444; Fax: (510) 528-3444.

Berrett-Koehler and the BK logo are registered trademarks of Berrett-Koehler Publishers, Inc.

Printed in the United States of America

Berrett-Koehler books are printed on long-lasting acid-free paper. When it is available, we choose paper that has been manufactured by environmentally responsible processes. These may include using trees grown in sustainable forests, incorporating recycled paper, minimizing chlorine in bleaching, or recycling the energy produced at the paper mill.

LIBRARY OF CONGRESS CATALOGING-IN-PUBLICATION DATA
Alternatives to economic globalization : a better world is possible /
John Cavanagh and Jerry Mander, editors.—2nd ed., updated and expanded
p. cm.
"A report of the International Forum on Globalization"
Includes bibliographical references and index.
ISBN 1-57675-303-4
1. International economic relations.
2. Globalization.
3. Economic development.
I. Cavanagh, John.
II. Mander, Jerry.
III. International Forum on Globalization. Alternatives Task Force.
HF1359 .A547 2004
337—dc22    2004046315

SECOND EDITION

08 07 06 05 04 03 04    10 9 8 7 6 5 4 3 2 1

Project management, design, and composition: BookMatters, Berkeley
Copyediting: Sandra Beris; Proofreading: Janet Reed Blake; Indexing: Ken DellaPenta

# Contents

# Boxes

# Preface to the Second Edition

Since mid-2002 when the original manuscript of the first edition of this book was completed, the world has gone through dramatic changes. The military responses to the terrorist attacks of 9-11 have polarized world opinion and the body politic, driving great wedges into what had formerly seemed to be firm alliances and bringing entirely new and unexpected power shifts among nations. This is reflected not only in military terms but in others as well, including economic alliances and power centers, creating a new context for discussions about globalization. In a world that is increasingly alarmed by U.S. unilateralism, we have seen counterbalancing efforts from new European alignments, new South American alignments, and new alliances of the world's poorest nations—all of these in reaction to the apparent reach by the United States toward furthering its vision of some kind of "democratic" military and economic empire under its own domination.

Another new important counterbalancing force is global civil society, as reflected in the massive street protests over both war and globalization. In early 2003, the *New York Times* termed global public opinion "a second superpower."

The ever more visible failure of the economic experiment we variously call *economic globalization, neoliberalism,* or *corporate globalization* to live up to any of its own announced goals—and despite rhetoric to the contrary, to be transparently and obviously indifferent to such goals, especially those benefiting the poor countries—has led the poorest nations on earth into a kind of rebellion against the richest nations. This burst forth in late 2003 at the

WTO meeting in Cancun and at the Miami meeting of the proposed Free Trade Area of the Americas. It is likely that the international public resistance to American unilateralism and militarism in Iraq emboldened the many previously coerced nations to rise against the phony deals and self-serving offers from the great powers, offers that they had clearly learned from previous WTO rounds were not designed to benefit them. But the net result is that two movements—peace and global justice—seem now to be flirting with merger; when one sees colonial behavior in both military *and* economic activity, the distinctions start to blur.

In any case it became clear to the authors of this volume that it was necessary to include a new context for the discussion of globalization, and we have done so in our new introduction, "Turning Point," which follows right after this preface. This introduction contains our reflections on the impacts of the Cancun and Miami debacles, as well as recent U.S. military adventures. (In addition to the text, there is a new box by Antonia Juhasz of the IFG staff concerning the way the military occupation in Iraq has been directly used to further a draconian free market ideology and to pry open pathways for global corporations.)

We are writing this in May 2004. As far as we know, *Alternatives to Economic Globalization: A Better World Is Possible* remains the only comprehensive attempt to answer the question most asked after Seattle: "If you are not for globalization, then what are you for?" Other documents address pieces of an alternative to economic globalization, but there has been no overall synthesis besides this one. This was and remains a central motivation for this book: to create a comprehensive menu of ideas and actions toward alternatives to economic globalization that are rapidly emerging at the local, national, and global levels.

We have made significant revisions throughout this second edition, adding several new chapters, considerable new material in prior chapters, and updates throughout.

Following the introduction, we have arranged the book into three sections. Part 1, "A System in Crisis," provides a critical look at the ideas and instruments of globalization. Chapter 1, "Conflicting Worldviews" speaks of just that: the enormous gap between the way globalists see the world and the way civil society tends to; that gap is at the root of many problems.

Chapter 2 describes the central theories of the globalization experiment and reports on the latest failures of these theories to realize their stated goals. (Readers of the first edition will find two new boxes, one on the relationship of globalization to climate change, by Edward Goldsmith of *The Ecologist,* and the other on a hot issue in the 2004 U.S. presidential campaign: outsourcing and job loss. This was written by Sarah Anderson and John Cavanagh of the Institute for Policy Studies.)

The third chapter examines the bureaucracies that emerged from the Bretton Woods meetings of 1944, when the current experiment in global design was conceived. We look closely at the performance of the World Bank, the International Monetary Fund, and the World Trade Organization, with passing references to other major trade agreements and their unfortunate consequences. There are also updated boxes: "Global Economic Apartheid," by Robin Broad and John Cavanagh, and "Argentina and the IMF and the World Bank," by Sarah Anderson.

Part 2 of the book, "Alternatives in Action," starts with chapter 4, which discusses the ten central principles that a new global economic system should further, a new hierarchy of values that is the opposite of the present one that places corporations and their profits at the top. Some of the principles have been expanded from the first edition.

Chapter 5 raises a new and controversial argument, that elements of the commons—both local and global—should be firmly excluded from the global trading system. Some of these elements, like freshwater, the oceans, the air and sky, and biodiversity, are things that human beings have always expected to share as the natural right of all people but are now seeing privatized by various means, with devastating outcomes. We also raise the issue of what we call "the modern commons" of government services that we have come to depend on in the modern world.

Chapter 6 looks more deeply at one of the more controversial stances we have collectively taken. We have concluded that a centralized global economic model not only does not work but *cannot* work. Its most intractable problem is that it has moved power, authority, and activity out of the hands of the people who are most directly affected in local communities. *Subsidiarity* is the word now being used to describe a reversal of power, away from the global toward the local. Whatever economic decisions can be made at the local level should be, and all systems should be designed consciously to favor decentralized local empowerment.

In chapters 7 and 8, we turn to discussions of what needs to be done to reform the most essential global operating systems: energy, transportation, manufacturing, and agriculture. These systems are where "the rubber hits the road," as it were, in terms of the effects of globalized systems on local options on an everyday basis. We focus on means of furthering *disconnection* from the global systems. (In the agriculture section we add two new boxes. The first, by Debi Barker, focuses on WTO biases against small farmers. The second, by Edward Goldsmith, describes how changes in agriculture away from industrialized systems can reduce climate change.)

We also discuss prevailing measuring systems (like the gross domestic product) by which societies now determine the success or failure of their operations. The current systems are a major problem because they emphasize corporate growth and resource depletion as positive indicators; we describe a significant list of alternative measurements that include sustainability and other values.

In chapter 8, we have added two entirely new sections. The first is on media, which is both an operating system and a system that influences all the other systems. The second, "Peoples' Alternative Initiatives," celebrates and describes more than two dozen organizations worldwide—only a sample of hundreds that could have been included—that have seized the day to redefine and control their own economic destinies.

Part 3 of this second edition, "Global Governance," looks at that issue and what to do about it. The problems at this time are rooted in global corporations and global bureaucracies, so we offer lengthy chapters on each. The central purpose of chapter 9 is to review ideas for reversing the powers of unelected global corporations that serve as the central driving force of society today, though they operate on values that are diametrically opposed to our own ten principles. We offer an extensive series of proposals to effectively diminish corporate power and change corporate structure.

Chapter 10 looks squarely at what to do about the Bretton Woods trio—the World Bank, the IMF, and the WTO. We argue strongly for *replacing* all of them with new international institutions, mostly under the auspices of a highly reformed and decorporatized United Nations system. These new institutions would operate in the many areas in which international agreements are still required: labor rights, human rights, environmental protection, laws of the sea, dispute settlement, information exchanges, technology, culture, and so on. The question is this: How do we design agencies that answer those needs, without attempting to extend power over local institutions and processes, and that operate in a framework of mutual, democratic accountability? We have many suggestions for your perusal.

Finally, the new chapter 11 discusses how you can personally get involved, offering a series of doable, practical ideas, mostly at the local community level, but some national and international possibilities as well. This menu of what you can do is posted at the IFG Web site (www.ifg.org) and we encourage you to download and distribute the chapter as a pamphlet. We also encourage you to e-mail the IFG other ideas you may have on what individuals can do. Finally, the book concludes with a new resources section—good organizations that need your support and participation.

## A Living Document

The process of creating this book began in January 1999, nearly a year *before* Seattle. Meetings were held among some thirty IFG board members and key associate members, twenty-one of whom have been writing papers and holding regular meetings to develop this consensus report. It was frankly an extraordinary undertaking to reach consensus among so many strong-willed individuals, and it was only possible because of the many years of collaboration and friendship among the authors as part of the International Forum on Globalization over the last decade.

Typical of any consensus document, not every contributor agrees totally with every other one, or with every idea contained in these pages. But all are in agreement on the overall direction of the arguments and with the overwhelming majority of points. It has been an inspiring process for each of us.

The first edition of this book, now in print in seven languages, was shared with thousands of citizen and policy groups throughout the world, and we are now involved in a global process of regional meetings to get direct feedback from these groups as well as public officials and to learn about the many new local initiatives that are already under way. The first meeting-symposium was held in Santiago, Chile, in April 2004 and another is set for Europe later in 2004, with others to follow in Asia, Africa, and North America.

The goal of these regional meetings is to promote dialogue, criticism, feedback, and further development of the concepts in this book, all for the purpose of their application and actualization. At a future moment we will offer yet a third edition, which will encompass what we learn from the regional meetings, and we will continue to project these ideas as aggressively as we can. The authors of this volume strongly believe that the ultimate success of citizen movements depends on their becoming more proactive in creating the world that can be. We view this report, therefore, as one that will constantly evolve: a living document.

## Acknowledgments

The authors would like to offer special thanks to David Korten and Sarah Anderson, who, in the final months of manuscript preparation, worked tirelessly to help refine, edit, and clarify many parts of it. We also need to give especially heartfelt thanks to Suzanne York of the IFG, who was the research director of this project—a difficult and time-consuming task—and Elizabeth Connor, who managed the manuscript preparation and did a magnificent job processing and coordinating the flows of information and drafts among all the far-flung participants. Others who contributed greatly to the discussions or gave feedback or specific language to particular parts of the report include Diana Alonzo, Agnes Bertrand, Brent Blackwelder, Anuradha Mittal, David Morris, Mark Ritchie, and Steve Shrybman. And for extremely useful feedback on the manuscript and editing ideas, thanks also to Peter Berg, Ernest Callenbach, Paul Hawken, and Michael Shuman.

Finally, we offer our acknowledgment and deepest thanks to IFG board member and cofounder Martin Khor and the Third World Network. No individual or organization has contributed more to our collective thinking and analysis before and throughout this process. Many of us think of Martin as our Paul Revere for his ability to warn us well in advance of crucial new developments in the World Trade Organization and other trade bodies, and to steer us toward viable alternative strategies. We are indebted to him.

And thanks also to Steve Piersanti and his tremendous team at Berrett-

Koehler, whose enthusiasm, professionalism, and good ideas have made this a better book. We also wish to thank our excellent copyeditor Sandra Beris.

FOR THE DRAFTING COMMITTEE:
John Cavanagh, Washington, D.C.
Jerry Mander, San Francisco
May 1, 2004

~

# A Note on Sources

Readers will note that we have not used footnotes in this book. Key sources are indicated in the flow of the text, and all sources can be found in the sources section on page 369. All URLs cited in this book were confirmed on March 23, 2004.

# Introduction

## *Turning Point*

THREE LANDMARK EVENTS in 2003 punctuated the end of "the Golden Era" of corporate-driven economic globalization, the domination of the so-called Washington Consensus, and the ability of the United States to unilaterally dictate the course of global economic and political affairs.

One key event took place alongside the sunny beaches of the Mexican resort city of Cancun. Thousands of delegates representing governments and nongovernmental organizations (NGOs) from all over the world, plus tens of thousands of protesters, joined trade ministers from all member countries of the World Trade Organization to see if global trade talks, shattered in Seattle in 1999, could be successfully revived. On September 14, 2003, they got their answer: the talks collapsed.

Three months later in Miami there was a second stunning failure for the advocates of the prevailing economic design: the breakdown of negotiations for a new Free Trade Area of the Americas (FTAA).

In both cases, the crucial factor was an unprecedented new alignment among dozens of the world's poorest countries paying heed to their outraged citizenries. In Cancun, for example, a powerful collection of nations called the Group of 21, led by Brazil, China, India, South Africa, Egypt, and sixteen others—representing over half of the world's population, and supported in the streets by tens of thousands of demonstrators at home and thousands in Cancun—refused to acquiesce to the self-interested positions and proposals of the world's richest and most powerful nations. Then, in

I

Miami, a new generation of national leaders from South American countries, including Brazil, Argentina, Venezuela, Ecuador, and Bolivia, held tightly together to demand that the United States change its policy on agricultural subsidies and its refusals to ease entry for South American products. They too were saying that they would not be manipulated by the great power to the North.

After nearly a decade, the poor countries of the world had clearly grasped that the current global economic system was never designed to be responsive to them, despite public relations rhetoric to the contrary from the rich countries.

To the degree these alignments sustain themselves in future situations, the world will be permanently changed.

The third landmark event was the overwhelming global reaction and resistance to the U.S. invasion of Iraq. On February 15, 2003, several million people of all nationalities, races, and religions took to the streets in hundreds of cities around the world in the largest peace demonstration in human history. All but a very few of the world's governments, mostly small states that are financially dependent on the U.S. government, refused to give *any* economic, military, or even verbal support for the U.S. action. Virtually all the governments that joined—most notably Britain, Spain, Poland, and Italy—did so over the strong objection of a substantial majority of their own citizens. This international resistance to American unilateralism and aggression held firm even among nations normally friendly to U.S. interests and supportive of the prior excursion into Afghanistan.

Thus emerged a new set of alignments led by Germany, Russia, France, and China that stood firmly against the increasingly transparent aspirations of the Bush administration to build a global empire through economic and military coercion.

These three landmark events were but the most visible demonstrations of the growing awareness on every continent of the failure of the present global economic system and its ruling institutions. The demand is growing for a global system grounded in new principles and institutions that embody values of justice, democracy, and sustainability.

The global movement for peace and justice is at a turning point. Though we must continue to criticize and detail the many ways in which the dominant economic paradigm creates grave problems for the world, we now also turn toward articulating new futures. A movement that was once reactive and critical of events is becoming increasingly positive and visionary. It will be the main thrust of the second edition of this volume to amplify these emerging visions and begin a process of developing new realizable strategies and ideas toward achieving a better, more democratic, and ecologically sustainable world.

## Cancun: The Outbreak of Democracy

The collapse of the WTO negotiations in Cancun was not widely anticipated. In response to the breakdown of the WTO process in Seattle, there were loud assertions at the intervening ministerial meeting in Doha, Qatar, in 2001 that henceforth the WTO's primary mission would be to serve the economic needs of the poor countries. It was thus generally assumed that the richest nations would make a few compromises to induce consensus and get negotiations on track. It was clear by the final days of the Cancun meetings, however, that the draft text participating nations were asked to sign was produced in the same insulting manner as in previous years—in private backroom huddles among the wealthiest nations who then sought to coerce the rest to accept. In Lori Wallach's words in *Foreign Policy*: "Developing countries were expected to provide more privileges for foreign investors, subjugate their government procurement policies to WTO disciplines, prioritize facilitation of imports over other domestic policy goals, and adopt uniform 'competition' policies that enable megaconglomerates to further consolidate markets."

But this time, the poor countries, aided by the work of a highly focused contingent of NGO representatives, negotiated as a bloc and would not accept a deal they had no part in creating, one that mainly served the corporate interests of the rich nations. In so doing, most of these governments were responding to long-standing and increasingly powerful campaigns by their own citizen groups.

For example, in the Philippines, small-scale farmers, factory workers, and antipoverty activists had spent years pressing the government to stand up for their interests at the Cancun WTO summit. Their message to the Philippine government was simple, and it was aimed at the heart of the WTO agenda:

- Don't let Cargill and other giant agribusiness firms from rich nations use their governments' ample farm subsidies to dump their corn, rice, and wheat on our markets at low prices, displacing millions of peasant farmers.
- In the era of Enron and WorldCom, don't give in to the U.S. government and corporate demands that vital public services like health care, education, and water be offered for sale to those same global firms.
- Don't agree to new negotiations that will further handcuff governments' ability to steer incentives away from foreign firms toward smaller, locally based domestic firms.

Many of these Filipino activists traveled to the Cancun WTO summit and were joined by an estimated ten thousand to fifteen thousand protesters from across Mexico and the rest of the world. Barricades manned by thousands of Mexican police prevented most of the protesters from getting within miles of the government officials who were supposed to be negotiating in their interest. Despite the barriers, the Third World representatives got the message.

One especially shocking event behind the metal barricades occurred among a contingent of South Korean farmers and students who were deeply frustrated by the unfair rules of the WTO. A farmer named Lee Kyung Hae, the former head of South Korea's farmers' union, plunged a knife into his chest on the meetings' opening day. Lee took his life to dramatize, in his own words, that "multinational corporations and a small number of big WTO members are leading an undesirable globalization that is inhumane, environmentally degrading, farmer-killing, and undemocratic." His suicide note lamented the dumping of subsidized food in poorer countries like South Korea by global corporations based in the rich countries. He asked for a global trade system that would allow poor country governments to offer adequate protection to their farmers.

The flashpoint of the WTO meeting was clearly agriculture. But the democratic revolt and its new alignments were about far more than that. Beyond the Group of 21, an even larger affiliation of nearly one hundred developing country governments banded together to make the case that the poorest of the poor nations should receive what they called "special and differential treatment" in global trade and investment rules. This represented a kind of affirmative action program, to make up in part for the prior ravages of colonialism and the grossly distorted trading system.

Yet another group, with participants from the first two groups, insisted that the WTO negotiating agenda should not be expanded to include a new list of rich country proposals intended to favor foreign investors over local investors. The rejected proposals would have prohibited governments from favoring local over global firms in public contracts, requiring firms to hire local workers, limiting the percentage of foreign ownership in domestic enterprises, or requiring foreign investors to keep some profits in the country. These proposed new rules would have deprived small countries of their remaining control over their own economies and placed their economic fate entirely in the hands of foreign owners. (Such rules are precisely what the U.S. Coalition Provisional Authority has proposed for Iraq. See also Box A, page 12.)

Overall, however, developing country negotiators inside the barricaded conference rooms and the protesters marching in the streets worked together to reject the "one size fits all" development model of the WTO. It would be hard to overestimate the sweeping implications of this new solidarity among poor and developing nations asserting their collective interests in global negotiations for the first time since the 1970s.

By derailing the globalization agenda of the WTO in Cancun, these poor country governments, together with an increasingly skeptical and restless global public, were not rejecting the necessity or wisdom of global rules on trade and investment. To the contrary, they were putting forward an abundance of alternative proposals—as spelled out in the chapters that follow—for replacing the obsolete WTO approach with fairer rules and institutions that operate according to a different set of values. A framework of intelligent and equitable rules is essential to allow governments to put legitimate checks and balances on trade and investment to fulfill their responsibilities to their own people—for example, efforts by Mexico, South Korea, and Japan to protect traditional farming practices considered vital to their cultures, by Brazil to produce affordable generic AIDS drugs to treat its AIDS victims, and by Bolivia to develop its natural gas resources in ways beneficial to its own citizens. Such new rules would shift the priority from increasing trade and investment at all costs to creating frameworks that build healthy communities, dignified work, and a clean environment.

## Miami: Regime Change in Latin America

The negative outcome of the Miami negotiations for a Free Trade Area of the Americas was more predictable. The countries of South America had gone through enormous political upheaval, much of it in reaction to the devastating neoliberal dictates of the World Bank, the International Monetary Fund, and the WTO. The promise that economic globalization will bring prosperity rings nowhere more false than in Africa and Latin America. But in Latin America people have been able to do something about it.

Five governments had recently been thrown out of office in South America, including in the region's largest economy, Brazil. In every case one of the primary issues that determined the voters' choice was the devastating failure of economic globalization, so-called structural adjustment, and poverty alleviation programs pressed on them by wealthier nations through the IMF, the World Bank, and the WTO. New governments prevailed in Venezuela, Bolivia, Ecuador, Argentina, and Brazil, all of them to varying degrees resistant to economic globalization. It would be fair to categorize the South American continent as the first major region of the world to turn away from neoliberalism in an active political way.

So when negotiations began in Miami in December 2003, similar issues to those that devastated Cancun immediately surfaced, with even less possibility of their being accepted by the people whose lives they would further devastate. It quickly became clear that if the United States continued to refuse to compromise on agricultural subsidies and other matters—for example, allowing Brazilian oranges into Florida (thus potentially costing President Bush that state in the 2004 elections) or allowing Brazilian steel into the U.S. Midwest (for the same reason)—no deal was possible.

Several South American countries, joined by Caribbean countries, held together as a bloc of resistance to the FTAA. Thwarted by the collective power of these nations, the United States has subsequently sought to use its power advantage over individual countries by turning from multilateral agreements to the negotiation of a complex set of bilateral agreements designed to achieve the same ends as the FTAA. The United States is also pressing hard for a new Central America Free Trade Agreement (CAFTA), although as we go to press it has not yet been approved by the U.S. Congress and has become a political hot potato.

The political turnaround in Brazil is particularly noteworthy. Brazil is now the world's fifth most populous nation (after China, India, Indonesia, and the United States) and boasts the world's eighth largest economy, although it has not yet been invited to join the powerful Group of Eight.

Brazil's economic success is in part a consequence of the fact that it never embraced the corporate globalization model as fully as many of its neighbors; it didn't privatize as much as many other countries, and it really only started opening its economy to foreign interests in the 1990s. Cognizant of the extreme suffering in neighboring Argentina, which applied the free market formula to the extreme, in October 2002 Brazilians firmly rejected the corporate globalization path by electing a former metalworker and union member as their president: Luis Ignacio da Silva, or Lula.

Lula's government was at the center of the Cancun rebellion against the established order. It led the Group of 21 and was involved in all of the developing country negotiating blocs, and its firm resistance was a major factor in the collapse of the talks. U.S. trade representative Robert Zoellick accused Brazil of leading the bloc of "won't do" countries.

Two weeks after Cancun, Lula used the venue of the United Nations General Assembly in New York to meet with the political leadership of India and South Africa to create an informal "Group of Three" that would continue to meet. So Lula convened the most powerful nations of the three vast continents of the global South (with China showing sympathy but eschewing leadership in Asia) and has potentially changed global power relations in so doing. In the weeks that followed, Lula's government expressed its discontent with the ongoing talks over a proposed Free Trade Area of the Americas, which the United States wanted to have modeled on the corporate-friendly North American Free Trade Agreement. Brazil's rejection of that model in Miami, as in Cancun, was decisive and has contributed to the growing sense of a waning U.S. ability to coerce smaller nations to its will.

The Iraq war experience provides an even more vivid illustration of this surprising demise.

## Iraq: The Failure of Empire

The common wisdom among the millions of people who have taken to the streets against the virtually unilateral U.S. invasion of Iraq is that the war has essentially been an attempt to further U.S. drives to achieve global empire. Actually, however, it is as much an expression that a U.S. empire that already exists—an *economic* empire—has begun a precipitous decline. Like most prior empires dating back to Rome, failing systems become desperate, trying somehow to save their far-flung, overextended lines of supply and control, and can become extremely dangerous. If economic controls start failing, then war is an option.

In a speech at the Heinrich Boell Foundation's McPlanet Conference in July 2003 in Berlin, Walden Bello summarized the U.S. problem this way: "The great problem for unilateralism is overextension, or a mismatch between the goals of the United States and the resources needed to accomplish the goals. Overextension is relative, . . . to a great degree a function of resistance. An overextended power may be in worse condition even with a significant increase in its military power if resistance increases by an even greater degree." Resistance has obviously been growing, as evidenced by those voices on the streets and the majority of governments opposed to the war and to U.S. economic domination.

But signs of failure for U.S. imperial aspirations were already apparent long before the Iraq war and even before Cancun and Miami. The Asian, Russian, and Argentine financial crises were all early signs of the unworkability of the model that was being imposed and its tragic impacts on poor countries. The defeat of the multilateral agreement on investment (MAI) was another indication of rising opposition, as victims of the model are no longer willing to continue to play the game. (In chapter 2, we provide an extensive critique of the system.)

The failures of the entire neoliberal project are built right into its underlying economic model because it requires certain unachievable conditions. In order to sustain itself, a globalized economy on the neoliberal model requires (1) a never-ending, always-expanding supply of inexpensive resources; (2) an ever expanding supply of accessible new markets; and (3) a steady supply of cheap labor to exploit. It also requires a multitude of compliant governments to collaborate on the project. Such conditions can be achieved in the short run, as they partly were, especially for the model's perpetrators in the 1980s and 1990s. But they cannot continue for long on a finite planet.

Many global resources are already seriously depleted and becoming expensive: oil is certainly among them. Iraq may offer a short-term solution, a cheap oil supply to keep the system going, but other resources are also running out: water, forests, fish, farmable land, and certain key minerals. All of these shortages will worsen if global climate change proceeds as predicted.

The power of empire is all the more precarious when resource supply lines reach thousands of miles across land and sea, as oil does, making them vulnerable to interruption by political change, war, terrorism, or breakdown and very costly to protect—as we now see in the desperate efforts of the United States to secure its long-distance supplies by military force. Exacerbating the problem is a national leadership so wed to oil that it refuses to turn to viable local renewable energy options.

Markets are also finite. In the United States, markets have largely stagnated; even the very rich can only buy so many private planes, luxury yachts, and trophy homes. And a middle class increasingly stretched by long working hours, falling wages, and increasing consumer debt can only buy so many cars, refrigerators, TVs, and DVD players. Companies seeking rapid growth find they need to cast elsewhere. So reaching for and prying open foreign markets is mandatory—whether through coerced trade agreements or military force.

As for cheap labor, it is less and less willing to be cheap or to accept the meager security it is offered by mobile global corporations. Even those labor organizations that had won decent conditions, as in the United States, are finding themselves caught in a competitive race to the bottom against the world's poorest and most oppressed workers. They have good reason to be resentful of the fact that corporate CEOs are making tens—or even hundreds—of millions of dollars annually while their own benefits and wages decline or stagnate.

And few governments are quite as compliant as they were only a few years ago.

*None of the preceding mandatory conditions for the success of neoliberalism is sustainable.* When a great power comes to realize that, more extreme means may be used to keep things afloat a bit longer.

As Walden Bello has written, the United States "is very wary of a process of globalization that is not managed by the U.S. [to] ensure it does not diffuse its own economic power." The Bush administration is actually two-faced on trade, as evidenced by the many U.S. protectionist moves, from agriculture to pharmaceuticals to steel. The motto of the United States, says Bello, may be "protectionism for the U.S. and free trade for the rest of us."

The war in Iraq is primarily an attempt to keep an overstressed U.S. economic juggernaut, one now gasping to sustain its huge need for resource flows and supply lines, breathing a little longer. It's a kind of CPR for a system that's having a hard time breathing for itself.

But it is also a metal-fisted warning to other nations of the region and the world about who's in charge, who comes first, and how we're going to live. Yet it is not as credible or convincing a statement as it may have been in the past.

## COALITIONS OF THE NONCOMPLIANT

By now the whole world has understood the falseness of the claims underpinning the Iraq war. We have learned about the "neoconservative" passion (among officials who are now high up in the Bush administration) to invade Iraq *ten years before 9-11*, and to reshape the Middle East into a free-market globalist framework intended to keep those resources flowing to the United States.

The Bush administration's 2002 "national security strategy," although wrapped in eloquent language about the need to protect and project "freedom," made an open declaration of its intent to pursue preemptive war to protect whatever a U.S. president might define as a U.S. interest. That doctrine explicitly equated "freedom" with free markets and free trade—even going so far as to suggest that "lower marginal tax rates," and "pro-growth legal and regulatory policies" are integral to its concept of freedom. Its implicit premise is that threats to the market freedom of U.S. corporations anywhere in the world are threats to U.S. security and may justify future preemptive war.

The Iraq war was the first physical implementation of this doctrine based on the premise that Iraq possessed weapons of mass destruction and was colluding with Al-Qaeda and other terrorist groups to use them against the

United States. The evidence, now well confirmed, that there were no weapons of mass destruction, no connection between Saddam Hussein and Al-Qaeda, no Iraqi threats to its neighbors, and no imminent Iraqi threat to the United States to justify a military response was simply ignored.

The U.S. performance in these matters was so poor that it has brought on a crisis of confidence and believability in all U.S. assertions and an extreme loss of moral authority, stimulating peoples and nations to band together in new ways in opposition to U.S. aims. Few nations supported U.S. policy, the U.N. Security Council did not back it, and public opinion showed opposition everywhere in the majority, often as high as 90 percent.

The United States invaded anyway and succeeded in eliminating the government of a corrupt and ruthless dictator, arresting Saddam Hussein, and occupying the country. It now seems highly unlikely, however, that any other announced goal will be achieved. It will not bring democracy or peace to the Middle East, and by increasing Middle Eastern resentment of Western nations has significantly worsened the world terrorist threat.

The consequences have been disastrous even for the United States, which finds itself increasingly isolated and discredited diplomatically, overstretched militarily, and on the verge of fiscal disaster as a consequence of growing federal budget and national trade deficits. In his assessment of the situation, James Webb, U.S. Secretary of the Navy under the Republican administration of Ronald Reagan, wrote in *USA Today* that by launching an unnecessary invasion of Iraq:

> Bush arguably has committed the greatest strategic blunder in modern memory. To put it bluntly, he attacked the wrong target. While he boasts of removing Saddam Hussein from power, he did far more than that. He decapitated the government of a country that was not directly threatening the United States and, in so doing, bogged down a huge percentage of our military in a region that never has known peace.

In a report published by the People-Centered Development Forum, *Global Civil Society: The Path Ahead,* authors David Korten, Nicanor Perlas, and Vandana Shiva describe the futility of imperial policy, whether by economic or military means in the modern world.

All imperial endeavors that are dependent on long-distance control, long-distance supply, and a high degree of suppression of alternative approaches are "inevitably self-defeating," they write. They argue for alter-

## BOX A: IRAQI "FREEDOM"—CORPORATE STYLE

*By Antonia Juhasz, International Forum on Globalization*

The U.S. invasion of Iraq was more than just a grab for cheap, steady oil supplies. In keeping with the U.S. national security doctrine, it was a test case and model for future actions to bring "freedom," by which was largely meant market freedom. Iraq was to be the poster child for the benefits of military muscle in the cause of free trade. Any doubts about this disappeared on September 15, 2003, when L. Paul Bremer, administrator of the Coalition Provisional Authority, issued Bremer Order No. 39, which imposed new rules for foreign investment in a "free" Iraq: rigidly neoliberal, highly beneficial to U.S.–based global corporations, but not so good for Iraqi freedom. As we go to press, by all accounts these Bremer orders have been incorporated into the operating rules of the new "sovereign" interim Iraqi government under Prime Minister Allawi. We anticipate they'll be sustained by future Iraqi governments in the shadow of U.S. authority.

The following are a few examples of the rules contained in Bremer Order No. 39:

- *Privatization:* The order allows full privatization of all two hundred of Iraq's state-owned enterprises. The initial list to be sold to private corporations included cement and fertilizer plants, phosphate and sulfur mines, pharmaceutical factories, and the country's airline.
- *One hundred percent foreign ownership:* The order allows for 100 percent foreign ownership of businesses in all sectors except oil and mineral extraction, banks, and insurance companies (discussed in following paragraphs).
- *National treatment:* The order states that "a foreign investor shall be entitled to make foreign investments in Iraq on terms no less favorable than those applicable to an Iraqi investor." This copies the "national treatment" provision of the WTO and other international trade regimes. As a result, the government of Iraq cannot favor local investors, businesses, or providers over foreign ones. It cannot require that U.S. companies with billion dollar reconstruction contracts hire any local contractors. It cannot require that qualified local Iraqi companies receive contracts over foreign-owned companies in order to boost the Iraqi economy.
- *Unrestricted repatriation of profits:* The order permits foreign investors to "transfer abroad without delay all funds associated with [their] investment, including shares or profits and dividends" (among others). Foreign investors can put their money wherever they like and take it out whenever they want to, "without delay."
- *Forty-year leases:* Iraq's government and businesses will be locked into contracts signed under these rules for forty years, with an option of unlimited renewal.

CONTINUED

Thus, order 39, as long as it continues, in effect allows U.S. corporations operating in Iraq to own *every* business, do all of the work, and send all of their money home. Nothing needs to be reinvested locally to boost the Iraqi economy or be targeted to help damaged regions, communities, or services. All the profits can go home with the foreign owners, and they can take out their investments at any time. No Iraqi need be hired, no public services need be guaranteed, no rights of workers need be protected, and no resources need stay in the country. Iraq and its people are reduced to raw materials to be exploited by U.S. corporations and the global economy.

Other relevant Bremer orders were 40 and 37:

- *Bremer Order No. 40* turns the banking sector from a state-run to a market-driven system overnight by allowing foreign banks to enter the Iraqi market and purchase up to 50 percent of an Iraqi bank. J. P. Morgan-Chase, the second-largest bank in the United States, which was implicated in the Enron scandal, has been awarded a contract to run a consortium of thirteen banks from thirteen countries that will constitute the Trade Bank of Iraq. The Trade Bank may be just the point of entry for J. P. Morgan, giving it "first dibs" on the full privatization yet to come.
- *Bremer Order No. 37* implements a flat tax in Iraq by providing for a marginal income tax rate of 15 percent

for both corporations and individuals. Historically, flat taxes reduce the tax burden on the poorest, increase the burden on the middle class tremendously, and drastically reduce the taxes paid by the wealthy.

The occupying authority also has big plans for trade liberalization. Iraq has already achieved "observer" status in the WTO, and Iraq's laws are being made 100 percent compliant with WTO rules. And a plan prepared for the Coalition Provisional Authority by Virginia-based BearingPoint, Inc., lists oil, "other natural resources," and luxury export-oriented agricultural crops such as "high-value fruit, vegetables, flowers, and seeds" as the leading exports.

The exact manner of dealing with oil investments and exports—a highly controversial issue—remains secret at this time. We do know that Chevron-Texaco gained the first contract to market Iraq's oil and has experienced enormous profit from that activity.

As of March 21, 2004, according to the *San Francisco Chronicle,* extensive reconstruction contracts were already given to such U.S. companies as Halliburton/KBR ($12.6 billion), Bechtel ($2.8 billion), Washington Group ($2.1 billion), Fluor ($1.1 billion), Perini ($1 billion), and Parsares ($974 million). Much of the reconstruction is of Iraqi infrastructures destroyed by the U.S. invasion.

Finally, President Bush announced plans for a new U.S.–Middle East Free Trade Area (MEFTA). Iraq will be a charter member.

native approaches, such as are contained in this book, that do not project power globally but root it locally.

> The viability of complex systems depends on localizing decision making and keeping interdependence within manageable limits. Elite globalization has created an unstable and ultimately self-destructive system, because it ignores this essential principle. The crisis of social and environmental system failure can be resolved only by the decentralization of power and control based on the principles of partnership and community. . . . Wise and rational leaders would by now have abandoned [the push toward empire] in favor of more constructive alternatives.

## New Awakenings

Given all of the preceding, now is clearly a moment for new directions. *A turning point.* The great news is that tens of millions of people around the world are not waiting around for governments or international bureaucracies or agencies to make better decisions—though we all struggle nearly daily to encourage that. As readers will discover in the chapters that follow, notably chapters 7 and 8, "Alternative Operating Systems," communities everywhere are challenging the assumptions of globalization's inevitability and resisting the efforts of specific countries to force it on them. But they are also seizing this moment as an opportunity to try new ideas, to reclaim powers long denied: the power to determine their own destinies, control their own economies, secure their rights to water, land, dignity, a healthy environment, and live in harmony, peace, and dignity.

So we begin this volume with a sense of cautious optimism about the prospects for citizens and their governments to construct alternatives to economic globalization. Whereas even a few years ago proposals such as we advance in these pages might have seemed wildly unrealistic to some, today they seem far less so.

In many ways this period may be akin to the 1960s and 1970s, when the development debate was still very vibrant. Local, national, and global alternatives flourished. During that period, civil society joined with Southern governments to sketch out alternatives that were implemented on the ground in many countries.

History is likely to view the corporate-driven globalization of the 1980s and 1990s as an anomaly, a time when a single dominant model was promoted *despite* its inherent unsuitability to the reality and needs of its time. Since the mid-1990s, the inevitability of the model's failure has become ever more evident, bringing drastic changes in the political scene that culminated in the turning point events of 2003. The World Bank and International Monetary Fund have come under tremendous criticism by civil society, governments, and even a bipartisan commission of the U.S. Congress (the Meltzer Commission, which released its report in 2001). In the wake of the Enron and WorldCom scandals, global corporations have lost a great deal of public trust. Global citizen alliances found new strength in the growing size and success of demonstrations around the world. Tens of thousands of representatives of civil society organizations now gather annually at the World Social Forum (WSF) to strengthen their alliances and share a new vision of a world that can thrive if it is freed from the grip of corporate globalization. And the spirit and principles of the WSF are being projected into a growing number of regional and national social forums all around the globe, engaging people by the hundreds of thousands in intelligent, focused dialogue on the world that is possible.

There are also the beginnings of an expanded alliance between civil society groups and some governments of the global South reminiscent of the 1970s alliance between citizen groups and the Group of 77 nations, which articulated and promoted their collective economic interests through proposals for a "New International Economic Order." The protests that contributed to a breakdown of the 1999 WTO meeting in Seattle emboldened some governments of Southern countries to be more forthright in their challenge to WTO procedures and proposals harmful to their national interests. The subsequent April 2000 protests in Washington, D.C., against the World Bank and the IMF called for debt relief and a rollback of structural adjustment policies. These protests coincided with a meeting of the Group of 77 heads of state in Cuba, where several of them issued statements sharply critical of the World Bank and the IMF, expressed support for the Washington protesters, and called for a transfer of some responsibilities for global economic policies from the Bretton Woods institutions to the United Nations. And at the negotiations around the Free Trade Area of the Americas, members of the Brazilian and Venezuelan government teams routinely ducked out of negotiating sessions to brief international civil society representatives on important developments.

Southern nations have much to lose from business as usual under the Bretton Woods regime and much to gain from new procedures like those proposed in this volume—especially debt relief, removal of structural adjustment conditions, and controls on speculative financial flows. These countries account for a majority of the votes in the United Nations General Assembly, a power they have previously been reluctant to use in defiance of the powerful Northern industrial countries. But the recent experiences in the WTO and the growing alliances with civil society are strengthening popular support in both the North and South for taking an independent stand in the interests of democracy, the environment, and the well-being of the poor.

There are precedents for a grand alliance of progressive Southern leaders, global civil society, and sympathetic politicians in the North with the power to achieve sweeping institutional reform at the global level. Years ago, similar alliances between progressives in the North and popular leaders in the former colonies resulted in the dismantling of the trans-Atlantic slave trade and later of the empires of Europe's colonial powers. Recent events give credence to the view that a new cycle of change is under way both at the institutional and grassroots levels, and that a new grand alliance may evolve with the potential to remedy the injustices of our time.

# PART ONE

# A SYSTEM IN CRISIS

*Sold to the world as a panacea for all problems, economic globalization has not lived up to its advertising. It has not lifted the poor; it has instead brought record disparities in income and wealth between rich and poor nations, and rich and poor within nations. It has greatly inhibited democracy and social justice; it has destroyed local communities and pushed farmers off their traditional lands. And it has accelerated the greatest environmental breakdown in history. The only real beneficiaries of globalization are the world's largest corporations and their top officials, and the global bureaucracies they helped to create.*

*Part 1 discusses the worldviews that brought this system forward and the reasons for its failure, reasons deeply rooted in the system's basic structure and design.*

CHAPTER ONE

# Conflicting Worldviews

THE MILLIONS OF PEOPLE who have taken to the streets in India, the Philippines, Indonesia, Brazil, Bolivia, the United States, Canada, Mexico, Argentina, Venezuela, France, Germany, Italy, the Czech Republic, Spain, Sweden, the United Kingdom, New Zealand, Australia, Kenya, South Africa, Thailand, Malaysia, and elsewhere in massive demonstrations against the institutions and policies of corporate globalization have often been met by skepticism or even hostility from the media. Rarely have mainstream media attempted seriously to inform the public on the issues behind the protests, usually preferring to characterize demonstrators as "ignorant protectionists" who offer no alternatives and do not merit serious attention. Many in the media have tried to reduce the complex issues involved to a simplistic contest between "protectionism" and "openness," or between "anarchy" and "an orderly democratic process." In North America and Europe, those involved in the protests are dismissed as spoiled children of privilege—selfish, ill-informed malcontents who would end trade and international cooperation.

Anyone who makes even the smallest effort to find out why millions of people from virtually every nation and walk of life have taken to the streets finds these simplistic characterizations to be untrue. As for the charge of being antipoor, the largest protests are in low-income countries, and most of those involved are themselves poor. The charges of isolation and xenophobia are equally uninformed; the resistance against corporate globalization is global in scope and is dedicated to international cooperation to achieve economic justice for every person on the planet. As for the charge of being antitrade, many of the movement's leaders are actively involved in the promotion of *fair* trade—in contrast to the often exploitative *free* trade they oppose—as a means of improving the economic conditions of poor people and their communities.

In fact, the resistance is grounded in a sophisticated, well-developed critique set forth in countless publications and public presentations, including, among many others, documents available from the International Forum on Globalization (IFG) and numerous books and articles by IFG associates. The critique is also available in the publications of a thriving independent media that tells the stories and communicates the opinions that the mainstream media so often ignores or dismisses. These independent information sources are gradually expanding public awareness and enlarging the constituency for transformational change, but they have not yet reached sufficient critical mass to force a reframing of the terms of the political debate still dominated by corporate media and interests.

The claim that the protestors offer no alternatives is as false as the other claims. In addition to the alternatives described in books, periodicals, conferences, and individual articles and presentations, numerous consensus statements have been carefully crafted by civil society groups over the past two decades that set forth a wealth of alternatives with a striking convergence in their beliefs about the underlying values human society should serve. Since 2001, tens of thousands have gathered annually in Porto Alegre, Brazil, or Mumbai, India, for the World Social Forum titled "Another World Is Possible" to carry forward this process of popular consensus building toward a world that works for all.

Perhaps the most obvious and straightforward alternative advocated by civil society is simply to place a moratorium on the negotiation of new trade agreements. More ambitious proposals—such as those presented in this volume—center on redirecting global, national, and local priorities toward the task of creating healthy, sustainable human societies that work for all.

Although many of the protests have centered on opposition to trade agreements, global civil society does not oppose trade. Humans have engaged in trade since the beginning of time and as long as two or more members of the species survive will surely continue to do so. What the protesters reject is the use by corporate interests of international trade *agreements* to circumvent democracy in their global campaign to strip away social and environmental protections that ordinary people have struggled for decades—even centuries—to put in place.

The issue is governance. Will ordinary people have a democratic voice in deciding what rules are in the best interests of society? Or will a small ruling elite, meeting in secret and far from public view, be allowed to continue to set the rules that shape humanity's future? If the concern of the decision makers is only for next quarter's corporate profits, who will care for the health and well-being of people and the planet?

These are increasingly serious questions for a great many people who live with the violence and insecurity that spreads through the world in tandem with growing inequality, an unraveling social fabric, and the collapse of critical environmental systems. It is this reality of social and environmental disintegration that has brought millions of people together in a loose global alliance that spans national borders to forge what may be considered the most truly global and inclusive social movement in human history.

## Different Worlds

The corporate globalists who meet in posh gatherings to chart the course of corporate globalization in the name of private profits, and the citizen movements that organize to thwart them in the name of democracy, are separated by deep differences in values, worldview, and definitions of progress. At times it seems they must be living in wholly different worlds—which, in fact, in many respects they do. Understanding their differences is key to understanding the implications of the profound choices humanity currently faces.

Corporate globalists inhabit a world of power and privilege. They see progress at hand everywhere, because from their vantage point the drive to privatize public assets and free the market from governmental interference spreads freedom and prosperity around the world, improving the lives of people everywhere and creating the financial and material wealth necessary to end poverty and protect the environment. They see themselves as champions of an inexorable and beneficial historical process toward erasing the economic and political borders that hinder corporate expansion, eliminating the tyranny of inefficient and meddlesome public bureaucracies, and unleashing the enormous innovation and wealth-creating power of competition and private enterprise.

Corporate globalists undertake to accelerate these trends as a great mission. They seek public policies and international agreements that provide greater safeguards for investors and private property while removing restraints to the free movement of goods, money, and corporations in search of economic opportunity wherever it may be found. They embrace global corporations as the greatest and most efficient human institutions, powerful engines of innovation and wealth creation that are peeling away the barriers to human progress and accomplishment everywhere. They celebrate the World Bank, the International Monetary Fund, and the World Trade Organization as essential and beneficial institutions for global governance engaged in the great work of rewriting the rules of commerce to free the market and create conditions essential to economic growth.

Corporate globalists subscribe to this worldview like a catechism. They differ among themselves mainly in their views of the extent to which it is appropriate for government to subsidize private corporations or provide safety nets to cushion the fall of the losers in the market's relentless competition.

Citizen movements, on the other hand, see a very different reality. Focused on people and the environment, they see a world in a crisis of such magnitude that it threatens the fabric of civilization and the survival of the species—a world of rapidly growing inequality, erosion of relationships of trust and caring, and failing planetary life-support systems. Where corporate globalists promote the spread of market economies, citizen movements see the power to govern shifting away from people and communities to financial speculators and to global corporations dedicated to the pursuit of short-term profit in disregard of all human and natural concerns. They see corporations replacing democracies of people with autocracies of money, replacing self-organizing markets with centrally planned corporate economies, and replacing diverse cultures with cultures of greed and materialism.

In the eyes of citizen movements, these trends are not the result of some inexorable historical force but rather of the intentional actions of a corrupted political system awash in corporate money. They see the World Bank, the IMF, and the World Trade Organization as leading instruments of this assault against people and the environment.

Ironically, the citizen movements seek many of the things the corporate globalists claim to offer but in fact fail to deliver: democratic participation, economies comprising enterprises that provide good jobs and respond to the real needs and preferences of their customers, a healthy environment, an end to poverty. However, where the corporate globalists seek a competitive global economy ruled by megacorporations that owe no loyalty to place or person, citizen movements seek a planetary system of economies made up of locally owned enterprises accountable to all their stakeholders. Citizen movements work for economic justice for all, international cooperation, vibrant cultural diversity, and healthy, sustainable societies that value life more than money.

Citizen movements recognize that corporate globalists *cannot* deliver on their promises because the narrow and shortsighted financial imperatives that drive their institutions are antithetical to them. Many corporate globalists may act with the best intentions, but they are blinded by their own financial success to the costs of this success for those who have no place at the table, including future generations.

Corporate globalists generally measure progress by indicators of their own financial wealth, such as rising stock prices and indicators of the total output of goods and services available to those who have the money to pay. With the exception of occasional cyclical setbacks in Latin America and elsewhere and declining per capita incomes in the poorest African countries, these indicators generally perform well, confirming in the eyes of corporate globalists their premise that their program is enriching the world.

In contrast, citizen movements measure progress by indicators of the well-being of people and nature, with particular concern for the lives of those most in need. With the exception of the highly visible pockets of privilege enjoyed by corporate globalists, these indicators show deterioration at a frightening pace, suggesting that in terms of what really matters, the world is rapidly growing poorer.

The U.N. Food and Agricultural Organization (FAO) reports that the number of chronically hungry people in the world declined steadily during the 1970s and 1980s but has been increasing since the early 1990s. The U.S. Department of Agriculture estimates that by 2008 two-thirds of the people of sub-Saharan Africa will be undernourished, and 40 percent will be undernourished in Asia.

In a world in which a few enjoy unimaginable wealth, two hundred million children under age five are underweight because of a lack of food. Some fourteen million children die each year from hunger-related diseases. A hundred million children are living or working on the streets. Three hundred thousand children were conscripted as soldiers during the 1990s, and six million were injured in armed conflicts. Eight hundred million people go to bed hungry each night.

This human tragedy is not confined to poor countries. Even in a country as wealthy as the United States, 6.1 million adults and 3.3 million children experience outright hunger. Some 10 percent of U.S. households, accounting for 31 million people, do not have access to enough food to meet their basic needs. These are some of the many indicators of a deepening global social crisis.

On the environmental side, a joint study released in September 2000 by the United Nations Development Program (UNDP), the United Nations Environment Program (UNEP), the World Bank, and the World Resources Institute assessed five ecosystem types—agricultural, coastal, forest, freshwater, and grassland—in relation to five ecosystem services—food and fiber production, water quantity, air quality, biodiversity, and carbon storage. It found that of these twenty-five ecosystem-service combinations, sixteen had declining trends. The only positive trend was in food and fiber production by forest ecosystems, which has been achieved by an expansion of industrial forest monocropping at the expense of species diversity.

Human activity—in particular, fossil fuel combustion—is estimated to have increased atmospheric concentrations of carbon dioxide to their highest levels in twenty million years. According to the Worldwatch Institute, an environmental think tank, natural disasters, including weather-related disasters such as storms, floods, and fires, affected more than two billion people and caused in excess of $608 billion in economic losses worldwide during the decade of the 1990s—more than the previous four decades combined. Three hundred million people were displaced from their homes or forced to resettle because of extreme weather events in 1998 alone.

It becomes more imperative to rethink human priorities and institutions by the day. Yet most corporate globalists, in deep denial, reiterate their mantra that with time and patience corporate globalization will create the wealth needed to end poverty and protect the environment.

Citizen movements counter that the policies and processes of corporate globalization are destroying the real wealth of the planet while advancing a primitive winner-takes-all competition that inexorably widens the gap between rich and poor. They reject as absurd the argument that the poor must be exploited and the environment destroyed to make the money necessary to end poverty and save the planet.

Many citizen movements embrace the present imperative for transformational change as an opportunity to lift humanity to a new level of possibility—the greatest creative challenge in the history of the species. Yet experience leads them to conclude that the institutions with the power to provide the leadership are neither inclined nor suited to doing so. Nor is there realistic cause for hope that leaders who are lavishly rewarded by the status quo and hold steadfastly to the view that there is no alternative will suddenly experience an epiphany.

The challenge of providing leadership to create a just and sustainable world thus falls by default to the hundreds of millions of extraordinary people in an emerging global civil society who believe a better world is possible—and who are forging global alliances that seek to shift the powers of governance to democratic, locally rooted, human-scale institutions that value life more than money. Although the most visible among them are those who have taken to the streets in protest, equally important and even more numerous are those struggling to rebuild their local communities and economies in the face of the institutional forces aligned against them.

## Economic Democracy

The current and future well-being of humanity depends on transforming the relationships of power within and between societies toward more democratic and mutually accountable modes of managing human affairs that are self-organizing, power-sharing, and minimize the need for coercive central authority. *Economic* democracy, which involves the equitable participation of all people in the ownership of the productive assets on which their livelihood depends, is essential to such a transformation because the concentration of economic power is the Achilles heel of *political* democracy, as the experience of corporate globalization demonstrates.

The defining political struggles of the twentieth century centered on a choice between socialism and capitalism. Both centralized the power of ownership in institutions that could not be held accountable: the state in the case of socialism and the corporation in the case of capitalism. Both worked against the classic liberal economic ideal of self-organizing markets, markets in which communities organize themselves to respond to local needs within a framework of democratically determined rules.

Although rarely noted, economic democracy is as essential to the efficient functioning of economies as sound public regulation. Because today's markets respond only to money, they are overly attentive to the wants of the rich and neglect the most basic needs of the poor. Economic democracy is also a necessary foundation of individual, community, and national economic self-determination—the ability to determine one's own economic priorities and the rules of one's economic life—because it helps secure a political voice for each person.

At the same time, there are real and often difficult trade-offs to be considered in the choice between local, national, and global rule making. For example, civil society has a strong commitment to raising social and environmental standards everywhere. To this end, some activists call for setting universal labor, health and safety, and environmental standards, possibly enforced with trade sanctions. They correctly point out that allowing different standards in an open, competitive global economy inevitably puts competitive pressure on everyone to lower their standards.

But others note that it is invariably the strong nations who advocate for uniform standards because they hold the power to impose self-serving rules of their own choosing on weaker nations. Furthermore, uniform international standards not only violate the democratic right to self-determination but also fail to take into account differing local conditions and preferences. Those on this side of the argument call for measures to secure the right of nations and even localities to adopt standards of their choosing appropriate to their circumstances, as long as they do not shift the burden of their decisions onto others.

Both positions are based on valid concerns. The differences relate in part to the extent of the priority given to economic self-reliance. The less the self-reliance of a community or nation, the greater its external dependence and the greater the need for globally uniform rules to avoid a downward pressure on standards everywhere. By the same token, the greater the self-reliance of a community or nation, the greater the scope for local flexibility and adaptation to local circumstances. Dialogue on these trade-offs in the IFG has led to a consensus tilt in favor of self-reliance and local self-determination.

Concerns about local self-reliance and self-determination have important implications for global governance. For example, in a self-reliant and local-ized system, the primary authority to set and enforce rules rests with the national and local governments of the jurisdictions to which they apply. The proper role of international institutions is to facilitate the coordination of national policies on matters where the interests of nations are inherently intertwined—global warming, for example.

Of course, a democratic commitment to self-determination means that ultimately it is left up to the people of every nation—if not every indigenous group or local community—to decide the extent to which they will inte-grate their own economy with the economies of other nations. The people of different countries will likely reach different decisions. The international interest is properly confined to ensuring that these decisions are made dem-ocratically, that economic relationships among countries are just and bal-anced, that no country builds up unpayable debts to the rest of the system, and that each national economy is secure against predatory interventions from foreign nations and corporations.

There is certainly a need for international institutions to facilitate coop-erative exchange and the working through of inevitable competing national interests toward solutions to global problems. These institutions must, how-ever, be transparent and democratic and support the rights of people, com-munities, and nations to self-determination. The World Bank, the IMF, and the World Trade Organization violate each of these conditions to such an extent that the authors of this book recommend that they be decommis-sioned and new institutions be built under the authority of a strengthened and reformed United Nations. These new institutions would be responsible for freeing Third World nations from the burden of unpayable international debts, helping all nations bring their international trade and investment accounts into balance with the global system, and working with national governments to establish the public accountability of corporations with operations that span national borders.

## Momentum for Change

Less than a decade ago, the claims of corporate globalists of the inevitability of their cause seemed credible to many. Talk of economic alternatives seemed little more than bravado. Today, although corporate globalization remains a formidable force, it no longer seems quite as invincible, nor discussion of alternatives quite as fanciful. Public consciousness of the pervasive abuse of corporate power has fueled the growth of a powerful opposition movement.

For example, secret negotiations during the 1990s toward a multilateral agreement on investment (MAI) under the Organization for Economic Cooperation and Development (OECD) were exposed and ultimately ended. U.S. President Clinton was twice denied the "fast track" authority he sought, which would have allowed him a free hand in negotiating trade agreements with minimal congressional debate and no amendment. (A Republican Congress finally did grant this authority to President George W. Bush in 2002, by three votes.) Efforts to launch a new round of trade negotiations at the 1999 WTO ministerial meeting in Seattle were disrupted, and the WTO was forced to expose its undemocratic nature by moving its 2001 ministerial meeting to Qatar, a remote monarchy where public protest is ruthlessly suppressed. In April 2000, police shut down much of Washington, D.C., to secure a World Bank–IMF meeting from protestors demanding the decommissioning of these institutions and the cancellation of Third World debt. A subsequent meeting of IMF and World Bank directors in Prague closed a day early, and a planned meeting in Barcelona was canceled. In 2001, pharmaceutical corporations were forced to make concessions allowing greater use of low-cost generic drugs in poor countries. And as chronicled in the introduction to this volume, in fall 2003 protesters joined some poor country governments in Cancun, Mexico, and in Miami to derail global and regional trade negotiations.

The evolving alliance of civil society organizations brings together union members, farmers, landless peasants, people of faith, women's organizations, youth organizations, small business owners, artisanal producers, economic justice organizers, prison reform advocates, environmentalists, AIDS and other health activists, politicians, independent media organizations, civil servants, the homeless, peace and human rights organizations, gay and lesbian groups, intellectuals, consumer advocates, and even a few corporate CEOs of every age, religion, race, and nationality. It is the product of a largely spontaneous awakening of millions of people to the reality that their future and the future of their children depends on exercising their democratic right to participate in the decisions that shape their future.

Unified by a deep commitment to universal values of democracy, justice, and respect for life, this alliance functions with growing effectiveness without a central organization, leadership, or defining ideology. It also takes different forms in different settings.

In India, activists seek to empower local people through the democratic community control of resources under the banner of a millions-strong Living Democracy movement. In Canada, hundreds of organizations have joined together to articulate a citizens' agenda that seeks to wrest control of governmental institutions back from corporations. In Chile, coalitions of environmental groups have created a powerful Sustainable Chile proposal that seeks to reverse that country's drift toward free markets and reassert popular democratic control over national priorities and resources. The focus in Brazil is on the rights of workers, the poor, and the landless. In Bolivia, a mass movement of peasants and workers has successfully blocked the privatization of water. In Mexico, the Mayan people have reignited the spirit of Zapata in a movement to confirm the rights of indigenous people to land and resources. French farmers have risen up in revolt against trade rules that threaten to destroy small farms. The construction of new highways in the United Kingdom has brought out hundreds of thousands of people who oppose this desecration of the countryside to meet globalization's relentless demand for ever more high-speed transport.

These are only a few examples of the initiatives and actions in defense of democratic rights that are occurring around the world. Some are purely local; others are national or international. Some seek major reforms to the current structures; others seek complete transformation. Some are short-term and address the debates of the moment; others are long-term and spell out new rules and institutions to advance sustainable societies. (See Box B by Martin Khor of the Malaysia-based Third World Network for further discussion of these different approaches to alternatives work.) But all are linked together in common rejection of the illegitimate power and false promises of global corporations and in a proactive commitment to revitalize democracy at local, regional, national, and global levels. Each contributes to an emerging vision of the healthy, just, and sustainable society that humanity has the means to create. Each adds its voice to a growing global chorus proclaiming the right of "We the people of planet earth" to create such a society.

---

### BOX B: COMMENTARY — CONFLICTING PARADIGMS

*By Martin Khor, Third World Network*

Let me put forward two conflicting paradigms that civil society is now facing and which require that we make some difficult choices about how we advance our work. The first paradigm involves the choice to work in the system of globalization, in which we feel we are trapped. If we do work within that system, we begin by asking: "Are the rules of the game fair, particularly to the weaker partners, or are they being twisted and manipulated by the strong partners in order to keep the weaker countries down?" If the latter, then we should fight for the reform of the rules of the game so that they can be more fair. We should monitor and be aware where the rules of the game go against the weak and the poor. In this first paradigm, we will be working and arguing within the parameters of the system and trying to tinker with it, because we may conclude that there is no choice, at least in the short run. And this may be an approach pragmatic people will take who are involved in, say, survival for the next five years or ten years.

But we realize that even as we work in that system and make it more fair for all the participants, that system may not last very long because of ecological limits. In other words, if we continue to emphasize high growth, but the growth is more equitably shared and the poor are made to come out better, still the whole system of industrialism goes on. So the debate is whether the textile mills should continue to be in London and provide jobs for British workers with high standards of living and security or whether they should be transferred to Bangladesh where child labor is exploited. But maybe it's better for the child laborer to be exploited than to be out of a job, and dead. It's that kind of debate that we may be entering into within this first paradigm. Is it fair for the Bangladeshi to be exploited in a factory or should he remain unexploited; should his labor standard go up? If his labor standard goes up he may lose his job because the factory may move back to London and the London worker will have the job.

So then the issue becomes this: maybe the factory shouldn't exist in London or Bangladesh either because industrialism is bad; perhaps industrialism is incompatible with the long-term survival of the world. This is the

CONTINUED

BOX B: CONTINUED

basis of the second paradigm—that this debate over North-South is irrelevant because in twenty or thirty years the whole system will blow up anyway. So, in the second paradigm, we work for Gandhi-style, community-based, self-reliant family units of production, trading mainly within the community and the region and only making occasional exchanges with the rest of the world, as needed.

Now if you are working within this second paradigm, you might say, "I don't want transnational corporations. I will use any methods to kick them out, and I will go back to emphasizing local production." So, if we are working from this second paradigm we would certainly come out with different policy conclusions than if we were working from the first paradigm, which is for fairer trade, fairer economic relations.

The debate on whether worker rights and environmental rights should be addressed in trade agreements is really contained in that first paradigm, while at the same time we must remember there is that second paradigm. But sometimes we borrow ideas from that second paradigm to buttress our arguments for the first paradigm, and vice versa, and we get confused. So as we work and debate which initiatives make sense, we should be explicit as to whether we are arguing from the first or the second paradigm.

Let us be clear that the real world is moving ahead in the first paradigm. Some of us may be fighting from within that paradigm to point out where

there are inequities, where there are double standards, and where there must be fairer terms of exchange, and so forth. I personally often work in the context of the first paradigm, whereas emotionally I really belong to the second one. So if we ask if we should trade with the rest of the world, we must make it very clear what our assumptions are and which paradigm we are proceeding from. Because at the end of the day, it is better if we can infuse the second paradigm into the first paradigm as a kind of transition.

For example, as we grapple with trade and environment under the first paradigm, we would do well to ask how we make the globalized system more environmentally sustainable as a transition toward the second paradigm. And to do it in such a way that the poor do not suffer and the costs of adjusting are borne by the rich.

I believe that for now we must always try to work in both paradigms. In this sense, we can devise a system that moves toward environmental sustainability in a socially equitable manner that will reduce income inequalities; resolve the poverty problem, but at the same time solve the environmental problem. Can trade mechanisms, systems of prices and products, and other things be devised so that we have this transition toward Paradigm Two? This is one of our greatest challenges.

SOURCE: Martin Khor, "Commentary." In John Cavanagh, ed., *South-North: Citizen Strategies to Transform a Divided World.* San Francisco: International Forum on Globalization, November 1995.

# CHAPTER TWO

# Design for Corporate Rule

THE ALTERNATIVES OFFERED in this volume grow from the widespread damage inflicted by corporate globalization over the past five centuries as it passed from colonialism to imperialism to postcolonial export-led development models. Since World War II, the driving forces behind economic globalization have been several hundred global corporations and banks that have increasingly woven webs of production, consumption, finance, and culture across borders. Indeed, most of what we eat, drink, wear, drive, and entertain ourselves with today are the products of global corporations.

These corporations have been aided by global bureaucracies that have emerged over the last half-century, with the overall result being a concentration of economic and political power that is increasingly unaccountable to governments, people, or the planet and that undermines democracy, equity, and environmental sustainability.

Advocates like to describe economic globalization as a long-term, inevitable process, the result of economic and technological forces that have simply evolved over centuries to their present form. They describe these forces almost as if they were uncontrollable, like forces of nature; they say that it's utopianism to believe things could be otherwise. To accept this inevitability, as most governments, academics, and mainstream media tend to do, would mean that no resistance is possible. But on the evidence of the hundreds of thousands of people who have demonstrated in Seattle, Quebec City, Porto Alegre, and Cancun, in Geneva and various other European capitals, in India, Japan, and Brazil, in Mexico, the Philippines, New Zealand, Argentina, the United Kingdom, and elsewhere, it should already be obvious that such passivity is no longer the norm.

It is true that global trade activity and concepts like free trade have existed for centuries in various forms. Although earlier versions were very different from the modern one in scale, speed, and form, the social and environmental outcomes have always been similar.

Modern globalization is not an expression of evolution. It was designed and created by human beings with a specific goal: to give primacy to economic—that is, corporate—values above all other values and to aggressively install and codify those values globally. In fact, the modern globalization era has a birthplace and a birth date: Bretton Woods, New Hampshire, July 1944. That was when the world's leading corporate figures, economists, politicians, and bankers met to figure out how to mitigate the devastation of World War II and prevent another Great Depression. They decided that a new centralized global economic system was needed to promote global economic development. This, they said, would prevent future wars, reduce poverty, and help the world rebuild.

The conferees at Bretton Woods saw themselves as altruists, though many had a large financial stake in the outcome. They decided that the ideal instrument to keep the pieces together would be the global corporation, supported by new bureaucracies and new rules of free trade. Out of the Bretton Woods meetings came the World Bank (originally called the International Bank for Reconstruction and Development) and the International Monetary Fund. Later came the General Agreement on Tariffs and Trade (GATT), which eventually gave birth to the World Trade Organization. (For more on these institutions, see chapter 3.) Other expressions of the model include the North American Free Trade Agreement (NAFTA), the European Union's Maastricht Agreement, the proposed Free Trade Area of the Americas (FTAA), and others.

Together these instruments are bringing about the most fundamental redesign of the planet's social, economic, and political arrangements since the Industrial Revolution. They are engineering a power shift of stunning proportions, moving real economic and political power away from national, state, and local governments and communities toward unprecedented centralization of power for global corporations, bankers, and the global bureaucracies they helped create, at the expense of national sovereignty, community control, democracy, diversity, and the natural world.

The good news is that all of this can be reversed or revised, if with difficulty. And the central purpose of this document is to help us move that process forward.

## Key Ingredients of the Globalization Model

Economic globalization—sometimes also referred to as *corporate globalization* or *neoliberalism*—has several key features:

- Promotion of hypergrowth and unrestricted exploitation of environmental resources and new markets to fuel that growth
- Privatization and commodification of public services and of remaining aspects of the global and community commons
- Global cultural and economic homogenization and the intense promotion of consumerism
- Integration and conversion of national economies, including some that were largely self-reliant, to environmentally and socially harmful export-oriented production
- Corporate deregulation and unrestricted movement of capital across borders
- Dramatically increased corporate concentration
- Dismantling of public health, social, and environmental programs already in place
- Replacement of traditional powers of democratic nation-states and local communities by global corporate bureaucracies

We begin with a review of some of these features of the economic globalization model.

### HYPERGROWTH

The first tenet of the globalization design is to give primary importance to the achievement of ever more rapid, never-ending corporate economic growth—hypergrowth—fueled by the constant search for access to new resources, new and cheaper labor sources, and new markets. This is why there is such excitement about China joining the experiment, because it offers all three: labor, resources, and markets. To achieve hypergrowth, the emphasis is on the ideological heart of the model—free trade—accompanied by deregulation of corporate activity. The idea is to remove as many impediments as possible to expanded corporate activity. In practice, such impediments are usually environmental laws, public health laws, food safety laws, laws pertaining to workers' rights and opportunities, laws permitting nations to control investment on their own soil, and laws attempting to retain national control over local culture. Viewed as obstacles to corporate free trade, such laws are open to challenge by new trade and investment agreements. As a result, while corporations are deregulated and freed, nation-states and local governments are harshly regulated and constrained, making it far more difficult for them to protect local jobs, identity, and tradition as well as national sovereignty and the natural world. (See Box C.)

Advocates of globalization like to argue that the beneficiaries of all this growth will be the poor because the increased wealth will "trickle down" to them. But as we will discuss later, all evidence shows that the opposite is true. The benefits of hypergrowth mainly trickle *up*.

---

## BOX C: PUBLIC INTEREST LAWS AS "IMPEDIMENTS" TO FREE TRADE

*By Debi Barker and Jerry Mander, International Forum on Globalization*

A major goal of the Bretton Woods institutions is to remove impediments, including public interest regulations, that might restrict corporate access to markets, labor, and resources.

WTO tribunals have an impressive record for challenging democratically created laws and standards, particularly environmental protections. The WTO's very first ruling was against the U.S. Clean Air Act, which set high standards against polluting gasoline. The act was found noncompliant with WTO trade rules and had to be softened.

Other controversial rulings have targeted other issues:

- The U.S. Marine Mammal Protection Act (particularly the provision that protects dolphins otherwise killed by industrial tuna fishing)
- The sea turtle protections under the U.S. Endangered Species Act
- The European Union's ban on imports of U.S. beef injected with growth hormones

Although only governments may submit WTO complaints, global corporations are almost always the driving force. In one of the most appalling examples, the U.S. government acted on behalf of Chiquita to challenge the Eu-

CONTINUED

## PRIVATIZATION AND COMMODIFICATION

A second tenet of the design is to push toward privatization and commodification of as many noncommodified nooks and crannies of existence as possible. This too is necessary to expand the terrain for economic activity and profit. The conversion process now includes formerly pristine elements of the global commons—elements that have until now always been far outside the trading system and that most of us have always assumed would remain the inalienable right of all human beings to retain in a noncommodified form. For example, the genetic structures of our bodies, and of all life, are now becoming "enclosed" as part of the commodity trading system through biotechnology, with the process greatly assisted by WTO rules on intellectual property rights. Similarly, indigenous seeds,

---

BOX C: CONTINUED

ropean Union's preferential treatment of banana imports from former colonies.

There is also a secondary chilling effect from this process. For example, the government of Guatemala canceled a public health law that had forbidden infant formula companies, notably Gerber, from advertising their products as being healthier than breast milk. And Canada canceled its ban on the import of MMT, a fuel additive that can damage nervous systems. In both cases the reasons were threats of suit under trade regimes. In the Gerber case the United States threatened a suit in the WTO. In the Canadian case, Ethyl Corporation threatened to sue Canada under NAFTA's investor-state provision—likely to be expanded in the FTAA agreement—which allows corporations, for the first time, to sue sovereign governments, not in domestic courts but in international tribunals. The Ethyl threat alleged an illegal "expropriation" by Canada because Canada's environmental safety

law diminished the firm's future profits. A similar case has been brought against the U.S. government over a California ban on another dangerous fuel additive, MTBE.

The net effect is that the whole process produces a mutual ratcheting downward of environmental, labor, or health standards in all countries. It's a kind of "cross-deregulation," a way that corporations can get their own governments to destroy laws in other countries, just as they pressure for deregulation domestically.

Advocates love to call it *free* trade, but what they really mean is freedom for global corporations but suppression of the freedoms for communities or nations to regulate or otherwise maintain primary values, like the environment, health, culture, jobs, national sovereignty—and democracy.

SOURCE: Debi Barker and Jerry Mander, *Invisible Government*. San Francisco: International Forum on Globalization, 1999.

developed and freely shared by agricultural communities for thousands of years, are now subject to long-term monopoly ownership by global corporations through patenting. Recent protests against the WTO's TRIPs (Trade-Related Intellectual Property Rights agreement) by farmers in India and by AIDS victims in Africa and elsewhere who are trying to get relief from high-priced patented medicines, have begun to shine a new light on some appalling aspects of this issue.

There is also a similar pressure to privatize freshwater—rivers, lakes, streams—probably the most basic element of sustenance, always considered a part of the commons. These too may soon be converted into part of the global trade system. All of these and others are being rapidly privatized and commodified as part of the globalization project to bring ever more raw material—more territory (geographic and biological)—into play for corporate access, investment, development, and trade. (See chapter 5, "Reclaiming the Commons," for more on these issues.)

Alarmingly, the privatization process is now also taking place in the realm of public services. Corporations argue that government is invariably bureaucratic, inefficient, and self-serving in contrast to the so-called efficiency, dynamism, and consumer responsiveness of the private sector. Thus, public services should be left to them. They make this argument even though they operate on an entirely different hierarchy of values than do governments. Privatization of public services is now an important part of both the proposed new FTAA agreement and the General Agreement on Trade in Services (GATS) within the WTO. The latter negotiations, currently ongoing, involve changes in many services that were until recently reserved for governments, like public broadcasting, public education, public health, water delivery and treatment, sewage and sanitation services, hospitals, welfare systems, police, fire, social security, railroads, and prisons. These may all soon be commodified, privatized, opened to foreign investment and domination, and eventually available only to those people who will be able to pay commercial rates for them. We could wind up with Mitsubishi running social security, Bechtel controlling the world's water, Deutschebank running the jails (and maybe the parks), Disney running the British Broadcasting Corporation, Merck running the Canadian health care system. It sounds far-fetched, but the threat is real.

There is also the commodification of money itself. Right now, the overwhelming majority of global transactions under the free trade system are not in goods and services but are financial. Money itself is a commodity for speculation. Modern information technology has made it possible to shift unimaginably large sums of money instantaneously across borders, anywhere in the world, without any controls on the transactions, by the stroke of a computer key. This has already had terrible destabilizing effects on many countries and was one of the precipitating causes of the 1997–98 financial crisis that began in Asia.

## ECONOMIC AND CULTURAL HOMOGENIZATION

The third tenet of economic globalization is to integrate and merge the economic activity of all countries into a homogeneous model of development—a single, centralized supersystem. Countries with cultures, economies, and traditions as varied as those of India, Sweden, Thailand, Kenya, Bhutan, Bolivia, Canada, Russia, and close to two hundred others are all meant to adopt similar tastes, values, and lifestyles. They are to be served by the same few global corporations, the same fast-food restaurants, hotel chains, and clothing chains; wear the same jeans and shoes; drive similar cars; receive the same films, music, and television shows; live in the same kind of urban landscape; and engage in the same kind of agricultural and industrial development schemes, while carrying the same personal, cultural, and spiritual values—a *global monoculture.* This trend is already visible to any traveler. Every place is becoming more and more like every other place. Cultural diversity is going the way of biodiversity.

Such a homogeneous model serves the efficiency needs of the largest corporations, which can act on a global plane, duplicating their production and marketing efforts on an expanded terrain and achieving the many efficiencies of scale that go with borderlessness. It's like the standard gauge railway of another era or, in today's terms, like computer compatibility. Among the primary purposes of the global trade agreements and bureaucracies is to make rules that ensure there are no blockages in the flow, that global corporations can move freely in all countries, and that economic homogenization and integration are accelerated.

## EXPORT-ORIENTED TRADE AND INVESTMENT

Corporate globalization favors orienting all national economies to export, lifting barriers to foreign investment, and removing all restraints on the free flow of speculative money across national borders. These preferences encourage production for sale to other countries over domestic sale, foreign ownership over domestic ownership, and financial speculation. These activities favor global corporations and financiers but leave people everywhere dependent for their livelihoods on the actions of absentee owners over whom they have no influence.

The underlying theoretical rationale for export-oriented production centers on the theory of *comparative advantage.* According to this theory, every country should produce only those products over which it has a relative advantage; thus, some countries now specialize in single crops like coffee, sugarcane, forest products, or high-tech assembly. Theoretically, they can meet their other needs by using the earnings from these specialized exports to buy goods and services over which others have an advantage.

Comparative advantage is a crucial component of globalization theory. It facilitates the replacement of diverse local or regional economic systems, including systems that may currently emphasize successful diversified, small-scale, industrial, artisanal, and agriculture systems that feature many small producers using mostly local or regional resources and local labor for local or regional consumption. The goal is to substitute large-scale monocultural export systems.

Going back to the mid-twentieth century, many countries of the world actively tried to do the *opposite* of specialization: they diversified their industrial and agriculture systems precisely in order to recover from a colonial period during which huge monocultural systems, such as pineapple plantations, coffee plantations, banana plantations, or, more recently, industrial assembly work were imposed on them. Once independent, the governments of many of these countries concluded that this kind of imposed specialization left them extremely vulnerable to political decisions abroad and to the shocks and whims of the market and commodity-pricing systems. As a result, they were sometimes unable to purchase necessities like health products and food, energy, and basic industrial needs. Naturally, they sought self-sufficiency in these items. Their preferred system was sometimes called *import substitution*, or simply *national self-reliance.* It was intended to help countries regain some degree of control over their domestic economies.

After Bretton Woods, and especially during the 1980s, the World Bank and the IMF put tremendous pressure on these countries to abandon self-reliance, a term that came to be synonymous with isolationism and protectionism. The World Bank and the IMF pressured them to open their borders to private investments by global corporations in a position to produce on the large scale appropriate for the export model. It became impossible for these countries to gain any financial aid from the bank or the IMF unless they submitted to structural adjustment programs (SAPs)—in other words, unless they redesigned their domestic systems to emphasize exports. The pressure worked. But after converting so much production to export, these same countries found that they were still subject to restrictions on imports by the wealthy countries. Many poor countries are now sorry they accepted the system and are joining the resistance to it.

Why did the World Bank and the IMF push so hard to achieve these goals? Here's the crux of the matter: *systems that emphasize local or regional self-reliance are extremely subversive to free trade, economic globalization, and hyper corporate growth.* These all depend on maximizing the number and scale of economic transactions. Local and regional production for regional consumption is the archenemy of globalization because it operates on an inherently smaller scale, and there are fewer steps in the process.

There is far less opportunity for global corporations if local populations or countries can satisfy their needs internally or regionally than if economic activity is designed to move back and forth across oceans, exporting, importing, or reworking it and then exporting it again, with thousands of ships passing each other in the night. That's what fuels global economic growth and provides opportunities for global corporate operations. But alas, it's also what destroys the environment fastest and makes countries dependent on external forces they cannot control.

Ironically, free trade theorists often invoke the names and theories of Adam Smith and David Ricardo in defense of these destructive export-oriented policies. Yet Smith had an explicit preference for small, locally owned enterprises. And Ricardo's theory of comparative advantage assumes that capital is immobile, confined inside national borders—a far cry from the current rules and theories.

Converting diverse local economies into export trade systems benefits global corporations but makes individuals, communities, and nations dependent and vulnerable. Society, communities, and the environment would all be better off if international institutions and agreements emphasized aiding local and national self-sufficiency rather than export production.

The agriculture sector is a prime example of the social and environmental problems of the export-oriented development model. Even in today's computer age, nearly half of the world's population still lives directly on the land, growing food for their families and communities, primarily staples and other mixed crops. These farmers replant with indigenous seed varieties and use crop rotation and community sharing of resources like water, seeds, and labor. Such systems have kept them going for millennia. But local systems are anathema to global corporations. So companies like Monsanto, Cargill, and Archer Daniels Midland are leading a chorus of corporate, government, and bureaucratic statements—often expressed in millions of dollars worth of advertising—that small farmers are not "productive" or "efficient" enough to feed a hungry world.

Nearly all the investment rules of the WTO and the big banks—and many more now being proposed—strongly favor global corporations and monocultures over local diverse farming for self-sufficiency. So where tens of thousands of small farmers once grew food to eat, giant corporations and global development schemes are converting the land to single-crop luxury monocultures run by absentee landlords.

Furthermore, these companies do not grow food for the local people to eat. Instead, they favor high-priced, high-margin luxury items—flowers, potted plants, beef, shrimp, cotton, coffee—for export to the already overfed countries. As for the people who used to live on these lands and grow their own foods, they are rapidly being removed. And because the corporate systems feature machine-intensive production, there are few jobs. Thus, the people who used to feed themselves become landless, cashless, homeless, dependent, and hungry. Communities that were once self-sustaining disappear; still-intact cultures are decimated. This is so even in the United States, where few family farmers are still in business.

Other environmental problems intrinsic to the shift to export include loss of biodiversity from emphasizing single crops for export and heavy use of pesticides. Where indigenous Filipinos, for example, once grew thousands of varieties of rice, a few varieties now account for the bulk of production, and the other varieties are disappearing. Mexico has lost more than 75 percent of its indigenous maize varieties. According to the Food and Agriculture Organization (FAO), the world has already lost up to 75 percent of its crop diversity because of the globalization of industrialized agriculture.

There are also external costs of industrial agriculture. Hailed as more efficient than small-scale farming, this is a kind of efficiency that ignores the costs of air, water, and soil pollution, toxic rivers, dead fish. Many public health problems from food-borne diseases are directly attributable to factory farming systems: infections from salmonella, *e. coli,* and *listeria* as well as Mad Cow disease, hoof-and-mouth disease, and others.

Finally, industrial agriculture brings the social costs of taking care of all the farmers who lose their livelihoods through this system; together, social and environmental costs rise into the billions of dollars. If you take all these external costs into account, does it make any sense to call this system "efficient"?

---

## BOX D: INTRINSIC ENVIRONMENTAL CONSEQUENCES OF TRADE-RELATED TRANSPORT

*By Jerry Mander, International Forum on Globalization, and Simon Retallack,* The Ecologist

The central feature of an export-oriented production model is that it dramatically increases transport and shipping activity. In the half-century since Bretton Woods, there has been about a twenty-five fold increase in global transport activity.

As global transport increases, it in turn requires massive increases in global infrastructure development. This is good for large corporations like Bechtel and Halliburton, which get to do the construction work: new airports, seaports, oil fields, pipelines for the oil, rail lines, high-speed highways. Many of these are built in areas with relatively intact wilderness, biodiversity, and coral reefs, or they are built in rural areas. The impact is especially strong now in South and Central America, where there have been tremendous investments in infrastructure development in wilderness regions, often against great resistance from native communities like the U'wa in Colombia, the Kuna in Panama, and many different groups in Ecuador. The problems also occur in the developed world. In the United Kingdom a few years ago, there were protests by two hundred thousand people against huge new highways jammed through rural landscapes so that trucks could better serve the global trading system. Both the indigenous protesters and the rural English were protesting the same thing—the ecological and social destruction of their region to serve globalization.

Increased global trade increases fossil fuel use as well, contributing to global warming. Ocean shipping carries nearly 80 percent of the world's international trade in goods. The fuel commonly used by ships is a mixture of diesel and low-quality oil known as "Bunker C," which is particularly polluting because of high levels of carbon and sulfur. If not consumed by ships, it

CONTINUED

Indeed, farmers are rapidly becoming the leaders of international resistance to globalization in many parts of the world. We have seen mass protests by rice farmers in Japan, Thailand, and the Philippines. There have been huge protests against Cargill, Kentucky Fried Chicken, and Monsanto in India, with millions of people on the streets. And a few years ago, a French farmer named José Bové drove his tractor into a McDonald's restaurant in France. Bové was protesting "bad food," he said, as well as the entire industrial agricultural system, the corporate takeover of small farms for export monocultures, and the destruction of traditional farming in France.

BOX D: CONTINUED

would otherwise be considered a waste product. The shipping industry is anticipating major growth over the next few years; the port of Los Angeles alone projects a 50 percent increase over the next decade.

Increased air transport is even more damaging than shipping. Each ton of freight moved by plane uses forty-nine times as much energy per kilometer as when it's moved by ship. A physicist at Boeing once described the pollution from the takeoff of a single 747 as like "setting the local gas station on fire and flying it over your neighborhood." A two-minute takeoff by a 747 is equal to 2.4 million lawn mowers running for twenty minutes.

Ocean pollution from shipping has reached crisis levels, and there have been direct effects of these huge ships on wildlife and fisheries. Even more serious, possibly, is the epidemic increase of bioinvasions, a significant cause of species extinction. With the growth of global transport, billions of creatures are on the move. Invasive species, brought by global trade, often outcom-

pete native species and bring pollution or health crises. In the United States, the emergence of the West Nile virus where it never existed before is due to increased transport activity. So is the spread of malaria and dengue fever.

Ocean shipping also requires increased refrigeration—contributing to ozone depletion and climate change—and an increase in packaging and the wood pallets used for cargo loading; these are little-noted but significant factors in increased pressure on global forests.

Global conversion of agriculture from diverse, small-scale local farms to giant, chemical-intensive industrial production for export markets has also brought terrible environmental destruction to lands and waters across the planet. (See also chapter 8.)

The central point is this: if you are going to design a system built on the premise that dramatically increased global trade and transport are good, you are guaranteed to bring on these kinds of environmental problems. They are *intrinsic* to the model.

# Beneficiaries of Economic Globalization

One might give the benefit of the doubt to the architects of this global experiment. Perhaps they actually believed that the system would produce the kind of rapid growth that would truly benefit the poor and the environment. We have certainly heard them repeat the homily over and over: "A rising tide will lift all boats." We continue to hear it from the heads of the WTO, the World Bank, and most countries' leaders. But is it true?

The problems begin with the assumption that hypergrowth can continue forever. How can exponential growth possibly be sustained, given the limits of a finite planet? Where will the resources—the minerals, the wood, the water, the land—come from to feed hyperexpansion without killing the planet and ourselves? The world's limits are already in view. How many cars and refrigerators can be built and bought? How many roads can cover the land? How many fish can be vacuumed from the sea before species disappear and ecosystems fail? How much pollution can the world survive? What about global warming, toxic dumping, ozone depletion?

There's another important question: Who actually benefits from this system? It's not the farmers who are driven from their own lands and made into homeless, jobless refugees in both the South and the North. It's not the urban dwellers who must deal with masses of displaced people jamming into cities looking for jobs. It's not the workers caught in downward wage spirals in both the North and the South. It's not indigenous peoples facing hordes of corporate invaders seeking the last resources. And it's surely not nature.

The actual beneficiaries are obvious. They are the exact opposites of those whom the advocates claim. In the United States, for example, during the period of most rapid globalization—the 1990s—the top corporate executives of the largest global companies made salaries and gained options in the many millions of dollars (often in the hundreds of millions), while real wages of ordinary workers barely rose. Sarah Anderson and John Cavanagh of the Institute for Policy Studies report that American CEOs were paid on average 458 times more than production workers in 2000, up from 104 times in 1991. The Economic Policy Institute's 1999 report by Lawrence Mishel and others says that median hourly wages are actually down by 10 percent in real terms over the previous twenty-five years. And in the industry that led the United States' recent boom—the computer industry—where some people famously made fortunes, 80 percent of assembly and production workers are temporary workers, earning $8 an hour with no benefits and no unions.

As for lifting the global poor, the U.N. Development Program's 1999 *Human Development Report* revealed that the gap between the wealthy and the poor within and among countries of the world is growing steadily larger. It blamed inherent inequities in the global trade system for this situation. In 2004, the International Labor Organization (ILO) of the United Nations confirmed that the gap between rich and poor was continuing to widen, "with countries representing 14 percent of the world population accounting for half the world's trade and investment." The United States, the world's richest country, was cited as having the widest gap in the world between rich and poor. The ILO report also indicated that in poor countries women's traditional agriculture has been hit especially hard by globalization. Even

---

## BOX E: IN THE UNITED STATES: THE ISSUE IS JOBS

*By Sarah Anderson, Director, Global Economy Project, Institute for Policy Studies, and John Cavanagh, Institute for Policy Studies*

Many Americans share the wide range of concerns about globalization that people around the world, in both the North and the South, are feeling. Like those in the Mexican state of San Luis Potosi, California legislators and others are outraged by international investment rules that allow global corporations like Metalclad and Methanex to undermine public interest regulations through investor-state lawsuits. As in Cochabamba, Bolivia, residents of New Orleans and other cities are fighting the pressure to privatize essential public services, such as water. And just as people in other nations resent the power of U.S. corporations to dominate their culture, media, and political systems, so too are Americans disturbed by the excessive influence of these firms on their own country.

Unfortunately, however, in a globalized system, the interests of a community in one place are often set against the corresponding community in another place. Loss of jobs in one place because of "outsourcing" can be seen as "economic development" in another. That is one of the tragic realities of a globalized system, which pits workers against workers in different countries.

In 2004 in the United States, these concerns intensified and became a key issue in the presidential election campaign. However, the fear that trade and

CONTINUED

investment liberalization throws American workers into competition with lower-wage areas with often poor labor rights and environmental enforcement has been a consistent driving force of activism and debate for more than a decade.

To calm Americans' job-related fears, proponents of agreements like the North American Free Trade Agreement have relied primarily on two claims. First, they argued that NAFTA would be a big net job creator because it would result in large U.S. trade surpluses with its NAFTA partners. Yet just the opposite has occurred. Even though U.S. exports to Canada and Mexico increased somewhat, the combined U.S. trade deficit with Mexico and Canada has increased about tenfold since NAFTA went into effect. Overall, the U.S. trade deficit in goods was $549.4 billion in 2003, the highest on record. China, since becoming a member of the WTO, has the largest trade surplus with the United States, at $124 billion in 2003. In response to the booming U.S. deficit, free trade supporters have changed their math, now claiming that it is valid to base job impacts solely on exports, without considering the displacement effects of increased imports. This argument has been undermined by the millions of U.S. manufacturing jobs lost during the past decade.

The second false claim made by supporters of the current approach to globalization is that U.S. workers who lose jobs in manufacturing have little to fear because of low overall U.S. unemployment rates and new, better opportunities in the service sector. However, according to the Department of Labor, one-third of workers who were displaced during the 1999 to 2001 period had not found jobs by 2002, and of those who were reemployed, more than half had to take a pay cut. This is not surprising, because virtually all the new jobs created during the 1990s were service-sector jobs, which on average pay 20 percent less than manufacturing jobs.

Of course, not all service jobs are in burger flipping and broom pushing. There are also high-paying careers in the health care and information technology fields that have been held up as the bright future of the U.S. economy. But now, even highly skilled computer programming, financial analysis, and X-ray reading jobs are going overseas. And this development, made possible by advances in information technology, has shaken the confidence of American workers who face a seemingly limitless shift of jobs from the United States to low-wage countries.

The top destination in the developing world for such outsourced service jobs is India, where the wage gap with the United States is more than twelve to one for telephone operators and about nine to one for medical transcribers, according to a 2003 study by the University of California, Berkeley. The next biggest developing-country draw for service work is China, which has rock-bottom wages but lacks India's English-speaking advantage, followed by Mex-

CONTINUED

ico, where the wage ratio with the United States is about eight to one.

McKinsey and Company, a consulting firm that helps U.S. corporations develop offshore operations, says that global pay gaps result in cost savings for outsourcers of at least 45 to 55 percent (after accounting for higher infrastructure and other costs). If this is true, figures in the Berkeley study suggest that companies could save around $300 billion a year if they outsourced all of the estimated fourteen million U.S. service jobs considered vulnerable to being shipped overseas.

The offshoring of white-collar jobs has stirred up questions about globalization among Americans up and down the income ladder. Whereas low- and middle-class workers have always tended to be skeptical of trade agreements like NAFTA and the WTO, according to a February 2004 poll by the University of Maryland, even among Americans earning over $100,000 a year support for actively promoting more free trade dropped from 57 to 28 percent between 1999 and 2004.

It is unclear whether this latest wave of insecurity over American jobs and globalization will lead to xenophobic, isolationist responses or more rational policies to help workers in the United States and elsewhere. Thus far, the focus of most of the U.S. debate has been on national measures to discourage foreign outsourcing of service jobs—for example, by banning offshoring of government contract work. In the long term, the best response is to focus on supporting sustainable economic activity in poor countries. This requires distinguishing between outsourced jobs that represent raw exploitation and those that may genuinely benefit workers and their communities. Some have argued, for example, that the flow of highly skilled software engineering jobs to India is a positive reward for that country's investment in higher education and that while these jobs are largely nonunion, conditions are far from sweatshop-like and often pay well by national standards. The goal should not be to deny workers anywhere the opportunity for dignified employment. Rather, the focus should be on the factors that make workers vulnerable to exploitation. These include the agricultural policies promoted by the World Bank, IMF, and WTO, which have wrenched millions of farmers off their land, creating a nearly bottomless pool of unemployed laborers desperate for jobs. Other factors that also keep wages artificially low are labor repression and the increased power of employers to pit workers against one another in a globalized economy. For Americans, a major challenge for the foreseeable future will be to recognize that it is in their self-interest to act in solidarity with their counterparts around the globe, as well as help both poor nations and the United States, to build strong local economies where needs are well satisfied without intervention by globe-spanning corporations. Only then can the economic divide that hurts people everywhere be narrowed.

the U.S. Central Intelligence Agency concurred. In its *Global Trends 2015* report, the CIA maintained that globalization will create "an even wider gap between regional winners and losers than exists today. [Globalization's] evolution will be rocky, marked by chronic volatility and a widening economic divide . . . deepening economic stagnation, political instability, and cultural alienation. [It] will foster political, ethnic, ideological, and religious extremism, along with the violence that often accompanies it." Such is already the degree of wealth concentration that the world's 587 billionaires are now worth more than the combined income of the bottom half of humanity.

The economic clout of global firms is equally staggering. As Sarah Anderson and John Cavanagh of the Institute for Policy Studies report, the combined sales of the top two hundred firms grew faster than overall global economic activity between 1983 and 1999, reaching the equivalent of close to 30 percent of world gross domestic product (GDP). Yet these firms employ only three-quarters of 1 percent of the global workforce. As they continue to grow larger and more globalized, they continue to replace workers with machines or buy up competitors and eliminate duplicate jobs. Such economies of scale are intrinsic to the free-trade, globalization design, just as environmental pollution is intrinsic to export-oriented trade. Large-scale mergers and consolidations—bigness—produce fewer jobs, not more jobs. Indeed, the ideologies and rules of economic globalization have destroyed the livelihoods of millions of people while eliminating basic public services. Despite this, according to the ILO study, corporations are paying less tax, consistent with neoliberal philosophies. "In the world's thirty wealthiest nations," said the ILO's 2004 report, "the average corporate tax fell from 37.6 percent in 1996 to 30.8 percent in 2003."

It is true that there are isolated instances where some improvement has been achieved in Third World countries. The Bretton Woods institutions often trumpet these examples. But it is also true that the benefits of this growth have usually been short-lived. Furthermore, nearly all of it goes to the elites in these countries and to the chief executives of the global corporations at the hub of the process.

Let's look at the so-called poster children of free trade, the Asian Tigers: Taiwan, South Korea, Singapore, and Malaysia. In these countries, improvement has come not by assiduously following the dictates of the Bretton

Woods institutions but often by doing the opposite of what they prescribe. Asian countries that have had some brief successes in developing their own economies did not cut all their tariffs as demanded by globalizing institutions, permit foreign entry without controls, or eliminate existing support for domestic businesses, local economies, and local agriculture. Instead, those countries first developed the ability to take care of their basic needs internally, rather than totally converting to an export-based production system.

By at first resisting the economic model pushed by Bretton Woods, some countries managed to stay free of the volatility of export markets. But when they finally succumbed to pressure from the IMF and the World Bank, they found their glory days quickly ending.

Indeed, most poor countries have never enjoyed much benefit from globalization. After three decades of strong doses of IMF and World Bank medicine and less than a decade of WTO policies, many have seen that globalization is a false promise. The policies are not designed to benefit them but to benefit rich industrial countries and their global corporations. For this reason, many of the poor nations of the world—notably from the Caribbean and Asia—held firmly together in opposition to the WTO in Seattle in 1999, only reluctantly agreed to further trade talks in Doha, Qatar, in 2001, and rejected new talks in 2003 in Cancun.

So much for the rising tide that lifts all boats. Clearly it lifts only yachts. (See also Box G in chapter 3.)

Hundreds of thousands of people are now convinced that it doesn't need to be this way; there is nothing inevitable about it. Globalization is driven by a set of rules and self-interested institutions that can be changed—if we have a democracy.

At its root, economic globalization is really an experiment, an economic model promoted by people who most benefit from it. As for the charge that those who are against it are utopian, obviously the globalizers have got things backward. To keep arguing as they do—that a system that homogenizes global economic activity and culture to benefit corporations, removes power from communities and puts it into global bureaucracies, marginalizes and makes homeless millions of farmers and workers, and devastates nature can survive for very long—*that* is utopianism. It's not going to work. It's far better that we seek other solutions.

## BOX F: GLOBALIZATION AND CLIMATE CHANGE

*By Edward Goldsmith,* The Ecologist

Climate change may be the most daunting problem that humankind has ever encountered, and economic globalization is accelerating it. The Inter-Governmental Panel on Climate Change (IPCC) now predicts a temperature change of up to 5.8 degrees centigrade during the twenty-first century. However, the IPCC did not take into account such added critical factors as the annihilation of our tropical forests and other vegetation, especially because of global trade and development models. These forests contain six hundred billion tons of carbon, almost as much as is contained in the atmosphere. Much of this carbon is likely to be released into the atmosphere in the next decades by the increasingly uncontrolled activities of the giant global logging companies. The director-general of the United Nations environment Program recently said only a miracle could save the world's remaining tropical forests.

Nor does the IPCC include damage to the world's soils from modern export-oriented industrial agriculture. Agriculture is now responsible for 25 percent of the world's carbon dioxide emission, 60 percent of methane, and 80 percent of nitrous oxide, all of them potent greenhouse gases. All the world's soils combined contain sixteen hundred billion tons of carbon, more than twice the amount now in the atmosphere. Much of this will be released within a few decades unless there is a

rapid switch to sustainable, locally oriented, largely organic agricultural practices. (See also chapter 8.)

The Hadley Centre of the British Meteorological Organisation has drawn even more frightening outcomes than IPCC. Hadley does take forest depletion and industrial agriculture into account in its recent models and concludes that the world's average temperature will actually increase by up to 8.8 degrees centigrade rather than 5.8 degrees over this century. Many other climatologists agree. If they are right, the implications are horrifying.

The IPCC tells us to expect a considerable increase in heat waves, storms, and floods and the spread of tropical diseases into temperate areas, which will not only affect human health but also that of our crops. It also tells us to expect a rise in sea levels of up to eighty-eight centimeters, which will affect (by seawater intrusion into the soils underlying croplands and by temporary and also permanent flooding) something like 30 percent of the world's agricultural lands. This will be especially disastrous for poor and small farmers occupying lowlands, such as in Bangladesh, and among island nations, although it will also threaten much of the U.S. coastline. But, of course, if the Hadley Centre's predictions are right, the implications are still worse than the IPCC expects.

Also worrying is the melting of the secondary Antarctic, the Arctic, and in

CONTINUED

particular, the Greenland ice shields, which is occurring far more quickly than was predicted by the IPCC. This will reduce the salinity of the oceans and may weaken or divert oceanic currents such as the Gulf Stream from their present course. This process could eventually lead to the freezing up of areas that at present have a temperate climate, such as Northern Europe, which could eventually resemble Labrador, on the same latitude. Ironically, global warming could also lead to extreme *cooling* in some locales.

(The British *Observer* newspaper reported in 2004 on a secret U.S. Pentagon study warning of the possibility "that European cities will be sunk beneath rising seas as Britain is plunged into a 'Siberian climate' as early as the first half of this century." The Pentagon's report apparently also predicts the possibility of nuclear wars, megadroughts, famine, and rioting across the world, in reaction. The authors of the study, including CIA consultant Peter Schwartz, a former head of planning at Royal Dutch/Shell, argued that climate change "should be elevated beyond a scientific debate to a U.S. national security concern," advice that was likely to fall on deaf ears in the Bush administration.)

Indeed, the effects of climate change are proceeding faster than predicted. Four years of drought in much of Africa have resulted in thirty to forty million people facing starvation. Drought in the American corn belt, the Canadian plains, and the Australian wheat belt may seriously reduce cereal exports, which will in turn affect the vast masses of people in Africa and elsewhere who are already facing starvation. The recent climate in Europe has also been dreadful. Floods in Germany in 2002 caused an estimated 10 billion euros in damages. The terrible storms in northern Italy, with hailstones the size of tennis balls, destroyed crops over a wide area in 2002. Drought in southern Europe has also drastically reduced harvests, destroying, for example, olive harvests throughout southern and central Italy.

All this is the recent result of no more than a 0.7 degree centigrade increase in global temperatures. What will things be like when we have to grow our food in a world whose average temperature has increased by two or three degrees, let alone by five to eight degrees as we are told might happen later in this century?

Even if we stopped burning fossil fuels tomorrow, our planet would continue to heat up for at least 150 years, which is the residence time of carbon dioxide, the most important greenhouse gas in the atmosphere, while the oceans will continue to warm for a thousand years. Our only choice is to take measures—and very dramatic ones at that—that can slow down the warming process so our planet remains partly habitable. This includes minimizing export-oriented products, with their commensurate fossil fuel use, and making drastic changes in agricultural production. But thus far industrial nations are not sufficiently attending to the problem, and some, like the United States and Russia, are ignoring it completely. Public protest is mandatory.

## The Role of the Media

Signs of the instability and unfairness of the globalization experiment are in view everywhere. Sadly, however, they are poorly reported. When the mainstream media does report a few crises created by globalization, it fails to help the public grasp that these crises are all rooted in the same problem—corporate globalization itself. Here are some examples.

- We read about environmental problems such as changes in the global climate, the melting polar ice cap, or habitat destruction. We read about ozone depletion, ocean pollution, and wars over oil, and soon we will probably read about wars over water supply. But rarely are these grave matters linked to the imperatives of global economic expansion now accelerated by free trade, the overuse of resources, and the consumer lifestyle that's being promoted worldwide by television and its parent—advertising. (See Box F, "Globalization and Climate Change.")

- The financial crises in Asia in 1997 to 1998 and in Argentina in 2001 to 2002 were often reported as being caused by incompetence, inefficiency, corruption, and cronyism in the countries involved. The gigantic bailout by the International Monetary Fund in Asia was made to seem like a beneficent act of charity toward our underprivileged, dysfunctional Asian friends, who had not yet achieved our own higher ethical standards. Rarely was it acknowledged that the money did not go to the citizens of those countries but rather was used to bail out the international bankers who caused the problem in the first place through reckless lending that created artificial economic bubbles. Nor did the popular media describe the role of currency speculators in the Asian crisis. Under the new rules of global free trade and deregulation, there are no controls over the massive movement of funds across borders, into countries, and back out of them. Since the advent of global computer networks, currency speculators have been able to move unimaginably huge amounts of money instantaneously and invisibly from one part of the globe to another, thus destabilizing currencies and countries and forcing nations to seek the radical solution of an IMF bailout. (We call it a "casino economy" when countries cannot control the rapid entry and exit of billions of speculator dollars.) If countries do make rules to

slow down the process—as have done Malaysia, Chile, and China—
they are often ridiculed by the economic establishment and the media
as well.

- The mainstream media does report on the anti-immigrant backlash,
whether led by a Pat Buchanan in the United States, a Jean-Marie Le Pen
in France, or a Joerg Haider in Austria. But it neglects to mention the role
of the international trade agreements in making life at home impossible
for those who migrate. Elsewhere we mention NAFTA's role in destroying the self-sufficient corn-farming economy of Mexico's Mayan people.
In India, Africa, and Latin America, megadevelopment schemes have displaced millions of indigenous people and small farmers to make way for
gigantic dams and other development projects. The result is that more
people join the landless, jobless urban masses.

- Terrible new diseases such as ebola, Mad Cow disease, *e. coli* infection,
and lately, the West Nile virus outbreak in the United States are thoroughly reported. But the connection between the outbreaks and the new
mobility that disease vectors are provided by global transport and development is rarely mentioned. The news stories also leave out the link to
factory farming practices and the globalization of industrial agriculture.

- We read about the appalling performance of Enron Corp. as it led the
process of energy deregulation, cheated its own workers while paying
bonuses to its top executives, and gave intimate advice to the U.S. president and vice president about energy policy and government appointments. What the popular media has not fully explained are the ways in
which Enron directly benefited from global bureaucracies like the World
Bank, which gave structural adjustment loans to poor countries, often on
the condition that those countries use that money to hire firms like
Enron to build domestic infrastructure and drive their economies. The
World Bank gave with one hand and took back for its friends with the
other. Nor did we read much about how Enron's behavior was not
unique; it is typical of the behavior of global corporations, and it is built
into their structure. Like other aspects of globalization, the problem is
systemic.

- We also read stories about the assaults on the last indigenous tribes in the
Amazon, Borneo, and the Philippines. Insufficiently reported are the
root causes—the need on the part of the globalization process for more

water or forests or oil or genetic resources in areas where indigenous people have lived for millennia and the equally desperate need to try to convert self-sufficient people into consumers. This too is part of the globalization process: the homogenization of conceptual frameworks, the monoculturalization of peoples and lands, the utter uniformity of the development model everywhere on earth.

All of these subjects are treated by the mainstream media as if they were unrelated. This is a disservice to an insecure public that is trying to figure out what is going on. People are not being helped to understand that dozens of major issues—overcrowded cities, unusual weather patterns, the growth of global inequality, the spread of new diseases, the lowering of wages as profits and CEO salaries soar, the elimination of social services, the destruction of the environment—are all part of the same global process. They are of one piece, a fabric of connections resulting from the world's new economic arrangement, all in the cause of an economic ideology that cannot serve social or ecological sustainability. (For a longer discussion of the problems of global media, see "Global Media" in chapter 8, page 230.)

CHAPTER THREE

# The Unholy Trinity

*The World Bank, the International Monetary Fund,
and the World Trade Organization*

THE THREE MAJOR GLOBAL INSTITUTIONS that create and express
the rules of economic globalization are the World Bank, the International
Monetary Fund, and the World Trade Organization, variously called the
"unholy trinity" or the "iron triangle." It is their fundamental job to align all
of the world's formerly disparate national economies behind a central
formula, to create the standard gauge railway by which corporate-led economic growth can more easily fulfill the mandate of Bretton Woods.

Each has its own basic function. The World Bank funds large-scale projects, promotes structural adjustment policies, and dominates the development
debate through its research department. The IMF presses similar economic
"reforms" through short-term emergency loans. And the WTO is the rule-
setter for global trade and investment. But they all work together to be sure
that all countries adopt identical visions, policies, and standards and keep in
line. And they all share the overall goals to deregulate corporate activity, privatize whatever is public, prevent nations from protecting natural resources or
labor or safety laws or standards, and open all channels in every country for a
free flow of investment and trade.

The thrust of those policies is perhaps most dramatically revealed in the
structural adjustment programs imposed on low- and intermediate-income
countries by the International Monetary Fund and the World Bank.
Structural adjustment requires governments to do the following:

• Cut government spending on education, health care, the environment, and
  price subsidies for basic necessities such as food grains and cooking oils.

- Devalue the national currency and increase exports by accelerating the plunder of natural resources, reducing real wages, and subsidizing export-oriented foreign investments.
- Liberalize (open) financial markets to attract speculative short-term portfolio investments that create enormous financial instability and foreign liabilities while serving little if any useful purpose.
- Increase interest rates to attract foreign capital that has fled its home country, thereby increasing bankruptcies of domestic businesses and imposing new hardships on indebted individuals.
- Eliminate tariffs and other controls on imports, thereby increasing the import of consumer goods purchased with borrowed foreign exchange, undermining local industry and agricultural producers unable to compete with cheap imports, increasing the strain on foreign exchange accounts, and deepening external indebtedness.

## The World Bank

According to its charter, the World Bank was created "to assist in the reconstruction and development of territories of member nations by facilitating the investment of capital for productive purposes" and "to promote the long-range balanced growth of international trade." The World Bank was originally intended to focus on financing the post–World War II reconstruction of Europe, using capital subscribed by member governments as guarantees against which it could borrow in international financial markets at favorable rates and then lend out for development projects. When Europe showed little interest in mortgaging the future of its economy to foreign bankers, the World Bank set about marketing its loans in the newly independent former colonies. At first, that too proved a hard sell. So the bank invested in training and education to indoctrinate scores of Third World bureaucrats and economists in an economic ideology that equates development with export-led economic growth fueled by foreign borrowing and investment—the basic fallacy that remains a cornerstone of its policy today.

Originally, the loans were used to finance infrastructure projects and imports beyond the means of the country's export earnings. Eventually, ever-larger new loans were needed just to service payments of interest and principle due on previous loans. The more the borrowing, the greater the need for still larger loans, and borrowing became something of an economic addiction. Aside from a handful of citizen watchdog groups, few paid attention to the burden these loans placed on domestic economies when the time came to repay.

During the 1970s, OPEC sharply increased oil prices and hence the cost of energy imports. Northern banks, awash with OPEC deposits, lavished loans on Third World countries—often with the encouragement of the World Bank. Soon the costs of debt service exceeded repayment capacity by such a wide margin that there was a threat of a global financial crisis. Beginning with Mexico in 1982, the IMF and the World Bank swung into action with structural adjustment as their primary response. Together they reoriented national economies to focus on debt repayment and to further open their resources, labor, and markets to foreign corporations. "Adjusted" countries came under great pressure to increase the export of their natural resources and the products of their labor, become more import-dependent, and increase foreign ownership of their economies. Once the countries accepted these conditions, the IMF and the World Bank rewarded them with still more loans, thus deepening their indebtedness—rather like a firefighter pouring gasoline on a burning house to stop the blaze.

The results have been disastrous not only in human and environmental terms but also in economic terms. In 1980, the total external debt of all developing countries was $609 billion; in 2001, after twenty years of structural adjustment, it totaled $2.4 trillion. In 2001, sub-Saharan Africa paid $3.6 billion more in debt service than it received in new long-term loans and credits. Africa spends about four times more on debt-service payments than it does on health care. (See Box G for a related discussion.)

In recent years, the World Bank has provided hundreds of billions of dollars in low-interest loans to subsidize the efforts of global corporations to establish control over the natural resources and markets of assisted countries. Corporations in the energy and agriculture sectors have been among the main beneficiaries. Often World Bank–financed roads, power plants, and electrical grids were built primarily to serve the global corporations establishing operations in the service area of the loan-financed facilities, rather than to serve the local populations. Indeed, as documented by the Institute for Policy Studies, the World Bank has become the major contributor to global greenhouse gas emissions through fossil fuel projects that

## BOX G: GLOBAL ECONOMIC APARTHEID

*By Robin Broad, American University, and John Cavanagh,*
*Institute for Policy Studies*

A careful analysis of social and economic data from the United Nations, the World Bank, the IMF, and other sources offers a shocking picture of trends in the global economy and the gap between rich and poor countries. There are two ways to measure what is happening economically between the North and the South. The first is to measure which is growing faster, and therefore whether the gap between them is growing or shrinking. The second is to measure financial resource flows between the two.

On the first issue the picture is clear: the North-South gap widened dramatically in the decade after 1982 as the Third World debt crisis drained financial resources from poor countries to rich banks. Between 1985 and 1992, Southern nations paid some $280 billion more in debt service to Northern creditors than they received in new private loans and government aid. Gross national product (GNP) per capita rose an average of only 1 percent in the South in the 1980s (in sub-Saharan Africa it fell 1.2 percent), while it rose 2.3 percent in the North.

Situating the lost decade of the 1980s within a longer time period reveals similar trends for some regions. According to the United Nations Development Program, per capita incomes in Africa were one-ninth of those in Northern countries in 1960; they had fallen to one-eighteenth by 1998. Per capita incomes in most of the rest of the developing world (Latin America and the Caribbean, and South Asia) remained at about one-tenth of Northern levels at the beginning and end of these four decades. Only in East Asia have developing countries closed the gap with the North.

Likewise, a look at various resource flows between the North and the South is instructive. Despite the perception of an easing of the debt crisis, the overall Third World debt stock swelled by around $100 billion each year during the 1990s (reaching $2.4 trillion in 2001). Southern debt service (which reached $331 billion in 2000) still exceeds new lending, and the net outflow remains particularly crushing in Africa. Although it is true that a series of debt reschedulings and the accumulation of arrears by many debtors have reduced the net negative financial transfer from South to North over the last few years, the flows remain negative.

Part of the reason why some analysts now argue that the debt crisis is no longer a problem is that since the early 1990s these outflows of debt repayments have been matched by increased inflows of foreign capital. Here too, however, a deeper look at disaggregated figures underlines the disconcerting reality. According to World Bank figures, roughly half of the new foreign

CONTINUED

BOX G: CONTINUED

direct investment by global corporations into the South in 1992 quickly left those countries as profits. In addition, foreign investment flows primarily to only ten to twelve Third World nations that are viewed as new profit centers by Northern corporations and investors. According to World Bank figures, more than 70 percent of investment flows in 1998 went to just ten of the so-called emerging markets: China, followed by Brazil, Mexico, Singapore, Thailand, Poland, Argentina, South Korea, Malaysia, and Chile.

The inescapable conclusion is that the North-South economic gap is now narrowing for about a dozen countries but continues to widen for well over one hundred others. Hence, without a major shift in policy, the world of the twenty-first century will be one of economic apartheid. There will be two dozen richer nations, a dozen or so poorer nations that have begun to close the gap with the rich, and approximately 140 poor nations slipping farther and farther behind.

As U.S. firms have shifted from local to national and now to global markets over the past half-century, a new division of winners and losers has emerged in all countries. The book *Global Dreams*, by Richard Barnet, cofounder of the Institute for Policy Studies, and John Cavanagh, chronicles how powerful U.S. firms and their counterparts from England, France, Germany, and Japan are integrating only about one-third of humanity (most of those in the rich countries plus the elite of poor countries) into complex chains of production, shopping, culture, and finance.

Although there are enclaves in every country that are linked to these global economic webs, others are left out. Wal-Mart is spreading its superstores throughout the Western Hemisphere; millions in Latin America, though, are too poor to enjoy anything but glimpses of luxury. Citibank customers can access automated teller machines around the world; the vast majority of people nevertheless borrow from the loan shark down the road. Ford Motor Company pieces together its new "global car" in Kansas City from parts made all over the globe; executives in Detroit worry about who will be able to afford it.

Thus, although on one level the North-South gap is becoming more pronounced for most Third World countries, on another these global chains blur distinctions between geographical North and South. These processes create another North-South divide: the roughly one-third of humanity who make up a "global North" of beneficiaries in every country, and the two-thirds of humanity from the slums of New York to the favelas of Rio who are not hooked into the new global menu of producing, consuming, and borrowing opportunities in the "global South."

SOURCE: Adapted and updated from Robin Broad and John Cavanagh, "Development: The Market Is Not Enough." *Foreign Policy, 101,* Winter 1995-96.

primarily benefit global corporations. Regional development banks such as the Asian Development Bank (ADB) and the Inter-American Development Bank have generally copied the World Bank's model.

## The International Monetary Fund

The International Monetary Fund (IMF) was originally created to work with member nations to implement measures to ensure the stability of the international financial system and correct balance-of-payment maladjustments. By the early 1980s, however, it took a different course. Rather than helping governments avoid currency crises, it has persistently pressured them to abandon the regulation of cross-border trade and financial flows, resulting in massive trade imbalances and reckless financial speculation.

IMF-sanctioned policies helped attract huge inflows of foreign money to what were called the "emerging market economies" of Asia and Latin America in the form of loans and speculative investment. As Walden Bello and Martin Khor have each documented, the rapid buildup of foreign financial claims set the stage for the subsequent financial meltdown in Mexico in 1994 and in Asia, Russia, and Brazil from 1997 to 1998. This is why: when it became clear that the huge financial bubbles the inflows had created could not be sustained and that claims against foreign exchange could not be covered, speculators were spooked and suddenly pulled out billions of dollars. Currencies and stock markets went into a free fall. Millions of people fell back into poverty. Then the IMF stepped in with new loans to bail out the foreign banks and financiers involved—leaving it to the taxpayers of the devastated economies to pick up the bill once the loan payments came due. In many instances, at IMF insistence, uncollectible private debts were converted into public debt.

Over the last two decades, structural adjustment programs were imposed by the World Bank and the IMF on close to ninety developing countries, from Guyana to Ghana. The objective of SAPs went beyond debt repayment or attainment of short-term macroeconomic stability, seeking nothing less than the dismantling of protectionism and other policies of government-assisted capitalism that their theorists judged to be the main obstacles to sustained growth and development.

Two decades after the first structural adjustment loan, the World Bank states that it has formally abandoned the entire program, replacing it with what it calls the "Comprehensive Development Framework." The new paradigm, according to a statement of the Group of Seven Finance Ministers and Central Bank Governors, has the following elements:

- Increased and more effective fiscal expenditures for poverty reduction, with better targeting of budgetary resources, especially on social priorities in basic education and health
- Enhanced transparency, including monitoring and quality control over fiscal expenditures
- Stronger country ownership of the reform and poverty-reduction process and programs, involving public participation
- Stronger performance indicators that can be monitored for follow-through on poverty reduction
- Assurance of macroeconomic stability and sustainability, and reduction of barriers to access by the poor to the benefits of growth

What brought about this shift in plans? Clearly, it was spectacular failure that could no longer be denied at the pain of totally losing all credibility. With dozens of countries under "adjustment" for over a decade, even the World Bank had to acknowledge that it was hard to find a handful of success stories. In most cases, structural adjustment caused economies to fall into a hole wherein low investment, reduced social spending, reduced consumption, and low output interacted to create a vicious cycle of decline and stagnation rather than a virtuous circle of growth, rising employment, and rising investment, as originally envisaged by the World Bank–IMF theory.

With much resistance from the bank's entrenched bureaucracy, President James Wolfensohn moved slowly to distance the bank from hard-line adjustment policies and even convinced some of his staff (grudgingly) to work with civil society groups to assess SAPs in the so-called Structural Adjustment Program Review Initiative (SAPRI). For the most part, however, the change of attitude did not translate into changes at the operational level because of the strong internalization of the structural adjustment approach among bank operatives.

Although self-doubt began to engulf the World Bank, the IMF plowed confidently on. Lack of evidence of success was interpreted to mean simply that a government lacked political will to push adjustment. Through the establishment of the Enhanced Structural Adjustment Facility (ESAF), the IMF sought to fund countries over a longer period in order to institutionalize more fully the desired free-market reforms.

It was the Asian financial crisis that finally provoked the IMF to make some cosmetic changes. In 1997–98, it moved with grand assurance into Thailand, Indonesia, and Korea with its classic formula of short-term fiscal and monetary policy cum structural reform in the direction of liberalization, deregulation, and privatization. This was the price it exacted from governments for financial rescue packages that would allow them to repay the massive debt incurred by their private sectors. Instead, a short-term crisis turned into a deep recession as governmental capacity to counteract the drop in private-sector activity was destroyed by budgetary and monetary repression. If some recovery is now discernible in a few economies, it is widely recognized as coming in spite of rather than because of the IMF.

For a world that had long been resentful of the IMF's arrogance, this was the last straw. In 1998–99, criticism of the organization rose to a crescendo. Criticism went beyond the IMF's stubborn adherence to structural adjustment and its serving as a bailout mechanism for international finance capital to its being nontransparent and unaccountable. Its vulnerable position was exposed during a recent debate in the U.S. Congress over a G-7 initiative to provide debt relief to forty poor countries. Legislators depicted the IMF as the agency that had caused the debt crisis of the poor countries in the first place, and some called for its abolition within three years. Said representative Maxine Waters: "Do we have to have the IMF involved at all? Because, as we have painfully discovered, the way the IMF works causes children to starve."

In the face of such criticism from legislators in the IMF's most powerful member, Clinton administration treasury secretary Larry Summers claimed that the IMF-centered process would be replaced by "a new, more open and inclusive process that would involve multiple international organizations and give national policymakers and civil society groups a more central role."

What does this mean? Is structural adjustment dead, and have the Bretton Woods institutions seen the light? The fact is, in the case of the IMF, as well as that of the World Bank and the Asian Development Bank, jettisoning the paradigm of structural adjustment has left them adrift, in the view of many critics, with the rhetoric and broad goals of reducing poverty but without an innovative macroeconomic approach. James Wolfensohn and his ex-chief economist Joseph Stiglitz talk about "bringing together" the "macroeconomic" and "social" aspects of development, but World Bank officials cannot point to a larger strategy beyond increasing lending to health, population, nutrition, education, and social protection to 25 percent of its total lending. The ADB is even more of a newcomer in the antipoverty approach, and a recent strategy paper is long on laudable goals. But even ADB insiders agree that it breaks no new ground in macroeconomic innovation. Most at sea are IMF economists, some of whom openly admitted to NGO representatives at the September 1999 IMF–World Bank meeting that so far the new approach was limited to relabeling the Enhanced Structural Adjustment Facility the Poverty Reduction Facility, and that they were looking to the World Bank to provide leadership.

It is not surprising that in such circumstances the old paradigm would reassert itself. For example, the IMF told the Thai government—already its most obedient pupil—to cut its fiscal deficit despite a very fragile recovery, and it pushed Indonesia to open its retail trade to foreign investors despite the consequences of higher unemployment. Similarly, technocrats of the ADB made energy loans contingent on the Philippine government's accelerating the IMF-promoted privatization of the National Power Corporation, even though consumers are likely to end up paying more to the seven private monopolies that will succeed the state enterprise. "It's the old approach of deregulation, privatization, and liberalization, but with safety nets," is the accurate description of one Filipino labor leader much consulted by the multilateral institutions. (See Box H for a related discussion.)

---

### BOX H: ARGENTINA AND THE IMF AND THE WORLD BANK

*By Sarah Anderson, Director, Global Economy Project, Institute for Policy Studies*

Argentina is one of the most dramatic cases of the economic collapse of a poster child of the IMF and World Bank. Its collapse provoked a popular uprising that culminated in the election of a new government—that of President Nestor Kirchner—which is now standing up to the Bretton Woods institutions and rejecting the neoliberal model.

Here's a snapshot of the story. With strong backing from the World Bank and IMF, in the early 1990s Argentina began to liberalize trade and financial markets and privatize virtually every public service (including the postal service). The government also tied its hands further by pegging the value of its currency to the U.S. dollar.

When the value of the U.S. dollar began to rise in the mid-1990s, things began to fall apart. Argentine exports lost competitiveness and industry began to decline, causing a jump in unemployment. Simultaneously, social security privatization under World Bank sponsorship led to a decline in govern-

CONTINUED

BOX H: CONTINUED

ment revenues, since contributions to social security were diverted to private pension funds. As revenues fell, the government turned to the IMF for help in meeting loan payments. In return, the IMF demanded deep cuts in public spending that further cut domestic demand and stoked social unrest.

Although Argentina's grossly overvalued currency was a major factor in the collapse, other free-market reforms exacerbated the problems. Once trade barriers and capital controls had been lifted, the government was powerless to address the looming trade deficit and the flight of capital. Privatization led to reduced access to services for the poor and the middle class. Millions lost health coverage as private international insurers pressured providers to cut costs. Argentine banks were sold to foreign firms, which cut back lending to small and medium-size enterprises. Stripped of protections, private employers were pressured to become "lean and mean" through mass layoffs. Along with the IMF and World Bank, they also lobbied for labor law reform that further weakened unions. All this fueled the anger that exploded in deadly riots in December 2001 and brought about the country's economic crash. Unable to meet debt service payments to foreign banks, Argentina declared the largest default in world history that same month.

The IMF never admitted any wrongdoing in Argentina. Instead, it blamed the collapse on excessive public spending and the currency peg, which it had initially supported and helped sustain but then claimed was a purely home-grown policy. Even as the economy was in a free fall throughout 2002 (GDP declined 12 percent), the IMF continued to demand increased austerity and other structural reforms as conditions for restarting lending to the credit-strapped country. A rising tide of public opinion against further concessions to the IMF pressured the government to assert that if the IMF didn't agree to defer loan payments, Argentina would default to the "international lender of last resort," just as it had to the private bankers.

In January 2003, the IMF board, which recognized that the IMF's credibility was in serious danger throughout Latin America, forced its management to concede to a "rollover" of Argentina's loans. The new government of Nestor Kirchner, which took power in May 2003, maintained this stance. It has successfully resisted pressure from the IMF and G-7 governments to offer a sweeter deal to private creditors and increase the government surplus by cutting public services in order to repay defaulted bonds. It has also bucked IMF and World Bank orthodoxy by renationalizing the postal service and other public services that the previous Menem government, the onetime darling of free-market fundamentalists, had privatized.

The Argentine experience is a lesson of the extreme dangers of the radical free market system, but it is also a lesson in the power of resistance. Although the people of Argentina continue to suffer, their unified opposition against the IMF and World Bank has had a positive impact.

# The World Trade Organization

The World Trade Organization (WTO) has emerged as the third pillar of the Bretton Woods system.

A very healthy debate was launched after World War II about the need for a global trade and investment institution that could help generate full employment, protect worker rights around the world, and protect against what were then referred to as "global cartels"—small groups of corporations that gained too much power over a sector. These broad-based goals were enshrined in a Havana charter that proposed the formation of an International Trade Organization (ITO). Rejected by the U.S. Senate on the grounds that its broad mandate would compromise U.S. sovereignty, only one element of the ITO, the General Agreement on Tariffs and Trade (GATT), was created instead, with the more narrow goal of reducing tariffs in goods and services and setting a handful of broad trade principles.

World trade grew dramatically following World War II, under the guidance of the GATT. While initially limited to this trade expansion mandate, the GATT evolved into an institution that promoted corporate rights over human rights and other social and environmental priorities.

In the early 1980s, economists and politicians, powered by the so-called Reagan Revolution and the Thatcher and Kohl ascendancies in Europe, began planning a new but dramatically different GATT negotiating round. Their goal was to expand the GATT disciplines to bind signatory governments to a set of multilateral policies regarding the service, government procurement, and investment sectors; to establish global limits on government regulation of environmental, food safety, and product standards; to establish new protections for corporate intellectual property rights granted in rich countries; and to have this broad panoply of one-size-fits-all rules strongly enforced over every level of government in every signatory country.

This agenda was translated into the Uruguay Round of GATT negotiations, a transformational undertaking pushed largely by U.S.-based global corporations and their allies in the U.S. government. When completed in 1994, the Uruguay Round replaced the old GATT trade contract with a new institution, the World Trade Organization. The WTO was given a built-in enforcement system more powerful than that of any previous treaty. This system, with closed tribunals of trade bureaucrats who determined if a country's laws exceeded the constraints set by the new rules, included automatic, permanent trade sanctions against any country refusing to comply with WTO demands. In short, the WTO took on the role of implementing globally much the same policy agenda that the World Bank and the IMF had already imposed on most of the Third World.

Proponents of the WTO argue that it is needed to regulate trade, prevent trade wars, and protect the interests of poor nations, but its actions tell a different story. (See again Box C for a list of some of the most controversial WTO rulings on environmental protections.) WTO panels have also ruled against Canada's cultural protections, which taxed U.S. magazines. India has been told it must change its national constitution because WTO rules do not allow it to provide its people with inexpensive generic drugs since it is considered unfair to foreign drug companies that profit handsomely from branded products. The WTO even takes for itself responsibility for determining whether it is permissible to label such products so consumers will know what they are buying and can assess the risks accordingly.

Given the claim that the WTO protects the poor and prevents trade wars, the 1999 WTO "banana wars" decision is especially revealing. Europeans were told by the WTO that they could not give import preference to bananas produced by two hundred thousand members of small banana farmer cooperatives located in the Caribbean because it was unfair to two giant U.S. agribusiness corporations, Chiquita and Dole, which grow bananas in Central America and control half the world's banana trade. When Europe refused to end its preference, the WTO sanctioned a retaliatory move by the United States to impose 100 percent tariffs on a wide variety of European exports. Thus, in a single case, the WTO struck down a preference for the poor and sanctioned a trade war.

Specifically, the WTO has served primarily U.S. government and corporate interests over developing-country and civil-society interests. Just as it was the United States that blocked the founding of the International Trade Organization in 1948 when it felt that this would not serve its position of overwhelming economic dominance in the postwar world, so it was the United States that became the dominant lobbyist for the comprehensive Uruguay Round and the founding of the WTO when it felt that more competitive global conditions had created a situation where its corporate interests now demanded an opposite stance.

Just as it was the threat of the United States in the 1950s to leave the

GATT if it was not allowed to maintain protective mechanisms for milk and other agricultural products that led to agricultural trade's limited coverage in GATT rules, so it was U.S. pressure that brought agriculture fully under the GATT-WTO system in 1995. The reason for Washington's change of mind was articulated quite candidly by then–U.S. Agriculture Secretary John Block at the start of the Uruguay Round negotiations in 1986: the "idea that developing countries should feed themselves is an anachronism from a bygone era. They could better ensure their food security by relying on U.S. agricultural products, which are available, in most cases, at much lower cost." Washington did not just have developing country markets in mind but also Japan, South Korea, and the European Union.

It was the United States that pushed to bring services under WTO coverage with its assessment that in the new burgeoning area of international services, particularly financial services, its corporations had a lead that needed to be preserved. It was also the United States that pushed to expand WTO jurisdiction to the Trade-Related Investment Measures (TRIMs) and Trade-Related Intellectual Property Rights (TRIPs) mentioned in an earlier chapter. The first sought to eliminate countries' ability to shape foreign investment policies to ensure national benefits. For instance, TRIMs targeted domestic laws regulating internal cross-border trade of product components among transnational corporation subsidiaries, which developing countries had passed in order to develop new domestic industries. TRIPs was designed to consolidate the U.S. advantage in the cutting-edge, knowledge-intensive industries.

It was again the United States that forced the creation of the WTO's formidable dispute-resolution and enforcement mechanism after being frustrated with what U.S. trade officials considered weak GATT efforts to enforce rulings favorable to the United States. As Washington's academic point man on trade, C. Fred Bergsten, head of the Institute of International Economics, told the U.S. Senate, the strong WTO dispute settlement mechanism serves U.S. interests because "we can now use the full weight of the international machinery to go after those trade barriers, reduce them, get them eliminated."

In sum, it has been Washington's changing perception of the needs of its economic interest groups that has shaped and reshaped the international trading regime. It was not global necessity that gave birth to the WTO in 1995 but rather the U.S. government's assessment that the interests of its corporations were no longer served by a loose and flexible GATT. In the course of the 1990s, what had been a U.S. idea spread to become the mantra of the wealthiest countries, then known as the G-7 (the United States, Japan, Germany, France, the United Kingdom, Italy, and Canada). From the free-market paradigm that underpins it to the rules and regulations set forth in the different agreements that make up the Uruguay Round to its system of decision making and accountability, the WTO is a blueprint for the global hegemony of the largest corporations based in the richest nations.

But what about the developing countries? Is the WTO a necessary structure—one that, whatever its flaws, brings more benefits than costs and therefore merits efforts at reform? When the Uruguay Round was being negotiated, there was considerable lack of enthusiasm for the process by the developing countries. After all, these countries had formed the backbone of the United Nations Conference on Trade and Development (UNCTAD; for more on this organization see chapter 10), which, with its system of one-country–one-vote and majority voting, was, they felt, an international arena more congenial to their interests. They entered the Uruguay Round greatly resenting the policy of the large trading powers to weaken and marginalize UNCTAD in the late 1970s and early 1980s. However, they had been promised that the WTO's multilateral rules and enforcement would stop the unilateral bullying by more powerful nations on trade matters.

Yet as the WTO began operations, it became evident that the imbalance in economic power had not been remediated. WTO rules were enforced only when countries spent millions of dollars to bring a case, and then the rules were enforced with trade sanctions. Many developing countries began to realize that they had signed away their right to employ a variety of critical trade measures for development purposes. In contrast to the loose GATT framework, which had allowed some space for development initiatives, the comprehensive and tightened Uruguay Round was fundamentally antidevelopment. This is evident in the following: in signing on to the WTO, Third World countries committed to ban all quantitative restrictions on imports and reduce tariffs on many industrial imports, and they promised not to raise tariffs on all other imports. In so doing, they effectively gave up the use of trade policy to pursue domestic objectives. The route that the newly industrializing countries (NICs) had taken to industrial status through the policy of import substitution was now removed.

The antidevelopment thrust of the WTO accord is made even more manifest in the TRIMs and TRIPs agreements. NICs like South Korea and Malaysia made use of many innovative mechanisms, such as trade-balancing requirements that tied the value of a foreign investor's imports of raw materials and components to the value of its exports of the finished commodity, and "local content" regulations that mandated a certain percentage of the components that went into the making of a product to be sourced locally.

These rules did indeed restrict the maneuvering space of foreign investors, but they were successfully employed by the NICs to marry foreign investment to national ventures. They enabled these countries to raise income from capital-intensive exports, develop support industries, and bring in technology, while still protecting local entrepreneurs' preferential access to the domestic market. TRIMs make these mechanisms illegal.

Proposals under consideration for future WTO action include expanding existing WTO prohibitions on trade in goods that forbid any public policies that give preference to local over foreign investors (including banking, media, and other service sectors) or to local over foreign suppliers. Also on the agenda are constraints on initiatives to protect national food security by shielding local farmers from foreign competition, to protect forest and water resources from exploitation by foreign corporations, and to regulate speculative movements of international money. Other WTO proposals would open the way to privatizing public services, such as public schools and health care, under the ownership of global corporations.

The WTO rules and enforcement system is regularly used by corporations and their allied governments to attack measures taken by governments to protect the health, safety, and culture of their people and to preserve the environment. Yet under WTO rules, governments take ever stronger steps to protect the profits and property rights of corporations and financiers. Although the WTO presumes to impose a one-size-fits-all set of rules constraining the public interest policies of WTO member nations, it does nothing to limit the excesses of global corporations and financial speculators—two priority regulatory needs. Instead, it regulates national and local governments to prevent them from regulating international trade and investment. In short, it regulates governments to protect corporations. (See Box I for a related discussion.)

## BOX I: THE HYPOCRISY OF THE NORTH IN THE WTO

*By Martin Khor, Third World Network*

There is perhaps no arena in which the United States and the other richest industrial countries fail more to practice what they preach than trade policy. For two decades, through their own dictates as well as through the World Bank, the IMF, the GATT, and now the WTO, they have uniformly preached that liberalization of Southern markets is essential. Just as consistently, they have failed to practice this dictum at home.

The old GATT system dealt with trade in goods. There were imbalances even in that system. For example, the largest economic sectors and export sectors of most developing countries are agriculture and textiles. Both still employ millions in the industrial countries, and both have been highly protected in most of these countries for decades.

Beginning in 1986, governments began the famous Uruguay Round negotiations that transformed the GATT into the WTO in 1995. At the core of the negotiations was a proposed trade-off. Developing countries would agree to a series of new issues in the WTO (services, intellectual property, investment measures) that would make the system more imbalanced and more intrusive (as the system moved from its traditional concern with trade barriers at the border to greater involvement with domestic economic and develop-

ment structures and policies). In turn, the developing countries were promised, the Uruguay Round would open up Northern markets for agriculture and textiles.

The North has insisted that the South keep its side of the bargain but has failed to deliver on its own promises. The developing countries have been under great pressure to liberalize their rules on imports and foreign investments as fast as possible from the industrial nations, the international financial institutions, regional trade arrangements with developed countries, and the WTO. Implementing their obligations under the WTO agreements has brought many problems for developing countries. Here are some examples:

- The prohibition of investment measures and subsidies has made it harder or impossible for the state to encourage and promote the domestic sectors.
- Import liberalization in agriculture threatens the viability and livelihoods of small farmers whose products face competition from cheaper imported foods, many of which are artificially cheapened through massive subsidy.
- The effects of a rigorous intellectual property rights regime include exorbitant prices for medicines and

CONTINUED

other essentials, patenting by Northern corporations of biological materials originating in the South, and higher costs for and lower access by developing countries to industrial technology.

• Increasing pressures on developing countries to open up their services sectors could deny the poor access to essential services.

These measures threaten to stop developing countries from industrializing, upgrading technology, developing local industries, protecting small farmers, achieving food security, and fulfilling health and medicinal needs.

The developing countries' problems arise from the structural imbalances and weaknesses of several WTO agreements. They have compiled a lengthy list of their problems of implementation and proposals for addressing them, and submitted these in the WTO. There has been progress on very few of the implementation problems. Some are on the post-Doha work program along with many other topics. The attitude of the developed countries seems to be that the developing countries entered into legally binding commitments and must abide by them or make new concessions to change them. Such an attitude does not augur well for the WTO, for it implies that the state of imbalance will remain, and if developing countries pay twice or pay three or four times, the

imbalances will become worse and the burden even heavier.

The new WTO rules also pose problems for the public in the rich countries, including the high cost of medicines and other consumer products due to patenting, and the threats to public services and management of natural resources such as water, as a result of services liberalization. The regional NAFTA agreement has also generated a host of problems and controversies, including corporations suing the state for expropriating their future profits as a result of measures on health and environmental or other grounds.

Meanwhile, the industrial nations have largely failed to deliver on their pledges to open up their own economies in agriculture and textiles. In most Northern countries, these sectors remain closed. In agriculture, tariffs on many items of interest to developing countries are prohibitively high (some tariffs are over 200 to 300 percent). Domestic subsidies in OECD countries have actually risen from U.S. $275 billion (annual average for base period 1986 to 1988) to $326 billion in 1999, according to OECD data published in 2000. The increases in permitted subsidies more than offset the decrease in subsidy categories under the agriculture agreement.

In textiles and clothing, only very few items that the developing countries export have been taken off the

CONTINUED

BOX I: CONTINUED

quota lists of Northern countries, even though more than half of the ten-year implementation period has passed. According to a submission at the WTO in June 2000 by the International Textiles and Clothing Bureau, only a few quota restrictions (13 out of 750 by the United States, 14 out of 219 by the European Union, 29 out of 295 by Canada) had been eliminated. Given this record, it is doubtful that the designated quotas will be removed by 2005.

In early 2002, the United States announced that it would be imposing tariffs of up to 30 percent on some of its steel imports in order to protect its domestic steel industry. This decision sent shock waves around the world, because it signifies the rise of unilateral protectionist actions in the world's richest country.

Developing countries are asked to bear for a little while the pain of rapid adjustment, with assurances that it will surely be good for them after a few years, whereas the developed countries that advocate this policy ask for more time for themselves to adjust in agriculture and textiles (and other products) that have been protected for many decades.

The fact that rich countries still argue that they need more time to protect their weak or uncompetitive sectors should make them sympathetic to the developing countries' increasing complaints that import liberalization and other obligations have damaged their

societies. But the governments of rich countries refuse to admit the truth of the matter and resist the demand of citizen groups and many Southern governments to change the system.

At the November 2001 Doha, Qatar, WTO ministerial meeting, developing countries raised many of these implementation issues. Instead, the largest developed countries pushed very hard to have the WTO expand its negotiating and rule-making mandate, including into new areas such as investment, competition policy, government procurement, and trade and the environment.

This attempt at expansion was strongly resisted by most of the developing countries (including regional groupings), which argued that (a) they were not yet ready to enter negotiations or consider agreements on these issues; (b) they did not adequately understand the implications of the proposed issues; and (c) from the limited understanding they did have, they were very concerned that new agreements in these areas would add to their already heavy obligations and further restrict their development policy options and constrain or reduce their development prospects. The Doha meeting ended with confusing language on both the implementation concerns of the developing nations and the desire for new issues by the developed countries. There is certainly no consensus in the WTO on how to move forward.

# Proposals

The Bretton Woods institutions have a distorted view of economic progress and relationships. Their embrace of unlimited expansion of trade and foreign investment in order to achieve economic growth suggests that they consider the most advanced state of development to be one in which all productive assets are owned by foreign corporations producing for export; the currency that facilitates day-to-day transactions is borrowed from foreign banks; education and health services are operated by foreign corporations on a for-profit, fee-for-service basis; and almost everything that local people consume is imported. When placed in such stark terms, the absurdity of this ideology becomes obvious. It also becomes clear who is served by such policies. Rather than enhancing the life of people and the planet, they consolidate and secure the wealth and power of a small corporate elite.

Harvard economist Dani Rodrik has pointed out that relevant data demonstrate that trade and investment liberalization do not necessarily bring increased economic growth or prosperity. They do, however, contribute to serious imbalances in the global economy, including alarming growth in inequality both inside and between nations. Alternative models that emphasize domestic production for domestic markets and that direct trade and foreign investment to the service of national needs hold greater promise.

Author William Greider has pointed out another, less noted imbalance that is encouraged by trade and investment liberalization—rapid expansion of production combined with the suppression of wages so that most workers cannot afford to buy the products they produce. As a result, there is a substantial surplus of production today. The world has dealt with this by looking to the United States as the buyer of last resort. For more than two decades, the United States has been buying far more from others than it sells to them and paying for the difference with money borrowed from foreign investors, primarily the Japanese. This actually puts the United States into a financial position similar to that of Asia, Russia, and Brazil just before their financial collapses in 1997 and 1998. On the other side of this troubling equation, we find country after country exporting goods and resources to support needless consumption in the United States while their own people lack the financial means to obtain even the most basic necessities.

Trade theory gives great importance to keeping international trade and payment accounts in balance if the exchange is to be mutually beneficial and economic relations are to be reasonably stable. British economist John Maynard Keynes, one of the chief architects of the Bretton Woods system, took this idea quite seriously. In 1942, he pointed out that we "need a system possessed of an internal stabilizing mechanism, by which pressure is exercised on any country whose balance of payments with the rest of the world is departing from equilibrium in either direction, so as to prevent movements which must create for its neighbors an equal but opposite want of balance."

Ironically, one of the IMF's original responsibilities was to help nations keep their international accounts in balance. Yet current policies of the World Bank, the IMF, and the WTO not only ignore this principle but also set in place conditions that prevent nations from honoring it. The result is imbalance, instability, inequality, and deprivation.

In the current economic system, liberalizing trade and investment and enhancing international competitiveness are seen as the means to growth, which, in turn, is seen as the key to prosperity and democracy. The following chapter outlines the principles of an alternative system that proposes democracy and rights as the means toward sustainable communities, dignified work, and a healthy environment. In chapter 10, "New International Structures," we offer specific ideas on a global governance system that operates in behalf of these principles.

# PART TWO

# ALTERNATIVES
# IN ACTION

*From the bottom up, a process of correction and readjustment is under way. Millions of people have risen to demand a new system and new ideas; many are already putting their ideas into practice. In part 2 we present a range of alternative expressions, from conceptual to practical: new principles that build a framework for a viable system that works for people and the environment rather than corporate profit; ideas for reclaiming the commons, which was once used by all peoples but now is largely privatized; concepts for achieving a meaningful power shift away from the global toward the local; and direct management where "the rubber hits the road," where the global economy starkly affects the local: energy and oil, transport, manufacturing, agriculture, media, and so on. Finally, we review a panoply of grassroots initiatives from around the world. Taken together, these events and actions reveal a new system bursting through from within the old.*

CHAPTER FOUR

# Ten Principles
# for Sustainable Societies

ON A RAINY DAY in late November 1999, environmentalists dressed like
turtles marched arm-in-arm with teamsters down the city streets in what has
become known as the Battle of Seattle, an extraordinary event that dead-
locked WTO negotiators and brought that powerful agency's momentum to
a standstill. These unlikely partners were joined by tens of thousands of
others—students, religious activists, women's rights activists, family farmers,
health activists, indigenous people, and economic justice organizers from
many countries—in what was baptized the Seattle Coalition.

In sifting through the thousands of pieces of literature produced by these
formerly disparate groups, we found that a fascinating pattern emerged.
Certain words cropped up time and again as core principles, no matter the
particular group or specific country in which the organization was based.

Almost all the authors of this volume were in Seattle, first at a giant
International Forum on Globalization teach-in, organized in Seattle's sym-
phony hall, and then on the streets. We all remarked on this commonality
in core principles.

The term *democracy* was perhaps the most common thread linking all the
groups, with different groups affixing different adjectives to try to give the
word a deeper meaning: *living democracy, participatory democracy, new democracy, people's democracy.* After democracy, *ecological sustainability* came next,
again often described in related terms. Most groups now also suggest *localization* and *subsidiarity* as key principles opposed to *globalization.*

As we pored over the documents and manifestos distributed in Seattle
and elsewhere, we found that ten terms were repeated most often as orga-

78 ALTERNATIVES IN ACTION

nizing principles, and we began to understand the basis for the movement that has alternately been described as "anti–corporate globalization" or "pro–global justice." It is this growing commonality among principles that allows this set of disparate groups with thousands of separate leaders and hundreds of different significant issues to be called a *movement*.

These principles stand in stark contrast to those that guide economic globalization, which are narrow and serve the few at the expense of the many and the environment. Economic growth has been the central goal of the IMF, the World Bank, and the GATT, as well as its successor, the WTO. Expanding international trade and investment flows has been viewed as an end in itself.

As part 1 explained, the governing ideology of the past half-century has been that unfettered trade and investment will bring prosperity, which will bring democracy. This ideology has guided the declarations of U.S. presidents from Harry Truman to George W. Bush, as well as the policy pronouncements of most leaders the world over, particularly since the 1980s. The persistent mantra of corporate and government leaders alike has been that to remain competitive in a global economy, governments must cut regulations and encourage the most favorable climate for foreign investment, often at the cost of worker rights and environmental integrity. In the words of Maude Barlow, the chair of the Council of Canadians, "Stateless corporations have given rise to corporate states."

The time has come to create healthy, sustainable societies that work for all. Healthy, sustainable societies vest power in institutions that measure their performance by their contribution to the long-term well-being of people, community, and nature and distribute power equitably among all of society's stakeholders. Such societies are measured by their essential qualities, primarily the well-being of all their people. Each sustainable community and nation seeks to achieve sufficient self-reliance in meeting basic needs—including food, shelter, clean water, energy, education, health, political participation, and culture—to assure the livelihoods, civil liberties, and sense of meaning and identity of each of its members.

## Core Principles

To achieve truly sustainable societies, all international, national, and regional economic policy rules and institutions should be designed to conform to the ten basic principles that are enunciated here.

## I. NEW DEMOCRACY

The rallying cry of the amazing diversity of civil society that converged in Seattle was the simple word *democracy*. Democracy flourishes when people organize to protect their communities and rights and hold their elected officials accountable. For the past two decades, governments have transferred much of their sovereignty into the hands of global corporations. The authors of this volume advocate a shift from governments serving corporations to governments serving people and communities, a process that is easier at the local level but vital at all levels of government. Lula in Brazil and Kirchner in Argentina, to note two hopeful examples, were elected on such a mandate and their success ultimately depends on their overseeing such a shift.

We use the terms *new democracy* and *living democracy* in part because *democracy* is equated in many minds with elections alone. As vital as fair elections are to democracy, we want to focus more attention on the dynamic processes initiated by civil society organizations around the world to instill new energy and meaning into democratic movements. In some countries, primarily in the Southern Hemisphere, these movements focus on winning community control over natural resources. In other countries, mainly in the North, they are striving to remove corporate money from politics and refocus government agendas on a citizens' agenda of rights.

Accountability is central to living democracy. When decisions are made by those who will bear the consequences—such as when a community democratically decides how to manage forests immediately around its homes on the watershed it depends upon for flood control and water—they are likely to give a high priority to the sustained long-term health of those forests because their own well-being and that of their children is at stake. This is not the case if the management decisions are in the hands of a foreign corporation whose directors live thousands of miles away, and furthermore, face a legal mandate to maximize short-term return to shareholders. The shareholders, in turn, may not even know they hold shares in this particular company, let alone the location of its forests. These circumstances lead directors to consider only the immediate profit that clear-cutting the trees will bring; they will neither see nor bear the costs of the flooding, mudslides, and disruption of local water supply that this choice will inflict on others. When health, labor, and environmental standards and the rules of foreign trade and investment are shaped by corporate lobbyists in secret negotiations in distant cities, those who will profit are well represented, but those who will bear the costs are not at the table, and their interests carry no weight.

The principle of new democracy means creating governance systems that give a vote to those who will bear the costs when decisions are being made. It also means limiting the rights and powers of absentee owners and ensuring that those who hold decision-making power are liable for the harms their acts bring to others. The dominant institution of the global economy—the publicly traded, limited liability corporation—violates these conditions by institutionalizing an extreme form of absentee ownership and by insulating the shareholders in whose name the corporation acts from liability for the harm these acts may inflict on others. It is an institutional form poorly suited to the needs of sustainable societies.

This volume includes dozens of examples of organized citizens launching "new democracy" initiatives (see particularly chapters 4, 7, and 8), and they are as diverse as the conditions that gave rise to them. Some are small and community-based, such as the seventy-six families who formed a fishing cooperative in rural Chile. Others are large, encompassing whole regions or countries, such as the Mondragón Cooperative Corporation in Spain, the Grameen Bank in Bangladesh (and now elsewhere), and the Landless Workers Movement in Brazil.

Some emerge from the collapse of market economies, such as the so-called horizontalism movement across Argentina that originated in the crisis of its IMF model in December 2001. Some are temporary processes designed to mobilize popular resistance to assaults on democracy, such as the 1998 Canadian inquiry to seek alternatives to the corporate-driven multilateral agreement on investment (see Box J). Some are citizen initiatives to stop or replace abusive corporate control of vital resources, such as the movement around water in Cochabamba, Bolivia.

Many others involve indigenous peoples reclaiming their autonomy over their lives, land, and resources. Some involve other communities asserting collective rights over seeds or other natural resources. Some, like Sustainable Chile (Box K later in this chapter), involve thousands of people in dialogues about the future they might create.

All of these efforts involve people organizing and taking risks to assert control over their lives and resources in order to advance the common good.

## BOX J: CITIZENS' AGENDA IN CANADA

*By Tony Clarke, Polaris Institute*

"All great social movements have been fired by a fierce imagination," declared a participant in the 1998 citizens' inquiry that was held across Canada in the wake of the collapse of the OECD negotiations for a multilateral agreement on investment (MAI).

The behind-closed-doors negotiations on the MAI at the OECD headquarters in Paris during the late 1990s had become a flash point for citizen activists in Canada. More than any other set of issues since the U.S.-Canada Free Trade Agreement and its sequel, NAFTA, the MAI had come to symbolize the massive resistance to, and the failures of, corporate globalization. When the Canadian government refused to heed the lessons of the MAI defeat in 1998, the country's largest public interest organization, the Council of Canadians, seized the moment.

Working in collaboration with some forty other national organizations, the council organized a series of public hearings in fall 1998 in eight Canadian cities. The series, called "The MAI Inquiry: A Citizens' Search for Alternatives," was conducted by a panel of commissioners including individuals who were both well known in the country and knowledgeable about globalization issues.

In preparation for the hearings, a *Citizens' Handbook,* designed to stimulate imagination about alternative ways to organize the global economy, was widely circulated. Highlighting the need to reorganize the global economy in terms of the three Rs of democracy—rights, rules, and responsibilities—the handbook included a citizens' report card to evaluate the performance of institutions like the WTO, the IMF, and the World Bank. While hundreds of civil society groups made submissions to the commissioners as they traveled across the country, thousands of individual citizens filled out and handed in their report cards.

During the public hearings, witness after witness emphasized the need for new organizing principles as the basis for transforming the global economy. These organizing principles included the following:

- *Recognizing people's fundamental democratic rights* as enshrined in the U.N. Declaration of Human Rights and the international covenants on economic, social, and cultural rights and on civil and political rights
- *Protecting the common good and heritage* affecting the lives and rights of all people, such as food security, labor standards, environmental safeguards, cultural integrity, public services, vital resources, and basic human rights
- *Building sustainable local communities,* where greater priority is put on employing local resources and people to produce goods and services for local and regional communities within ecological limits

CONTINUED

## 2. SUBSIDIARITY

Economic globalization entails first and foremost the delocalization and disempowerment of local communities and economies. Yet a high percentage of people on earth still survive through local, community-based activities: small-scale farming, local markets, local production for local consumption. This traditional system has enabled these people to remain in control of their economic and food security, and it also maintains the viability of their communities and cultures. Even in developed countries, most livelihoods have traditionally been connected to local economic production. Economic globalization is rapidly dismantling this, favoring instead economies based on export with global corporations in control.

---

BOX J: CONTINUED

- *Restoring the political sovereignty of governments,* such as the powers to determine economic, social, and environmental objectives for national development and the capacity to ensure that transnational corporations meet these priorities
- *Reasserting the democratic control of citizens* through new forms of participatory democracy whereby citizens become effectively involved in international policymaking on trade, investment, and finance

As the final report of the citizens' inquiry demonstrated, there is no shortage of imagination when it comes to reorganizing the global economy to serve the democratic rights of people and ensure the survival of the planet. No blueprint or platform for transforming the global economy was laid down before the hearings. Instead, people were encouraged to come forth as individuals and groups to present their own ideas and proposals for discussion and debate. Through this process, a variety of creative initiatives emerged:

- *Harnessing transnational corporations* and making them more accountable by requiring a more rigorous screening process on their operations
- *Renegotiating trade agreements* like NAFTA and the WTO by reopening the contentious areas but, if no satisfactory changes result, proceeding to invoke the abrogation clause
- *Reregulating foreign investment* to serve objectives and priorities for national development
- *Controlling speculation in financial markets* by adopting "speed bump" measures to regulate the inflows and outflows of capital
- *Curbing the threat of capital flight* by governments developing a more creative negotiating strategy with transnational corporations and encouraging strategic use of workers'

CONTINUED

This brings destruction of local livelihoods, local jobs, and community self-reliance.

It is necessary to create new rules and structures that consciously favor the local and follow the principle of subsidiarity—that is, whatever decisions and activities can be undertaken locally should be. Whatever power can reside at the local level should reside there. Only when additional activity is required that cannot be satisfied locally should power and activity move to the next higher level, that of region, nation, and finally the world. Site-here-to-sell-here policies and the grounding of capital locally should be codified. Economic structures should be designed to move economic and political power downward—toward the local rather than in a global direction. (In Europe, calls by IFG members and others that globalization be

---

**BOX J: CONTINUED**

pension funds as an alternative source of capital

In short, the citizens' inquiry provided the grounds for people to come together and begin reclaiming democracy and the commons through a process of outlining proposals for transforming the global economy. For most participating citizen activists, this is an important part of building a new democracy movement in Canada and around the world.

But the Council of Canadians soon realized that this was not a one-shot endeavor. Building a citizens' agenda is an ongoing process. Nor is it sufficient to focus energy on the global economy without at the same time developing proposals and strategies to change the structures of economic policymaking and governance at national and local levels. What's more, developing a citizens' agenda for social transformation should not be confined to the membership of one organization alone. To be effective, the process must be carried out in a broad alliance with a variety of civil society organizations and groups.

Accordingly, the council set up a task force to design and implement a three- to five-year plan of action to build a citizens' agenda for social transformation in Canada. The plan focused on developing an agenda for transformation on three tracks: local, national, and international. The council did not develop this citizens' agenda process in a vacuum. On the contrary, steps were taken to learn from the experiments that have taken place in other countries, such as the Sustainable Chile project, the Via Panchayat movement in India, and the peoples' budget process that has been instituted by the metropolitan government in Porto Alegre, Brazil. In this way, the citizens' agenda was meant to be stimulated by, and contribute to, the building of a global civil society movement.

replaced by greater emphasis on protecting and rebuilding local economies has had its first political success. United Kingdom Green members of the European Parliament were elected in 1999 on a manifesto that called for a "protect the local, globally" route to localization.)

Subsidiarity respects the notion that sovereignty resides in people. In other words, legitimate authority flows upward from the populace through the expression of their democratic will. Thus, the authority of more distant levels of administration is *subsidiary,* or subordinate, to the authority of more local levels, which allow a greater opportunity for direct citizen engagement. Decisions are properly made as close as feasible to the level of the individuals who will bear their consequences. Most of the affairs of self-reliant local economies are properly left to local people and institutions; issues such as global warming that demand collective action on a global scale necessarily require a greater involvement from global institutions.

The principle of subsidiarity recognizes the inherent democratic right to self-determination for people, communities, and nations as long as its exercise does not infringe on the similar rights of others. This right is properly secured through (a) the local and national ownership and control of resources and productive assets; (b) local and national rule-making authority in a system in which more central levels of authority support the local in achieving self-defined goals; and (c) local and national self-reliance in meeting essential needs with local and national resources to the extent feasible. Greater local ownership, political authority, and self-reliance mean less external dependence and vulnerability to exploitation—and the reduction or elimination of winner-takes-all competitive struggles for jobs, markets, money, and physical resources that are central to the global economic system. It does not, however, mean isolation. Sustainable societies are good neighbors that reach out to engage in cooperative, peaceful, and mutually beneficial relationships with all people through trade, cultural exchange, and the sharing of information and technology.

The principle of subsidiarity is so central to sustainable societies that chapter 6 of this volume is dedicated to the subject, spelling it out in some detail and offering a glimpse of the rich debate about this issue.

## 3. ECOLOGICAL SUSTAINABILITY

All life on earth is dependent on the vibrant health of the planet's life support systems, and the maintenance of its biodiversity. The ultimate measure of long-term viability for an economic system must finally be whether it is able to meet genuine needs of people without diminishing the ability of future generations to meet theirs and without diminishing the natural diversity of life on earth. So any sustainable society must be certain that (a) rates of resource exploitation do not exceed rates of regeneration; (b) rates of resource consumption do not exceed the rates at which renewable replacements can be phased into use; and (c) rates of pollution emissions and waste disposal do not exceed the rates of their harmless absorption. (Rates of GDP growth, or wealth increases, are not appropriate standards and may actually illustrate imbalances). Compromising any of these three conditions puts the well-being of future generations and planetary life at grave risk.

Unfortunately, economic globalization is intrinsically harmful to the environment because it depends for its own viability on an *opposite* set of standards: ever-increasing commodity consumption, expanding resource use, and increased disposal of polluting waste in oceans, land, and air. As described earlier, a primary feature of globalization—export-oriented production—is intrinsically damaging because it brings increased global transport activity and therefore increased fossil fuel use, refrigeration, packaging, and very costly and ecologically destructive new infrastructures such as dams, ports, roads, airports, canals, pipelines, and so on. In the agriculture realm, the switch to industrialized export systems also brings soil and water pollution, pesticide poisoning, and genetic pollution from genetically engineered plants. And by the rules of globalization's bureaucratic instruments, globalization also accelerates commodification and privatization of resources that are fundamental to life, such as freshwater; it appropriates global commons like air and oceans as dumping grounds for wastes; it inhibits the ability of nations to make their own environmental and health regulations; it separates farmers and traditional peoples from their historical connections to land by substituting industrial systems while dismissing far more earth-friendly worldviews and practices; it is a primary instrument in the spread of invasive species, including deadly mosquitoes and other organisms; it substitutes homogeneity and monoculture for biodiversity; and it directly serves unregulated corporate power.

None of this activity is sustainable. Most of it is *inherently* unsustainable. The problems will not get fixed without profound fundamental changes in all aspects of the formula and behavior.

No lesser light than Maurice Strong—who presided over the original Stockholm Conference on the Human Environment in 1972 and the Earth Summit of 1992 but is as much a mainstream businessman as an environmentalist—has seen the issues clearly. In his book *Where on Earth Are We Going?* he writes: "The environment isn't just an issue, something to be fixed while everything else remains the same. Ecological destruction is a sign of the imbalance in the way our industrial civilization sets its priorities and governs itself. . . . Globalization is creating new wealth at an unprecedented scale while increasing the dichotomy between industrial capitalism's victors and victims."

## BOX K: SUSTAINABLE CHILE

### By Sara Larrain

Over a decade ago, Augusto Pinochet was forced out of power through a plebiscite, and Chile began rebuilding a more democratic government. However, the democratically elected leaders in Chile have largely continued to support policies that contribute to an inequitable and unsustainable society. Although Chile is often cited as a model of macro-economic success, a number of Chilean NGOs, academics, and civil society groups continue to raise serious questions about what this "success"—based on the authoritarian implementation of neoliberalism—has meant for the environment, the poor, and the common good.

In response to growing concerns, the Institute for Political Ecology, the National Network for Ecological Action, and the University Bolivariana be-gan the Sustainable Chile project in 1997. Over the course of a year and a half, the project coordinated with a number of civil society groups, churches, and academics to articulate a citizens' agenda for a sustainable Chile based on social equality, environmental sustainability, and strengthened democracy. In addition, more than five hundred civil society leaders represented their communities in workshops held in a number of Chilean cities, in which they elaborated on regional diagnostic studies of sustainability problems facing their regions and formulated concrete proposals to address the issues.

Throughout this process, participants articulated the ways in which poverty, inequality, unequal distribution of wealth, exploitation of natural resources, pollution, and limited demo-

CONTINUED

If we are going to reverse paths in the future—and given the already-emerging crisis of climate change and others, it must be in the *near* future—a redesigned system is mandatory, one that observes the fundamental rules of ecological sustainability. We already know the goals. The great need now is for a new system that reverses a current dominant hierarchy of values that places corporate profits and wealth creation at the top and leaves sustainability out of the mix. That is a formula for disaster. The survival of the earth and all natural systems is basic and cannot be compromised.

## 4. COMMON HERITAGE

There exist common heritage resources that constitute a collective birthright of the whole species to be shared equitably among all. We believe that there are three categories of common heritage resources.

---

BOX K: CONTINUED

cratic institutions represent serious threats to sustainability in Chile. The citizens' agenda expresses these concerns and priorities of Chilean civil society and proposes a number of remedies, ranging from redistributing income, reducing military spending, reforming national environmental and fishing laws, and stabilizing copper production to reforming the 1980 constitution, written by the Pinochet regime, abolishing an amnesty law designed to ensure impunity for human rights violators, and creating a national youth program. The agenda also includes proposals for protecting indigenous lands and waters, such as by creating a national registry of indigenous lands and water sources and national oversight mechanisms for land and water concessions, offering tax exemptions to indigenous owners of water sources, and ratifying ILO Convention 169 on the protection of indigenous rights.

The process of elaborating the citizens' agenda brought together diverse groups throughout Chile and thus strengthened civil society. The agenda is intended to serve as a basis for further discussion and dialogue among citizens and politicians throughout Chile. Sustainable Chile project organizers hope that it will not only contribute to a public debate but also be used as a tool to mobilize the social and political will to put their proposals into action to establish a new Chilean society based on sustainability. Similar exercises have been conducted in Brazil, Uruguay, and Argentina (in 2002) under the Sustainable Southern Cone program.

SOURCE: Adapted from *For a Sustainable Chile: A Citizen's Agenda for Change.* Santiago: Sustainable Chile Program, 1999.

The first category includes the water, land, air, forests, and fisheries on which everyone's life depends. The second includes the culture and knowledge that are collective creations of our species. Finally, more modern common resources are those public services that governments perform on behalf of all people to address such basic needs as public health, education, public safety, and social security, among others. All of these common heritage resources are under tremendous strain as corporations seek to privatize and commodify them.

Together, these three categories of resources form the foundation of all real wealth. After all, without them there is neither life nor civilization. Healthy societies acknowledge and reward individual contributions to increasing the useful productivity of natural resources or expanding humanity's common pool of culture and knowledge. At the same time, they recognize that no individual created the natural wealth of the planet or the whole of any underlying body of knowledge.

Where property rights to common heritage resources are used to secure the livelihood rights of individuals, it is recognized that any right to the use of a common heritage resource carries a corresponding moral obligation to act as its steward on behalf of all. Similarly, the accumulation of such rights must not infringe on the birthright of others to their equitable share in the common inheritance. Efforts by persons or corporations to monopolize ownership of an essential common heritage resource, such as water, a seed variety, or a forest, and exclude the needs of others should be deemed unacceptable.

Our belief that these categories of common heritage resources should be treated differently in the global economy opens up a vast and fascinating debate over how to manage them. Chapter 5 of this volume is devoted to that debate.

## 5. DIVERSITY

A few decades ago, it was still possible to leave home and go someplace where the architecture was different, the landscape was different, and the language, lifestyle, dress, and values were different. Today, farmers and filmmakers in France and India and millions of people elsewhere are protesting to maintain that diversity. Tens of thousands of communities around the world had perfected local resource management systems that worked but are being under-

TEN PRINCIPLES FOR SUSTAINABLE SOCIETIES

mined by corporate-led globalization. Yet cultural, biological, social, and economic diversity are central to a dignified, interesting, and healthy life.

Diversity is key to the vitality, resilience, and innovative capacity of any living system. So too for human societies. The rich variety of the human experience and potential is reflected in *cultural diversity*, which provides a sort of cultural gene pool to spur innovation toward ever higher levels of social, intellectual, and spiritual accomplishment and creates a sense of identity, community, and meaning. (See Boxes L and M.) *Economic diversity* is the foundation of resilient, stable, energy-efficient, self-reliant local economies that serve the needs of people, communities, and nature. *Biological diversity* is essential to the complex, self-regulating, self-regenerating processes of the ecosystem from which all life and wealth ultimately flow.

*(continued on page 94)*

---

## BOX L: CULTURAL DIVERSITY: THE RIGHT OF INDIGE-NOUS PEOPLES TO REMAIN DIFFERENT AND DIVERSE

*By Victoria Tauli-Corpuz, Indigenous Peoples' International Center for Policy Research and Education*

There are still some three hundred million indigenous people on the earth. We represent more than five thousand distinct cultures and six thousand languages. According to the United Nations Environment Program, indigenous peoples account for a majority of the world's remaining cultural diversity.

But economic globalization presents a grave threat to our continuing existence, just as much as it threatens the biodiversity of our forests and fields. Globalization is really a continuation of the colonization we were subjected to for five hundred years. In the past, swords and guns were used to quell our resistance and take our lands. The colonizers also used government laws and institutions, schools, and churches to make our ancestors despise our cultures and deny our identities. Today the forces of globalization continue to regard our rights, our political systems, our economic systems, and our culture and knowledge systems as backward, unrealistic, and romantic. But the true explanation for the aggression toward us is that we occupy the last remaining places on earth where resources abound and biodiversity and cultural diversity thrive. Our continued existence stands in the way of their "progress."

The indigenous worldview respects Mother Earth and reveres the sacredness of life. We believe in reciprocity with nature and in sharing nature's gifts

CONTINUED

BOX L: CONTINUED

among peoples and generations. Ours is a collective identity with collective ownership of forests, waters, and lands. These are antithetical to individualism, private property, modernization, and global capitalism.

For indigenous peoples, keeping our territorial or ancestral lands is the most important thing; it determines our identity. This is where our ancestors walked and learned everything that they left for us. This is where we have forged our relations with nature and created social bonds with each other. This is why we resist cultural homogenization and globalization.

Pressures to take our lands and resources have led to conflagrations worldwide. Because of the trade-liberalizing rules of the WTO, corporations are rapidly invading our communities. The U'wa in Colombia are fighting oil development on their lands; the pygmies in Rwanda and Burundi are battling logging concessions; the Igorot, Mangyan, and Lumad in the Philippines are fighting mining on ancestral lands. The Penans of Sarawak, the Cree of Canada, and the Mapuche of Chile are all fighting World Bank dam projects. And these are only a few examples.

Yet our minerals, logs, waters, and biodiversity are not enough for them; now they also want our collective knowledge and our human genes. Corporations are all over native lands, prospecting for seeds we have developed or for our knowledge of the cosmetic and pharmaceutical properties of forest plants. They take this knowledge home and patent our plants. This "biopiracy" even extends inside our bodies to our gene structures: they are surreptitiously collecting blood samples from our people without telling us why. They call it the Human Genetic Diversity Project, but we call it the Vampire Project. Biopiracy is legitimized by the WTO's Trade-Related Intellectual Property Rights agreement, which confirms the rights of individuals and corporations to patent life forms in defiance of our traditional beliefs and practices.

Our ancestors told us that land is sacred, that animals and plants are our relatives, and that it is our duty to ensure that they are defended for the next generations. Our resistance to these efforts to homogenize us must be supported— our right to self-determination and our right to be allowed to remain different and diverse. Legal instruments that conflict with our indigenous values, cosmologies, lifestyles, and customary laws should not be imposed on us from any outside body. These are not decisions for the WTO or the IMF or the World Bank. We fight for the right to define ourselves and to maintain our continued existence as indigenous peoples on our own ancestral lands.

One important way in which we are fighting to protect ourselves is by urging member states of the U.N. Commission on Human Rights to adopt the

CONTINUED

U.N. Draft Declaration on the Rights of Indigenous Peoples. But even more important is to raise the awareness of indigenous peoples all over the world about our rights as distinct peoples. All forty-five articles of the declaration are equally critical, but I will highlight just a few of them:

- Indigenous peoples have the right to self-determination. By virtue of this right, we freely determine our political status and freely pursue our economic, social, and cultural development (Article 3).
- We have the collective and individual right to maintain and develop our distinct identities and characteristics, including our right to identify ourselves as indigenous and to be recognized as such (Article 8).
- We have the right to practice and revitalize our cultural traditions and customs. This includes the right to maintain, protect, and develop the past, present, and future manifestations of our cultures, such as archeological and historical sites, artifacts, designs, ceremonies, technologies, visual and performing arts, and literature, as well as the right to restitution of cultural, intellectual, religious, and spiritual property taken without our free and informed consent or in violation of our laws, traditions, and customs (Article 12).
- We have the right to maintain and

develop our political, economic, and social systems, to be secure in the enjoyment of our own means of subsistence and development, and to engage freely in all our traditional and other economic activities. Those who have been deprived of their means of subsistence and development are entitled to just compensation (Article 21).
- We have the right to maintain and strengthen our distinctive spiritual and material relationship with the lands, territories, waters, coastal seas, and other resources that we have traditionally owned or otherwise occupied or used, and to uphold our responsibilities to future generations in this regard (Article 25).
- Indigenous peoples are entitled to the recognition of the full ownership, control, and protection of our cultural and intellectual property. We have the right to special measures to control, develop, and protect our sciences, technologies, and cultural manifestations, including human and other genetic resources, seeds, medicines, knowledge of properties of fauna and flora, oral traditions, literature, designs, and visual and performing arts (Article 29).
- We have the right to our traditional medicines and health practices, including the right to protect vital medicinal plants, animals, and minerals (Article 24).

CONTINUED

• We have the right to own, develop, control, and use the lands and territories, including the total environment of the lands, air, waters, coastal seas, sea ice, flora and fauna, and other resources we have traditionally owned, occupied, and used. This includes the right to the full recognition of our laws, traditions, and customs, land tenure systems, and institutions for the development and management of our resources. States should provide protective measures to prevent any interference with, alienation of, or encroachment upon these rights (Article 26).

• Indigenous peoples have the right to determine and develop priorities and strategies for the use of our lands, territories, and other resources, including to require that states obtain our free and informed consent prior to the approval of any project affecting these, particularly in connection with the development, utilization, or exploitation of mineral, water, and other resources (Article 30).

• We have the right to the recognition, observance, and enforcement of existing treaties, agreements, and other constructive arrangements concluded with states or their successors, according to their original spirit and intent and to have states honor and respect these. Conflicts and disputes that cannot otherwise be settled should be submitted to

competent international bodies agreed to by all parties concerned.

These and many other elements of the U.N. declaration are a good starting point in our efforts to protect our cultures and lands. This draft declaration was adopted by the U.N. Subcommission on Prevention of Discrimination and Protection of Minorities in 1994. Until now, however, the U.N. Commission on Human Rights has not adopted it because of opposition from governments. The most obstructive government is that of the United States. Even though it is not being adopted by the higher U.N. bodies, we are now using it as the international standard and framework for the protection of our rights. It is becoming an international customary law on indigenous peoples. The Philippine Indigenous Peoples Rights Act, which was passed in 1997, is almost a clone of this draft declaration.

We ask the support of our friends in the global justice movement to put pressure on the U.N. member states to adopt this draft declaration. We also ask you to help push for national legislation to protect our rights and to use this as the overall framework. Our greatest contribution to the struggle against globalization and homogenization will be for us to protect and develop further the diversities in our cultural and biological heritage as well as the diverse worldviews and economic and political systems that we have nurtured and sustained.

## BOX M: CULTURAL DIVERSITY: THE RIGHT OF NATIONS TO RESIST CULTURAL HOMOGENIZATION

*By Maude Barlow, Council of Canadians*

I do not want my house to be walled in on all sides and my windows to be stuffed. I want the culture of all lands to be blown about my house as freely as possible. But I refuse to be blown off my feet by any.

—Mahatma Gandhi

In Latin America, Asia and the Pacific, Africa, and the industrialized world, the power of corporate-led globalization results in young people demanding Nike sneakers, Gap clothes, the latest CDs, Michael Jordan T-shirts, baseball caps, and other consumer goods popular in the world's most dominant economic power. Hollywood movies, the global music industry, television, and mass-market books spread a homogeneous culture. Around the world, North American corporate culture is destroying local traditions, knowledge, skills, artisans, and values. When combined with the destruction of the habitat of aboriginal peoples in many parts of the world, this assault on local cultures is having a profound impact.

Technology is also advancing one culture and one language. The United States has more computers than the rest of the world combined. English is used on 80 percent of Web sites, yet fewer than one in ten people worldwide speak the language. Everywhere, Internet access divides educated from illiterate, men from women, rich from poor, young from old, and urban from rural.

For many countries feeling the deadening and homogenizing impacts of economic globalization, cultural diversity and the right to protect it from the forces of globalization have become as important a fight as preserving biodiversity. Governments and people around the world are increasingly concerned about a global cultural homogenization dominated by the American and Western values and lifestyles carried through the massive U.S. entertainment-industrial complex.

Many societies, particularly indigenous peoples, view culture as their richest heritage without which they have no roots, history, or soul. Its value is other than monetary; to commodify it is to destroy it. There is a growing sentiment in many parts of the world that culture is not just another product like steel or computer parts. Through funding programs, content regulations, and other public policy mechanisms, many countries have encouraged their own artists and cultures and tried to maintain some space for their own intellectual creations. Still others are looking to these models in order to promote local cultural expression.

In contrast, the entertainment-industrial complex sees culture as a business—a very big business—that

CONTINUED

should be fiercely advanced through
international trade agreements like the
World Trade Organization. This industry combines giant telecommunications
companies, movie studios, television
networks, cable companies, and the Internet working together in a complex
web that includes publishing, films,
broadcasting, video, television, cable
and satellite systems, megatheater pro-
ductions, music recording and distribution, and theme parks.

Mass-produced products of American popular culture are the biggest U.S.
export, according to the United Nations'
1999 *Human Development Report.* A huge,
well-organized coalition has formed that
links the U.S. entertainment, media, and
information-technology sectors together in a kind of common front to oppose
cultural protections in other nations.
Companies like Time-Warner and Disney have powerful friends on Capitol
Hill and in the White House, and they
work closely with the U.S. government,
which, in turn, has taken a very aggressive stand in protecting their interests.

For many years, the U.S. State Department has used a variety of trade
remedies to consistently strike down
nation-state and local rules aimed at
protecting local and national culture.
In recent years, the battle has heated up
as more and more countries adopt
measures to support their own artists
and cultural producers.

Speaking before a House committee
in early 2000, then–U.S. trade representative Charlene Barshefsky was as determined as ever to use trade agreements
to promote American corporate-enter-
tainment interests. "We are developing
proposals for a wide range of sectors
where our companies have strong commercial interests, including audiovisual
services and telecommunications. Our
companies are poised to be among the
primary beneficiaries from stronger
commitments at the WTO," she said.
This quote clearly expresses the dilem-
ma in culture: How can you maintain the
free flow of intellectual creations and art
while promoting diversity?

The debate is not only about the
right of states to maintain existing policies and programs.

CONTINUED

Global corporations abhor diversity because for them it is a source of
inefficiency and uncertainty, and most of all, it is a drain on profits. They seek
to reduce costs and increase market control through cultural homogenization,
economic specialization, and elimination of unprofitable species. These corporations profit from economies of scale, reduced management costs, and the
increased dependence of individuals and communities on the products and
services they find it profitable to sell. Corporate logos replace authentic local
cultures as the primary source of personal identity. Communities that once
created their means of livelihood through local enterprises, using local labor

BOX M: CONTINUED

More fundamentally, it is about the right to develop new ones and to adapt or amend others as our society evolves. The measures adopted worldwide are generally not about protectionism because most of the markets remain open to the cultural products of others. It is about finding ways to provide choice so that in the deluge of cultural products available, citizens can choose to watch, listen to, or read a book, magazine, film, or sound recording that reflects their own local reality. Overall, the debate is exactly about cultural diversity.

As civil society movements form all over the world, so too is the cultural community developing international links to fight for its survival. In September 2000, a global network of NGOs concerned about cultural issues met in Santorini, Greece, and formed the International Network for Cultural Diversity. More than 160 organizations in more than thirty countries initiated this network and are committed to becoming a powerful voice in the coming decades.

Many in the cultural community believe it is now time for a new international instrument to deal with this emerging issue. In this spirit, in March 2002 the International Network for Cultural Diversity put forward a draft "Convention on Cultural Diversity." The network believes that to succeed this instrument must have an equivalent status to trade agreements; it cannot be subservient. It would recognize the importance to all nations and peoples of maintaining cultural diversity, contain only those commitments that are appropriate to culture, and set out rules on what kinds of measures countries can use to promote diversity. Challenges and disputes under the new charter would need to be judged by cultural experts, not trade bureaucrats.

The instrument would have to be self-defining: what constitutes a matter of cultural significance to one nation may not to another. These definitions must be allowed to change over time because we cannot know today what form cultural expression will take in the future.

NOTE: With special thanks to Garry Neil.

and resources to meet local needs, now must depend on the sale of their labor and resources for whatever the market will bear to distant corporations over which they have no control. Biological vitality is sapped by the loss of biological diversity, which creates an ever growing, unsustainable dependence on the input of expensive and often toxic fertilizers and pesticides. People and communities pay the price for loss of the services that nature once provided for free; corporations and their distant absentee owners reap the profits.

Diversity may be bad for corporate profits, but it is essential for healthy, sustainable, vital communities.

## 6. HUMAN RIGHTS

In 1948, governments of the world came together to adopt the United
Nations Universal Declaration of Human Rights, which established certain
core rights such as "a standard of living adequate for . . . health and well-
being . . . , including food, clothing, housing and medical care, and necessary social services, and the right to security in the event of unemployment."
Building on this declaration, governments negotiated two covenants in subsequent decades, one on political and civil rights and the other on economic,
social, and cultural rights.

Over much of the past half-century, people have struggled to press their
governments to advance these rights, which remain as central to human
development today as they were in the beginning. The goal of trade and
investment should be to enhance the quality of life and respect core labor,
social, and other rights.

Traditionally, most of the human rights debate in the United States and
other rich nations has focused on civil and political rights. Although we
agree that it is the duty of governments to ensure these rights, we believe
they also need to guarantee economic, social, and cultural rights. This
assertion has some important implications. For example, as chapter 5
explains, we believe that every person has the right to clean and safe
water. That leads us to conclude that water should not be commodified or
privatized for sale at market prices and that it is the obligation of government to guarantee safe water supplies. We recognize that many governments are corrupt and unaccountable, but this does not lead us to the conclusion that the private sector is a better guarantor of rights. Rather, it
reinforces our resolve to press accountability on governments at every
level.

Some suggest that this principle of human rights can conflict with the
second principle, subsidiarity. Their reasoning is that some local societies
follow practices that violate human rights, such as female genital mutilation
and other violations of the right against gender discrimination. We believe
that when these two principles clash, then universal human rights should
trump local assertion of authority that violates those rights.

## 7. JOBS, LIVELIHOOD, EMPLOYMENT

The United Nations Universal Declaration of Human Rights affirms every person's "right to work, to free choice of employment, to just and favorable conditions of work, and to protection against unemployment." Most of the people in the world ensure the livelihood of their families through work outside the formal sector. In indigenous societies, the majority participate in activities that offer sustenance but are often not integrated in the national or global market. In rural areas, most make a living off the land, often engaged in subsistence agriculture or small-scale entrepreneurial activities that do not offer regular incomes. In urban areas, most people in poorer nations make ends meet without regular jobs or incomes. In each of these cases, corporate globalization is displacing greater numbers of them from dignified livelihoods than it is helping. The reversal of globalization policies that displace farmers from their land and fisherfolk from their coastal ecosystems is central to the goal of a sustainable world.

The Universal Declaration of Human Rights also affirms that everyone "has the right to form and to join trade unions." Over the past eight decades, the U.N. International Labor Organization has elaborated over one hundred conventions that further specify basic labor rights. Yet this same organization points out that today some 30 percent of workers are unemployed or seriously underemployed. Many of those who work do so under brutal, exploitative, and dangerous conditions. One of the most dynamic social movements confronting corporate-led globalization is organized labor, which has gathered over one hundred million workers around the world into trade unions. Millions more join together in associations of informal sector workers. These movements, rooted in a struggle for these core rights, are a cornerstone of the social movements that are creating economic alternatives.

Hence, sustainable societies must both protect the rights of workers in the formal sector and address the livelihood needs of the greater numbers of people who subsist in what has become known as the informal sector, as well as those who have no work or are seriously underemployed.

## 8. FOOD SECURITY AND SAFETY

Communities and nations are stable and secure when their people have enough food, particularly when these nations can provide their own food. People also need safe food, a commodity that is becoming increasingly scarce.

Some of the strongest citizen movements around the world today are fighting the juggernaut of globalized industrial agriculture. Monopoly control of food and seeds by a small number of corporations threatens millions of farmers and the food security and safety of tens of millions of people. Global rules of trade now favor the industrial agriculture model, rapidly destroying small-scale farmers who produce staple foods for local consumption. Globalized industrial agriculture is driving small farmers off the land and replacing them with pesticide and machine-intensive monocultures producing luxury items for export at great environmental and social cost. Meanwhile, biotechnology brings a host of new ecological and health risks.

New rules of trade must recognize that food production for local communities should be at the top of a hierarchy of values in agriculture. Local self-reliance in food production and the assurance of healthful, safe foods should be considered basic human rights. Shorter trade distances and reduced reliance on expensive inputs that need to be shipped over long distances are key to a new food system paradigm. (See also chapter 8.)

## 9. EQUITY

Under the current rules, economic globalization has widened the gap between rich and poor countries, between the rich and poor in most countries, and between women and men. The social dislocations and tensions that result have become among the greatest threats to peace and security the world over. Greater equity both among nations and inside them would reinforce democracy and sustainable communities.

Reducing the growing gap between rich and poor nations requires first the cancellation of the illegitimate debts of poor countries. It also requires the replacement of the current institutions of global governance with new ones that include global fairness among their operating principles.

As for inequities within nations, a key flaw of the current dominant system is that markets respond to the wants of those with money and disregard even the most basic needs of those who do not have the means to pay. Extreme inequality in income and ownership distorts the allocation of economic resources, excludes all but the very rich from meaningful democratic participation, undermines institutional legitimacy, and creates social instability.

Economic globalization disproportionately hurts women too. Women make up the majority of the small-scale food producers who still provide most of the planet's nutritional needs. Hence, they suffer the most from a globalized agricultural system. Likewise, most of the workers on the global assembly lines of Nike, Dell, and other global corporations are women, so they suffer most from the sweatshop conditions in many of these workplaces. Whether farm or factory workers, women are the primary household workers and caregivers, and the majority of this work is unpaid. And just as the lowest rungs of the global assembly lines are made up primarily of women, corporate CEOs and global bureaucrats are overwhelmingly male, reinforcing the unequal-gender pay scale.

The claim of economic globalization advocates that those who accumulate great wealth take nothing away from those less fortunate is at best disingenuous. When those who have the money to enjoy meat-rich diets cause the market to redirect available supplies of grain away from the tables of people who cannot pay in order to feed livestock to provide meat to those who can, they contribute to the dynamics of hunger. When banks foreclose mortgages on family farms and put them up for sale to corporations to grow crops for export, they are depriving the displaced families of their means of livelihood and often condemning them to a marginal, dependent existence as landless laborers or sweatshop workers producing products for export that they cannot afford themselves. When the rich buy opulent second, third, and fourth homes, they drive up the price of land and housing and force the less fortunate onto the street. Those who profit from clear-cutting hillsides contribute to the floods that sweep away the homes and crops of those living below. Those with the wealth to engage in profligate energy consumption contribute to the storms that kill and displace hundreds of thousands of people living on coastal lowlands in Bangladesh and elsewhere. The idea that the good fortune of the rich has no consequences for the plight of the poor may comfort the consciences of the rich, but it is not true.

In an increasingly crowded world with finite environmental limits, the human species confronts an increasingly painful trade-off between expanding the profligate material consumption of the wealthy and meeting the basic needs of everyone.

Because equity is essential to social health, healthy societies set a floor on the bottom and a cap on the top, while striving to maintain true equality of opportunity and balance between incentive and equity. A century ago, the celebrated financier J. P. Morgan, himself no paragon of virtue, asserted that a company's top executive should not make more than twenty times the income of the lowest-paid worker. As we have mentioned earlier, in the year 2000 in the United States, the average CEO made 458 times the income of the average worker. There are a plethora of policy options to improve the incomes of both industrial and rural workers. And there are sensible proposals to remove incentives that encourage excessive executive pay.

Social justice and greater equality—among nations, within nations, between ethnic groups, between classes, and between women and men—are cornerstones of sustainable societies.

## 10. THE PRECAUTIONARY PRINCIPLE

We live at a time when corporate-driven scientific and technological innovation is affecting the environmental, social, and political milieu as never before. Great technological change takes place with little advance understanding of its impacts, and virtually no process for democratic evaluation, often until it is far too late to reverse a technology's negative effects. The twentieth century brought us the automobile, chemicals, plastics, nuclear energy, air travel, television, computers, bioweaponry, space exploration, and more recently biotechnology, nanotechnology, and wireless communication, to name only a few of the innovations. Each of these is already bringing massive change on social, economic, and political fronts. Much of that change is beneficial, but there has also been a degree of pollution and an ecological impact that were never publicly considered and that may bring great hardships, illness, and dislocations for generations to come. Most important, *none* of these changes were brought to the world in a democratic manner, with full exposure of the potential negative outcomes, which range from climate change, to ocean pollution, to chemical poisonings, to space weaponry, to globally centralized and concentrated communications, and so on. Nearly all were introduced either because of military or market considerations without regard, exposure, or discussion of negative potentials. Whenever new technologies were described at all, it was always about benefits, in sometimes utopian language. "Nuclear energy is safe, clean, unlimited." "Biotechnology will feed the world." "Antibiotics will end disease." Downsides are not apparent until much later.

In recognition of this problem, the 1992 Declaration of Rio, signed by country participants at the Rio Earth Summit, codified the precautionary principle as international law, as follows: "In order to protect the environment, the precautionary approach shall be widely applied. . . . Where there are threats of serious or irreversible damage, lack of full scientific certainty shall not be used as a reason for postponing cost-effective measures to prevent environmental damage."

The International Forum on Globalization strongly endorses this principle as basic to rational, democratic decision making. Obviously, it sometimes takes many years for "scientific proof" of harm to be established, and the precautionary principle places the onus of proof on the technology's or the process's proponents to prove that it is safe *before* it is generally introduced. As in the old adage, "Better safe than sorry." Or the more recent cautionary about problematic technologies: "Guilty until proven innocent."

Precaution even in the absence of absolute certainty of danger and the deliberate shifting of burdens of proof to proponents are two fundamental components of the precautionary principle. Two other important ones are that where doubt exists, preference should always be given to alternatives and that there must be full public participation at all levels of decision making.

Although the precautionary principle is considered controversial by some, many countries have begun to accept and codify it. Germany and Sweden have already done so, and wide application of the precautionary principle has also been made in Australia, Scotland, and Norway, among others. In February 2001, the European Commission, a branch of the European Union, also took a helpful stance: "When there are reasonable grounds for concern that potential hazards may affect the environment, human, animal, or plant health, and when at the same time the data preclude a detailed risk evaluation, the precautionary principle has been politically accepted as a risk management strategy." Alas, however, not by all.

The United States, for example, has famously refused to apply the principle in the case of climate change, arguing that science has not yet proven that human activity is the cause—a very lonely and dangerous view. The United States has also sued, under WTO rules, to overturn the European Union's ban on the import of beef products treated with artificial growth hormone, which is suspected of increasing the risk for cancers. The ban on these beef products was itself an expression by the EU of the precautionary principle.

Here we have yet another area where the WTO represents a major problem. Under WTO rules, safety regulations must be based on "risk assessment," which requires governments to present categorical proof of harm from new technologies and techniques before they may ban a usage. Without such categorical proof—which the EU did not have in the case of its ban on beef containing hormones—preventive measures qualify as "illegal barriers to trade," and may be overturned. If such WTO rules had been in place in the 1950s, the U.S. Food and Drug Administration would not have been able to ban the use of the drug thalidomide, which caused severe deformities in babies in many countries (including in Europe) where it had been approved and widely used and whose culpability was not finally proven until thirty years later.

Quite a few U.S. laws actually do apply the precautionary principle, though not by name. These include the Clean Water Act, the National Environment Protection Act, the Occupational Safety and Health Act (OSHA), and the Pollution-Prevention Act of 1990, though WTO rules may someday be used to challenge these policies. Meanwhile the United States is using those same WTO rules to threaten action against precautionary policies of other governments. In addition to the beef hormone case, this has lately happened with regard to genetically engineered export foods, phthalates in children's PVC toys, and certain electronic technologies.

Universal acceptance and adoption of the precautionary principle is thus essential if citizens, through their democratically elected representatives, are to have the right to learn about, decide upon, and control the risks that they or the natural environment should be exposed to. Global trade bodies should either codify and incorporate the principle, as was done at Rio, or at least take no restrictive stance when countries apply it.

## Applying the Principles to Globalization

These ten principles seem to be mirror opposites of the principles that drive the institutions of the corporate global economy. The imperatives of this powerful system create a self-reinforcing drive toward the privatization and monopolization of common heritage resources; the centralization of power and authority for the few who are shielded from legal accountability for the impact of their decisions on the well-being of people and planet; a life-and-death competition that divides the world into big winners and even bigger losers; the unaccountable externalization of costs; the destruction of cultural, biological, and economic diversity; and the disregard of deadly risks to human and environmental health. It is time to reclaim the power taken by the institutions of corporate globalization and replace them with institutions and rules that better serve the needs of people and planet.

We offer the ten organizing principles as a basis for determining which rules, incentives, policies, and institutions can support sustainable societies. Because much of the globalization debate has centered on international trade and investment, it is appropriate to examine how these principles for sustainable societies translate into principles for international trade and investment. The following paragraphs, adapted from a statement of the Interfaith Working Group on Trade and Investment, convened by a number of U.S. faith-based organizations, offers some ideas on this subject.

- *International trade and investment systems should respect the legitimate role of democratic governments at all levels.* In collaboration with civil society, governments should be allowed to set policies on the development and welfare of their people. This means respecting the right of every community and nation to democratic self-determination, including the right to determine the terms—in cooperation with other communities and nations—under which they wish to enter into trade with others or invite others to invest in their economies. Because such decisions have far-reaching consequences for the well-being of every member of society, they should be worked out through transparent democratic processes involving the participation of all levels of government and civil society. Participation of the most vulnerable stakeholders is especially important.

- *International trade and investment systems should safeguard the global commons and respect and promote human rights, the rights of workers, women, indigenous peoples, and children.* The rights of local communities to protect and use their natural resources to secure the needs of their people in a sustainable manner need to be respected. Societies need rules to protect the public interest. As in any area of human activity, international trade and investment are properly regulated to that end—preferably by the democratically chosen governments of the nations and communities involved. Any international agreement on trade and investment should properly support such local and national regulation.

- *Finally, all international agreements should support the goal of creating sustainable societies.* This will require changes in past practice that will be addressed more fully in subsequent chapters.

Surely, it is time for a new approach.

# CHAPTER FIVE

# Reclaiming the Commons

## *What Should Be Off-Limits to Globalization?*

AS RECENTLY AS two decades ago, large parts of the world were not part of economic globalization. The majority of people in the world still lived off the land with little dependence on outside markets. In many rural areas, seeds were exchanged as the collective property of the community, not the private property of Monsanto or Cargill. Of the three hundred million indigenous people in the world, most lived in complete isolation from global trade activity. Municipal water systems were usually under local government or community control. Much of the economic activity in the Soviet Union, Eastern Europe, and China was not linked to global markets. Most developing countries restricted foreign investment in their banking, insurance, and other critical economic sectors. Most stock markets were national, closed to global investors. Even though global corporations clamored to enter each of these domains, national and local governments and communities maintained strong barriers.

All of that has changed. Under two decades of market fundamentalism, introduced by Ronald Reagan, Margaret Thatcher, Helmut Kohl, and their counterparts elsewhere, the boundaries came crashing down. Some of this was seen in dramatic fashion on CNN in living rooms around the world, such as the destruction of the Berlin Wall. Some happened in the face of remarkable citizen opposition, such as the passage of NAFTA in 1993 and the WTO in 1994. Other battles over the global spread of corporate control occurred on the local stage, such as the determined fight by Bolivian workers and peasants to keep the municipal water system in Cochabamba out of the hands of Bechtel and the struggles of Indian peasants against the Cargill and Monsanto assertions of property rights over their seeds. During these two decades, global corporations—with the strong support of many national governments—forcefully asserted their right to any market anywhere. And today their reach has extended into virtually every domain of even remote rural communities around the world.

One of the most critical points of unity among the authors of this document is that this encroachment of corporate globalization into every aspect of life and the environment must stop. We seek to shift the framework of the overall debate on globalization in this sense: we believe that many aspects of social and economic life around the world should be off-limits to the processes of economic globalization. In this chapter, we offer the beginnings of a framework for choosing which arenas should be off-limits to which aspects of economic globalization.

On one level, there is already agreement across the spectrum of the globalization debate that certain goods and services should be kept out of trade. For example, governments around the world have created a global convention to ban trade in hazardous wastes. Likewise, there is a global convention against the trafficking of endangered species. And there is growing global action against the trafficking across borders of women sold into sexual bondage.

Now, the International Forum on Globalization would like to expand the debate beyond these pernicious goods to include the rights of peoples and obligations of nations concerning what has traditionally been called *the commons*.

In this chapter, we offer an overview of the many notions of the commons around the world and spell out the current threats of economic globalization to commons such as freshwater, the genetic commons, communal lands, and others. We then introduce the concept of the modern commons— that is, the role of governments in carrying out a sacred public trust to perform certain key services that were once the province of communities and families but have been captured by and subsumed into the nation-state. We argue that selling off these services to global corporations—which operate on an entirely different set of priorities than the public interest—is a grave violation of these modern commons, many of which should never be commodified. We argue that they are also obligations of governments as trustees of the common rights and services of people. Finally, we offer a few ideas on how the commons might be protected from the worst aspects of economic globalization.

We offer these suggestions in the spirit of opening up a complex discussion. We do not pretend to present the final answers.

## Understanding the Commons

Much of the thrust of economic globalization over these decades has been driven by global corporations pushing to develop and market every type of natural resource. In a world where natural resources were already seriously overexploited, corporations have attempted to convert every remaining nook and cranny of the natural world and human experience into commodified form.

Now, areas of life traditionally considered out of bounds are being considered for monetized activity, private ownership, or global trade. These are aspects of life that had been accepted since time immemorial as collective property, or the common heritage of all peoples and communities, existing for everyone to share as they have for millennia. These are what have been known as *the commons.*

Obvious among them are the air we breath, the freshwater we drink, the oceans and the diverse wildlife and plant biodiversity of the world, the genes all creatures pass to following generations, the stores of human knowledge and wisdom, the informal support systems of the community, the seeds that communities use for replanting, the public square, shared languages and culture, and among indigenous peoples, communal lands that have been worked cooperatively for thousands of years.

Some commons are gifts from the bounty of nature and are crucial to the survival of people and the earth. Most cultures have innumerable rituals to celebrate these gifts and rules or taboos against harming them. Other commons are new, including, for example, the broadcast spectrum or the Internet. Still others are ancient, such as the common grazing meadows of Africa, Europe, and Asia; folklore; and cultural artifacts.

Some commons may be thought of as global, such as the atmosphere, the oceans, outer space, and because they have no territorial claimants, Antarctica and the moon. Others may be thought of as community commons: public spaces, common lands, forests, the gene pool, local innovative knowledge with respect to medicinal plants, and seeds that communities have developed over centuries.

Author Jonathan Rowe of California's Tomales Bay Institute points out that the key characteristic of all aspects of the commons is that they belong to everyone. No one has traditionally had exclusive rights to them. We have inherited them jointly; they are our common heritage. They "are more basic to our lives than the state or the market," says Rowe. He goes on to say, "One cannot imagine a life without air fit to breathe, oceans rich with life, free clean water, a vibrant biodiversity. These are things we have always taken for granted. The commons have the quality of always having been there, one generation after another, available forever to all."

Later in this chapter, we will advocate for yet another category—the "modern commons" of public services like health, water purification and distribution, education, and information, each of which was once achieved informally within small local and indigenous communities that have since been absorbed by the state and are also now on tap for privatization.

The modern nation-state has also taken onto itself the collective security of its citizens, which in a less technologically oriented and mobile world was once the province of communities. In that context, we need to discuss the varieties of security protection that a modern state is obliged to offer in addition to its obvious military roles. Since adopting the Universal Declaration of Human Rights in 1948, the United Nations has helped governments define basic human rights. Governments are obligated to protect human rights, as well as food security, as fundamental to life. Protection of cultural diversity is also a basic duty and right. Nothing in the global trading system should ever be permitted to reduce these fundamental priorities. (At present, many elements of the WTO and other trade agreements work directly against countries that try to protect these fundamental rights, which we now propose as part of the modern commons.)

Precise categorization of each type of commons is difficult to achieve because many cross several categories—for example, river water (which may pass through several regions and countries), biodiversity (which may be local or national), the broadcast spectrum (which may be local, national, or international), and the genetic structures of life. Similarly, protections against trade that destroys the commons—toxins, armaments, and so on—must be national and international.

Nonetheless, the purpose of this discussion is to lay on the table one central principle: *Any global trading system needs to recognize and yield to the primary notion that not every aspect of experience should be subject to its centralized rules, and many aspects should never be included in global trade or investment of any kind or in the rules that govern trade and investment.*

Such complex questions are usually omitted from discussions about global trading systems, which usually keep their focus on new resources, expansion, and profit. But these questions must be addressed if any kind of social or environmental sustainability is to be obtained. How can communal spaces be effectively protected? Do any effective instruments now exist? What new ones can be proposed? How do we define the areas of the commons, common heritage, or government services that should *never* be subject to trade—or at least never be subject to the authority of global agreements that impinge on local or national sovereignty? What are the obligations of nation-states in the modern world? What goods are too dangerous—toxins, weapons, and drugs, for example—to be allowed into the global trade system at all? Should we establish taboos for certain kinds of trade?

## Current Threats to the Commons

The conversion of the commons into commodified, privatized, "enclosed" form has been under way for centuries. (See the following section, "The Tradition of the Commons," for more on the history of this subject.) In the current context, the main engines of this conversion are the global corporations and the global bureaucracies that increasingly have served these corporations. With the help of the new global trade and finance bureaucracies, corporations are finding opportunities in some virgin territory that most humans never thought could possibly be fodder for corporate enterprise. Here are a few examples.

### THREATS TO THE FRESHWATER COMMONS

Unthinkable as it may seem, freshwater—a common heritage basic to the survival of all human beings—is being opened up to private ownership, commodification, export, and trade. It's as if water were an ordinary commodity, like new computer parts or car tires, rather than a shared, irreplaceable, and limited resource needed by all creatures of the earth.

In many parts of the world, the rights to freshwater in rivers, streams, and lakes are being sold to giant transnational corporations like Bechtel, Vivendi, and others. (Before its collapse, Enron was also a main player in water deals.) These firms have started charging users for every drink of water or liter of irrigation. For people who cannot pay the fees—and many cannot—they, their families, and their fields go thirsty.

Private corporations around the world have identified freshwater as the last great untapped natural resource to be exploited for profit. They are quickly taking control of water and water services to kick-start trade in what authors Maude Barlow and Tony Clarke have labeled *blue gold*. Indeed, water is becoming just as important as a prior era's black gold—oil.

Companies have been able to proceed aggressively because water has been defined as a tradable commodity by both NAFTA and the WTO. Once the tap is turned on—that is, once any deals are made by *any* state or municipality in a country to privatize water or water services—the tap cannot be turned back off without violating corporate rights. The WTO contains specific provisions prohibiting the use of export controls to prevent the export of water, and NAFTA contains a clause (chapter 11 of NAFTA) that gives companies the right to sue governments for lost *future* profits. This applies, for example, in cases where governments try to stop water export. Water services are also among those slated to be labeled as a commodity in the new General Agreement on Trade in Services (GATS), under a new category called "Environmental Services." (For more on this, see the later section "Threats to the Modern Commons.")

Once water is privatized, commodified, and put on the open market, it is not available to everyone who needs it but only to those who pay. Right now, contrary to popular understanding, most of the world's freshwater is used by corporate industrial agriculture and in manufacturing, such as in the computer industry for manufacture of computer chips. Relatively little is left for drinking or small-scale farming.

Some 460 million people worldwide are now dependent on private water corporations; this is up from only 50 million in 1990. But growing at equal speed is resistance to water privatization. A powerful global citizens' movement is demanding recognition that access to the freshwater commons and control of it is a basic human right. These are some brief examples from around the world:

*Argentina*

In 1993, the World Bank required Argentina to privatize its water systems as a condition of its loan. The world's largest water company, Suez, took over through a subsidiary, Aguas Argentinas. The World Bank, the IMF, and other lending agencies funded 97 percent of that $1 billion water privatization, and residential water rates *increased by 88.2 percent.* In 1997, Suez was charged with failing to improve and expand services as promised. In 2003, it was also charged with not fully treating much of the sewage it transported, and with dumping untreated sewage into Argentina's rivers. Water in seven districts in Buenos Aires was found to be "unfit for human consumption." In response, thousands of citizens have blocked roads in protest, and demanded congressional oversight and cancellation of the privatization contract.

*Bolivia*

As in Argentina, the World Bank in 1999 made water privatization of Bolivia's third largest city, Cochabamba, a condition of debt reduction. Bechtel Corporation got the contract, via its subsidiary, Aguas del Tunari, and increased water rates by as much as 200 percent. Virtually overnight, families earning only $60 per month faced water bills of $20 per month. A new protest organization soon formed, called the Coordination in Defense of Water and Life. At first the government defended Bechtel, using deadly force in some cases. But in April 2000, the protest was so extensive and powerful that Bechtel abandoned the project. It also responded, however, with a $25 million lawsuit against Bolivia for "lost profits" under a Bolivia-Netherlands investment treaty that mirrors NAFTA rules. (The outcome is still pending.) Meanwhile, workers, citizens, and local officials have been successfully running the water company themselves for more than three years via a communal system, favoring *access* not *profit.* The Bolivian experience has given great courage to groups in other countries seeking similar outcomes.

*South Africa*

To help pay for its transition out of apartheid in 1994, South Africa accepted loans and conditions from the World Bank and the IMF, which "advised" the privatization of the country's water. The resultant price increases led to 10 million households having their water cut off in 2001 alone. Millions of poor township dwellers had little choice but to use untreated river water for their needs, bringing cholera outbreaks affecting more than 140,000 people. A powerful peoples' movement, the Anti-Privatization Forum, is now demanding an end to privatization and the return to guaranteed water for all.

### India

Three communities in India—Kerala, Maharashtra, and Uttar Pradesh—are experiencing severe water shortages as a result of Coca-Cola's overexploitation of common groundwater resources around its facilities. Coca-Cola is also dumping wastewater into the ground, polluting the scarce water that remains. Villagers are left without adequate water for farming and drinking and must seek water from miles away. In Sivagangai, Tamil Nadu, residents are organizing to stop a proposed Coca-Cola facility based on the experiences of villagers in other regions. Thousands of people across India argue that Coca-Cola has proven itself an unfit neighbor that should leave the country.

### Canada

Rich in water resources, Canada was one of the first countries to face a direct challenge to its rights to control its own water based on a corporation using a rule from a trade agreement. In 1998, Sun Belt Water Inc. gained a contract to export large quantities of water from British Columbia to California. The citizens of B.C. protested, however, launching a successful campaign to ban the export of bulk water from their province. Stopped at the provincial level, Sun Belt has sought recourse in NAFTA using the infamous "Chapter 11" investment code-protections of the agreement. If Sun Belt wins, either B.C. will have to reverse the ban or the government of Canada will have to pay the company $220 million for the right to protect its own water. Later, in July 2003, the citizens of Vancouver forced their government to scrap a planned privatization of Vancouver's water system.

### United States

Eighty-five percent of the water systems in the United States are still publicly owned and operated. Global water corporations hope to change this equation. They are enticing financially strapped cities with promises of reduced costs and increased services. A few have succumbed. However, the U.S. movement against privatization is growing, working directly with activists around the world who have fought these same corporations. A recent example is the success story of Stockton, California. In January 2004, a judge ordered the city of Stockton to rescind its water privatization contract with OMI-Thames after concerned citizens, armed with proof of the devastating impacts of water privatization globally, brought a lawsuit. The judge ruled that the city violated California's Environmental Quality Act by not conducting an environmental review of the risks of water privatization.

The global resistance is growing. In January 2004, in New Delhi, Vandana Shiva, together with the Polaris Institute, Council of Canadians, and Public Citizen, co-hosted a meeting of activists from sixty-three countries. The meeting launched the Peoples' World Water Movement, an international collaboration "to stop the theft of the world's water." Participants pledged to build international solidarity around water struggles and to create a framework for action, including (1) the guiding principle that "water is life"; (2) the reaffirmation of water as a fundamental human right and the development of an international convention on freshwater at the U.N.; (3) resistance to the corporate takeover of public water commons on a for-profit basis; (4) campaigns to stop the theft of groundwater by corporations and to reject global trade rules that encourage corporate water takings from communities; (5) increasing public opposition to destructive dams and river diversion projects; and (6) empowerment of local communities to develop and employ locally appropriate methods of sustainable water management and develop water stewardship as an alternative to the commercial destruction of the freshwater commons.

## THREATS TO THE GENETIC COMMONS

Another commons that few people ever thought could be subject to privatization and development is the genetic commons—the vast building blocks of all life on earth. Yet this too is now subject to reinvention through genetic engineering and transformed into patentable commodities.

The late David Brower of Earth Island Institute once called the genetic commons "the last untapped wilderness on earth," but that is no longer true. Like our great forests, the genetic commons are on the verge of rampant commercial intervention. In some areas, like agriculture, the process is well under way. Third World agriculture activists call it *biopiracy*. (See Box N.)

According to Andrew Kimbrell of the International Center for Technology Assessment, "Corporations are now scouring the globe seeking valuable plant, animal, and human genes that they can claim as their own private property, as if they invented them. Thousands of gene patents have already been given to corporations, which are now able to patent whole life forms and own them."

Most of this activity falls within the life science industries. Corporations like Monsanto, Novartis, Du Pont, Pioneer, and others have benefited enormously from the WTO's TRIPs agreement, which confirms their ability to patent plant and seed varieties according to their genetic makeup. Even though these varieties were developed over centuries by indigenous farming communities that shared them with one another freely in a process that is at the core of these cultures, now fees must be paid to use them.

Global corporations insist that this valuable genetic material should not be locked up by small communities but that the whole world should have access to it. Indeed, corporations use the language of the global commons until such time as they confirm their monopoly patents on the material. At that point, all arguments in defense of the commons are abandoned. Instead, the corporations then argue that *they* should be permitted to lock up these genetic materials through patents in order to have a chance of recouping their research investment—for the benefit of all humanity.

Pharmaceutical corporations are especially eager for access and the rights to patent genetic materials. Their representatives travel the globe, exploring traditional native remedies in jungles and fields. They also extract blood and scrape "buccal mucosa" from the skin of native peoples wherever they can, hoping to find genes that contain natural resistance to certain maladies. Usually they accomplish this without disclosing why they are doing it or how much profit they stand to make from their findings and their patents. Among indigenous peoples, the right of "free and prior informed consent" has now become a major international demand before governments can bring in development projects and before companies are permitted to enter.

The cynicism of such practices became especially clear when global pharmaceutical corporations refused to set aside the rules of the WTO's TRIPs agreement in South Africa to permit low-cost, locally developed AIDS drugs to be substituted for the expensive patented varieties they controlled. Only after intense global protest did the patent holders agree to lower prices for AIDS victims there. But the TRIPs rules remain in force for all other instances.

The authors of this document believe that seeds, medicines, and other genetic materials that have been developed in communities for centuries or millennia should always be subject to community control. Any agreement with outsiders to use these materials must be on the basis of fair and equal negotiations on a case-by-case basis, after full discussion of all the relevant facts.

---

## BOX N: FROM COMMONS TO CORPORATE PATENTS ON LIFE

*By Vandana Shiva, Research Foundation for Science, Technology, and Ecology*

During the Uruguay Round negotiations of the GATT, the United States succeeded in forcing its own patent system onto the world through the WTO. U.S. corporations had a major role, having drafted and lobbied on behalf of the Trade-Related Intellectual Property Rights agreement (TRIPs). As a Monsanto spokesman said about the lobbying effort, "The industries and traders of world commerce have played simultaneously the role of patients, diagnosticians, and prescribing physicians."

TRIPs not only made U.S.-style IPR laws global, but also removed critical ethical and moral boundaries by including life forms and biodiversity into patentable subject matter. Living organisms and life forms that are self-creating were thus redefined as if they were machines and artifacts made and invented by the patentee, despite the fact that the corporations made only minor modifications in their labs—just enough to redefine them as "inventions." Intellectual property rights laws and patents then give the patent holder a monopolistic right to prevent others from making, using, or selling these "inventions" even if the seeds were originally developed by local farmers. Seed saving by farmers had thus been redefined from a sacred duty to a criminal offence: stealing corporate "property." And all practices of sui generis ownership of seeds and other forms of local biodiversity were directly undermined. Article 27.3(b) of the TRIPs agreement, which relates to patents on living resources, was basically estab-

CONTINUED

lished by the life sciences companies to confirm themselves as "lords of life." Life science corporations now claim patents on genes, plants, animals, and seeds. Ciba Geigy and Sandoz have combined to form Novartis; Hoechst has joined with Rhone Poulenc to form Aventis; Zeneca has merged with Astia; Du Pont has bought up Pioneer Hi-Bred; and Monsanto now owns Cargill seeds, DeKalb, Calgene, Agracetus, Delta and Pine Land, Holden, and Asgrow. Eighty percent of all genetically engineered seeds planted are Monsanto's intellectual property. Monsanto also owns broad species patents on cotton, mustard, and soybeans—crops that were not invented or created by Monsanto but that have evolved over centuries of innovation by farmers of India and East Asia working in close partnership with the biodiversity of nature.

This process of patenting life forms is truly perverse, in many ways:

*Ethical perversion:* Current IPR laws permit the claim that seeds, plants, sheep, cows, or human cell lines can be classified as "products of the mind" created by Monsanto, Novartis, Ian Wilmut, or PPL. This ignores that living organisms have their intrinsic self- organization; they make themselves, and hence cannot logically be reduced to the status of inventions and creations of patent holders. They cannot be owned as private property because they are our ecological kin, not just genetic mines.

*Criminalization of saving and sharing seeds:* Recognizing corporations as owners of seed through intellectual property rights converts farmers into thieves when they save seeds or share with neighbors. Monsanto actually hires detectives to chase farmers who might be engaging in such theft and bring them to court.

*Encouragement of biopiracy:* Biopiracy is the term the South now uses for the theft of biodiversity and indigenous knowledge through these patents. It deprives the South in three ways:

• It creates a false claim to novelty and invention, even when the knowledge has actually evolved since ancient times. Biopiracy is intellectual theft, robbing Third World people of their creativity and their intellectual resources.
• It diverts scarce biological resources to monopoly control of corporations, depriving local communities and indigenous practitioners. Biopiracy is resource theft from the poorest two-thirds of humanity, who depend on biodiversity for their livelihoods and basic needs.
• It creates market monopolies, excluding the *original* innovators from their rightful share of local, national, and international markets. Instead of preventing this organized economic theft, WTO rules under TRIPs protect the powerful and punish the victims. In a dispute initiated by the United States against India, the WTO forced India to change its patent laws and grant exclusive marketing rights to foreign corporations on the basis of foreign

CONTINUED

BOX N: CONTINUED

patents. Since many of these patents are based on biopiracy, the WTO is in fact promoting piracy through patents.

Over time, the consequences of TRIPs for the South's biodiversity and the Southern people's rights to their diversity will be severe. No one will be able to produce or reproduce patented agricultural, medicinal, or animal products freely; the livelihoods of small producers will be eroded and the poor will be prevented from using their own resources and knowledge to meet basic needs of health and nutrition. Royalties for the use of these patented items will have to be paid to the patentees and unauthorized production will be penalized, thus further increasing the debt burden.

Indian farmers, traditional practitioners, and traders will lose their market share in local, national, and global markets. For example, the U.S. government recently granted a patent for the antidiabetic properties of *karela, jamun,* and *brinjal* to two nonresident Indians, Onkar S. Tomer and Kripanath Borah, and their colleague Peter Gloniski. The use of these substances for control of diabetes has been everyday knowledge and practice in India for ages. Their medical use was documented long ago in authoritative treatises like "The Wealth of India," "The Compendium of Indian Medicinal Plants," and "The Treatise on Indian Medicinal Plants."

If there were only one or two cases of such false claims to corporate invention on the basis of biopiracy, they could be called an error. However, biopiracy is an epidemic. Plant species like *neem, haldi, pepper, harar, bahera, amla, mustard, basmati, ginger, castor, jaramla, amaltas,* and *new karela* and *jamun* have now all been patented. The problem is deep and systemic; it calls for a systemic change, not case-by-case challenges.

Some have suggested that biopiracy happens because Indian knowledge is not documented. That is far from true. Indigenous knowledge in India has been systematically documented, and this in fact has made piracy easier. Even the folk knowledge, spread orally in local communities, deserves to be recognized as collective, cumulative innovation. The ignorance of such knowledge in the United States should not be allowed to convert corporate biopiracy into invention.

The potential costs of biopiracy to the Third World poor are very high because two-thirds of the people in the South depend on free access to biodiversity for their livelihoods and needs. In India, 70 percent of seeds are saved or shared farmers' seed; 70 percent of healing is based on indigenous medicine using local plants. When corporations steal and control those genetic resources through patents, the poor are directly deprived.

SOURCE: Vandana Shiva, "War Against Nature and the People of the South." In Sarah Anderson, ed., *Views from the South: The Effects of Globalization and the WTO on Third World Countries.* San Francisco: International Forum on Globalization, 2000.

## THREATS TO COMMUNAL LANDS

In hundreds of cultures around the world, the notion of private, individual land ownership is anathema. Communal land ownership—or no land ownership—is traditional practice and belief among indigenous and farming communities on every continent. This worldview is fundamental to these millions of people, their cultures, their agriculture, and their economic, political, and spiritual practices. In peasant farming communities of South America and Asia and in indigenous communities everywhere, the notion that an individual or corporation could legally gather under its own authority large fruitful tracts of land—thus depriving the people who shared it for millennia—is outrageous beyond all understanding.

Native American activist Winona La Duke has described the land ownership issue among indigenous peoples by pointing out that in her own Ojibway culture, the term *nishnabe akin* means "the land to which the people belong." It is a notion that is the exact opposite of Western ideas about land ownership. It is also at the heart of many teachings about humans and land being in *relationship* with each other, with reciprocal obligations.

In contrast, the new trade agreements and policies of international banks and corporations are designed to delegitimize the authority of any such reciprocal arrangements and to solidify private ownership so that land can be more easily bought and exploited. For example, one of the specific demands of the United States in NAFTA negotiations with Mexico was that Mexico break up the traditional *ejidos* of the Mayan corn farmers, the system of communal land ownership that was established after the successful peasant revolution of the early 1900s that was led by Emiliano Zapata.

The history of the "enclosure" of the commons is largely devoted to the privatization of communal lands throughout the planet. In most places, the process is so far along that it is rarely publicly argued. However, this has begun to change as mass movements like Brazil's landless peasant movement (Landless Workers Movement) and other such movements around the world have demanded dramatic land reforms and redistribution under the principle that land, like water, is basic for sustenance.

## PRIVATIZATION OF THE BROADCAST SPECTRUM

The electromagnetic spectrum is another extraordinary gift of nature—wave energy radiating from space and from the earth—an intricate, highly complex part of the earth's ecological web, but one directly affecting the health and evolution of all plant, animal, and human life. Gamma rays, X rays, ultraviolet, infrared, and visible light, short- and long-wave radio and television frequencies, CB radio and telephone, radar signals, microwaves (among many others) all occupy their portion of the spectrum. Only appreciated and understood by science in the last few centuries, EMS surely qualifies as a global commons of a kind, a radiation wilderness, one could say, aspects of which—or their uses—are extensively regulated by individual nation-states. Often regulation is in the interests of serving all people, but in this case it's now in the interests of global corporations.

For our purposes in this document, we are mainly concerned with the frequencies occupied by the *broadcast* spectrum, representing a minor portion of the electromagnetic field: radio and television, the heart of the global communications infrastructure. (Most of the issues relevant to broadcasting, and also the Internet, yet another kind of commons, will be discussed in greater detail in chapter 8, "Alternative Operating Systems (2)." But it is useful to introduce the broadcast spectrum briefly here as well as part of our more comprehensive look at the commons.)

Policies about uses of the broadcast spectrum commons have varied greatly among nations. Some have accepted the broadcast commons as part of their public trust obligation and have given the highest importance to its "public service"—that is, its public education and information capabilities—permitting only a very limited percentage of private commercial ownership. This has been the case in some European countries, notably England, France, and Germany, and the Scandinavian countries, which have emphasized noncommercial and public interest applications. Similar stances have been taken by Canada and New Zealand. In England, France, and Germany, roughly half of radio and television broadcasts are noncommercial/public interest/publicly financed offerings. This is the case despite the huge pressures of the Thatcher-Reagan years to privatize all or most broadcasting.

At the opposite extreme from the European examples have been the appropriation of the entire broadcast commons by dictatorial and one-party governments for their own purposes. This was certainly the case until recently in Eastern Europe and parts of Asia and South America, though most of these are now moving rapidly in the direction of commercialization. Some countries have turned over their entire broadcast spectrum to private commercial enterprise, basically giving up on any meaningful trustee role.

As is the case with many aspects of the commons, the U.S. performance has been mixed. An initial instinct toward democratic and public service uses of broadcasting, going back to the 1920s, lost its momentum in the late twentieth century and is now rapidly in reverse.

The Federal Communications Act of 1934 (FCA) was created ostensibly to bring order to the ever more crowded and static-filled open airwaves of the early broadcast system. The act created the Federal Communications Commission (FCC), which had authority to issue license agreements for specific frequencies. Many groups fought strongly to maintain a highly democratic access to the airwaves, and the 1934 act did stipulate that all licensees must use the public airwaves "to serve the public interest, convenience, and necessity." It also stipulated that ownership of the broadcast frequencies was *not for sale;* the airwaves remained in the public's domain, with the FCC acting as trustee.

(Among the public service standards that later evolved for commercial franchises was the fairness doctrine, which obliged licensees to air both sides of controversial issues—environmental, public health, work standards, and so on. And all broadcasters had to submit to yearly performance reviews proving they had acted in the public interest.)

Regrettably, however, in exchange for these presumably useful broadcast contributions, *U.S. licensees paid nothing at all.* Plus, they were permitted to sell airtime for advertising, and to keep the profits from that. Back in the early 1930s, before television, this surely could not have seemed the spectacular boondoggle that it would later become. Nor was it clear that the power and scale of both the commercial broadcasting industry *and* its sibling, the advertising industry, would eventually become the dominant arbiters of information and culture flow in society, influencing democratic processes and public policy as nothing ever before.

Meanwhile, noncommercial "educational" broadcasters struggled to survive against the steadily increasing powers of commercial interests. They functioned at the margins of the system, in areas of the broadcast spectrum that commercial interests did not yet cover, developing AM broadcasting in the 1920s, and then FM radio and UHF television later on. But as soon as it seemed that money could readily be made from those frequencies, commercial broadcasters used their political powers to seize the reins. Still, in the 1960s, under a liberal democratic regime, Congress finally passed the Public Broadcasting Act of 1967, which led to the creation of the Corporation for Public Broadcasting (CPB), and soon after, the Public Broadcast Service (PBS) and National Public Radio (NPR). But they were severely handicapped from the start.

Unlike some of the public broadcast systems in Europe, such as the BBC, public funding was pathetically weak, so as not to represent true competition for the commercial system. By now, after years of steady cuts, public funding represents only about 10 percent of public broadcast, far less than European counterparts.

Meanwhile, commercial broadcasters were becoming ever more responsive to their blossoming advertising profits, and they pressured successive administrations and congresses to eliminate most regulations, including the fairness doctrine. Broadcasters also pressured for fewer controls on their ability to buy up additional franchises and broadcast outlets in the same market, and other markets around the country. By 1983 about fifty media conglomerates grew to control half of all broadcast media in the United States; by 1993 only twenty firms controlled half the media, and today it's ten. These are mostly the same megacorporations that control about 70 percent of all global media—most notably Time Warner, Disney, and Fox. (Much more about media concentration can be found in chapter 8.)

The passage of the 1996 Telecommunications Act, pushed hard by the Clinton-Gore administration to gain favor with media moguls, and the more recent 2003 rulings by the FCC and by Congress, pushed hard by the Bush-Cheney administration (for the same reasons) have made a bad situation far worse. Media scholar and activist Robert McChesney of the University of Illinois calls the 1996 act "one of the most important federal laws of this generation," made even more remarkable, albeit predictable, by the fact that the corporate media, strongly in support, scarcely reported the issue at all, except in the back of the business pages. "The overarching purpose of the 1996 Telecommunications Act," says McChesney, was "to deregulate all communication industries and to permit the market, not public policy, to determine the course of the information highway and the communications systems." The combination of the 1996 act and the 2003 FCC rulings have made it possible for already giant media corporations to vastly expand their franchises, locally and nationally, so that one company can utterly dominate local markets while reaching up to 50 percent of the total U.S. audience, and with minimal fear of any regulatory controls. So licenses originally obtained for nothing to operate the public airwaves have now obtained value in the *billions* of dollars.

Thus, although the airwaves were originally codified as a public commons they have now been nearly totally privatized in the United States. Even public broadcast institutions like PBS are virtually privatized because federal funding has been so diminished that the only option has been to turn to private corporations for funding. So we now see real commercials playing on these "public" channels. Meanwhile, the public trust and caretaker role of the FCC has largely been abandoned. Though the people still technically *own* the airwaves, the trustee is clearly squandering the public's interest.

The net result has been a substantial homogenization and narrowing of political and cultural perspectives offered by media and received by the public, a general trivialization of program content—a "dumbing down," as it were—and a laissez-faire attitude on the part of the "trustee" except when the occasional naked breast might flash on the screen. That is about the only time the FCC steps in to "protect" the public.

The situation in the United States differs from that in most other countries, which have taken the trust obligation toward the broadcast commons more seriously. However, all countries now face very accelerated efforts within the World Trade Organization to smooth out all variations and to apply pressures toward privatization that are nearly uniform and total. For example, if successful, negotiations in the General Agreement on Trade in Services (GATS) within the WTO will make it far more difficult for any nation to make effective rules slowing down foreign investment by gigantic global media corporations who buy up local and national broadcasters, as well as any rules that reserve parts of the spectrum for noncommercial, publicly funded broadcasting, wherever that still exists. In fact, under new rules of the WTO, such public funding of public service outlets may soon be categorized as "illegal subsidies," or "unfair trade practices," and banned. PBS and NPR, for whatever one feels they are worth, might lose their remaining protection as broadcast channels designed to serve the public interest or prevent further commercialization. The same could soon happen to public broadcasting in all countries. And a world where only eight corporations already control the great majority of all broadcasting, and other media, may see even further centralized control of information. (We will come back to this subject in chapter 8.)

## APPROPRIATION OF THE GLOBAL COMMONS
## FOR WASTE SINKS

Ownership and privatization are not the only threats to the commons. There is also the effective appropriation of particular global commons as free dumping grounds and waste sinks for the activity of global corporations.

The atmosphere, oceans, and even outer space have become dangerously polluted, freely appropriated by oil, energy, shipping, and toxic industries as convenient sites to dump effluents and wastes. In the case of automobiles, ships, and the fossil fuel industry, it is an intrinsic result of the technologies that effluents rise to the atmosphere.

When similar pollution takes place in a local commons or inside national borders—say, local smokestack emissions or runoff into rivers—government agencies exist specifically to try to do something about it. This is not to say these agencies do a good job of regulating such activity—often they do not—but at least they offer an authority to address the matter and a place where citizens may focus their complaints.

When it comes to the global commons, however, few such agencies exist. There have been some efforts over the last half-century to apply some pollution regulations. The Kyoto Protocol on Global Warming, the Montreal Protocol on Substances That Deplete the Ozone Layer, the United Nations Convention on the Law of the Sea, the Stockholm Convention on Persistent Organic Pollutants agreement, among other multilateral environment agreements (MEAs), are efforts to control impacts on global commons. But all have suffered from tremendous political resistance, weak regulatory regimes, and poor enforcement ability. Still, MEAs remain one hope for rational international recognition, on a case-by-case basis, of the collective rights to maintain the commons in a condition that serves all people and the planet's other species.

An important problem, however, is that when such agreements do begin to make progress in limiting corporate activity, the World Trade Organization can threaten to negate them by asserting its own superior authority on behalf of the primacy of global trade activity. For example, at the November 2001 WTO ministerial meeting in Doha, Qatar, the WTO made explicit its intentions to codify its superiority to MEAs, potentially wiping out generations of effort.

Other solutions to the problem have also been proposed. They include a variety of trust agreements where certain commons would be held as the explicit property of all people in trust for the future. Any encroachments would have to go through very complex permission procedures, thus at least slowing and making visible the problems before they occur.

Sadly, there are hundreds of examples of threats to the commons of the kind we have given here. All reflect increased global pressure on remaining pristine areas. Fortunately, however, there is also increased popular resistance to these encroachments. New methods and instruments must be found or created to prevent continued destruction.

## The Tradition of the Commons

In most parts of the world, the tradition of the commons is ages old, though it varies from place to place and culture to culture. These are a few examples.

### EUROPE

In Europe, the concept of the commons dates back at least fifteen hundred years. It referred to commonly shared areas of land and resources enjoyed by all members of village communities, including pasture for the grazing of animals, water from streams and lakes, and all the products of field and forest that people used to sustain their lives.

In some parts of Europe, concepts of the commons were formally codified. The most remarkable example goes back to the Roman Doctrine of the Public Trust, codified in 529 A.D. as Codex Justinianus, after the emperor of that period, who said: "By the laws of nature these things are common to all mankind: the air, running water, the sea and consequently the shores of the sea."

The public trust doctrine was applied in many instances over the next millennium and a half, and still emerges as "common law" in specific cases throughout Europe and elsewhere, most recently in Hawaii. (There, a case of the rights of indigenous people to free-flowing water was decided in favor of the natives, using the public trust doctrine as the basis for the suit.)

According to San Francisco scholar and journalist Mark Dowie, the doctrine "waxed and waned depending on the political climate" in Europe. Though feudal lords and kings sometimes used military force to appropriate village pastures and water from lakes and streams, there were also numerous cases of "liberal noblemen" who applied the public trust doctrine to lands, woods, and fields for use by serfs and commoners.

In the eleventh century, a French law decreed that "the public highways and byways—running water and springs, meadows and pastures, forests, heaths, and rocks are not to be held by Lords; nor are they to be maintained in any other ways than that their people may always be able to use them." Centuries later, according to Dowie, King Alfonzo X of Spain added harbors to the preceding list of public domains. In 1225, in England, the Justinian doctrine was recodified in the Magna Carta and forced upon King John after his defeat at Runnymede. The treaty stipulated that no king could grant private hunting and fishing rights to favored earls and dukes, cutting off the commons from people who relied on them for their livelihood. "The fences and weirs that had been built to keep riffraff out of the rivers and forests were torn down and the English commons provided sustenance to all commoners" for centuries thereafter, writes Dowie.

As late as the seventeenth century, colonial powers in North and Meso America adopted varieties of English, French, and Spanish doctrines of the public trust as the common law of their colonies. And the idea was maintained in the original thirteen American colonies, "which granted state governments sovereign rights to common land and sovereign responsibility for its care," according to Dowie. Some states wrote a form of the ancient code directly into their constitutions. For example, the following is from the Pennsylvania state constitution, which still exists:

> The people have a right to clean air, pure water, and the preservation of the natural, scenic, historic, and aesthetic values of the environment. Pennsylvania's public natural resources are the common property of all the people, including generations yet to come. As trustee of these resources, the Commonwealth shall conserve and maintain them for the benefit of all the people.

Three other states created similar constitutions, and even now call themselves "commonwealths"—Massachusetts, Virginia, and Kentucky—using language similar to the European codes.

Nonetheless, in parts of feudal Europe, the commons generally deteriorated over time. As trade developed between regions, and especially with the rise of a large Europe-wide market for wool, many lords and merchants sought to ensure and expand their own supply by privatizing more and more of the common areas, most importantly land. As they succeeded in enclosing ever larger areas, peasant communities began to lose access to resources they had previously taken for granted. Self-sustainability became more difficult. Rather than remaining as subsistence farmers who also traded in local markets, peasants increasingly became "cottagers"—small artisanal producers—or sought day labor jobs with large landowners whose lands they had formerly shared.

The Enclosure Act in early nineteenth-century England for the first time made the hunting and gathering of food from the commons illegal, as private property rights took precedence. Millions of subsistence farmers were also removed from their lands. And with the Industrial Revolution cottage industries also declined, so people had little choice but to become factory workers with no connection to the land anymore. Thus, peasants evolved into proletariat.

Some mainstream economists have justified and praised this conversion of the commons to private property as a way of establishing clear ownership and therefore the ability to protect resources from exploitation. But this justification for what was essentially robbery of shared common resources ignores two important facts. First, the people whose lives depended on the commons were almost always excellent caretakers of it and remained so over many centuries. In fact, it was basic to the survival and success of the commons that the entire community shared its values as well as its sustaining virtues and helped protect and preserve it. Second, the people who enclosed the commons, appropriating it for private use, were nearly always outsiders, absentee owners with little personal dedication to nurturing, conserving, or taking care of these resources for the future. The reason they sought private ownership was to exploit the resources as fast as possible. They did not try to own it in order to save it, the assertion of mainstream economists notwithstanding. Rather, they usually pillaged and polluted it.

With the advent of corporate ownership and rights of private property, ownership was made still more abstract or removed from resources, which were increasingly understood only in quantifiable, objective terms. Forests, for example, were no longer appreciated for their community sustainability, the biodiversity they fostered, or their spiritual contexts. Instead, they became "board-feet," ripe for exploitation. That is certainly the situation we face today, in its most amplified form.

### INDIGENOUS COMMUNITIES

In other parts of the world terms like *commons* were not well known, but the concepts of shared community use and protection of common resources are basic, endemic, understood, and respected by entire societies.

Among indigenous peoples around the world, virtually all political, social, and spiritual values have traditionally been so deeply intertwined with the values and teachings of the natural world that these societies say they are inseparable. It is not really a question of a community commons, as understood by the Europeans. It is more that all creatures—human as well as plant and animal—are directly related, equal, and with equal rights to exist in a fulfilling manner. All economic, political, and spiritual teachings are rooted in that primary relationship.

It is little wonder, therefore, that invading societies—at least those that did not actually slaughter the native populations—made enormous efforts to undermine and destroy their commitment to their traditional relationships to land and nature. That was the only way they could succeed in getting their hands on the resources they desired. (See also Box L, page 89.)

Native peoples were pushed to separate from their lands in hundreds of different ways. Primary among these efforts was the aggressive attempt to undermine traditional religious values and cosmologies as well as traditional native stories and teachings about the need to live in harmony with, and as part of, nature. The actions of missionaries throughout the Americas, the Pacific Islands, and Africa are well known in this context. They actively helped shift the traditional value system toward a new and more hierarchical view of humans and nature and toward the individualistic notion of private property. In the United States, Australia, and elsewhere, "reeducation" also played an important role—that is, young people were forcibly removed from their traditional communities and placed into boarding schools that did not allow native languages or teachings. The result was a kind of self-loathing that undermined native cultures and their traditional collective economic values.

Equally important were legal maneuvers, such as requiring adjudicatory land title. Since native societies did not traditionally conceive of themselves as "owners" of land but as part of it as a community, "title" and "ownership" of land were an absurdity, but one which they were required to address. The histories of the relationships between invading and native societies are replete with stories of how legalistic maneuvering succeeded in separating Indians from millions of acres of land they had formerly enjoyed in a collective manner. These acts of removal and separation continue to this day, notably in the United States.

One particularly appalling recent example is the U.S. Congress's creation of the Alaska Native Claims Settlement Act (ANCSA), purported to be a guarantor of native land rights in Alaska, where these rights had never been abrogated. In fact, ANCSA was the final step in extinguishing the native relationship and rights to enjoy the lands in the traditional manner. Rather than Native Alaskans being granted title, or simply granted recognition of "aboriginal rights of ownership" as requested, the Alaskan lands were divided and made into native corporations, managed by native boards of directors, who were given ownership of the lands. But in order to survive, these corporations needed to cut down their forests or exploit their minerals just as any corporation would. These corporate acts, albeit carried out by natives, were contrary to their prior indigenous values. So for the larger society, the desired outcome was achieved: the communal relationship to nature was removed and replaced by an exploitative one, thus providing new fodder for global corporations.

The global invasion of communally held native lands—which has happened on every continent and continues today—has had terrible outcomes, from destruction of the traditional reciprocal relationship between humans and nature to major social breakdowns.

The conflict of values endemic to these pressures over ownership of common lands and resources was very well described in the pamphlet *A Basic Call to Consciousness,* published in 1978 by the Iroquois Nation (the Hau de no sau nee), in a submission to the U.N. Conference on Indigenous Peoples. Here are some short excerpts:

> The majority of the world does not find its roots in Western culture or tradition. The majority of the world finds its roots in the natural world, and it is the natural world, and the tradition of the natural world, which must prevail.
>
> . . .
>
> The original instructions direct that we are to express a great respect, an affection, and gratitude toward all the spirits which create and support life. When people cease to respect and express gratitude for these many things, then all life will be destroyed.
>
> . . .
>
> To this day the territories we still hold are filled with trees, animals, and the other gifts from the Creation. In these places we still receive our nourishment from our Mother Earth. Many thousands of years ago, all the people of the world believed in the same way of life, that of harmony with the universe. [But] the way of life known as Western Civilization is on a death path on which their own culture has no viable answers.
>
> . . .
>
> The Indo-European people who have colonized our lands have shown very little respect for the things that create and support life. We believe that these people ceased their respect for the world a long time ago. The air is foul, the waters poisoned, the trees dying, the animals disappearing. Even the systems of weather are changing. Our ancient teachings warned us that if Man interfered with the natural laws, these things would come to be.
>
> . . .
>
> The traditional native people hold the key to the reversal of the processes in Western Civilization. Our culture is among the most ancient continuously existing cultures in the world. We are the spiritual guardians of this place. We are here to impart this message.

### ASIA

Traditional societies everywhere on the planet share values similar to the ones expressed by the North American Iroquois leadership. Concepts like

Mother Earth combined with belief in nonhierarchical, nonownership-based, communal relationships to field and forest can be found among all peoples who still live in a direct relationship with the earth.

Most people in India today still derive their livelihoods and meet their survival needs from the biological resources of the country, as forest dwellers, farmers, fisherfolk, healers, and livestock owners. Indigenous knowledge systems in medicine, agriculture, and fisheries are the primary basis for meeting their food, health, and cultural needs. In these traditional communities, the biodiversity of the forests and fields and the historic inno-vations of plant life for food and medicinal purposes have never been seen as the individual property of any person or family but as community resources available to all people. None can be excluded, and neither the state nor any other economically powerful entity can monopolize use of any aspect of the commons, biologically or intellectually.

There is a vibrant struggle in India today over the commons—not only the biological commons (land, forests, water) that have been the basis of sus-tainability for a great majority of India's population to the present time but also the *intellectual commons*. This refers to the cumulative knowledge that agricultural communities have collected and freely shared for centuries, as well as the innovations they have achieved in developing plant varieties for food and medicine. Global biotech and pharmaceutical companies have been aggressively patenting these examples of the intellectual commons, preventing their common use, and privatizing them for their own purposes. This invasion has led to a level of outrage on the part of India's farmers, indigenous people, and peasant communities that has brought literally mil-lions of people onto the streets in protest against the World Trade Organization's TRIPs agreement, which protects the rights of corporations to engage in these practices.

Community rights to control the biological and intellectual commons are recognized in law as sui generis rights—equivalent to a patent, but recog-nizing roots in a community rather than an individual. This system is based in part on usufruct rights, which entitle farmers and laborers access to resources needed for their own sustenance, such as common pastures, water, and biodiversity. Sustainability and justice are inherent in such a system of usufruct rights because there are physical limits on how much any one person can labor; hence, there are limited returns for labor, unlike capital and private property.

The battle over the biological and intellectual rights of farmers in India, and against the WTO's TRIPs agreement, comes at the end of a long and painful history of prior enclosures of the commons in India. The policy of deforestation and enclosure of the commons in India began in 1865, when the Indian Forest Act authorized the government to declare forests as "unmeasured" lands or "reserves" for state use. This began what was called the scientific management of forests, but it was really the first step in a long series of moves to separate forests from people and convert them to commodities available for private ownership. Peasant communities that had formerly sustained themselves based on the forests' resources were forced to produce indigo instead of food and pay taxes for salt. They experienced the rapid erosion of their usufruct rights to food, fuel, and livestock pastures, as well as forests and sacred sites. This was a primary cause of their later impoverishment, which led directly to their resistance to further erosion of their common rights by global biotech corporations.

## Threats to the Modern Commons

In most developed countries, it is hard to remember the time when the central political and economic unit was the local community or when resources were commonly shared. Over the past several centuries, political, economic, and technological evolution in much of the world has conspired to bring far more specialization and industrialization of economic activity, far less economic and social self-reliance, and far greater dependence on dominant centralized political units—cities, states, provinces, and national governments—to provide for the common fundamental needs and services that people require, such as education, transportation, health care, environmental protection, security, and the certainty that there will be sufficient food, housing, and work.

All governments now acknowledge their responsibility in these matters, though they perform them with varying levels of success. Canadians and Danes tend to believe their governments have performed well, at least until recently, whereas Russians and Burmese may not feel this way. Most governments get mixed grades on these matters—good in some ways, bad in others. The United States, for example, has kept its economic and sanitation performance generally high but has been very poor in matters of health care and transportation, and its delivery of these services is marked by extreme inequality. Maude Barlow's book, *Profit Is Not the Cure*, details the impact of the World Bank, the IMF, the WTO, and their market-opening policies on the erosion of health care services all over the world, and she chronicles the private sector firms that have benefited. Two decades of these policies have left a legacy of unequal access and health crises for the poor worldwide.

The United Nations Universal Declaration of Human Rights asserts that in addition to the services that nations are expected to perform, governments are also expected to ensure certain basic human rights, religious and political freedoms, and the right to *meaningful* work at fair wages with human dignity. In fact, the U.N. declaration asserts that every person on the planet has an "inherited right to citizenship," which includes health care, education, and work. Moreover, every government has the duty to *defend* the fundamental human rights of every one of its citizens, even beyond its borders. Such assertions also imply that governments have the duty to protect their own ability to perform these services and ensure these fundamental rights against attempts to weaken them.

The authors of this report believe that these services and protections qualify as a kind of "modern commons," in which the state has assumed the responsibility for the common good that once resided in local communities. Even as more power devolves back toward the local—an outcome most of us support—we believe that states have a vital role to play in protecting the community stewardship of both traditional and modern commons. The performance of these responsibilities, however, is now under tremendous threat from global economic institutions.

Great pressure is being applied to national governments by corporations and global bureaucracies to privatize and commodify most public services. Global corporations seek to put them in the same category of commercial activity as toothpaste, cars, real estate services, or movies, provided by private industry at market rates.

Yet there are profound differences between the sacred trust arrangement of governments to provide for basic needs and rights and the private, contracted provision of products, entertainment, and commercial services. Corporations operate from a hierarchy of values that requires profit and growth. Yet as corporations make inroads as providers of health, education, water, or food security, the delivery of these services will go only to people who can pay the market rate. The many who cannot will essentially fall out of the system. *Hence, we would argue that any acts that separate governments from their obligation to provide for all people regardless of economic status are to be prevented.*

Similarly, any efforts by global bureaucracies to *require* that governments privatize such services should be resisted by governments and activists alike—and ultimately banned. At this moment, the current WTO negotiations in Geneva over the expansion of the General Agreement on Trade in Services (GATS) are a case in point.

If the GATS agreement is finalized, then most of the services we have listed here as fundamental rights of citizens and obligations of governments will be subsumed under the new rules of GATS. In other words, corporations will have the right to establish a commercial presence and operate what have until now been domestic services inside countries. These include health care, elder care, child care, water purification and delivery, education, prisons, domestic rail and air transportation, public broadcasting, parks, museums and cultural institutions, social security and welfare programs, and public works of all kinds. As mentioned in chapter 2, the United States or Canada might find ExxonMobil running public broadcasting while Mitsubishi runs social security; France might have Disney operating the Louvre; Enron or WorldCom could be running the German health care system; and Shell Oil could be in charge of the Japanese railroads and perhaps child rearing as well. Such outcomes are not unrealistic: as we already mentioned, U.S. giant Bechtel was on the verge of running a significant piece of Bolivia's water delivery system until recently, nearly causing a revolution because of its prices to the poor.

The U.N. Covenant on Economic, Social, and Cultural Rights includes the right to education and health. Of all services, these are shaping up as the most potentially lucrative for the global corporations pushing the GATS agreement. Global expenditures on education now exceed $2 trillion, and global expenditures on health care exceed $3.5 trillion. Global corporations are aiming at nothing less than the dismantling of public education and health care systems. Already they have succeeded in lobbying over forty countries, including all of Europe, to be listed in the GATS.

The obligation of governments to provide services for their citizens may soon be reduced to whether some distant corporation will or will not charge an affordable rate for people to send their children to school or to a doctor. In our view, no global agreement should have the power to forcibly intervene in the trust agreement between governments and citizens.

Of course, there are many other threats to basic social programs and services and basic rights to food and health, aside from the upcoming GATS agreement. In chapter 2 we discussed the structural adjustment programs of the World Bank and the International Monetary Fund. To be eligible for development loans or debt relief, dozens of developing countries were forced to abandon a multitude of social programs and allow for-profit foreign corporations to enter, commercialize, and privatize these operations to the detriment of local people.

We have also discussed the WTO's TRIPs agreement, which enables global corporations to claim intellectual property rights over the genetic heritage of people and communities and to redefine the role and form of agriculture. Farming and the community way of life it has sustained are becoming dominated by global corporations that have rendered farmers dependent on them for seeds, fertilizers, pesticides, and herbicides. Structural adjustment programs have also played a big role in this shift in agriculture, requiring nations to convert their farms to export-oriented, specialized production and permit entry of global corporations that accelerate the process. This has driven farmers off lands where they formerly grew food for their communities and has increased hunger and migration.

Because food security is one of the most fundamental human rights, every government has an interest in ensuring it as an essential foundation for social stability and public health. We believe this means that no development banks or trade agreements should be given the right to *require* that any country revamp its agricultural production systems, allow foreign entry and investment, or open itself to cheaper food from abroad to its own detriment. Of course, any country may choose to allow such entry if conditions warrant, but it should not to be *forced* to do so.

Cultural diversity and integrity is another area that can be seen as part of the commons and is arguably a fundamental right that should be protected by nations. It too is now threatened in many ways by global trade agreements. The right of social, religious, cultural, and indigenous groups to preserve their practices, beliefs, artifacts, and artistic expressions is crucial to maintaining diversity within and among nations and in the world. This also applies to the efforts of nation-states to prevent foreign domination of their own national cultural expressions, through media and artistic creations. Many countries, notably Canada and France—both deeply concerned about retaining film and television industries in domestic hands—have been fighting strenuously to retain their rights to protect their own cultures.

Current WTO trade law subjects culture to the disciplines of the agreement, including "national treatment," "most favored nation," and the prohibition against quantitative restrictions. (All of these WTO rules open up countries to foreign media and other cultural products, often to the detriment of local cultural expressions, which can be overpowered.) There have been several complaints over culture at the WTO since its inception. All have had the effect of limiting the right of a state to protect its cultural industries. The most significant was a 1997 ruling in which the United States successfully forced Canada to abandon protections of its magazine industry, even though American magazines already made up 85 percent of all of those available at Canadian newsstands. Then–U.S. trade representative Charlene Barshefsky said the decision would serve as a useful weapon against Canada's and other countries' protection of their film, books, and broadcasting industries. (See Box M in chapter 4.)

The United States is taking such a hard line because any exemption for Canada would set a negative precedent for other countries, especially in the developing world, where cultural protection is an emerging issue. The fact that the effort to undermine these protections failed at the Seattle WTO ministerial meetings does not mean the problems are over. Both the GATS and the TRIPs agreement will have a direct impact on the telecommunications sector, including the Internet, digital and e-commerce spheres, public broadcasting, patents, trademarks, and copyright law. All are now on the table. They should be taken off.

In sum, we argue that in all of the preceding issues, nation-states and communities should not be subjected to the rules of global trade agreements or multilateral institutions like the WTO or the IMF. Trade in these areas should be subject to national and local decision-making processes alone. Only in this way will it be possible for nations to act on behalf of the common interests of their citizens and to fulfill their own obligations to them.

# Three Proposals to Reempower the Commons

Businessman Peter Barnes, former president of Working Assets, Inc., and now a director of the Tomales Bay Institute in California, likens the commons to "the dark matter of the universe. It's everywhere, but we don't see it. The only economic matter we see is the kind that glistens with dollar signs."

In other words, those aspects of nature or ordinary life that still function as commons—running freshwater, the atmosphere, the public market, biodiversity, the oceans, and the Internet—mostly do not enter into economic calculations, although corporations and global bureaucracies are pushing hard to be sure that they soon do, via privatization and enclosure.

According to Barnes, "The great challenge for the twenty-first century is, first of all, to make the commons visible; second, to give it proper reverence; and third, to translate that reverence into publicly owned property rights and legal institutions that are on a par with private property." At least.

So the central idea is to graduate the powers of the public commons at least to a balanced position with those of the marketplace and then devise strategies to strengthen further its importance, viability, and systems of preservation.

In this section, we offer proposals in three areas where there is work being done to improve the equation between the powers of the private and those of the public commons. The first proposal is to diminish the power grab over the commons and the authority of the global trade and finance bodies; the second is to increase the authority of the multilateral environment agreements and the international bodies that act on behalf of the commons; and the third—where we will hear further from Barnes—is to examine and strengthen some trust arrangements that might effectively protect the commons, and add power to its authority.

The proposals follow.

## I. REVERSE THE POWERS OF GLOBAL TRADE BODIES OVER THE COMMONS AND EXCLUDE CERTAIN ASPECTS OF THE COMMONS FROM THE TRADING SYSTEM

Global trade bodies now have an immense and increasing role in accelerating the invasion of the nonmonetized, nonprivatized commons. We have mentioned the impending rules of the General Agreement on Trade in Services (GATS), which undermine the ability of nation-states to protect modern-commons services: water delivery, public broadcasting, education, welfare, culture, even security and military systems. All may be deprived of their present level of public trust protection, or stewardship laws, and placed under private control. A *second* factor is the emerging investment rules of the WTO, which will increase the ability of global corporations to enter countries freely and seize financial control and management of local or national commons.

A third set of factors are the policies of the World Bank and International Monetary Fund's structural adjustment programs, which often require that governments privatize services and local public commons as conditions for loans. And a fourth problem is the recent assertion by the WTO of its supremacy over multilateral environment agreements (MEAs), such as the Kyoto Protocol and the Convention on Biological Diversity, requiring that such agreements to protect the global commons conform to corporate-oriented trade rules. (MEAs will be discussed in the next item.)

The following ideas and proposals suggest effective mechanisms and rules to diminish the global bureaucracies' powers over the commons and suggest areas of the commons that must remain outside the global trading system.

### The Authority of Trade Agreements Must Be Narrowly Defined

Global trade bureaucracies and international financial agencies should not have authority over state or national decision making when it comes to the commons, natural heritage resources, the preservation of national choice in domestic services, or fundamental human rights. Trade and investment agreements should not be allowed to require a national or state government to privatize or commercialize remaining areas of the commons or public services or to force countries to open up these areas to foreign investment and competition either by imposing rules requiring governments to conform or penalizing them for not doing so.

### Decisions on Common Property Resources and Public Services Should Be Local or National

Decisions about common property resources and public services should be reserved to the localities and nations involved, consistent with the principle of subsidiarity (see chapter 6). Local commons are the province of local communities. National commons should be subject to national democratic decision-making processes. Global commons should be addressed by multilateral agreements on issues of sustainability and equitable access. No commons—whether local, national, or global—are the proper subject of a multilateral trade agreement. Decisions about the ownership, control, and operation of fundamental public services—including health care and hospitals, water management and delivery, natural resource use, education, transportation, public broadcasting, agriculture and food security, culture, social security, welfare, military, police, and jails—should be specifically excluded from multilateral trade and investment agreements.

Some nations and communities may determine that it is in their public interest to contract for private operation of some of these resources and public services. Indeed, there is sometimes a role for private ownership and markets to play in the management, allocation, and delivery of certain common heritage resources—including land, seeds, and water—but only in a framework of effective, democratically accountable public regulation that guarantees fair pricing, equitable access, quality, and public stewardship. However, decisions in these matters are properly local or national and have no place being prescribed by global trade and investment regimes concerned only with advancing private commercial interests. Nor is it acceptable for any international agreement to dictate actions by local or national jurisdictions that would result in excluding individuals or communities from equitable access to services and resources, such as clean water, that are essential to life and health.

*Things Fundamental to Life and Human Survival*
*Should Not Be Privatized or Monopolized*

Certain aspects of the commons that are basic to survival should not be privatized or subject to trade agreements. These include the atmosphere, bulk freshwater, and the genetic and molecular building blocks of life (including the human genome). It may be permissible to patent truly distinctive seed varieties created by privately funded research, for a limited period of time, but the patenting of naturally occurring seeds or seed varieties developed by farming communities or by publicly funded research should not be allowed.

*Some Aspects of Life Should Not Be Patented or Otherwise Monopolized*

Here we include some areas of life that *are* now partly privatized and traded but should never be subject to corporate *patent* rights or monopoly ownership as offered by TRIPs. At present, these include genes, seeds, plant varieties, and animal breeds—with the possible exception of temporary rights to the exclusive production and sale of distinctive plant and animal varieties created through privately funded breeding programs. The general principle is this: no patents on life. There is also a need to rethink patent rules on life-sustaining pharmaceuticals—for example, AIDS drugs—to ensure fair pricing and access by all who need them, without regard to financial means.

*The Right of Countries to Choose Not to Import or Export Goods They Deem Harmful and Pernicious Should Be Protected; Trade in Certain Pernicious Goods May Properly Be Prohibited by International Agreement*

A country properly has the right to ban the import or export of certain goods that it considers presents a threat to health and safety, including genetically modified organisms (GMOs), toxins, weapons, and addictive drugs, as well as tobacco and alcohol, for which existing trade agreements now prohibit exclusions. Some currently traded goods are so harmful to the environment, public health, safety, peace, and the global commons that it may be appropriate to create an international agreement to ban them entirely. Candidates would include toxic and nuclear wastes, endangered species, land mines, and sex workers. Such issues, however, are appropriately addressed by international forums and agreements devoted specifically to these topics, not by specialized trade bodies or trade and investment agreements.

## 2. STRENGTHEN THE REACH AND ENFORCEMENT OF MEAS AND OTHER PROTECTIVE TREATIES AMONG NATIONS

At this time, the only meaningful protection for some aspects of the global commons resides in the United Nations' multilateral environment agreements (MEAs). These include the Kyoto Protocol to the U.N. Framework Convention on Climate Change, the Montreal Protocol on Substances that Deplete the Ozone Layer, the U.N. Convention on Biological Diversity, the

U.N. Convention on the Law of the Sea, the Outer Space Treaty of 1967, the Antarctic Treaty (1959), the U.N. Convention on Straddling and Highly Migratory Fish Stocks, the Stockholm Convention on Persistent Organic Pollutants, and in another vein, the International Telecommunications Union (which assigns radio frequencies to individual nations, and supervises their use), among others.

All of these agreements may have been directly undermined by the World Trade Organization's assertion at the Doha ministerial meeting of 2001 that its own rules should take priority over them. According to the WTO, when there is a conflict between the rules, WTO rules trump the MEAs, which means that trade ministers rather than environment ministers decide the ultimate use of the resources. In turn, it means that corporate interests determine what happens to the world's common resources, even though it is these very corporate interests themselves that are rapidly destroying the environmental commons. If left unchallenged, this WTO policy will be disastrous for environmental governance on the planet and will weaken the most effective mechanism that now exists for protection of the global commons.

The international community, and the governments (many from the Third World) that led the diplomatic fights to establish MEA treaties, have yet to fully respond to or grasp the potential threats posed by the WTO. Some international NGOs, notably the IFG, *have* developed full programs to address the problem. But any new political coalition to defend MEAs clearly must also go well beyond the environmental community and include rural poor peoples' movements, farmers, indigenous peoples, fisherfolk, and so on, whose livelihoods depend on the commons. Broad inclusion of these movements could raise some sticky issues. For example, among indigenous groups, land ownership is traditionally communal and noncommodified. But some MEAs and trust arrangements commodify certain natural processes, as in the case of carbon trading in the Kyoto protocol and in some trust arrangements that include market-based applications. Nonetheless, all groups are unifying around the demand that the United Nations, not the WTO, should be the forum in which the fate and powers of MEAs are decided.

One important step toward a solution on indigenous issues would be the ratification of the U.N. Draft Resolution on the Rights of Indigenous

Peoples, which well articulates indigenous rights and protections. It should have final status equal to all other international treaties, including MEAs. (See also chapter 4, Box L.)

Most important in all our efforts must be to increase the enforcement powers of MEAs. The World Trade Organization has been given real power to levy economic and political sanctions on any government that defies its rules, but many MEAs lack such powers. Balance needs to be restored. Also, MEAs as they exist today are products of complex negotiations among nations and may not cover their subject area thoroughly, as we have seen, for example, with the many loopholes in the Kyoto protocol. Nor are there MEAs for every endangered aspect of the commons. Nevertheless, MEAs are presently the most viable international model for environmental governance.

Finally, MEA bureaucracies must build into their own constitutions specific language that asserts that their rules *supercede* any created by global trade bodies such as the WTO. Already, the Biosafety Protocol of the Convention on Biological Diversity has included such language in its basic agreement, which will surely lead eventually to a bitter battle with the WTO. It is a battle that governments and every MEA bureaucracy need to initiate, and win.

To help alleviate these limits of MEAs, some officials, scholars, and activists are proposing augmented governance mechanisms, such as a world environmental court. For example, Michael Meacher, who was environment minister in the U.K. government from 1997 to 2003, argues strongly for the viability of such a court as "the supreme legal authority" for settling issues regarding harms to the global environmental common. "The basis of its legal operations," says Meacher, "would be a global environmental charter specifying the ecological conditions which must be met if the biosphere is to be allowed to operate within tolerable elasticities from its natural functioning." In addition, says Meacher and others, we need a strengthened United Nations Environment Program (UNEP). Three fundamental changes are required for it to be effective: (1) it must be well funded by contributions from national governments based on a percentage of the gross domestic product of each nation; (2) it needs to operate at least on the level of environment ministers, who will not just talk but will make concrete decisions that are binding upon all nations; and (3) it must have authority at least equal to that of the WTO. Finally, the sanctions and penalties for breaches of the rules must be severe enough to serve as true deterrents to further destruction of the commons.

## 3. APPLY MODERN TRUST MODELS

Peter Barnes argues that a variety of trust models are the most practical long-term form of protection for local and global commons, at least where domestic laws or international accords or treaties, such as MEAs, prove inadequate. He argues that trusts have operated successfully for centuries, and that their fundamental rules make them uniquely appropriate instruments to operationalize protection today and keep common resources safe from the ravages of the market.

Trusts may be held by the state—as, for example, in the public trust model described in an earlier section—or they may be separate institutions with appointed trustees. In all cases, the managers or trustees must follow certain rules—for example, to sustain fiduciary responsibility, to operate with undivided loyalty on behalf of the trust's beneficiaries, *not* to favor the present generation over future generations, to prevent the depletion of the protected resource unless mandated otherwise, and to remain transparent and accountable at all times, among other conditions. These operating standards for trusts make them structurally the opposite of corporations, whose goals are usually to attempt to maximize short-term benefits. In fact, the rules of corporate law make it mandatory that corporate executives place profit as the primary value and scarcely include such values as resource protection or community welfare. We will look first at the public trust doctrine, and then turn to a variety of other models, with examples of where they have worked effectively.

### Doctrine of Public Trust

This concerns the inherent *obligations* of the state, or government, to protect the people's interests in the commons, especially in the case of such life-giving resources as water, air, biodiversity, wildlife, forests, and so on, although they may also include public education, public broadcasting, transportation, and the like—aspects of what we have called the modern commons.

As mentioned earlier, the Doctrine of Public Trust dates back to Roman times, continued through the Middle Ages in France, Spain, and England,

and was codified within the Magna Carta. In Europe, the public trust doctrine not only confirmed the rights of so-called commoners to enjoy the fruits of the land, waters, forests, and so on but also stipulated that while governments or kings could technically own public lands, they did so in trust for the public, and with an obligation to protect the public's common usages. According to Mark Dowie, this is where the notion of sovereign property was born. "With sovereignty came the unavoidable duty of state stewardship, a concept that survives today in all manifestations of the doctrine." Further, according to Dowie, "government could not relinquish such public trust obligations to any private party."

The public trust doctrine remained viable through the period of North American colonialism and in fact is still recognized as common law in the United States and elsewhere. Dowie cites numerous cases of its application. For example, nineteenth-century New Jersey fisherpeople protested the privatization of coastal and estuarine oyster beds, from which their communities had freely gathered food for centuries. The legal question became whether these estuaries and oyster beds, when privatized, could exclude common usage. The case finally went to the U.S. Supreme Court, which decided that the use of the oyster beds was protected under the public trust doctrine, even though that doctrine had never been codified in the United States. A decade later, the California Supreme Court ruled that property rights in water "consist not so much of the fluid itself, as the advantage of its use." In other words, common usage is protected.

"In 1892 came the granddaddy of them all," reports Dowie. "In *Illinois Central Railroad v. Illinois*, the U.S. Supreme Court held that a state legislature could not grant ownership of land under navigable waters to a private party." Water and the ground beneath it, said the court, "is a title held in trust for the people of the state, that they may enjoy the navigation of waters, carry on commerce over them, and have liberty of fishing therein, from the obstruction or interference of private parties."

Later cases invoking the public trust doctrine have included the famous Mono Lake decision, in which the California Supreme Court ruled that waters from that lake could not be diverted for private development uses that might injure not only tidelands but also, according to reporter Dowie, "lakes, rivers, riverbeds, wildlife habitat, and recreation."

The public trust doctrine was also applied in a recent case involving the

Hudson River Valley in New York State, where General Electric Corporation, which for decades had been dumping millions of tons of toxins on lands adjacent to the river, was finally deprived of its private property rights because of its effect on the river water. Public trust case law held that tidal resources and wetlands held by the states in trust for the people include lands that are privately owned; the public trustee may never legally relinquish the public's rights in those lands. The same logic was used in the Hawaiian Waiahole ditch decision, affirming the state's obligation to protect indigenous rights to water.

So, the Roman Doctrine of Public Trust is alive and well, though right-wing advocates of property rights *uber alles* are challenging the doctrine wherever they can and have even tried to use it to their own benefit. In one case cited by Dowie, for example, "a Texas-based oil company was denied a permit to drill for crude in California, [but] sought a reversal, arguing that domestic oil was, now more than ever, as vital to the public as water." That case is pending.

Dowie's view is that "ecological integrity [should be] established as a public trust right in all states." The question is this: Could a doctrine that acknowledges the public's right to real property be used to service "all aspects of the sometimes invisible larger commons"? Dowie says that such "public trust litigation is likely to succeed only with intensive community activism and public education."

*Ideas for Novel Trusts*

Peter Barnes advocates a design of modernized trust institutions that can protect the commons just as well as the public trust doctrine once did. He agrees that it will require mounting public pressure from NGOs and public officials to achieve, but if so, the trust model could come to occupy a legal position comparable to corporations.

Trusts are sufficiently flexible to be designed in dozens of differing forms, for different purposes. In every variant, the central obligations of trustees remain these: acting only on behalf of the public beneficiaries, not depleting the resource, acting in an open manner, and so on, as amplified earlier. All of those standards are the opposite of resource management by market factors, as now, or even by the state (which is often beholden to commercial interests).

The design of some trusts, for example, could prohibit all but the most noninvasive uses of certain commons—wilderness regions or parks. Other forms could focus on the kinds of commons that allow sustainable use, without diminishment of the commons. These are appropriate for fisheries, rivers, forests, and the atmosphere. "The challenge," in business terms, says Barnes, "is to live off income without diminishing capital." A common law precedent is "the riparian principle," which once applied broadly to rivers and streams in England and early America. This permitted water to be used but *not owned* by those adjacent to it, with water quality and volume undiminished. An example of this is the Pacific Forest Trust, which buys conservation easements from private forest owners, who thenceforth can continue to harvest trees but within strict limits that prevent overcuts, ecologically harmful practices, and development.

Other kinds of trusts could allow free unlimited usage of an undepletable commons, as, say, with the Internet. Still others, concerned with depletable but highly valued resources could define a predetermined level of maximum use, with all fee income from such use going to the public beneficiaries. Examples of the latter include the Alaska Permanent Fund, through which every Alaskan now receives a yearly dividend from oil and gas leases. Unfortunately, the downside of such arrangements is that they may provide incentives for the public to support increased oil consumption.

Less problematic examples include California's successful Marin Agricultural Land Trust, which is designed to maintain the rural character of a farming region threatened by sprawl and development. The trust buys conservation easements from small farmers using public and private funds. This ensures that the agricultural land use remains and that farmers may survive and continue to operate and own their small farms. Similarly, the Oregon Water Trust acquires previously allocated water rights and uses them to augment flows of rivers and streams for environmental health.

Barnes's favorite example is his own Sky Trust model (also discussed in "Energy Systems" in chapter 7), in which a global commons—the atmosphere—is put into a global trust for control of its use as a pollution dump site.

"The Sky Trust is based on the premise," says Barnes, "that the sky belongs to everyone and must be held in trust for future generations. It requires polluters to purchase expensive emission permits from a trust representing all citizens of the world. The trust's income can be used for public purposes or rebates to citizens through equal dividends" in the manner of the Alaska Permanent Fund. The difference between the Sky Trust and the Alaska fund is that trustees would set a strict maximum usage, reflecting ecological limits, while charging very high fees. Thus polluters would have to pay significantly—at present they pay nothing for this kind of pollution dumping—and then might also have to raise prices for polluting products— say, cars, or the output of smokestack factories. Thus pollution is discouraged, and so is consumption of polluting products. Meanwhile, any money that is finally raised from fees is divvied up among publics, or used for public purposes.

Of course, there remains the question of how we get from here to there. Where is the political will to achieve models that might effectively remove some part of the public commons from having its fate solely determined by market forces? Public outrage and organizational and political pressure are mandatory in these matters, but such trust models offer an opportunity for expressing viable alternative systems. Meanwhile, they can help achieve compromise solutions in a difficult context: privatization, rampant growth, and corporate political domination, all of which are the roots of the problem.

The way to proceed, finally, is on all fronts. The firm removal of global, local, and modern commons from the global trading system is the first prong of a unified effort to strengthen the viability of the commons and separate it from market forces. Preservation and expansion of the powers of the MEAs are vital. And trusts of various kinds can make inroads too.

CHAPTER SIX

# Subsidiarity

*Recalling Power from the Global*

IT IS THE MAJOR CONCEIT, or gamble, of the proponents of economic globalization that by removing economic control from the places where it has traditionally resided—in nations, states, subregions, communities, or indigenous societies—and placing that control into absentee authorities that operate globally via giant corporations and bureaucracies, all levels of society will benefit. But as we have seen in earlier chapters, this is not true, and it is a principal reason why so many millions of people are angrily protesting.

The captains of globalization are driven by what is still essentially an economic ideology. They operate on a macro scale removed from the everyday realities of local conditions or awareness. They lobby for their ideas and theories as though they were viable and cogent, as if they themselves were expert visionaries and managers of their new centralized global architecture. They continue to praise their formulas despite the numerous spectacular breakdowns they have caused: the Asian financial crisis, the Russian financial crisis, the near-economic meltdown of Brazil, and the collapse of the Argentine economy, along with the global increase in poverty, hunger, inequity, dependency, and powerlessness. These theories do not work and cannot work; the main beneficiaries, unsurprisingly, remain the global corporations and economic elites that have instituted these processes.

As we have seen, the central modus operandi of the globalization model is to delocalize controls over economic *and* political activity in a systematic appropriation of the powers, decisions, options, and functions that through history have been fulfilled by the community, region, or state. Another modus operandi of globalization is anonymity. On the other hand, it is a principal virtue of localization that it restores face-to-face, knowing relationships of trust to economic transactions.

When sovereign powers are removed from the local and put into distant bureaucracies, local politics must also be redesigned to conform to the rules and practices of distant bureaucracies. Communities and nations that formerly operated in a relatively self-reliant manner, in the interests of their own people, are converted into unwilling subjects of these larger, undemocratic, unaccountable global structures.

Meanwhile, millions of people all over the world continue to go to work every day, trying to maintain their traditional small-scale, artisanal, or indigenous livelihoods. In fact, the local economy is the foundation for most communities, whether North or South, rich or poor. Even traditional economists like Paul Krugman acknowledge that most U.S. cities are locally rooted because of the expanding service economy. Yet these local economic activities are under constant attack. They are increasingly subject to, and dependent on, mysterious eruptions and gyrations in the larger system. These may include the vagaries of distant export markets, fluctuations in prices and exchange rates, abilities of national governments to service interest payments on loans, and centralized decisions about international capital flows, commodity specializations, and the like—decisions made by authorities in Washington, Geneva, Brussels, Rome, and Tokyo without the slightest nod to democratic processes. At the local level, such mundane issues as the price of coffee, tomatoes, oil, wheat, or rice depend on these unfathomable distant factors. Financial assets such as stocks and bonds, as well as prevailing wage rates for labor, are also governed less and less frequently by local conditions and instead fluctuate according to the manipulations of economic networks by financiers and corporations.

But most affected of all, tragically, is democracy itself and all its institutions.

If democracy is based on the idea that people must participate in the great decisions affecting their lives, then the movement of basic life decisions to distant venues—particularly venues that abhor democratic participation, openness, accountability, and transparency—brings the death of democracy. If local economic activity is something that people have been able to do for themselves, globalization is something done *to* people rather than *by* them.

We have reached the end of the road for that process. It's time to change directions.

## Understanding Subsidiarity

Because globalization is the problem, then logically a return to the local is inevitable—a reinvigoration of the conditions by which local communities regain the power to determine and control their preferred economic and political paths. Instead of shaping all systems to conform to a global model that emphasizes specialization of production, comparative advantage, export-oriented growth, monoculture, and homogenization of economic, cultural, and political forms under the direction of transnational corporate institutions, we must reshape our institutions to favor exactly the opposite.

The operating principle for this turnaround is the concept of *subsidiarity*—that is, favoring the local whenever a choice exists. In practice, subsidiarity means that all decisions should be made at the lowest level of governing authority competent to deal with them. Global health crises and global pollution issues often require cooperative international decisions. But most economic, cultural, and political decisions are not international and can be made at the national, regional, or local levels, depending on the issue. Power should be encouraged to evolve downward, not upward. Decisions should constantly move closer to the people most affected by them. Wherever economic production, labor, and markets can be local, they should be, and rules should help achieve that. International, regional, and subregional trade will continue to exist, of course, but it should serve as a final resort, not as the purpose of the system.

All systems should emphasize local production and consumption rather than be deliberately designed to serve long-distance trade. This means *shortening* the length of lines for economic activity: fewer food miles, fewer oil supply miles, fewer travel-to-work miles. Technologies should also be chosen that best serve local control, rather than megatechnologies that operate globally. (The authors of this volume prefer solar, wind, minihydro, micropower, and conservation over nuclear and oil; we prefer small-scale local agriculture and local markets over globalized industrial agriculture for export markets.) Firms should continue to operate, but only within the confines of a "site-here-to-sell-here" policy, and investment and capital should remain rooted in the community, constantly recycled, and locally controlled.

We want to clarify that such self-reliance does not mean autarky. Indeed, there is a compelling argument that many healthy local economies will continue to have exports and imports, but spread among hundreds of items, none of them critical to the survival of the community. North Dakota's electricity sector provides a good example. Some are now urging that if North Dakotans want to become energy independent, they should build large-scale wind farms. Then, if they found themselves dependent on imports of wind machines, they might develop a local wind-machine industry. If they did this, they would likely depend on imports of metals and parts. Thus, the process never ends, but a process of import substitution steadily leads toward a more diverse, healthy, and self-reliant economy.

Where commons are found to exist—water, land, biodiversity, local knowledge—these should remain the property of the community as a whole. Wherever indigenous activities or effective nonmonetized activities continue to occur, these should be respected and encouraged as legitimate economic forms, providing real services to people and communities if not to global corporations and the market. The goal can no longer be individual or corporate wealth; rather it must be community self-reliance, public health, equity, accountability, and democracy. (See chapter 4 for more on this issue.)

Clearly, a reversal of this kind—consciously favoring the local over the global—will not sit comfortably with the largest and most powerful institutions in the world, all of which depend on the larger global system, long supply lines, expanding trade, and centralized absentee control. Those are the forms that were made in their image, as it were, and that offer maximum profit opportunity. But citizen groups and general populations around the world are making their own preference clear, and that is to move in the direction of reempowerment of local communities. Farmers, workers, unions, small businesses, consumer groups, peasant organizations, environmentalists, human rights advocates, and all groups seeking functional democracies are already working to reverse course. They will not be denied, but they need help in doing more faster.

One important reason why these people will not be denied has to do with the economics of local, small-scale alternatives. As we have noted, small-scale alternatives are already generating most of the goods and services people need in a cost-effective manner, and many trends suggest that their role will expand. Among others, the most salient trends are these:

- Distribution costs are getting proportionately larger than production costs (suggesting opportunities, as in food, for creating cheaper products through direct marketing).
- Global transportation costs will rise as oil prices rise, to begin to reflect real costs that have until now been externalized (see chapter 7), and as green taxes are enacted.
- Niche marketing increasingly favors local producers who best know local consumers.
- The shift from goods to services inherently favors local business.
- The growth of computers and the Internet makes it easier to run complex businesses from anywhere, including the home basement.
- Large corporations are generally worse places to work than smaller ones.
- Terrorist threats increase the importance of unhooking from the corporate-global juggernaut and returning to local self-reliance.

Elsewhere in this volume we describe changes in key global institutions consistent with the kinds of shifts we speak about here. For example, we describe desirable changes that are occurring in the dominant Bretton Woods institutions, in corporate structures, and in the essential operating systems of society like energy, transport, and agriculture. Here we get down to issues of the *scale of governance* and processes to bring economic and political power back toward the communities and nations from which they have been lifted.

## The Road to the Local

Localization attempts to reverse the trend toward the global by discriminating actively in favor of the local in all policies. Depending on the context, the *local* is defined as a subgroup within a nation-state; it may also be the nation-state itself, or occasionally, a regional grouping of nation-states. In all cases, the idea is for power to devolve to the lowest unit appropriate for a particular goal.

Policies that bring about localization are ones that increase democratic control of the economy by communities or nation-states, taking it back from the global institutions that have appropriated it. These policies may enable nations, local governments, and communities to reclaim their economies, make them as diverse as possible, and rebuild stability into community life—to achieve maximum self-reliance nationally and regionally in a way that ensures more sustainable forms of development.

(One disclaimer: We are aware that localization is not a panacea. Localization does not *guarantee* democracy or equality or human rights; it just makes them far more likely. Smaller communities offer people greater access to the sources of power and greater opportunity for positive outcomes. However, history offers many examples of ruthless opportunism even on the local level, and advocates like the National Front in France and Joerg Haider in Austria offer a current warning. What is sure, however, is that globalization offers *no opportunity* at all for democratic empowerment. We have a better chance with smaller-scale systems. We will return to this later.)

To move in the direction of localization will require a complete change in society's assumptions and will also require a long time and many steps. But to get our thinking started, we mention here a few points that have been spelled out by Colin Hines in his book *Localization: A Global Manifesto,* Michael Shuman in *Going Local,* and Helena Norberg-Hodge in her chapter on localization in Jerry Mander and Edward Goldsmith's *The Case Against the Global Economy.*

### REINTRODUCE SAFEGUARDS THAT WERE TRADITIONALLY USED TO PROTECT DOMESTIC (LOCAL) ECONOMIES

Traditional safeguards include tariffs, import quotas, investment restrictions and rules, and nontariff barriers concerning health, worker and environmental, and investment standards. All of these protections instituted by national governments have been the direct target of global trade rules established by the WTO and other bureaucracies intent on undermining local authority and its ability to maintain self-reliance.

### CHANGE SUBSIDY POLICY

Presently, countries offer huge subsidies for infrastructure development, especially for large-scale energy, transport and communications, and other megadevelopment schemes, as well as for the externalized costs of pollution-creating activity. Such policies should be wholly reversed to favor vital local enterprises such as small-scale organic agriculture for local markets, small-scale energy and transportation infrastructures (solar, wind, small-scale hydro, and so on, dedicated bus lanes, and pedestrian and bicycle accommodations), as well as community banking and development and loan funds. Municipal governments should screen local subsidies to test for local ownership and local import replacement. These subsidies include loans, loan guarantees, bonds, capital improvements, and so on. Subsidy programs of this nature would benefit from two further requirements, that they be duly noticed and bid upon (to prevent backroom dealing and to encourage transparency) and that they be performance-based (you get the tax break after you produce the promised jobs).

### PUT NEW CONTROLS ON CORPORATE ACTIVITY

Such new controls would include site-here-to-sell-here policies for manufacturing, banking, and other services, whether domestic or regional. Localities should have the right to require any of the following: changed composition of corporate boards to include labor or environmental or other local stakeholders; limits on corporate freedoms to buy other businesses, especially in other locales; strict limits on mobility and capital movement; loss of corporate personhood laws, which give corporations the rights of ordinary citizens without the responsibilities; abandonment of limited liability rules that protect corporate shareholders from liability for crimes; requirements for public transparency; and so on. (See chapter 9 for more on corporate personhood and limited liability laws.)

### GROUND CAPITAL AND INVESTMENT IN THE COMMUNITY

Profits made locally should remain primarily local. Outside direct investment is permissible and desirable only when geared toward local conditions and requirements. The Canadian labor-sponsored investment funds (LSIFs) offer a good example of how to ground capital. LSIFs invest pension funds exclusively in businesses that are labor-friendly and environmentally friendly and are locally owned in the provinces. The key to their success is that the government must be able to provide tax breaks to those who put money into these funds. There is also a great potential role for the selective investment of public pension funds and surplus revenue funds of public entities. Also desirable are the new local money systems designed for community use. Later in the chapter, we return to the issue of capital and investment.

## MAKE MAJOR CHANGES IN TAXATION POLICIES

Increases in resource taxes as well as the introduction of pollution taxes are needed for extraction and depletion of natural capital like forests, water, and minerals. These will more accurately reflect the true costs of corporate development activities and put the onus on corporations to cover currently externalized costs subsidized by governments. Other taxes would include the introduction of "Tobin taxes" on speculative financial transactions. (The fact that they are now untaxed has increased their volume and the great harms they cause.) There should also be a reassessment of current policies that tend toward greater tax breaks for large-scale enterprises than for smaller, local ones (including elimination of investment tax credits and accelerated depreciation allowances now enjoyed by big businesses to the detriment of smaller ones). Much of the income from such changes in tax policy could help finance the shift to localization.

## INCREASE DIRECT PUBLIC PARTICIPATION IN POLICYMAKING

Increased participation helps ensure equity and diverse viewpoints. This is a primary feature of localization: it makes possible a greater level of direct democracy.

## REORIENT INTERNATIONAL AID AND TRADE RULES

The domestic policies that influence those changes should also be revised so that they contribute to the rebuilding of local rather than global economies, particularly through enhanced global transfer of information and technology. Self-reliant communities may turn out to be the best actors for spreading the capital, technology, policies, and experience necessary to help partner communities in other countries become self-reliant. This is a fundamentally different paradigm for development and development assistance.

### INSTITUTE NEW COMPETITION POLICIES

At present, global competition policy as reflected in the rules of the WTO and other bureaucracies enhances competitive opportunities for global corporations forcing their way into local and domestic domains. Under localization policies, global corporations that continue to exist will no longer have such access unless they conform to all local investment rules, including the requirement to keep capital local. Competition among local firms, however, will be strongly encouraged in order to stimulate innovation. Localities should have the right to encourage (not force) citizens to buy local. Local labeling should be permitted, as well as selective government purchasing of local goods and services.

### ENCOURAGE SOCIAL COHESION
### AND LOCAL ECONOMIC RENEWAL

The push toward the global has left most local communities bereft of viable local instruments that encourage local environmental and social values. It is crucial that attention be paid to the quality and vitality of local culture and community programs on housing, livelihood, sustainable lifestyle, and a safe and healthy environment. Attention must focus on everything from land use and zoning considerations to microlending, development trusts, credit unions, community transport activity, community recycling, community self-building schemes, and myriad conservation activities that are all required aspects of the overall shift in approach. Not least important is a reformed educational system that grasps and can convey the values of this alternative system.

## Investment and Finance Issues

An equally important issue in the viability of local economic systems is how and whether sufficient capital can be found to keep them operative and innovative. Clearly, in a local economy, the operating costs are entirely different from those in a globalized economy. Measurements of successful performance are not based on traditional economic growth figures like GDP and GNP, but rather on more subjective social and environmental characteristics that also include the value of not cutting down the forests and not putting vast dollars into security and military expenditures (which count as GDP). Conversely, they give *positive* value to unpaid and nonmonetized aspects of a local economy that are reflected in personal care, household labor, self-sufficient livelihoods (sometimes based on barter), and the general goal of community self-reliance rather than individual or corporate wealth.

At least for a long while, however, capital and investment factors will continue to play major roles, so it is necessary to address them. Here are some of the ideas that are being studied to help such a system work.

## CAPITAL

We mentioned in the previous section that localization advocates seek to keep capital local. Capital flight has been the death of more than one otherwise viable community, and it must be prevented. Among the measures that may be considered are these: reintroduction of exchange controls; reregulation of banks and finance institutions so that greater advantages are achieved through local investment than flight; introduction of very high "speed bumps" that penalize investors who move money in and out of investment opportunities rapidly and prevent them from exporting more than a small percentage of their funds; 100 percent reserve requirements for banks seeking to create money through loan policies; introduction of Tobin-type taxes to hold down speculative investment and instabilities caused by frequent movement of money; higher margins for purchasing bonds; and restrictions on the use of derivatives to require that banks have cash or liquid assets in reserve to back up such contracts.

· Governments also can and should put deposits in community-friendly banks to support their expansion. They can and should create new kinds of secondary markets for financing the new, local economy. Also, because a great deal of savings in most economies go into equities, incentives and subsidies that encourage local reinvestment are critical. Michael Shuman suggests that some of the most intriguing opportunities for these types of local initiatives are through consortiums of like-minded municipalities. Community reinvestment is a good example. By definition, a community that reinvests 100 percent locally cannot achieve geographic diversification in its portfolio, which increases risk. One solution is for several communities to aim for 90 percent local reinvestment, with the remaining 10 percent invested in the others' funds. All the funds would therefore support local business. A similar case can be made for intermunicipal cooperation to promote fair trade, serve as a clearinghouse for local currency exchanges, and put together flexible manufacturing networks for goods that require larger economies of scale for production or distribution.

## TAXATION

We have already discussed several tax changes intended to reduce capital flight and speculation and to recover formerly externalized costs that the public sector has had to pay. We have also mentioned elimination of special tax breaks for large-scale enterprises and the need to *increase* taxes on energy use and natural capital.

Other important changes include less taxation on labor, which has had the undesirable effect of encouraging corporations to eliminate workers as a way of reducing taxes. Such taxes now include payroll or income taxes, social welfare taxes, and value-added taxes, among others.

Capital gains taxes should be *increased*, especially for short-term holdings. Far more preferential treatment should be offered for taxes on income that is based on productive work compared with passive earnings based on moving money between investments.

Governments can severely limit tax evasion by forcing public disclosure of corporate finances, especially global taxes paid or avoided; closing national and global tax loopholes; penalizing and eventually eliminating tax havens; monitoring and halting intracorporate financial transfers used to avoid paying national taxes (for example, transfer pricing); and imposing tax penalties for downsizing or relocation.

## NEW RULES OF INVESTMENT

The present rules of globalized finance and investment encourage moving control away from the communities that need to have it. Capital has been made almost completely mobile so it can always move wherever profit opportunity is greatest. Mobility of capital—which, as we mentioned in chapter 2, was opposed by the original gurus of free trade David Ricardo and Adam Smith—has required that local communities change their economies and their priorities to appeal to foreign capital investment and then follow their negative strictures from structural adjustment programs to draconian loan conditions.

Subsidiarity and localization require a reversal of that formula to emphasize and favor local direct investment over foreign investment. Where foreign investment continues to be sought, local communities should control its conditions. The goal is to redirect all benefits to the local community, including jobs, local livelihoods, services, local urban community development, small-scale energy, manufacturing for domestic and local markets rather than export, and the like. For example, governments could impose capital penalties on firms that depart a community, rather than the current policy in many municipalities of allowing the firm to write off the moving expenses.

*Favoring Local Direct Investment*

Colin Hines has proposed an alternative investment code for foreign investors, with some of the following new directives. Preferential treatment should always be given to local direct investment; this reverses such WTO rulings as most favored nation status, which outlawed local preferences and smoothed the way for massive dependency on investors. Investments may continue to be encouraged, but only if they have the effect of increasing local employment with decent wages and otherwise serve to improve the quality of local life. All investors should respect basic human rights and protect the environment as top priorities.

Existing laws that give preferential treatment to foreign or absentee owners of community enterprises must be rolled back over a few years time span.

Under the provisions of an alternative investment code, states and communities would be explicitly *permitted* to impose a code of performance requirements (again in direct opposition to current WTO rules) as follows: require a certain percentage of domestic content or local content in all manufactured products; require a given level of local personnel and respect for labor and environmental standards; protect enterprises that serve community

needs from any unfair foreign competition; give preference to locally produced goods.

Other reversals of current policies now imposed by trade agreements and
the Bretton Woods institutions would include these:

- Communities need some leeway in setting rules on investors that can
  result in expropriation if the investor breaks its promises. To prevent
  abuse of such rules, a community should have the right to impose a wide
  range of potential expropriation rules only before an investment is made;
  existing firms could be given a few years' notice.
- Governments should also be able to set limits on the amount of capital
  and profit that may be expatriated to source countries by foreign
  investors. Citizen groups and community institutions should be granted
  rights to sue investors for violations of this investment code. All judicial
  proceedings on these matters should be open and transparent.

*Encouraging Long-Term Local Investment*

With conditions made more difficult for capital movement and a new set of
requirements for responsible performance, the opportunities and advantages
formerly enjoyed by foreign direct investors will be reduced, and there will
be a desirable swing toward local direct investment and the goal of keeping
money recycling productively within a community.

To encourage the shift to local long-term investment, the following
measures would be helpful:

- Offer higher tax breaks for long-term local investment and create severe
  tax penalties for rapid capital movement (especially among foreign
  investors).
- At the local level (including the national level), give central banks authority to directly influence the structure and profitability of local banks,
  favoring those that support local investment for local development.
  National policy should encourage increased market regulation, establish
  small banks designed for microlending, and increase the emphasis on
  credit unions, Local Exchange Trading Systems (LETS), and tax breaks
  for the breakdown of large-scale enterprise into smaller, decentralized,
  locally owned operating units. Central banks could also set lower dis-
  count rates for community-friendly banks.

- Close down all offshore banking centers where capital hides from banking and securities laws or from national or state income taxes. National banking systems would be prohibited from honoring the transfers of offshore capital.
- Encourage long-term savings in local banks by offering higher interest rates there, thus providing local banks with additional development funds for local projects.

## Response to Critics of Subsidiarity

In the face of the globalization juggernaut and its widely propagated utopian visions, advocates of more decentralized, localized alternative paths tend to meet fierce criticism and disbelief about the viability of such solutions.

We have already mentioned that advocates of globalization assert that local systems are less democratic than the advancing global political constructs. We have already agreed that local governance does not guarantee democracy, human rights, equity, or good governance. We join others in citing examples where local governance has been authoritarian, oppressive, even brutal. Nevertheless, bringing governance and economies down to smaller-scale systems—where people are closer to the sources of power—offers far greater opportunity and promise for democratic participation than the present model. There are many examples of this throughout the world, some among indigenous populations, some in smaller communities, and some in large cities such as Brazil's Porto Alegre and Curitiba (for more on this, see chapter 7). Globalization, on the other hand, offers no democratic promise. Globalization actually *guarantees* absentee rule by giant corporations that are designed to act solely in their own economic interests and have no real concern about conditions faced in the daily lives of most people. The real choice, therefore, is between allowing corporate-led systems controlled from faraway cities and attempting to strengthen forms that may bring power back to the local, where opportunity for democracy, equity, and attention to local social and environmental conditions still exists. The better choice seems obvious to the authors of this report, though vigilance is mandatory.

As for defining and upholding human rights, that is the preserve of appropriate international agreements among nations, which have sufficient powers to institute sanctions of the kind that helped bring down the white racist regime in South Africa a few decades ago. Keep in mind that subsidiarity envisions a role for higher-order rules, whether national or global. It just insists that these rules be few and truly consensual, especially if they are going to restrict local action. It is worth noting that such sanctions as were applied in South Africa would now be far more difficult to introduce because they are nearly outlawed by the rules of the WTO. In fact, such sanctions would be explicitly banned by the new FTAA agreement or any reiterations of the proposed multilateral agreement on investment (MAI) that was fought off by activists a few years ago. Many of the elements of the MAI continue to resurface in other agreements, including the WTO's proposed new investment agreement. (If such rules had been in place twenty years ago, Nelson Mandela would likely still be in jail. So much for the globalizers as protectors of human rights.)

Other critiques of localization are essentially restatements of the many theoretical benefits of global free trade: that wealth will "trickle down" to the poor, that prices will be lower, and that greater diversity (of products) will exist in the marketplace. On the first point, that globalization lifts people from poverty, this is manifestly, tragically false. As chapter 2 of this volume explained, the benefits of globalization actually trickle up to the very wealthy. It accelerates gaps between rich and poor within countries and among countries. (A special report by the IFG, *Does Globalization Help the Poor?* provides more data on this phenomenon.) As for globalization bringing a greater diversity of products, that may be the case for some product categories and some segments of society that can take advantage of expanded choices in foreign cars, designer clothing, and exotic cheeses and meats, for example. But in many cases, localization increases the diversity of products: we think it is better to have one thousand microbreweries than one Coors, and many varieties of tomato and potato rather than the industrial, single-crop variety. In any case, for most people who are simply trying to feed their families, product diversity is an abstraction. Meanwhile, cultural diversity and biodiversity—which affect everyone—are actively suppressed by the globalization model.

It is true that the global marketplace does sometimes bring cheaper products in sectors where competition still exists. This is because the rules of free trade encourage free entry of foreign agricultural and manufactured goods, sometimes with lower prices. However, these lower prices do not signify a new efficiency brought by globalization. Often they signify export dumping (when domestic overproduction threatens high domestic prices and profits). They are also the result of high levels of direct subsidies, of subsidies through infrastructure development, or of the outlandish subsidies caused by the externalization of environmental or social costs of industrial monocultures, as explained earlier. If these subsidized costs—which ultimately are paid for by taxpayers and ordinary people—were actually included in the price of commodity imports, they would not be cheaper. Even if they *were* cheaper, however, is it better social policy for a country or community to sacrifice the vitality and cohesion of its economic system—especially the production of food staples, which also has important environmental and cultural benefits—on the chance that consumers can save pennies at the supermarket? We think not. Indeed, today local companies may offer lower prices, and local banks may offer lower rates, yet these entities fare poorly because of the superior marketing clout of giant firms and banks.

In any case, all of this activity is based on the tenuous theory of comparative advantage. Under comparative advantage concepts, the viability of economic systems depends entirely upon whether the importing community can pay for its imports with the earned income from export items in which it has this so-called comparative advantage in production. In practice, this neat formula rarely works. Export markets are variable, volatile, and unreliable. More than one nation is now facing a hunger crisis caused by the failure of comparative advantage theories, as export prices crash.

Others argue against localization by positing that small businesses usually pay lower wages and offer fewer benefits, and few are unionized. In fact, this is often untrue. Over time, as small companies grow, early employees usually get big salary boosts and increased benefits. Another argument is that it is harder to regulate one hundred mini-mills than one giant smokestack. Perhaps this is true, but weigh against this the political clout of the giant, which eliminates regulation, and the fact that local residents are usually the best judges of local smokestacks. Finally, there is the argument that some communities are better endowed than others. This is certainly true. Hence, redistribution mechanisms are needed.

Obviously, any nation or community's security would be better enhanced if its own people could grow their own foods—at least ensuring thereby their

SUBSIDIARITY 163

survival free of market idiosyncrasies—and also manufacture as many of their other needs as possible before entering global markets. The goal of societies should not be to find cheaper prices for products but to find the means to ensure that all the needs of all people are met and that a satisfactory and stable life is perpetuated within a system that does not collapse from being part of the volatile global market. If people grow their own food, produce their own necessities, and control the conditions of their lives, the issue of price becomes irrelevant.

CHAPTER SEVEN

# Alternative Operating Systems
# (1)

IN CHAPTER 4, we listed ten principles that should set the standards for all economic activity: democracy, subsidiarity, ecological sustainability, common heritage, diversity, human rights, sustainable livelihoods and employment, food security and safety, equity, and the precautionary principle. These principles guide our recommended changes in the institutions that form the basic architecture of the global economy. No longer should bureaucracies and global corporations operate on *their* set of values, placing economic growth and corporate profits at the top of a hierarchy that does not take crucial social and ecological norms into consideration.

But our discussion would be incomplete if we did not recognize that the problems do not reside only in the bureaucracies and corporations that presently deprive citizens and nation-states of the ability to act on their own behalf. They are part of the fabric of the practical operations of society, especially in its most important economic systems: energy, agriculture and food, transportation, and manufacturing.

It should not come as a surprise that each of these sectors has adopted standards, or forms of production and distribution, that are anathema to the core values that we propose should govern society. In fact, they are entirely compatible with—indeed they exude the same fundamental values as—the larger globalizing forces. They are all part of a single integrated megastructure that *is* the global economy, which extends into our nations and communities. It will not be possible to build more sustainable international structures without redesigning many of the world's key operating systems.

It is not the purpose of this report to issue a full analysis of every economic operating system in our society; we save that for another day. But in this chapter and the next, we will examine six key elements: the four systems we have mentioned—energy, agriculture, transportation, and manufacturing, which are the primary structures of day-to-day economic life in modern society—the measurements and indicators that society now uses to evaluate its overall performance, and finally, the media. All of these systems, like the entire global bureaucratic architecture, must be changed to reflect a new hierarchy of values that we hope will eventually dominate all economic activity.

Over the next few years of this exploratory process, we will be directly involving grassroots organizations throughout the world in a multiyear program to amplify and helps "actualize" this work. (Toward the end of chapter 7 we cite two grassroots initiatives that are already seizing the reins to achieve change.)

## Energy Systems

No domain of global economic activity does greater social, environmental, and political harm than today's dominant energy systems, from source to waste. Yet, ironically, there is no area so susceptible to satisfactory, short-run conversion and excellent available alternatives.

New energy production in most parts of the world today, but especially in the Western industrial nations, is based on fossil fuels: oil, coal, and natural gas, augmented in some places by large-scale hydroelectric and nuclear power. Production is highly concentrated on a global basis. In petroleum, for example, a handful of gigantic oil companies and a small number of global production cartels among the oil-producing nations control much of the world's supply and pricing.

Global trade and finance bureaucracies have consistently made rules and policies that strongly favor fossil fuel production above all other options, to the detriment of the many viable alternative systems that would be far more appropriate and efficient and far less environmentally, socially, and politically damaging.

The only alternatives to the fossil fuel—based production that the Bretton

Woods institutions now find acceptable are either large hydroelectric dams or nuclear energy. Both of those share with fossil fuel systems the inherent large-scale centralized attributes that make them appropriate processes for global enterprises alone to control. They both also share the same strong potential for environmental and social catastrophes. So they offer little in the way of alternative possibilities.

Each of the energy systems named has environmental problems that are well enough known that it is probably not necessary to repeat them here, except to mention what is specifically looming as the major crisis of our time and is a direct result of fossil fuel production: rapid and devastating climate change. No world problem demands more immediate attention than this because it will otherwise overwhelm any efforts to achieve sustainable future societies, and it threatens the survival of humans and other species. Nonetheless, fossil fuel production continues to be subsidized by nation-states at a phenomenal rate, amounting to $300 billion globally. The United States alone directly subsidizes these energy systems at more than $20 billion annually. Even this figure, however, does not begin to cover the *full* costs of fossil fuel systems, including staggering environmental damage and the immense investment in military programs to protect vulnerable supply lines as well as the often corrupt oil-producing nations, not to mention actual wars, as in Iraq.

Despite the many environmental, social, and political dangers of fossil fuel systems, major international financial institutions have consistently rewarded enthusiastic financiers and promoters of fossil fuel and other large-scale energy systems, especially in the developing world.

According to a report by the Institute for Policy Studies (IPS) authored by Jim Vallette and Daphne Wysham, the World Bank has financed $13.6 billion worth of energy products since the Rio Earth Summit in 1992, including fifty-one coal, oil, and gas-fired power plants and twenty-six coal mines. These projects will emit thirty-eight billion tons of carbon dioxide over their lifetimes, nearly double the emissions of all countries combined in 1996. Meanwhile, less than 3 percent of the World Bank's energy budget is devoted to alternative, renewable energy systems. Between 1992 and 1998, it spent over twenty-five times more on fossil fuel projects than on renewable energy. As for conservation programs, the bank spent nothing at all despite the many simple programs (like switching a country from incandescent to fluorescent lightbulbs) that would have eliminated a high percent of large-scale fossil fuel developments and would have been faster and cheaper. But the immediate beneficiaries of the World Bank's projects are global corporations, which have been granted 95 percent of the contracts; they would gain nothing from conservation.

The Overseas Private Investment Corporation (OPIC) and the Export-Import Bank (Ex-Im)—U.S. export credit agencies (ECAs) that use taxpayers' monies to subsidize U.S. commercial interests in developing nations—have also devoted billions of dollars to fossil fuel–based energy projects. According to IPS, the cumulative support for coal, oil, and gas projects by Ex-Im and OPIC between 1992 and 1998 totaled $23.2 billion. These projects will ultimately release 29.3 billion tons of carbon dioxide over their lifetimes. There is a similar story for the British Export Credit Guarantee Department, which has backed coal-fired plants in China as well as enormous plants in India, Indonesia, and elsewhere, thus effectively subsidizing such companies as Shell, Amoco, Mitsubishi, Enron, and Texaco.

In most cases, multilateral development banks ignore renewable energy projects and undermine localized systems of production and consumption that could reduce overall energy consumption. Thus, by emphasizing fossil fuel development to meet the demands of globalization, the World Bank and the other development agencies are playing a lead role in accelerating climate change.

Besides these global development and lending bureaucracies, as well as the oil-producing cartels and the oil companies themselves, the most important actors in this crisis are the most developed nations. The United States has been the leading consumer and promoter of fossil fuel usage and the main opponent of meaningful reforms. It even declined to sign the very modest reforms outlined in the Kyoto Protocol on Global Warming, which was endorsed by most other countries.

The United States now uses about 25 percent of the world's oil production, even though its population represents only about 4 percent of the global total. The oil is used largely to service U.S. automobile and other fuel-intensive transportation systems. So dependent has this country become on oil shipments from faraway places—notably Saudi Arabia, which has 25 percent of the world's known oil reserves—that it spends an estimated $25 to $35 billion a year to militarily protect a corrupt Saudi regime and other Middle Eastern sources. Meanwhile, domestic opportunities in the United States for easing the dependency on foreign oil by converting to alternative renewable energy forms have been resisted by the government, and particularly by the oil-friendly George W. Bush administration, as too impractical or expensive (as if wars were not).

Some scholars and critics—notably the London-based New Economics Foundation (NEF) in its report *The Environmental War Economy,* written by Andrew Simms—argue that Western industrial nations have already so overused their proportional share of the global fossil fuel supply and have caused so much more than their proportional share of pollution within the "global atmospheric commons" that they owe a major "ecological debt" (as well as a financial one) to the less developed countries of the world. Many Southern countries agree, and they go so far as to argue that such agreements as the Kyoto protocol must drastically reduce energy use in Northern countries, whereas less developed Southern countries should be granted some time to make up for prior exploitation that has hindered their development. (Southern countries also put forward the argument that in addition to the oil-based ecological debt, Northern countries owe them a major debt based on their ravaging of the biodiversity of the South for some five hundred years. See Box N in chapter 5 for more on this.)

The concept of a global atmospheric commons is amplified by Peter Barnes, founder of Working Assets. In his book *Who Owns the Sky?* Barnes proposes a system by which all citizens of the world are given recognized "property rights" over the atmosphere. They would have rights to determine whether "use" may be made of the atmosphere by any commercial players or whether alternative energy forms are a better choice. If permission is granted for some level of atmospheric pollution—presumably an amount that is tiny by today's standards—high fees would be paid by the commercial parties for this right, and those fees would ultimately go back to individual citizens on an equal basis, per capita by country. Barnes argues that this would reverse present subsidies and unaccountability for energy development and create a disincentive for this form of energy.

Perhaps the most problematic systemic aspect of the global oil-based economy is the inherently long and highly vulnerable supply line between producers and consumers.

The oil must be moved by some combination of supertankers crossing oceans and truckers crossing countries on public highways, or else through vulnerable oil pipelines that traverse thousands of miles of terrain, often in fragile wilderness regions and indigenous lands. These pipelines also span several nation-states with varying political and military climates and varying degrees of protection.

Each of these modes of transport can (and has) brought enormous geopolitical and ecological problems, including recent oil wars. Worst of all, the very length of these supply lines combined with the extreme volatility of oil make them spectacularly vulnerable to deliberate disruption. For example, one oil pipeline running through Colombia's jungles has been bombed more than four hundred times by varying sides of a three-way war that is presently waging there, causing ecological havoc. In Alaska, a lone gunman fired rifle shots into the Alaskan pipeline a few years ago, spilling thirty-five hundred barrels of oil over the fragile tundra. As for the other methods of transport, readers know the many examples of oil tankers spilling their cargo into the ocean and onto beaches, killing wildlife and destroying delicate aquatic ecosystems. The sheer length of these supply lines have made it necessary to spend enormous sums to try to protect them militarily as well as to subsidize cleanup costs. These subsidized costs do not show up in the price of oil at the pump.

Finally, of course, who could possibly forget that its volatility made jet fuel the perfect choice of terrorists on September 11, 2001, when it was delivered by hijacked airplanes with horrifying results? Those attacks on New York and Washington, D.C., in turn led to a war in Afghanistan costing tens of billions of dollars. Tens of billions more are being spent to rebuild Afghanistan and to cover the *annual* costs of U.S. homeland defense. And of course September 11 was used as justification for the U.S. attack on Iraq, at a probable ultimate cost of hundreds of billions of dollars. It is surely fair to include some of these expenses when reckoning the whole bargain that is involved in oil dependency.

## THE PROMISE OF ALTERNATIVE ENERGY SYSTEMS

There is no longer any reason for this unsustainable situation to persist— that is, none other than the immense pressures by the oil companies themselves as they seek to maintain state and global institutional interventions on their behalf. Considering the social, environmental, and security problems intrinsic to fossil fuel–based economies, it is a wonder that this form of energy production has survived to the present at all.

A number of countries have already shown that it is possible to eliminate dependency on electricity generated from nuclear power, which also poses an unnecessary threat to the health and security of millions of people around the world.

- Italy shut down all five of its nuclear reactors between 1987 and 1990, after the accident at Chernobyl and a vote by the Italian people in a referendum against nuclear power.
- Following a referendum in 1980, Sweden announced that it would phase out its twelve nuclear reactors, which generated half of the country's electricity. The first has already been closed as this volume goes to print. A second will close by 2003. New capacity will come largely from energy conservation and wind power.
- Belgium announced in 1999 that it would phase out its seven nuclear reactors, which generate nearly 60 percent of the country's electricity, between 2015 and 2025.
- The Netherlands is closing down its two nuclear reactors by 2003.
- Germany pledged in 2000 to close down all of its nineteen nuclear reactors, which generate 30 percent of its electricity, by 2021. Wind power will replace them.

Right now, most of the technology needed for a complete transformation of our energy infrastructure is already available. We can increase energy efficiency many times over and meet all our remaining needs with a mix of renewable resources: solar, biomass, geothermal, minihydro, micropower turbines, and most imminent and important, wind energy and hydrogen fuel systems; the latter is directly applicable to cars, trucks, airplanes, ships, and all other modes of transit.

None of these alternative technologies are difficult to develop or esoteric; in fact, all are already in use in many places. For example, Denmark already gets 15 percent of its total electricity from wind turbines. Hydrogen and solar energy systems are already powering the U.S. space program and many other military programs. In Germany, BMW is already operating and selling hydrogen-powered cars with conventional engines that are far more efficient than gasoline-powered cars. In Japan, Mazda is converting its rotary engine to hydrogen; it will be ready in 2004. DaimlerChrysler, Ford, Honda, Toyota, and GM are also developing hydrogen fuel cell cars. And the Rocky Mountain Institute—an important technology think tank and research institute directed by Amory Lovins—has completed design and construction of a prototype hydrogen fuel cell "hypercar" that will be inexpensive, has most of the safety and performance features of standard cars, and is claimed to achieve the equivalent of ninety-nine miles per gallon using hydrogen. (See Lovins's book *Hypercars: Materials, Manufacturing, and Policy Implications.*)

Hydrogen has none of the geopolitical problems of oil, and it is *not* scarce. It is, in fact, the most plentiful element in the universe and can be converted directly from water. It can be unlocked from water by electrolysis, using electrical energy from wind turbines, or it can be reformed from natural gas. The process is relatively simple; it does not pollute—its only tailpipe emission is water—and *no global cartel can control it.*

To accelerate the conversion to hydrogen fuel cells, Alvin Duskin, founder and former chief executive of U.S. Windpower Corporation, who now heads the San Francisco–based Committee for the Conversion of the Oil-Based Economy, has made an audacious but viable proposal: use the American upper plains states of Montana, North Dakota, and Minnesota to create a "Saudi Arabia of wind." Duskin says there is more than ample wind blowing steadily across those states "to convert the entire U.S. transportation sector from oil to hydrogen fuel cells within twenty years." It would take only relatively small government support to achieve this, "infinitesimal compared to what the U.S. now spends on war and security to protect oil supplies."

Predictably, the Bush administration has other ideas. In 2003, while giving lip service to the idea of a long-term transition to hydrogen fuel cells, the president announced that he planned to emphasize that the conversion be achieved via huge subsidies to natural gas and oil suppliers. The net gain, as far as the atmosphere is concerned, would therefore be nil, but for his colleagues in the oil industry it would be one of their greatest windfalls. It would also greatly benefit military contractors who will need to stay very busy helping increased U.S. war efforts to protect oil supplies.

Other countries, however, are taking all new ideas very seriously and are moving forward impressively in some areas, particularly in Europe and Canada.

*European Examples*

The British government has sharply separated itself from U.S. policy in the climate area, announcing plans to reduce overall carbon emissions by at least 60 percent by 2050, using a variety of means including major incentives and pressures upon industry. Also, Prime Minister Tony Blair has joined Sweden's Prime Minister Goran Persson to propose that the whole European Union adopt the same 60 percent goal. EU policymakers have already initiated an ambitious legislative agenda introducing Europe-wide emissions trading, and other reductions from improved equipment standards, demand-side management, bio-fuels, and fluorinated gasses, which will be mandatory for all EU nations.

A 2003 report, *Leading by Example: Successful Strategies for Cutting Greenhouse Gas Emissions*, by Michael Northrop of the Rockefeller Brothers Fund (New York), cites an additional long list of unilateral efforts now under way among European countries, and others. Germany, for example, has already reduced its emissions by 19 percent below 1990 levels, and German officials now predict a 40 percent reduction by 2020. Germany is also moving quickly to develop renewable power, recently adding some 1200 megawatts from new wind turbines. In addition, the German government is offering low-cost loans and other incentives to small businesses and homeowners for energy retrofits, efficiency improvements, renewable energy generation, and innovative finance schemes that the German government believes will have the added advantage of making the German economy stronger and more competitive.

Northrop's report also indicates that Sweden has committed to a 50 percent reduction in greenhouse gas emissions by 2050. France's target is a 75 percent reduction by 2050, and Denmark has pledged a 21 percent reduction by 2010. Denmark also plans a new series of large-scale offshore wind farms in the North Sea and the Baltic that will generate half of the country's power by 2030. Iceland has begun work to become the first country in the world to use hydrogen fuel cell technology to displace *all* of its present fossil-fuel usage by 2030. And the Netherlands is also developing a detailed 50-year plan for similar greenhouse gas reductions.

*Canadian and Australian Examples*

Meanwhile, across the ocean in Canada, Lester Brown, founder of the Worldwatch Institute, reports that the David Suzuki Foundation (Vancouver) and Climate Action Network have produced a remarkable plan that would cut carbon emissions by 50 percent before 2030. In Canada's most populous province, the Ontario Clear Air Alliance has published a plan to eliminate coal-burning power plants by 2015. "The plan is now supported by all three major political parties in Canada," according to Brown.

Michael Northrop cites the example of the Canadian province of Manitoba, which has made reducing GHG emissions "the centerpiece of a comprehensive economic development plan." Manitoba has instituted an array of measures to reduce short- and long-term emissions, eliminate coal from its energy mix, increase funding for energy efficiency, encourage substitution of ethanol into gasoline, develop wind and geothermal power, introduce low-impact hydro, and begin transitioning to hydrogen fuel cells for transport. Manitoba has also joined with the provinces of Ontario and Saskatchewan to assess development of a national clean energy grid in Canada that could distribute wind and low-impact hydro throughout the country via long-distance transmission lines. "Through these actions," writes Northrop, "Manitoba believes it can generate thousands of new jobs and be a zero-net-emissions economy in only twelve to fifteen years."

The Canadian government is firmly behind this kind of effort. It recently granted (U.S.) $250 million toward grants to help municipalities develop ideas for reducing GHG emissions. Already some 103 Canadian cities and countries have announced their determination to reduce GHG emissions, while Toronto became the first city in the world to commit to a 20 percent reduction below 1998 levels, saving $2.7 annually via energy efficiency.

Similar action is being taken in Australia, where 175 municipalities, home to two-thirds of the country's population, are participating in a Cities for Climate Protection program. Forty-two of these municipalities have already implemented local abatement plans; according to Northrop, "This is the fastest pace of any group in the world."

In a 2002 progress report, Australia cited 780 actions including building retrofits, street lighting efficiency, vehicle efficiency, methane capture, and green purchasing practices. Meanwhile, the province of Victoria has introduced more than sixty measures expected to reduce emissions by 7.5 percent by 2010.

This kind of *subfederal* action seems now to be spreading all over the world. (We will report on similar activity in the United States at the end of this chapter.)

Clearly, change is under way. Lester Brown has said that "electricity and hydrogen can meet all the energy needs of a modern society." And Seth Dunn, also of Worldwatch, in his paper "Hydrogen Futures," predicts a nearly complete transition from fossil fuels to hydrogen within a century, although it could be argued that we should move much faster than that if we are to save the global climate. Dr. Ty Cashman, former secretary of energy of California, says that "an informed global public may be all that is required to bring an end to the climate-destabilizing fossil fuel era." And former energy executive Alvin Duskin says, "The only thing limiting the immediate conversion is the assumption that hydrogen is more expensive to produce than oil, but only if you ignore the repeating military costs from protecting oil suppliers and fighting wars, and the environmental costs from cleanups of oil spills and the like. If you delivered those costs to the pumping station, hydrogen would already be far cheaper. In any case, within a few years the unit price will be lower than gasoline, no matter how the costs are calculated."

In a comprehensive report, *Energy Innovations: A Prosperous Path to a Clean Environment,* the Cambridge, Massachusetts–based Union of Concerned Scientists (UCS), founded by the late Nobel laureate Dr. Henry Kendall, undertook a thorough analysis of steps needed to make a transition from fossil fuels to an energy future without the myriad political, economic, environmental, and social harms that are inherent in the present model. In addition to endorsing most of the alternative systems already mentioned, UCS cites advances in membrane technologies, advanced gas turbines, and integrated green building designs that would further reduce dependency on either fossil fuels or nuclear sources. UCS also suggests a highly innovative set of new tax strategies that could reallocate costs to motivate higher energy efficiency and lower emissions while avoiding any overall increase of taxes and fees.

Other well-circulated tax ideas include a so-called carbon tax on fossil fuels and a Tobin tax on all international financial transactions. This latter tax could be earmarked directly for the conversion away from a fossil fuel economy. It should be remembered that thirty years ago, production tax credits helped kick-start a vital new turn to solar and wind. But when oil prices plummeted and Ronald Reagan took office, all that changed. It must now be revived again.

All of the preceding is aside from the great contribution that could be made to this transition from even minimal efforts at direct energy conservation. Andrew Simms, of the New Economics Foundation, points out that energy has been conserved on a mass scale with enormous success in many countries in periods of crisis. During World War II, for example, the United Kingdom reduced its fossil fuel use by 80 percent, yet still mounted a major military effort. The United States had similar results on the occasions in its history when energy conservation became a national priority—unlike the present, when additional consumption is the national goal. In recent years, countries such as Germany, Japan, and Sweden have drastically reduced their energy use without notable diminishment in lifestyle. Indeed, such changes would likely bring a far more peaceful, healthful existence within newly stabilized and localized democratic systems.

If we converted now to this kind of combination of new energy sources for all electricity and transportation, we would immediately achieve the following positive outcomes:

- Greenhouse gas emissions (global warming) would be reduced by at least 30 percent in two decades, and much more after that.
- Dependency on expensive, environmentally disastrous long-distance shipment of petroleum would be eliminated.
- The powers of corrupt, undemocratic governments and gigantic industry cartels would be undermined.
- Vulnerability to oil price and supply shocks that bring global economic crises would be reduced.
- Military expenditures for the protection of oil-producing nations and the supply lines that connect them to their customers would be reduced.
- New jobs in more labor-intensive localized alternative energy fields would be created.
- The primary contributor to air and land pollution as well as acid rain would be eliminated.
- The impact on indigenous peoples of the world, whose lands are often targeted for exploitation and invasion for their oil reserves, would be lessened.
- Vulnerability to accidents or terrorist attacks would be reduced. (Most experts believe that a hydrogen-powered jetliner striking a skyscraper would have produced no explosion at all.)

The reports we have cited here are only a few of dozens of recent reports and books that demonstrate why a transition from fossil fuels is practical, viable, and desirable. (See the sources, at the end of this volume, for many more.) Clearly, there is no longer any reason to continue to be held hostage to an energy system that has, as part of its inherent package, such grave environmental, political, and military challenges and benefits only large corporations and political tyrants. We have the technologies and know-how to convert to energy forms that offer permanent benefits to the environment, public safety, and democracy.

To increase the political viability of this transformation, many NGOs and some government agencies are circulating draft domestic sustainable energy statutes, as well as draft international treaties, to establish independent international agencies to work with and lead governments in making these changes. Among the more comprehensive and widely circulated is an international sustainable energy fund statute prepared by the New York–based Global Resource Action Center for the Environment (GRACE). A full draft was released at the World Summit on Sustainable Development in Johannesburg in August 2002 (see www.gracelinks.org). The fund would support sustainable energy programs for the world's two billion poor and would finance them with the savings from the phaseout of government subsidies to fossil fuels. Imagine the impact if such a fund were established and the fossil fuel lending of the international financial institutions and government export credit agencies were eliminated.

Michael Northrop argues that the people of most states and local municipalities are way ahead of national politicians, especially in the United States. "Growing evidence suggests that a real movement has begun at the *subfederal* level to lower greenhouse gas emissions, often at rates equal to or better than those proposed in any international accord." He offers a comprehensive list of grassroots, municipal, state, and even corporate actions in the United States that go well beyond anything the federal government is doing. The following are a few examples from the list:

- Six New England states, together with five eastern Canadian provinces, have agreed to reduce greenhouse gas emissions by 70 to 80 percent, to help stabilize the global climate.
- California, the world's fifth largest economy, has sharply reduced allowable carbon emissions from automobiles to well below the Kyoto standard. It has also improved building codes, adopted energy-efficiency

standards for household appliances, increased state funding for energy efficiency, established tax credits for solar and wind power systems, and set up the country's first registry for GHG emissions data. It has also created the largest state-funded energy research program and has set up a unique program to export clean energy technology abroad. California's program is so effective that the Bush administration has attacked it and is trying to create new federal laws to override California's.

The California cities of San Francisco and Oakland have made similar dedicated moves, and also mandated a short-term switch to renewable systems for 40 percent of their energy needs, while self-constructing renewable energy infrastructures.

(Randy Hayes, past president of the Commission on the Environment in San Francisco, reports that the city has also mandated plans for the following: 20 percent reduction of $CO_2$ emissions by 2012; zero waste by 2020; and 100 percent production of electricity from renewable sources by 2030. San Francisco also passed a $100 million bond issue for renewable energy and efficiency projects. It established the world's first "Hydrogen City" program, the first tidal power project in the San Francisco Bay Area, and the first precautionary principle ordinance in the United States, as well as instituting bans on GE foods in city services, toxics in city parks, arsenic-treated wood in the city, and mercury thermometers. Hayes is now working with the city of Oakland to institute similar new measures.)

- New York State has announced an emissions reduction target of 10 percent below 1990 levels by the year 2020 and a goal of 25 percent of the state's electrical generation from renewable resources by 2012. New York has also adopted California's tough auto emissions standards, and a series of tax credits and incentives to lower emissions across the board.
- Massachusetts has adopted the country's first law regulating carbon emissions from power plants, created a Renewable Energy Trust Fund for energy efficiency, instituted a $CO_2$ offset program for new utilities, and is planning a full series of conservation and efficiency measures.
- The states of New Jersey, Connecticut, Pennsylvania, Maine, New Hampshire, Rhode Island, and Vermont are all developing comprehensive long-term clean energy programs.

- Twelve states have created a Clean Energy States Alliance, which is aiming to build a robust domestic clean-energy market, using joint strategies to accelerate production of solar and wind technologies, hydrogen fuel cells, and other technologies. The alliance is seeking investors as partners.
- Forty states have introduced new metering rules that allow excess energy generated at home by solar, wind, fuel cells, or other renewable systems to be returned to the energy grid for use elsewhere. This reduces the cost to households wanting to invest in renewables.
- At the city and county levels, 144 municipalities have committed to major reductions in greenhouse gas emissions, as well as complete energy efficiency programs, retrofittings, and other programs. Portland, Oregon, for example, has increased public transit by 65 percent since 1990, and recycling by 55 percent. Portland has also created strong public-private partnerships for energy efficiency in residential and public buildings. The city estimates that these efficiency programs have saved city businesses and residences more than $300 million since 1990.

Northrop's report offers many more examples of municipal and state actions, as well as innovative schemes by associations of hospitals, faith communities, universities, and other like-minded communities. Most compelling, says Northrop, is that these moves are extremely cost-effective and even profitable: "Companies and cities, in particular, appear to be able to document direct cost savings from their energy-efficiency programs."

There are also encouraging signs that even some large corporations are altering policy. Du Pont, for example, cut its GHG emissions by 67 percent between 1990 and 2000, and hopes for a total 75 percent reduction from 1990 levels. NorskeCanada has cut emissions by 54 percent below 1990 levels and by 2005 expects to be 75 percent below 1990 levels. Swiss Re announced it will be "greenhouse neutral" by 2013. Other notable efforts are being made by BP, IKEA, Stora Enso (Finland), Alcoa Aluminum, Shell International, Cinergy, and Nuon. Most promising is that all have reported major cost savings from these programs.

Another impressive initiative was announced in March 2004 by a new coalition of American Indian leaders and 150 American cities interested in climate protection. Twenty-three Indian reservations in the Great Plains have the potential for as much as 200 gigawatts of wind power. The

Intertribal Council on Utility Policy says it is working with 150 U.S. cities that are part of Local Governments for Sustainability to help them convert from nonrenewable energy to wind. (A remarkable new report by native activist Winona La Duke, *Indigenous Peoples, Power, and Politics: A Renewable Future for the Seventh Generation,* documents the history of Indian reservations in the United States being used as energy resource colonies, and the current push to reverse that in favor of locally controlled renewable systems.)

Although these examples of grassroots actions are still insignificant on the larger plane, they do signify an awakening public. And getting the United States to take real action is critical. Although the rest of the world community is willing to take action without the United States, a strengthened subfederal reductions movement connected to federal policymaking could speed the transition along.

## Transportation Systems

In the previous section, we briefly mentioned some implications of an expanded global transportation infrastructure. Built to service the global economy, it brings a multitude of negative consequences. With export production as a central feature of free trade, there has been a massive increase in ocean shipping, highway transport, air cargo transport, rail, and so forth, with a tremendous corresponding increase in infrastructure development. The latter includes new highways, seaports, airports, canals, and pipelines, often built in pristine wilderness areas, on coral reefs, in indigenous lands, and in rural communities. Considerable social problems have resulted in some instances, but the environmental problems are also crucial, not the least of which is the dramatic acceleration of climate change.

### THREE PRIMARY MODES

Let's look briefly at the three primary modes of transport.

#### Ocean Shipping

Ocean shipping has expanded more than tenfold since the 1950s, primarily because of increased commodity export activity from economic globalization. Ocean shipping accounts for more than 90 percent of commodity trade shipments, with the industry consuming more than 140 million tons of fuel annually, polluting oceans, destroying wildlife, and emitting carbon dioxide. Particularly problematic is that most ocean shipping is fueled by very low-quality oil known as "Bunker C," an extremely heavy polluter. Many experts predict a doubling of transoceanic shipping activity over the next ten years.

### Air Transport

A smaller amount of cargo is shipped by air than by sea or by land; it is by far the least efficient means of transporting goods to market. Nonetheless, air cargo is the fastest growing transport sector. Boeing forecasts a tripling of air cargo activity by 2017. The results would be dire for the environment. As mentioned in Box D in chapter 2, each ton of freight that moves by air uses forty-nine times as much fuel per kilometer as the same goods carried on ships. Worse, aircraft emissions are made at high altitudes, where the impact of emissions on the greenhouse effect is maximized.

Increases in air miles and new airports are the result not only of shipments of commodities but also of an exponential increase in business and tourist air travel in the global economy. Between 1980 and 1996, the number of tourists traveling internationally increased from 260 million to 590 million, and they traveled mostly by air. This growth, in turn, increases tourist infrastructures to service the larger population of travelers: development in pristine places of new hotels, golf courses, marinas; use of high-speed boats and off-road vehicles; construction of entertainment and restaurant complexes; and so on. In some parts of the world, this invasion of tourists has been extremely unwelcome because it often pushes indigenous populations away from traditional sustainable livelihoods in agriculture and fishing. Some lose their ability to survive while others are converted into maids, waiters, and bellboys serving wealthy foreign tourists. The cultural impact is devastating. The new ecotourism trend has not improved matters much, though some native communities are attempting now to make compromises that they believe they may somehow be able to control.

### Trucking

Freight movement across land has also increased sharply because of economic globalization. Europe, for example, has seen a tripling of transborder truck traffic, from four hundred billion ton-kilometers in 1970 to twelve hundred billion in 1997. The conversion of agriculture to industrial production for export has drastically increased "food miles," or the distance that food travels from source to plate, often amounting to thousands of miles in the global economy at great environmental cost. (See "Agriculture and Food Systems" in the next chapter.) From 1986 to 1991, for example, the distance that food traveled increased by 19 percent over previous levels, even though the total volume of food shipment was up only 8 percent.

In the United States in 1994, trucks traveled 182 billion miles on U.S. interstate highways, whereas total intercity truck transport was about 900 billion miles.

To accommodate such a spectacular increase in truck travel, vast new networks of highways and railroads are being built all over the world. The European Union alone is building twelve thousand kilometers of new highways to help further market integration throughout Europe. A similar picture prevails globally.

About 60 percent of the world's use of oil goes directly toward transportation activities, and this percentage is increasing annually.

## SUBSIDIES

None of this growth in transport activity could take place without the hundreds of billions of dollars that governments spend on transportation subsidies. We have already mentioned $300 billion in direct subsidies worldwide for fossil fuel production, including tax incentives for oil companies. These subsidies are an important reason why prices at the pump stay relatively low. But if we included the money that governments around the world invest in roads, rail, airports, seaports, and other transportation infrastructures, the direct subsidies to oil companies would be dwarfed. *If that kind of gigantic subsidy regime went instead to public mass transportation systems and alternative transportation schemes, many of our problems would be solved.* The reason they do not comes down to the immense power of global corporations to control governments and international bureaucracies.

Like nearly every aspect of the globalization model, the transport industry is characterized by oligopolistic conditions in every sector. Ten automobile companies account for about 65 percent of global car and truck pro-

duction; nine oil companies account for about 80 percent of petroleum production. According to the U.S.–based Institute for Policy Studies, of the one
hundred largest economies in the world—this includes nation-states as well
as giant corporations—twelve are oil or automobile companies. These companies illustrate the advantages of global scale augmented by favorable rules
and free entry interventions from global economic bureaucracies like the
WTO.

It could be argued that the most important single act to improve the
health of the planet and the quality of urban life would be to lessen the volume of international and long-distance transport. This goal can only be
achieved by consciously reversing present priorities favoring large-scale
export-oriented global economies and instead invoking the principle of *subsidiarity:* emphasizing local economies, using local resources and labor, and
primarily benefiting local communities. As we have said earlier, we do not
suggest eliminating international trade, only that it become the last option
rather than the first. It should be saved for the times when local needs cannot be locally satisfied. The net result of this conscious reversal toward subsidiarity would be a swift downturn in export and import activity, a diminishment of the volume of transport activity, and a quick benefit for the
global atmosphere and climate and global ecosystems and habitats. It could
also mean a revival of local economies, especially if savings in subsidies now
directed at global transport infrastructures were used for local infrastructures
servicing local needs. In turn, this would mean a diminishment of the powers of global energy and oil companies and the kinds of geopolitical problems that result from this situation.

## THE PRIVATE CAR

Although every means of transport has intrinsic problems, the private automobile has the greatest impact of all. By now it should be clear that one of
the worst decisions ever made by modern society was to embrace the concept of the private car and the internal combustion engine at the turn of the
twentieth century, and then to glorify it, subsidize it, and design all of life
around it.

Even in less developed nations, the private car has become the predom-
inant factor in the organization of everyday life. Urban environments have

been centered on accommodating it, finding ways to move it without congestion, parking it, regulating its speed, controlling its dangers. And yet its impacts are unabated. According to the World Resources Institute, in 1990 there were already 580 million four-wheeled motor vehicles on the road; by 2010, the estimate is 800 million.

Automobile companies have been exceedingly effective in creating advertising images of the joys of private car ownership as the apex of social achievement, even in poverty-stricken countries. In the United States, as elsewhere, automobile companies in the early and mid-twentieth century were able to lobby governments to destroy very workable and sustainable transportation systems—light rail, in particular—and to replace them with highways, new infrastructures, and auto accommodations. This happened especially in California, notably in Los Angeles and San Francisco. A wonderful light rail system that bound together the entire San Francisco Bay Area was eliminated, only to be replaced twenty years later by a new, very expensive Bay Area Rapid Transit System (BART) that does not cover sufficient area and is far more costly to use. In the United States, urban passenger transportation systems are now more than 90 percent auto-based.

Automobiles have been the primary technology in the post–Industrial Revolution era to reorganize life on earth and bring us to the urban situation we are now in.

Problems with the automobile do not begin and end with the fuel it uses or with how efficiently it operates. True, it would be hard to imagine any technology less efficient than a large structure built of steel, rubber, and hundreds of other materials, weighing 2,000 pounds, to carry a single passenger weighing 150 pounds while burning enormous quantities of gasoline to do so. But the ramifications of the car are far broader than that.

Aside from a dependence on oil, the private car uses more scarce resources in its construction than any other product on earth. Highways and concrete now cover virtually every region of the developed world and much of the rest of the world too. Noise from cars is omnipresent, even in wilderness regions, comparable to a society-wide case of tinnitus. The many kinds of pollution that automobiles bring include smog, acid rain, lead poisoning, ozone depletion, and others. The problem of solid waste disposal for used automobiles, which is often toxic, is also reaching crisis proportions, especially as automobile manufacturers continue to bombard us with appeals to throw away cars we may have only recently purchased.

Some of the world's most diversely interesting cities are being rapidly homogenized in service to the car. Mexico City, London, Manila, Bangkok, Rome, Paris, Athens, Sao Paulo, Tokyo, Madrid, Jakarta: like New York, Chicago, and Los Angeles they are being rapidly ruined by the domination, congestion, smog, noise, and danger from cars. According to a report by Logan Perkins, published in *Livable Cities,* more than fifty thousand people in the United States alone are killed in automobile accidents annually, with pedestrians counting as one-fifth of those. Throughout the world, the experience of urban life is being unified but at the lowest common denominator—a new standard of unpleasantness and dysfunction. All this is to benefit a small number of gigantic automobile and oil companies who have actively, over decades, lobbied against and otherwise destroyed alternative systems.

### ECOCITIES

Recently, there have been a series of important ecocity conferences as urban areas try to gain control of their transportation systems and other ecological and social problems caused by the present trend of sprawl—housing that requires longer distance transport, usually by private car, and separates life's functions. Jobs are a hundred miles from home, shopping is somewhere else altogether, and public places are largely absent.

Already, some cities have moved to the forefront of these experiments in redesigning transportation, notably Porto Alegre and Curitiba in Brazil (see Box O) as well as Copenhagen, Stockholm, and Portland, Oregon, among others. Once democratic processes are under way, solutions are not complex, and they have the advantages of being less costly than present systems and far more convivial. The goal is obviously to reduce the impacts of the noisy, dangerous, gas-guzzling, dominant global transportation technologies and replace them with more efficient (in terms of material and energy consumption per capita) public transit systems. These include a combination of high-speed rail (for long-distance travel) and, for cities, light rail, buses that can run on fast dedicated lanes, and greater emphasis on bicycles for short-distance private travel. These can be augmented by taxis—over the long haul they are far cheaper to use than cars—or by flexible jitney and shuttle services. Accommodations for the private car might eventually cease. In addition, cities around the world have already begun to experiment to varying degrees with excluding cars from parts or all of the city. Amsterdam allows no private cars at all in most of the city center, while accommodating bicycles, light rail, and very small lorries needed for business purposes, as well as canal barges. In Copenhagen, 32 percent of all trips are by bicycle. And throughout Western industrial countries, bicycle riders are undertaking demonstrations on wheels—often under the banner "Critical Mass"—demanding dedicated bike paths, access to public transportation with their bikes, and other accommodations.

Lester Brown of the Worldwatch Institute predicts that bicycle manufacture, like industries devoted to hydrogen energy and solar and wind energy, will be among the great growth industries of the near future. "Because the bicycle is nonpolluting, is frugal in its use of land, and provides the exercise much needed in sedentary societies, future reliance on it is expected to grow," says Brown. "As recently as 1965, the production of cars and bikes was essentially the same, but today more than twice as many bikes as cars are manufactured each year. Among industrial countries, the urban transport model being pioneered in the Netherlands and Denmark, where bikes are featured predominantly, gives a sense of the bicycle's future role worldwide."

There are some regrettable anomalies, however. With the opening to free market activity in places like China, and especially now with China's admission to the WTO, it will soon be experiencing exactly the opposite of the positive steps that we've described. Major global automobile companies are eager to move their production facilities to low-wage China and to push hard for tax breaks and other accommodations, to convert China from a country where the bicycle has been the favored transport device to the private car. This kind of pressure is also being applied in Vietnam.

Of course, it will be helpful in the long run, in order to reduce dependence on the private car, to redesign urban environments altogether so they are no longer spread out across great distances, as are Los Angeles, London, and Bangkok. There are so many good new ideas for altering such arrangements. *The ultimate goal is to reduce the distance that people need to travel, just as we also try to reduce the distance, in other contexts, that goods need to travel from source to market.*

Among the emerging ideas are the reinvigoration of urban minicities—cities within larger cities. This effectively attempts to reestablish the smaller-scale townships that existed for centuries but later merged into metropolises. London, for example, merged dozens of smaller towns, like Richmond, Hampstead, Stratford, and Kensington. New York merged Brooklyn, Chelsea, The Bronx, and so on. Tokyo has likewise merged towns that were formerly disconnected. Now the idea is to design smaller minicities that are fully integrated and offer jobs, parks, communal spaces, residence, entertainment, even wildlife. This requires thinking of cities as three-dimensional rather than "flat," with taller buildings, smaller streets, many pockets of convivial spaces and markets, urban gardens, and larger open spaces surrounding them. According to Richard Register, president of Urban Ecology

---

### BOX O: CURITIBA: AN ECOLOGICAL CITY

By Simon Retallack, The Ecologist

Although it is nearly impossible to make large modern cities fully sustainable, there are examples of cities that have accomplished significant ecological achievements. Freiburg in Germany is one such case. Another is the city of Curitiba in Brazil. As Paul Hawken and Amory and Hunter Lovins explain in their book Natural Capitalism: The Next Industrial Revolution, Curitiba, a city with the population of Houston, has been revolutionized under the stewardship of its mayor, Jaime Lemer.

The downtown was made into pedestrian streets and covered with tens of thousands of flowers; low-income houses were built near jobs, shops, and recreation; schools, clinics, and shops were built in the suburbs to minimize travel; new buses were built and bus lanes created to provide a highly efficient, reliable, comfortable, rapid, and entirely self-financing public transport system that is now used by three-fourths of the city's commuters; and cyclists use one hundred miles of well-designed, traffic-separated bike paths. As a result, Curitiba now has no traffic problem, has the cleanest urban air in Brazil, and saves seven million gallons of fuel a year.

Sixteen large new parks were created and hundreds of thousands of trees planted, and regulations and tax incentives were created to protect and increase private gardens and woodlands, so that public green space in the city has expanded from 5 to 581 square feet per person in twenty-five years. The city has recruited over five hundred nonpolluting industries, which provide one-fifth of its total jobs. They are all required to dispose of their solid wastes on their own land to encourage firms to reduce, reuse, and re-

CONTINUED

in Berkeley, California, "Tall buildings and dense downtowns are not a cut-and-dried negative like smog or toxic waste, abject poverty, or epidemic disease. In the right context, and built in an ecologically well-tuned manner, heights and densities of a relatively high level are part of the solution to a long list of problems. For example, they save acreage for agriculture and nature; promote energy-saving, non- or low-polluting pedestrian, bicycle, and transit access; make commerce and culture and social diversity of all kinds easily available; and can be built to provide multilevel solar greenhouses, rooftop gardens, fruit trees along streets, restored creeks, and renewed biodiversity within a city."

In his book *Ecocity Berkeley*, Register writes: "Instead of thinking of going places, think in terms of being places. That is, think in terms of estab-

---

BOX O: CONTINUED

cycle. In fact, nearly everything is recycled in Curitiba, not least because of an initiative that now has 70 percent of households sort recyclables for three-times-weekly curbside collections. As a result, landfill use has been reduced significantly, together with threats to groundwater. Families can get garden plots in the suburbs to grow food for their own use and sale—the city even offers instruction in home-growing medicinal plants—and environmental education starts in early childhood and is integrated across the curriculum. Consequently, a city has been created that is both enormously pleasing to live in and probably more ecologically sustainable than any other in the world.

But people elsewhere on the planet do not have to wait for an inspirational mayor to win office and transform their cities. Groups of people have long collectively decided to pursue ways of life that are ecologically sustainable, inde-

pendent of the unsustainable world that surrounds them. One such movement that has sprung up in recent times is the Landless Workers Movement (MST) in Brazil, one of the country's largest and most dynamic social movements. As Jan Rocha explains, on the land that they have occupied, many farm organically and set up cooperatives to produce milk, fruit, flour, and other products. In Sao Paulo, MST settlers are planting thousands of saplings to counteract the erosion produced by the years of deforestation by ranchers. In the Amazon, they have begun replanting mahogany and native species such as the jaborandi to counter the effects of slash-and-burn agriculture. The MST has also organized protests against genetically modified soya planted illegally by large farm operations in the south, and MST schools foster environmental awareness. (For more on MST, see the section "People's Alternative Initiatives" in chapter 8.)

lishing desirable places close to one another. Transportation is what you have to get to places that are inconveniently located; the less the better. The less [transport] that is necessary, the healthier your life and your environment. If diversity is designed into the city, commuting is minimized, [and] local and long distance travel can be reserved for special occasions."

The end of flat cities sprawled over the landscape and their replacement with three-dimensional, taller, denser environments that emphasize footpaths, bike paths, public transit, urban gardens, restored creeks, universal recycling, and use of building materials and energy systems that are ecologically appropriate are subjects now under discussion in hundreds of communities around the world. Such ideas are examples of a kind of "devolution" in urban design that expresses a changed focus, away from dependence on ecologically and socially damaging transport systems, and a furthering of the concept of subsidiarity.

Lester Brown summarizes it this way: "An economy that is in sync with the earth's ecosystems will contrast profoundly with the polluting, disruptive, and ultimately self-destructing economy of today—the fossil fuel—based, automobile-centered, throwaway economy."

## Manufacturing Systems

A major development over the last half-century is that manufacturing processes in just about every country in the world have become ever more interconnected within a global production system that is increasingly complex, geographically far-flung, and in the control of relatively few global corporations. Manufacturers around the globe employ hundreds of millions of people in sectors as diverse as apparel, automobiles, and shipbuilding. But in any given product line, each country's involvement has tended to be only one cog in a larger "global assembly line."

Few countries carry production from start to finish. In the United States, for example, textiles, autos, electronics, food manufacturing, and many other industries are constructed as part of a long process, where discreet parts are shipped back and forth across the world in ships, processed or assembled in different places—often on different continents—and then finally sold in markets thousands of miles from their material sources or the factories where they were built. A car, for example, may contain production elements from as many as sixteen countries. A large apparel company usually sub-contracts to hundreds of manufacturing facilities in dozens of countries. As we have already discussed, the amount of global shipping that such a system requires represents a major social, public health, and environmental threat in itself.

This shift in production away from traditional local systems, where countries were able to produce products from start to finish, has had a tremendous impact on domestic governance systems and prerogatives. Under globalization, countries' laws may be subordinated to WTO trade and investment rules that assist global corporations to operate efficiently in this new manner. The shift has also had effects on labor and the environment.

Workers of the world find this new arrangement unfortunate from many perspectives. With corporate mobility accelerated by globalization rules, and with manufacturers now free to roam from country to country and to invest freely in resources and production facilities, workers in every industry in every country have lost some of the leverage provided by once powerful domestic labor unions. One aspect of the weakened powers of labor unions was very much on public display during the U.S. presidential campaign of 2004. The problem of global "outsourcing," where corporations send some job functions that were formerly domestic to other countries, particularly in the telecommunications, insurance, and manufacturing fields, was angrily cited as having significant responsibility for the tremendous loss of jobs over the past several years in the United States. As unions have weakened relative to global corporations, workers have been pushed into wage competition with workers in other countries, bringing a downward spiral of wages and working conditions everywhere. Under a globalized manufacturing system, labor unions are daily threatened with pressures to allow worker "give-backs" and wage concessions for people trying to keep jobs on this global assembly line, often managed thousands of miles away. In fact, the existence of strong labor unions in a country can often be sufficient reason for global corporations to stay away altogether, since there are many other countries that are less worker-friendly. The net result is to create a greater power imbalance between corporations and workers than ever before, making it more difficult to counter sweatshop conditions or abusive practices. However, the rising global justice movement has supported unions and other worker movements through a series of public campaigns against apparel, footware, and other firms that have used sweatshop labor. (Many IFG associates are participating in a more intense investigation of labor and globalization issues in a dialogue organized by Focus on the Global South, which brings together union and NGO leaders from around the world.)

Chapter 6 describes the principle of *subsidiarity*—bringing power and economic activity toward the local. Subsidiarity can help correct at least some of the injustices of a production system in which power imbalances are inherent in the design of large-scale, stateless corporate manufacturing that functions without any transparency or accountability. Corporations that are more locally rooted, as chapter 9 describes, would need to face the fact that the workers are also customers and neighbors—a far different arrangement than the global one.

But if democracy and workers' rights are directly affected by the present global manufacturing system, there is an even larger context to consider. Present global manufacturing processes are also a direct threat to all life on earth, and to sustainability. The rest of this section will focus on those issues.

In 1981, Lester Brown defined a sustainable society as one that is able to satisfy its needs without diminishing the chances of future generations. The same definition was used by the World Commission on Environment and Development (in the Brundlandt report). By that definition, current manufacturing processes are leading society in exactly the opposite direction than it should be headed.

At present, global manufacturing and production processes consume more than 220 billion tons of resources annually, all taken from the earth's "natural capital"—oceans, forests, plants, plains, soils, mines, and all other aspects of biodiversity.

Standard production practice today is for resources to be gathered wherever on earth they are, then processed, formed into usable products, and shipped back and forth across the planet. A high percentage of the materials are wasted in the mining and manufacturing parts of the cycle, as well as through shipping, and again when the finished products are discarded. We call this whole process the "take-make-waste" cycle.

Physicist Fritjof Capra, in his recent book *The Hidden Connections: A Science for Sustainable Living*, offers a comprehensive argument for why it does not have to be this way. He asserts that new concepts of systemic practice have the potential to convert nearly 100 percent of the present waste production into raw materials for further economic activity, in a continuously beneficial cycle that does not deplete the planet. The new view suggests that "all waste is food" for further technical activity or, if it is organic matter and properly handled, for recycling back to nature's own processes.

Many of the ideas that Capra and others propose are entirely compatible with the primacy of subsidiarity as applied to manufacturing. A far more localized, democratic, community-oriented system would avoid most of the social and environmental pitfalls now inherent in the global system.

The following is a short list of some of the principles now being proposed for a more sustainable manufacturing process.

### FULL COST ACCOUNTING

The depletion of forests and topsoils, overfishing of the oceans, and the dissemination of toxic wastes into soils, rivers, and oceans are currently being accounted for in two misleading ways. First, resource depletion and mining are measured as being *beneficial* to gross national product (GNP) and gross domestic product (GDP) because they are indicators of increased economic activity. In fact, however, they ought to be considered negative factors because they decrease the long-term ability of societies to sustain themselves. (See further discussion on this subject in the last section of this chapter, "Standards of Measurement.") Second, these depletions and toxic outfalls bring significant costs for cleanup or renewal, costs that are invariably externalized. That is, corporations creating these costs do not pay for them; taxpayers pay through government cleanup programs. These amount to government subsidies of wasteful practices by corporations. It is little wonder, therefore, that natural resources corporations make billions in profits: their resources are essentially free.

Nor do corporations have to pay for the external social costs that derive from their activities—costs of health care from toxic processes and pollutants, costs of welfare for people driven from farmlands or forests. Bringing externalized costs back where they belong, into the operating costs and balance sheets of corporations and into the prices of products they produce, might do more than any other single change to create a realistic measure of impacts and costs on the earth, people, and communities.

But President George W. Bush announced that the U.S. government will no longer require corporations to pay their share of the cleanup costs—amounting to many billions of dollars—for toxic Superfund sites in the United States. Either taxpayers will pay, or the environment will not be cleaned at all. Sadly, this approach is typical in the United States and\in most other countries too.

A transition to full cost accounting is a crucial component of a socially or ecologically sustainable society.

### CLOSE THE LOOP DESIGN: ZERO WASTE

New industrial models are now being developed that attempt to mimic nature's fundamental design principle—no longer a cycle of "take-make-waste" but one that approaches production as a whole system, leaving no waste at all. This is sometimes called a "closed-loop system." Fritjof Capra puts it this way: "The principle 'waste equals food' means that all products and materials manufactured by industry, as well as the *wastes* generated in the manufacturing process, must eventually provide nourishment for something new. A sustainable business organization would be embedded in an 'ecology of organizations,' in which the waste of any one organization would be a resource for another. In such a sustainable industrial system, the total outflow of each organization—its products and wastes—would be perceived and treated as resources cycling through the system."

"To realize how radical an approach this is," Capra says, "we need to realize that our current businesses throw away most of the resources they take from nature. For example, when we extract cellulose from wood to make paper, we cut down forests but use only 20 to 25 percent of the trees, discarding the remaining 75 to 80 percent as waste. Beer breweries extract only 8 percent of the nutrients from barley or rice for fermentation; palm oil is a mere 4 percent of the palm tree's biomass; and coffee beans are 3.7 percent of the coffee bush."

Capra says that new ecological "clusters" of industries have already sprung up in many parts of the world and are actively being promoted by such organizations as Zero Emissions Research and Initiatives (ZERI), founded in Europe by Gunter Pauli in the 1990s. "Taking nature as its model," says Capra, "ZERI tries to eliminate the very idea of waste." That is, it tries to achieve zero net material consumption and therefore causes virtu- ally no pollution or resource depletion. It also brings a major reduction in health problems that result from incineration and dumping.

Amory and Hunter Lovins and Paul Hawken make a distinction between two kinds of waste, biological and technical. *Biological nutrients* must always be put back into nature to be consumed by microorganisms and naturally enrich soil processes. Many production elements, notably packaging, which now accounts for about half of the planet's solid waste disposal, can be con- verted into biologically degradable materials. Meanwhile, *technical nutrients* must be designed to be recovered and put back into technical cycles. "Every output of manufacturing should be either composted into natural nutri- ents or remanufactured into 'technical nutrients,'" say the Lovinses and Hawken—in other words, either flowed back into nature or flowed into becoming raw material ("food") for the next manufacturing cycle. There should never remain a necessity to dispose of industrial wastes because all waste should be incorporated into new resources as part of the basic design of the system. Using closed-loop models, there would be no materials thrown away, no toxic dumping, no smokestacks or emission pipes causing pollution downstream. This may sound expensive or difficult, but it is a form of whole-system engineering that is already being effectively applied in many parts of the world and is becoming big business.

In 1996 in the United States, the so-called remanufacturing industry showed revenues of $53 billion, far more than many durable goods sectors. Many other countries are providing incentives for industries to think along these lines; Germany and Japan both require manufacturers to be responsi- ble for their products and processes *forever*—a policy exactly opposite to President Bush's policy cited here. And at least one international agree- ment, the Basel Convention, has prohibited any transboundary shipment of hazardous waste materials. (The United States has refused to sign.) In any case, the ban should be extended to all exporting of wastes through encour- aging systemic designs that include reintegration of wastes.

The ZERI organization has already initiated more than fifty projects on five continents in very diverse settings. Its work among Colombian coffee farmers helps illustrate the method.

The global market has recently left coffee farmers in deep trouble as prices have dropped dramatically. But because coffee farmers have until now only used about 3.7 percent of the plant and wasted most of the rest as wastewater and caffeine-contaminated compost, there was an opportunity to put the waste to work. Coffee biomass can be used profitably to cultivate tropical mushrooms, feed livestock, compost organic fertilizer, and generate energy.

Capra explains as follows: "When the coffee beans are harvested, the remains of the coffee plant are used to grow shiitake mushrooms (a high-priced delicacy); the remains of the mushrooms (rich in protein) feed earthworms, cattle, and pigs; earthworms feed chickens; cattle and pig manure produces biogas and sludge; the sludge fertilizes the coffee farm and surrounding vegetable gardens; while the energy from the biogas is used in the process of mushroom farming."

So rather than concentrating on the global coffee market, local farmers generate several revenue streams in addition to producing locally used produce and animals, while creating new jobs in the community. Only the shiitake mushrooms are grown for export. The net results are beneficial to the environment and the local community; there are no high investments and no need for farmers to give up their livelihoods based on the volatility of the export markets.

"Technologies in the typical ZERI clusters are small-scale and local," remarks Capra, "and the places of production are close to those of consumption, thereby radically reducing transportation costs."

Paul Hawken adds an interesting illustration of a systemic approach to manufacturing design by the Tunweni Brewery in Namibia:

This is a beer made from local sorghum, the only such beer in the world. Three times each day sewage and plant effluents are washed out, and then used to flush nearby pigpens into a "biodigester," thus eliminating any breeding of flies, while also producing a clean humane environment for pigs. Caustic soda from the washdown neutralizes the acidic manure. Meanwhile, the solid waste and spent grains are used to cultivate mushrooms. Not only does this help produce a new valuable crop, but the cultivation process converts the ligno-cellulose into carbohydrates, increasing the economic value of the spent grains. Part of the residue is then fed to pigs, and part is held back for earthworm farming, an eventual source of protein for the pigs. Meanwhile, the biodigester creates methane gas that will help diminish the fuel costs of the brewery, while the partially mineralized water released from the biodigester is used to grow algae that can also be fed to livestock. From the algae basins, the water goes to fishponds. Because of the high level of nutrients in this enriched water, there is no longer a need to buy fish food. Later, water from these fishponds can be used to irrigate crops.

What is also important about this example—in addition to the 100 percent elimination of waste in the production cycle—is that every step of the way, the use of waste cuts costs, provides "food" for new processes and products, and increases employment. It also encourages a full cycle of small-scale economic activity and its benefits within the local community.

### REINVESTMENT IN NATURAL CAPITAL

Until society is able to institute a universal closed-loop design, manufacturers must face the fact that global resource depletion is endangering their own continued functioning. Ironically, a shift in manufacturing policy toward active replenishment of resources is actually proving profitable to companies that try it because it ensures long-term supply and viability at far less cost than dependency on long-distance supply lines.

Among recent examples is a power company that plants trees to offset carbon emissions from its power plants. A ranching company in New Mexico adopted New Zealand's so-called management-intensive rotational grazing; this requires that cattle be kept on the move, thereby not over-grazing any single area and mimicking the natural behavior of plains animal herds before industrialization. In California, rice farmers flood their fields after harvest to create seasonal wetlands, supporting millions of wild fowl, replenishing groundwater, and improving fertility. In addition, the farmers are able to bale and sell rice straw rather than burn it because its high silicon content makes it a useful construction material.

These companies, among dozens of others, are finding that profits often increase from restorative methods, though too few companies yet follow the practices, and governments do not provide sufficient incentives for this approach. Perhaps as more economic activity localizes, where impacts are more visible and easily experienced, where the local commons is the economic base of the community, such ecologically and financially viable approaches will gain increased practice.

## CHANGES IN MANUFACTURING SCALE

Changes in energy, transportation, and agriculture systems will make them more compatible with local economies and eliminate the wasteful resource uses that go with long-distance supply lines, marketing, and travel. Localizing production and manufacturing will also serve ecological and democratic goals.

Paul Hawken has described recent changes in the Emilia-Romagna region of Italy, "where a sharp loss of mass-production jobs (geared to an export-oriented economy) since 1970 has been countered by a phenomenal growth in small businesses." In this region of four million people, there are 325,000 registered businesses. A combination of small artisanal firms, local labor unions, governments, and trade associations have cooperated to jointly purchase materials and share services and market assessments while also instituting common standards and quality assurances.

This activity is a further expression of the efforts of small manufacturers to "cluster" into "horizontal networks" to share resources. Firms that might have been competitive with one another come together for mutual benefit and to effectively combat the scale or size of much larger external corporations seeking to make inroads in the local market.

## CHANGES IN TECHNOLOGICAL SCALE

Megatechnologies require megainvestments and megamanagement. They are invariably biased toward absentee, usually global, ownership and operation, run by principles that are anathema to communities and democratic governance. If manufacture is to be more community based and designed to be smaller, then all technological systems and infrastructures need to be appropriately designed and scaled. Local infrastructures for reuse, recycling, and recovery of materials are mandatory, as well as a strong emphasis on local energy systems, including solar, small-scale electrical generation, wind, and local hydro, operating on a scale that fits the needs of small, flexible manufacturing processes.

A shift is required in the types and scale of technology at every level of economic activity. The essential issue should always be whether the technology is suited to megascale operation or whether it is better suited to local application, household use, and community-based systems. By such measures, technologies like nuclear power and long-distance delivery of oil for energy would be at the bottom of a list of energy systems topped by such local systems as those named earlier. The same could be said for transport or agricultural technologies.

Shifts in technological scale must also be accompanied by the principle that polluters must pay for damages they cause—no more externalization. And the *precautionary principle* described in chapter 4 should apply to every technological intervention. All technologies should be assumed potentially guilty of harms until proven innocent, a reversal of present standards.

Insurance liability coverage is a crucial indicator for precautionary standards: if the insurance industry refuses coverage, that is a clear signal of danger and unsustainability. At present, the risks endemic to nuclear power, genetic engineering, and large-scale chemical production, for example, have all been *externalized*, with governments and taxpayers assuming all the risk for insurance companies that refuse to cover losses beyond a certain amount. The nuclear and genetic engineering industries are specifically protected by law from the full risk of coverage of their inventions. Now the insurance industry itself is seeking government support to make up for the failure of "reinsurance" industries (those that insure insurers) to go beyond certain amounts.

The argument given for governments assuming the risks of catastrophic events is that losses might be so enormous that no corporation or insurer could possibly cover them. The cost of a nuclear catastrophe, for example, could be in the hundreds of billions of dollars. However, it is part of the central logic of a reformed, decentralized, and localized economic system that if catastrophic risk is a possibility from any industrial process, the precautionary principle should apply. If the risk is beyond the means of the perpetrators, then it should not be permitted.

### GREEN PROCUREMENT

Other helpful changes would be the aggressive promotion among local governments of green procurement and so-called ecologically preferable purchasing programs at every level of economic activity. These would stand in direct opposition to the current rules of the World Trade Organization, the

World Bank, and the IMF, each of which discourages local preferences as well as preferences for certain production processes, even in the name of ecological sustainability, such as ecolabeling for sustainably harvested forest products.

Finally, it is worth noting that many of the principles indicated here—recycling, zero waste, small scale, local control—already are standard economic practice in the less developed world, often bringing significant local successes. The major problems with these systems have emerged largely because of the global bureaucracies that try to *undermine* traditional local production systems to favor global corporations, and because of the inherent unsustainable nature of globalized industrial production.

## Standards of Measurement

So far in this chapter, we've talked about three of the key economic systems of our society—energy, transportation, and manufacturing—to help us all think through the kinds of shifts needed for our society to break the hold that corporate globalization has on our options. We discussed some changes that would help set us on the path in a more democratic, equitable, environmentally sustainable direction. In this final section of the chapter, we discuss a related matter: how society measures the success of these systems and its overall economic performance.

Not surprisingly, the primary unit that currently measures our success—gross domestic product—does so in terms that are compatible with the expansive goals of corporate-driven globalization while marginalizing all other ways of judging how we are progressing as a society. This gives corporate globalization a powerful tool to convince us that the direction we are going in is a good one when it isn't. By other standards, we are doing poorly.

### GROSS NATIONAL PRODUCT AND GROSS DOMESTIC PRODUCT

The GDP came into use in the mid-1980s, when it replaced the previous gross national product. We will come back to that important difference a little later in this section.

Both measurements are rooted in the World War II period, when U.S. economists were trying to find a way to measure the speed at which productive capacity in the country was increasing to meet war production needs. It was a useful measure at that time for that purpose, but its continued application is leading to distorted analyses and conclusions that exacerbate all the problems described in the earlier sections of this chapter.

GDP measures societal performance by one economic standard, the market value of the aggregate of all economic production—that is, the rate at which resources are converted to commodities and sold, the activities that go into that process, and all other paid services and activities in the formal economy. The assumption is that as GDP grows, society is better off: GDP growth brings progress and national well-being. Politicians run for office promising to increase GDP, and most domestic and international agencies use it as their standard of success.

However, the system is tragically flawed because it measures the wrong things and does not measure what it should measure. Clear-cutting of forests, strip-mining of mountaintops, construction of toxic dumpsites: all show up in GDP as positive indicators. So does expansion of military hardware and activities, prison construction, war, crime (and resources devoted to prevent it), as well as reconstruction from natural disasters.

Long-distance shipping of goods across oceans is seen as a good thing because it adds many layers of economic activity, from production to port to shipment to delivery. Local production for local consumption, involving less shipment (and less environmental impact), is seen as less productive because it does not contribute as much to GDP.

Unpaid household labor, care for the sick and elderly, self-sufficient food growing within communities—activities often carried out by women—do not contribute to GDP because little money changes hands, so they do not get counted. The same is true when anyone decides to keep land, forests, or other pristine areas as biodiversity preserves. This does not show up as a positive act. Razing the forests or putting copper mines on that land or converting it to mechanized agriculture or housing developments would add to GDP.

As David Korten likes to point out, using GDP as the standard of economic or social health "makes no more sense than taking the rapid expansion of one's personal girth as an indicator of improved personal health.

Applying such a standard to society's economic priorities has led to a gross distortion of economic priorities and resource allocation that is helping to lead the world toward social and environmental collapse."

In their article "The Need for New Measurements of Progress," which appears in Jerry Mander and Edward Goldsmith's *The Case Against the Global Economy*, authors Clifford Cobb and Ted Halstead (then of Redefining Progress, an organization that has been a leading voice critiquing the GDP measurement) point out: "GDP is the statistical distillation of the worldview of conventional economics. It basically assumes that *everything* produced is good by definition. It is a balance sheet with no cost side of the ledger; it does not differentiate between costs and benefits, between productive and destructive activities, or between sustainable or unsustainable ones. It is a calculating machine that adds but does not subtract. It treats everything that happens in the market as a gain for humanity while ignoring everything that happens outside the realm of monetized exchange regardless of its importance to well-being." The authors conclude: "To do otherwise, economists generally say, would be to make 'value judgments.' But refusing to make such judgments is a judgment in itself."

## THE IMPORTANCE OF INCLUDING THE NEGATIVE

GDP not only excludes beneficial nonmonetized economic activity but conveniently (for corporations) leaves out the actual costs to society of some activities—now and in the future—of this growth. Most alarming is the failure of GDP to account for the *depletion* of natural capital—topsoil, minerals, forests, rivers, life in the seas, the atmosphere—whose diminishment impoverishes the future of any society. Herman Daly of the University of Maryland, a former World Bank official, bemoans this failure of GDP and points out that natural capital is the basis of all real wealth in the world.

Cobb and Halstead agree: "When a timber company harvests an ancient redwood forest, the GDP rises by the market value of the wood. But it takes no account of the economic, environmental, and social costs involved in the loss of the forest." GDP actually treats resource overuse as *income* rather than *depletion*, thus creating a spectacular distortion in any effort to make judgments about the long-term health of any economy.

Similarly, the changeover of food-growing activity from small-scale, local, organic systems to industrial agriculture has increased pesticide use and fossil fuels and the need for long-distance transport. All are positive indicators for GDP. But they have serious health effects, causing illnesses of all kinds. Amazingly, however, these health effects also show up as positives in the GDP because they increase doctors' fees, hospital services, ambulances, medical machinery, drugs, and so on. (The messes created by the use of pesticides and oil require expensive cleanup operations, but these too are positive for GDP.) So from the point of view of GDP, public health problems are a good thing, not a bad one.

Particularly in higher-income countries, a significant portion of economic growth (increased GDP) comes from sales of such things as bottled water, which is actually a response to the *decline* in the purity and safety of water supplies. Another example is the increased demand for security systems to compensate for what is also a negative trend in society.

In the perverse world of GDP accounting, even a strong, stable family life contributes nothing to the economy. A divorce, however, generates lawyers' fees and probably means that at least one more new household will need to be furnished and fitted with commodities—a plus for GDP. A woman who bears her own child counts for nothing to GDP, but if she hires a surrogate to bear her child, that fee adds to GDP—as do the commissions and fees for lawyers, doctors, and other intermediaries. A parent who stays home to care for his or her own children counts for nothing. Parents who take a job to pay for day care add to GDP. All too often, GDP growth is actually a measure of social or environmental deterioration, not progress.

There are also countless cases of mining companies that extract gold and other minerals from the lands of indigenous peoples, using methods that kill topsoil, poison local water, and dump enormous piles of rocky waste into riverbeds. Human and natural losses can be enormous, and the sources of livelihood of the local people may be destroyed for generations to come, but GDP accounts record only the returns from the sale of the ore and the costs of mining it.

Military activity provides the supreme example. All additions to military hardware or personnel salaries or university research on weapons systems add to GDP, though they surely also add to the instability and insecurity in society. Once this hardware is actually used in war, then great destruction takes place, which requires later redevelopment and reconstruction—yet another plus for GDP, although the entire cycle of activity has been negative from start to finish. Death and destruction and pollution from this activity are not measured at all. So a country that becomes warlike may be assumed to be in better economic health as a result, receiving increased investment and other financial benefits.

## GDP'S BIAS AGAINST THE THIRD WORLD AND THE POOR

The Gross Domestic Product Index is designed to be helpful in measuring economic growth from year to year, and most economists argue that growth is crucial to lifting the world's poorest countries and peoples. We believe that this assumption is false and misleading. Ecological degradation of the kind that is measured as positive by GDP actually has devastating impacts on the poor because it reduces the resources—forests, lands, water, biodiversity—that poor people depend on, reducing their ability to live self-sufficiently and increasing their poverty. In any case, GDP reveals nothing about *who benefits* from growth, which is an essential question.

GDP makes no distinction between the production of goods and services that might actually help the poor—basic foods, health services, water, housing, education, job training, and so on—and the production of more luxuries for the rich—fancy foods, hotels, golf courses. This is yet another way in which GDP is useless as an indicator for society's performance. It is all too common for the deprivation of the poor to actually *increase* during periods of rapid economic expansion, because such growth often results from a systematic transfer of productive resources from the weaker elements of society to the rich and powerful. This is a common experience in low-income countries today, where many development projects—often financed with loans from the World Bank and its regional sister development banks—involve appropriating the lands on which poor people depend for their livelihoods and converting them to use for dams, tourist resorts, industrial agriculture and forestry estates, housing developments, and so on, which are designed to benefit people already better off than those displaced. Through this process, control of productive assets is consolidated in the hands of the capital-owning classes, and wages are depressed as the pool of wage labor expands among the displaced peoples. By the logic of economic growth and the GDP index, all this counts as progress.

The numbers clearly bear this out. In a recent report by the International Forum on Globalization titled *Does Globalization Help the Poor?* more than one hundred quotes from economists, researchers, scholars, and journalists show that during the thirty-year period of the world's most accelerated economic growth (1960 to 1990), the gap between the rich and poor within countries and among countries greatly increased. (See Box G in chapter 3.) Many of the sources for these data were actually the institutions that have pushed for rapid economic growth via globalization, including the World Bank, the IMF, the United Nations, and even the CIA.

GDP measurements have another direct negative impact on the South. Much of the production there takes place in the informal sector—community and household collaboration and exchange—and in subsistence agriculture. None of it appears in national accounting ledgers. The net effect of the invisibility of this activity is to open the door to development agencies that can argue for more "productive" economic approaches, such as increased foreign investment for capital-intensive infrastructures, industrial agriculture, high-tech assembly operations, and the like. All of these might create better numbers for GDP purposes and add to the illusion of progress, but they directly undermine traditional economies, cultures, and self-reliant systems. A type of small-scale financial support for local activities would make less of a splash for World Bank development figures but be far more beneficial for local people.

Finally, we mention an even more subtle though insidious manipulation that occurred in the mid-1980s, when the official measurement system switched from gross national product (GNP) to GDP. According to Clifford Cobb and Ted Halstead, this switch produced a "fundamental shift that exaggerated the contributions of multinational corporations. Under the old GNP, the profits of multinationals were attributed to the nation in which the corporations were based. If Goodyear owned a factory in Indonesia, the profits generated there were included in the U.S. GNP figures. Now, however, under GDP, the profits are included in Indonesia's figures, *even though the profits come back to the U.S.*"

This shift in strategy has made it seem as if Southern countries were growing in wealth, when actually the multinationals have been walking off with the profits for the benefit of their Northern investors. Southern countries get nothing. According to Cobb and Halstead, "Suddenly, multinationals seemed an unqualified boon. . . . It has brought an even greater social and ecological cover-up for the social and ecological costs of globalization."

## MEASURING WHAT MATTERS

Recently there has been a trend toward using indices like the Dow Jones Industrial Average and the Nikkei Index; in some quarters they are replacing GDP as the most closely watched economic indicators. TV and radio stations in some countries issue hourly reports on market fluctuations, with significant commentaries. However, stock prices are an even less meaningful indicator of human well-being than GDP. Only a tiny portion of the world's people own stock (although roughly half do in the United States), and as the collapse of the stock bubbles in the late 1990s along with the continuing corporate scandals reveal, there may be little connection between stock prices and substantive value. A rise in share prices increases the financial power of those who own the shares relative to the financial power of those who don't, but this is largely negative for society—a source of growing injustice—if there is no corresponding increase in productive capacity.

But we have also had a burst in very promising new efforts to develop new and better sets of indicators that would more accurately measure the things that matter. Readers can learn more details about some of them by contacting the International Institute for Sustainable Development of Canada, Environment Canada, the United Nations Development Program, or Redefining Progress (U.S.). These organizations have also joined with the World Bank and the U.N. Division for Sustainable Development in a comprehensive listing of some of these initiatives. (See *http://iisdl.iisd.ca/measure/compindex-asp.*) We offer a brief review of their suggestions here.

## GENUINE PROGRESS INDICATOR

This is one of the better-known alternatives to the GDP, developed by Redefining Progress, of Berkeley, California. The GPI would include many factors now left out of GDP: resource depletion, pollution, long-term environmental damage, housework and nonmarket transactions, positive adjustments for growth in leisure time, negative adjustments for unemployment and underemployment, income distribution (positive adjustment for greater equity in the system, negative adjustment for greater disparity), positive adjustment for greater life span of durables and infrastructure, negative adjustment for defensive expenditures (those that try to maintain a given level of service without adding anything, such as pollution control devices and medical and material costs of auto accidents), and positive adjustment for sustainable investment (which encourages domestic over foreign investment and investment from savings rather than borrowing).

Results from the GPI index compared with the GDP index vary from country to country but generally show that GPI rose more or less in tandem with GDP until about 1980. Then it sharply declined. The GPI is a big improvement over conventional GDP accounting because it begins to make visible the negative consequences of pursuing growth without accounting for costs and depletions.

## COMMUNITY ACCOUNTING SYSTEMS

Building on the work of Philippine economist Sixto Roxas, his country has become an important center of efforts to create true community accounting systems that take the household, rather than the enterprise, as the basic accounting unit. The differences are fundamental because in many instances the interests of the individual firm are at odds with the interests of the household and community. For example, a business benefits economically by hiring the fewest possible workers at the lowest possible wage. In contrast, the household benefits economically from having its members fully employed at the highest possible wage. The business benefits from selling its products at a high price, the household from buying at a low price.

Many investment projects may be highly profitable to a firm or individual yet very costly for the community—clear-cut logging for export, for example, or so-called export processing zones. The latter expropriate land, dominate local government decision making, enjoy tax holidays, demand fully developed infrastructure that must be paid for by local taxpayers, make priority claims on local water supplies and power generation, have few linkages to the local economy other than hiring labor at low wages, and contaminate local land and water supplies with their toxic wastes. Firms that operate in export-processing zones generate handsome profits that immediately go abroad, without compensating the community for the costs it incurs.

In contrast, community accounting systems take the household and community as the basic accounting unit and assess the costs and benefits of economic activity from a community perspective. At all levels, the community-based accounting system defines an economy that is inseparable from its habitat and corresponds to a local government responsible for managing the economy and its natural resource base.

The community balance sheet shows local natural resource stocks as *assets*. Production processes, such as in agriculture, forestry, mining, fisheries, trade, and services, create flows between asset accounts, firms, and households to reveal the consequences in terms of resource depletion and the distribution of benefits. Clear-cutting a forest is reflected immediately in the reduction of relevant community asset accounts. Unmet household needs are identified; resource flows into and out of the community are revealed; and the link between the community's well-being and the health of its local ecosystem is highlighted. This results in a perspective on investment decisions that is very different from the one provided by conventional methods of project assessment. Communities can more accurately assess the impact of proposed investments on the community balance sheet and negotiate with outside investors and trade interests accordingly.

Community-based accounting systems are also an important tool for implementing the principle of subsidiarity, because they allow local jurisdictions to see more clearly when trade offers real advantages to the community over local production—and when it does not. A substantial degree of self-reliance is encouraged, yet the community also remains open to beneficial trade and outside investment.

## LOCAL INDICATORS INITIATIVES

Many communities around the world have undertaken local initiatives to compile indicators of community social and environmental health. Redefining Progress identifies more than two hundred such efforts in the United States alone. Citizen led, they tend to focus on the kinds of communities in which people want to live. Recognizing the complexity of the human and natural systems involved, these initiatives make no effort to arrive at a single indicator. Many of those chosen reflect a highly sophisticated appreciation of the interplay between natural and human systems. Rarely do they include economic growth.

For example, the main indicator of social and environmental health chosen by Sustainable Seattle is the size of the seasonal spawning run of wild salmon. There is an almost primordial recognition that the condition of the wild salmon is a measure of the health of the watersheds on which all of the region's life depends. Toxic chemicals, loss of forest cover, disruption of stream flows, and urban sprawl all contribute to diminishing the salmon runs.

Sustainable Seattle's measure of stream quality is equally sophisticated. Rather than using a conventional test of the presence or absence of contaminants, it uses what is known as a benthic index of biological integrity, a measure of the diversity and density of bottom-dwelling (benthic) invertebrates. These are the mayflies, stoneflies, worms, mussels, and other groups of insects and invertebrates on which fish, birds, amphibians, and others rely for their food. The cleaner the water, the more they thrive.

Indicators of the number of pedestrian- and bicycle-friendly streets, open spaces near urban villages, reduction of fuel consumption and vehicle miles traveled, increased participation in gardening, and library and community center use all reflect a concern with the physical and social quality of urban life. Indicators of local farm production, employment concentration, and community reinvestment reveal the value placed on economic diversification and local ownership. A strong equity thrust is revealed in the decision to include indicators of unemployment, personal income distribution, number of hours of work required to meet basic needs, and the prevalence of low birthweight infants, children living in poverty, adult literacy, and racial equity in justice (disparities in the rate of arrests by race, for example).

Other useful indicators and reports include these:

• The Environmental Sustainability Index (includes twenty indicators on environmental sustainability)
• The Living Planet Index (indexes animal species and ecosystem change)

- The Ecological Footprint (estimates consumption of natural resources)
- The Compass of Sustainability (provides a Sustainable Development Index)
- The Dashboard of Sustainability (provides a Policy Performance Index)
- The Wellbeing Assessment/Barometer of Sustainability (measures human and ecosystem well-being together)

(The above list is from James Gustave Speth's *Red Sky at Morning: America and the Crisis of the Global Environment.* Web addresses for all organizations mentioned in this chapter can be found in the resources included at the end of this book.)

All of the new indicators described here, and others, reject the argument that the well-being of society depends mainly on economic growth. Only the interests of economists, financiers, corporation heads, and others like them are served by economic expansion. When the poor speak for themselves, they speak of their need for secure rights to the land and waters on which they depend for their livelihoods, decent jobs that pay a living wage, and health care and education for their children. Some say they need money, but rarely, if ever, do they say, "We need economic growth and rising share prices."

One of the best ways to assess the health of any society may be with indicators that show the condition of the most vulnerable among us—children, the poor, the elderly. When infant mortality rates are low, everyone is literate, the poor and elderly are nourished and housed, crime rates are low, voter turnout is high, and community events are well attended, then we are probably looking at a healthy society—no matter the GDP, GNP, or Dow Jones average.

# CHAPTER EIGHT

# Alternative Operating Systems (2)

IN THE PREVIOUS CHAPTER we spoke about three central, related, operating systems of contemporary society—energy, transport, and manufacturing— and a fourth, the way we measure the success or failure of the other three, using the wrong standards for judgment. We charted new courses for all. In this chapter, we will discuss two more crucial operating systems—agriculture and media. Although these two are not as closely related as the previous group, each of them has a crucial influence and role everywhere on earth, and each is at an important point of crisis. It is mandatory that we address and correct the present direction of both of them.

And then, finally, we present a series of examples of groups that have decided to set their own course and put into practice their visions for alternative economic and social activities on a local and regional level. Would that there were room for many more of these examples, because they are models and inspirations for all of us.

## Agriculture and Food Systems

If globalized energy systems are the primary cause of the world's environmental and geopolitical crises, then the undermining of small-scale, diversified, self-reliant, community-based agricultural systems and their replacement by corporate-run, export-oriented monocultures has been the primary cause of landlessness, hunger, and food insecurity. Furthermore, this conversion of agriculture is increasing rapidly as agriculture corporations spend billions of dollars annually in lobbying, advertising, and public relations efforts to promote trade policies that accelerate it. Such corporations argue that industrial agriculture is more efficient than traditional farming and has a better chance of feeding a hungry world. Yet all the evidence consistently shows the contrary; industrial farming's so-called efficiencies are sustained only by large government subsidies. And it causes more hunger than it solves.

We described this problem briefly in chapter 2, but to maintain a perspective on the scale and importance, we will examine it more closely here. Roughly half of the world's people still live directly off the land, growing their own staple foods, feeding their families and communities. They use indigenous seed varieties developed over centuries; they have perfected their own fertilizers, crop rotation, and pest management. Their communities have traditionally shared all the local commons, including water, labor, and seeds. They have been exemplary in preserving the biodiversity necessary for community survival. As one United Nations Environment Program (UNEP) report observed, "In India, peasants grow over forty different crops on localities that have been cultivated for more than two thousand years without a drop in yields, yet have remained free of pests" (quoted in Darrell Posey's *Cultural and Spiritual Values of Biodiversity*).

The same UNEP report cites many indigenous peoples for their "agro-ecology" approaches over millennia. Their procedures are "based on ecological knowledge and understanding" and are "highly efficient and productive and inherently sustainable. They have successfully adapted to difficult environments with innovative techniques for irrigation, drainage, soil fertility, frost control, and disease management." In Central America, for example, ingenious raised-bed systems known variously as *chiampas, waru waru,* or *tablones* have overcome truly terrible environmental conditions and have been successful in feeding the population without ecological damage. Similar locally appropriate systems are found in Africa, the Andes region, South Asia, and many other places.

Indigenous and peasant systems have also preserved traditional medicinal plants still used by a majority of the world's population, though these medicinal plants are now being fiercely hunted and patented by global corporations.

The UNEP report concludes that "modern agriculture" has become "one of the major threats to the indigenous and local communities as well as to biodiversity, healthy ecosystems, and food security." Yet no matter how successful it has been, small-scale community agriculture remains anathema to global corporations and trade bureaucracies.

As explained earlier, local systems, small owners, indigenous systems, and family farming cannot be made compatible with global corporate operations, and so we face the very aggressive international campaign to undermine small farmers, get them off their traditional lands, and make way for industrial agricultural systems, absentee owners, and the introduction of luxury monocultures for export markets. The net outcome is that once-viable, self-reliant communities are being increasingly made landless, homeless, cashless, and hungry; there are few jobs available in an industrial model that emphasizes machine- and pesticide-intensive production or biotechnology. Meanwhile, food-growing activities that had been the economic, social, and spiritual heart of community life are decimated, the core fabric of the culture along with them. This has been true as much in the United States as everywhere else in the world. Thus, once self-reliant farmers become dependent on welfare systems for survival or flee to already overcrowded cities, searching for the rare factory job in competition with all the other new arrivals.

---

## BOX P: WTO BIAS AGAINST SMALL FARMERS

*By Debi Barker, International Forum on Globalization*

The collapse of the World Trade Organization Cancun ministerial meeting in September 2003 was mainly due to the blatant unfairness of the rules in the WTO's agreement on agriculture (AOA). WTO rules, along with loan conditions imposed by the International Monetary Fund and the World Bank have increased hunger, poverty, loss of farming and rural livelihoods and are destroying ecosystems throughout the world. In Cancun, a group of developing countries, then referred to as the Group of 21, maintained that they would not negotiate any new issues (that is, further trade liberalization policies) until the unfair rules in agriculture were addressed—something that had been promised ever since Seattle.

The plight of Third World agricul-ture is directly linked to a system of unfair global rules that allow rich countries to protect and subsidize their big farms and food companies, while at the same time pressuring developing countries to open their markets to cheap food imports. The food is sold to the poor countries at prices below cost (known as *dumping*) because of the ability of rich nations to provide *export subsidies*. Poor nations cannot afford to subsidize exports, so they are at an extreme disadvantage.

Export dumping is one of the most common problems faced by developing countries. Industrial countries annually dump millions of tons of highly *subsidized*, and thus falsely cheap, food commodities into developing countries, thus destroying many self-reliant food economies and farmers' livelihoods by the

CONTINUED

millions. For example, Mexican farmers can no longer compete against U.S. products (primarily subsidized maize and cotton); Haitian and Honduran rice farmers lost their farm incomes when they reduced their tariffs, according to the rules of the WTO and the IMF, and were suddenly faced with an influx of subsidized U.S. rice; and Jamaican dairy farmers cannot compete with cheap subsidized milk powder from Europe. U.S. subsidized cotton has wiped out the cotton market in many African countries, particularly Mali, Benin, and Burkina Faso, which have lost twice as much from the drop in cotton prices as they receive in U.S. foreign aid.

Such examples result from a combination of: (1) loan conditions imposed by the IMF and World Bank, and the WTO stipulating that developing countries *must reduce or eliminate tariffs and open their markets* to the cheaper, subsidized foreign food commodities; (2) WTO rules that further reduce the right of poor countries to enact import tariffs and quotas, to protect local farmers; and (3) WTO rules that ban subsidies, except for certain rich countries' subsidies that allow them to export cheaply.

In sum, the developing countries have been stripped of mechanisms to safeguard their food base and rural livelihoods, while rich countries and corporations are effectively allowed to subsidize export commodities that are then dumped in poorer countries.

Under the WTO trade system, rich Northern countries have actually been allowed to increase subsidies since the

WTO's inception. From 1995 to 2001, dumping increased in four major U.S. commodities—from 23 percent to 44 percent in wheat, 9 percent to 29 percent in soybeans, 11 percent to 33 percent in maize, and 17 percent to 57 percent in cotton. Direct subsidy payments to European Union (EU) farmers have also increased and contribute to commodity dumping from the North to the South. The net result has been devastated farm communities in poor countries, which led to the coalition of developing countries who stood up to the North in Cancun.

After the collapse of the WTO talks in Cancun, U.S. trade negotiators were quick to point out, defensively, that *all* countries are required to cut subsidies and tariff rates. It is true that the WTO outlines a time schedule and guidelines by which developed countries must cut subsidies and reduce tariffs; however, the subsidies that most benefit exporters—large industrial farms and giant agribusinesses—are not on the table, and certain key Northern commodities are also exempt from tariff reductions. (These are protected under a complicated scheme referred to as "Green, Amber, and Blue boxes." This is where the influence of industrial agriculture corporations is clearly seen; many are key advisers to WTO agreements.)

While millions of farmers from developing countries have been devastated by the policies of trade agreements and international institutions, the majority of farmers in the North are not faring

CONTINUED

BOX P: CONTINUED

well either. Net income for U.S. farmers in 2001 was 36 percent lower than in 1989. Figures from the European Union are similar. A recent survey of United Kingdom farming districts found that the average farmer is earning only £3.60 per hour, below the UK minimum wage. Both the United States and the EU are losing record numbers of farm operators because they cannot compete with the large industrial farms.

This is primarily because the subsidy system enshrined in the WTO, favoring huge agribusiness interests over smaller farmers, is paralleled by domestic farm policies in the North, such as the U.S. Freedom to Farm Act and the EU's Common Agriculture Policy (CAP). U.S. farm subsidies have soared to more than $20 billion per year, up from the average of $9 billion per year in the early 1990s (pre-WTO). Yet less than 20 percent of U.S. farmers receive 86 percent of the total dollars of U.S. subsidies. Two-thirds of farms (the small ones) receive no subsidies at all. In 2002 the EU CAP comprised roughly $50 billion, almost half of the EU budget. As in the United States, only around 20 percent of EU farmers receive subsidies.

As the EU adds more "accession" countries, many are concerned about their agriculture base. Poland, for example, has 2.5 million small farmers. Following current EU policies, which discriminate in favor of large farms, many may be forced off their lands to make way for larger, more "viable" units.

If subsidies are one major issue, another is *low commodity prices* that farmers receive, bringing financial ruin to millions of farmers in both the North and the South. This problem also stems from the bias of most global rules toward giant agriculture corporations. These corporations have been able to concentrate their domination over many of the world's agricultural commodities and control global prices and supply. A handful of companies now trade virtually all the world's corn, cotton, wheat, and soybeans, with trade in coffee, sugar, and other tropical specialty crops also highly concentrated. The near-monopoly exists in both farm supplies (seeds, chemicals) and in food processing and distribution. This leaves small farmers in poor countries subject to the whims of corporations, commodity brokers, and the market, and generally unable to get fair prices for their products. Where once small farmers were able to grow food to use and to share locally, the ultimate control over their livelihoods is now in the hands of distant forces.

The net result of the whole process is increased poverty and landlessness among farmers in the South *and* the North, devastation to the environment from industrial agriculture practices, and lower food safety and nutrition.

The role of global institutions and trade agreements should be to ensure fairness in international trade. Multilateral rules are needed that protect the weak from the powerful. New fair trade rules, along with domestic and international policies that favor the local over an unaccountable undemocratic international scheme, are urgently needed.

Those who are able to continue farming find themselves pushed to the least productive soils or must submit to feudal arrangements with large export-oriented landowners who control supplies, production methods, and prices and try to squeeze the small producers as much as possible in order to keep costs low and profits high. Most important, these absentee owners do not grow diverse food crops for local families and communities to eat but rather emphasize luxury monocultures, like cut flowers, potted plants, cotton, coffee beans, shrimp, beef, luxury vegetables, soybeans, and so on, meant to be directly shipped to countries where the majority are already overfed. Land that once fed millions of poor families now feeds the overfed.

That such an export-based system can be promoted as helping to feed the world by companies like Monsanto and Archer Daniels Midland through billions of dollars in advertising is highly cynical. Victims of this free-market propaganda can be found throughout the world. As the Institute for Food and Development Policy (Food First) has reported, even during the time of the greatest acceleration of global trade in food, the past thirty years, world hunger has increased at a rate even higher than population growth. There are now nearly eight hundred million hungry people in the world.

Indeed, many countries report increasing poverty and hunger at exactly the same time as they experience vigorous growth in agricultural exports. In Thailand, for example, agricultural exports were up by 65 percent between 1985 and 1995, but the proportion of the population below the poverty line increased during that period to 43 percent. In Bolivia from 1985 to 1990 there was spectacular growth of exports, but 95 percent of the rural population still earned less than a dollar per day. In the Philippines, there has been an enormous increase in the acreage devoted to growing cut flowers for export, with a corresponding decline in acreage for food staples like rice and corn. Approximately 350,000 rural livelihoods have been destroyed by the shift. The Philippines, which had long been self-sufficient in rice, saw rice imports leap tenfold in the late 1990s, increasing dependency and hunger.

In Brazil during the 1970s, when soybean exports increased phenome-nally—to be shipped to Japanese and European markets for animal feed—hunger also increased from one-third to two-thirds of the population.

During the 1990s, Brazil actually became the world's third largest agricultural exporter, with the area devoted to industrial farming of soybeans growing by 37 percent from 1980 to 1995, displacing millions of small farmers in the process. Meanwhile, per capita production of the staple rice fell by 18 percent, increasing hunger and poverty.

Vandana Shiva summarized the situation at the 2002 People and Planet Conference in Kingston, Ontario, remarking that the root causes of hunger and poverty are by now obvious: "A combination of loss of land and loss of control of local resources like water, seeds, and biodiversity. All of these are basic to farming communities but are now in the hands of global corporations." She adds with irony, "The food security of the United States and other wealthy food-importing countries depends largely on the destruction of other people's security."

The shattering of established social arrangements and cultures also leads to tribal and ethnic hostilities, as people are thrown into competition for scarce lands and resources. In the Indian state of Punjab, for example, Hindus and Muslims were traditionally cooperative and peaceful. But they turned to violence against each other partly because of the pressures of the so-called Green Revolution—the World Bank–backed, corporate-driven shift to chemical- and machine-intensive production of the 1960s and 1970s. This mode of production required massive increases in use of freshwater, which was already scarce, thus creating competition for its availability. Similar conflicts have taken place in Africa over resource scarcities exacerbated by World Bank–inspired industrial monocultural production for export using vast amounts of water for irrigation.

Industrial agriculture is one of the world's greatest consumers of the planet's scarce freshwater. Commercial hybrid seeds for wheat require twenty times more water than traditional wheat varieties developed and grown in India. The massive infrastructure needed to divert water to industrial agriculture farms also has devastating environmental impacts, and chemical fertilizers and pesticides degrade water and soil, contribute to loss of species, poison air, and have other dire results. According to Steven Gorelick, writing for the U.K.–based International Society for Ecology and Culture (ISEC), governments subsidize water used in industrial agriculture, either directly or by paying for massive irrigation projects. This has, for example, encouraged the growth of water-intensive monocultures in such formerly desert areas as California's San Joaquin Valley, where industrial farms could not exist without water subsidies.

As for efficiency, global industrial agriculture can be called efficient only if the long list of hidden and overt subsidies that industrial societies provide agribusinesses are ignored. In ISEC's report *Bringing the Food Economy Home,* authors Helena Norberg-Hodge, Steven Gorelick, and Todd Merrifield cite a long list of subsidies in the large industrial nations, including export promotional supports as well as massive funding for research, education, and application of biotechnology and chemical- and energy-intensive monocultures. According to the report, many governments "directly subsidize pesticides and chemical fertilizers as a means of encouraging large-scale agriculture for export." Most of these countries are doing this at the urging of World Bank and IMF policies and because of pressure from global corporations. During the 1980s, for example, China's annual pesticide subsidies averaged some $285 million, Egypt's $207 million, and Colombia's $69 million. Pakistan devoted about 75 percent of its total agricultural budget to subsidize chemical fertilizers. But little support was given for smaller-scale organic methods.

Industrial agriculture also depends upon huge infusions of largely subsidized energy for operation of farm machinery and production of pesticides and fertilizers. Present estimates are that three times more energy is used to produce food in the industrial agriculture model than is derived from consuming it. In Canada, on-farm energy use grew by 9.3 percent between 1990 and 1996. In developing countries, during the height of the Green Revolution—1972 to 1982—total use of energy for agricultural production rose by 30 percent, not counting energy used for transport, marketing, or packaging of agricultural products.

Mechanized, modern tools of farming that require expensive hybrid seeds, biotech seeds, fertilizers, chemicals and pesticides, tractors, and other energy-rich systems have been pushed by the World Bank, the IMF, and the WTO but have been a main cause of the desperate situation of small and peasant farmers worldwide, leading to rising debt, increased hunger, the abandonment of small farms, and an epidemic of farm suicides.

In addition, there are gigantic hidden subsidies from the "externalization" of cleanup costs resulting from industrial agricultural processes: poisoned soils, rivers, estuaries, wildlife habitats, and so on. Industrial agriculture is also a major contributor to climate change because it depends on long-distance shipping to distant markets. The average plate of food eaten in Western industrial food-importing nations is likely to have traveled fifteen hundred miles from its source. Each one of those miles contributes to the environmental and social crises of our times. Shortening the distance between producer and consumer has to be one of the crucial reform goals of any transition away from industrial agriculture.

"If these subsidies for the large and global were redirected toward appropriate smaller-scale, more localized producers," says the ISEC report, "the shift toward more ecological and equitable food economies would be given a major boost."

Globalization has exacerbated this situation immeasurably, as global trade and investment rules strongly favor global agribusinesses. WTO rules also permit subsidies to exporters and commodity traders but not to the small-scale production that is characteristic of the South. The scales are strongly tipped in favor of the largest corporations. These circumstances and policies at the national and international bureaucratic levels have brought about a degree of corporate mergers and concentration in agriculture that is equal to any industry, including oil. For example, according to the ETC Group, by 2000 five grain-trading companies controlled 75 percent of the world's cereal commodity market (and its pricing). In the United States, four cattle processors controlled 80 percent of the U.S. market (double their share in 1980), whereas five food retailers controlled nearly 50 percent of retail food sales.

All of this leaves small producers and farmers caught in a terrible trap, as both their inputs for farm production and their outlets for distribution are controlled by an ever-smaller number of giant corporations, which also control commodity price markets. Any system that deliberately sets out to separate from their lands the farmers who have been feeding their families and local communities, replacing them with ecologically unsustainable export production from absentee landowners, is absurd on its face—and tragic for millions of people. In the name of "progress," family farms and rural communities are being driven to extinction. Millions of people are being pulled off the land and moved into ever-expanding cities. This process must be reversed, and it can be. (See Box Q.)

ACTIONS AND POLICIES TOWARD ALTERNATIVE SOLUTIONS

Millions of people around the world are mobilizing to reverse the global-ization of industrial agriculture. Millions of farmers in India alone have protested corporate biopiracy of their biodiversity and their seeds, and the eventual commercial patenting of indigenous varieties. (See chapter 5 for more on biopiracy.)

The movement also includes tens of thousands of farmers in Japan, the Philippines, Bolivia, Germany, and most significantly, the growing interna-tional movement of landless peasants throughout the Third World who are demanding a meaningful land reform process. In Brazil, for example, the landless peasant movement (Landless Workers Movement, or MST) has won actual title to over fifteen million acres of farmland that are able to serve

---

## BOX Q: RETURNING TO AN AGRICULTURE THAT PROTECTS THE ATMOSPHERE

### By Edward Goldsmith, The Ecologist

Industrial agriculture is responsible for 25 percent of the world's carbon diox-ide emissions, 60 percent of methane gas emissions, and 80 percent of ni-trous oxide—all major gases causing climate change. (See also Box F, chap-ter 2.) These can be drastically curbed by abandoning the present industrial agriculture model, and pursuing tradi-tional, sustainable agriculture systems that have provided abundant food and maintained ecosystems for many cen-turies. Here are some steps we can take:

Nitrous Oxide
In the last few decades tropical rain-forests have been cut down at an alarm-ing rate; mainly for conversion to an in-dustrial agriculture export crop or for cattle grazing. Millions of tons of ni-trous oxide emissions are the result. Ni-

trogen fertilizers, a staple of industrial agriculture, are another major source of nitrous oxide, contributing as much as 10 percent of total annual nitrous oxide emissions. Centuries-old alternatives in-clude mulch, manure, and other such low-tech, "on-farm" fertilizers that de-liver healthy soils and abundant crops.

Methane and Carbon Dioxide
Methane emissions are dramatically in-creasing because of flood-irrigated, nitrogen-dosed rice fields and the sub-stantial increase in industrially raised livestock—cattle, in particular. Cattle fed high-protein grain diets emit con-siderably more methane gas than grass-fed cattle. Organic rain-fed rice fields emit significantly less methane.

Carbon dioxide emissions are large-ly caused by loss of soil carbon to the

CONTINUED

250,000 families. The Brazilian government has recognized that legalizing MST land occupations—especially when lands were formerly idle—is far less costly (even including compensatory payments to prior landowners) than to have millions of people in abject poverty, without food, without work, edging toward violence, terrorism, and public health disasters, and filling overcrowded cities even further. (See also the later section of this chapter, "Peoples' Alternative Initiatives.")

Nor is the movement against globalized industrial agriculture confined solely to the poorest nations. Western industrial nations are also seeing small farmers and artisanal producers increasingly sacrificed to production and distribution rules and standards that favor large, monocultural, industrial producers while inhibiting the options of small farmers. For example, French farmer José Bové has become an international leader protesting these

---

BOX Q: CONTINUED

atmosphere. Modern industrial agriculture contributes to this by such practices as deforestation and drainage of wetlands, deep plowing that exposes the soil to the elements, use of heavy machinery that compacts the soil, use of fertilizers and pesticides that destroy soil structure, overgrazing leading to desertification, and the practice of growing monocrops on a large scale.

Using manures, composts, mulches, and cover crops such as forest bark, straw, or other organic materials that are fed back into the soil not only reduces nitrous oxide but is effective in preventing loss of soil carbon. These fertilizers also reduce soil-borne diseases and increase crop productivity. According to the United Nations Food and Agriculture Organization (FAO), a system of agroforestry—planting trees in or near crops—is a good means of maximizing absorption of carbon by the soil.

High energy intensiveness in industrial agriculture further contributes to increased carbon dioxide emissions. A recent study in the U.K. concluded that nonmechanized, or traditional, systems of agriculture in England and Germany used seven times less fossil fuels than industrial production.

Modern irrigation is especially energy intensive. When water is extracted from a depth of more than thirty meters, pumped irrigation requires more than three times as much fossil fuel energy for corn production as rain-fed cultivation. Our dependence on perennially irrigated land is largely due to commercial hybrid seed varieties, as well as genetically modified seeds, which require much more water, just as they require more chemicals. Farmer-saved seeds that have been developed and selected over millennia to succeed in specific local climates and geologi-

CONTINUED

cal configurations have longer roots that can dig deep into the soil to find sources of moisture that the short-rooted commercial seeds cannot utilize.

Water used for irrigation presently consumes nearly 70 percent of all the water used worldwide, and this figure is projected to double in another twenty years. The water scarcity that has resulted leads to pressure to privatize. (In the Indian state of Orissa, water prices have increased tenfold due to privatization, and small farmers can no longer afford it.)

Prior to industrialized agriculture, many regions had developed effective, nonintensive water systems. Some food producers still use such systems—water catchment, low-flow irrigation, and other such methods—low-cost, low-tech methods that foster high food production and maintain watersheds.

Most industrial agriculture production is for export markets—this translates into massive increases in the use of fossil fuels for transport, packaging, and long-distance preservation. One-eighth of world oil consumption goes toward transport, with food products accounting for a considerable slice of this.

Such travel and trade in food are completely unnecessary. This is referred to as "the great food swap"—ships pass in the night, one carrying grain from the United States to India and one loaded with grain from India to the United States. This system benefits the handful of corporate grain traders but creates great food instability around the world. Localized food production and distribution is one answer to reducing fossil fuel transport.

If traditional agriculture systems have successfully provided food and fiber for millions over many centuries, why are we undertaking such a radical transformation of food production, one that threatens the very atmosphere of the planet?

A World Bank report notes that "small holders are outstanding managers of their own resources—their land and capital, fertilizer and water." But the report goes on to lament: "The farmers had to be induced to produce for the market, adopt new crops, and undertake new risks. . . . Until enough subsistence farmers have their traditional lifestyles changed by the growth of new consumption wants, this labor constraint may make it difficult to introduce new [export] crops."

In other words, we destroy successful local agriculture systems to bring profits to wasteful industrial agriculture corporations, risking planetary health. It is imperative that we immediately move away from an industrial food system that depends on intensive use of chemicals, water, and fossil fuels toward a localized model based on traditional, ecologically sustainable practices. This is not only desirable to contain climate change but is also the best way to ensure food security and food safety, preserve wildlife and other species, maintain biodiversity, and protect our soil, water, and air.

rules in Western countries. Together with leaders of Southern movements, he has been joined by public health officials and environmentalists around the world in a common cause—seeking new policies that favor small-scale diversified farming and healthier food.

The campaign to achieve meaningful change must be simultaneously carried forward on the international, national, and local levels. We frame our discussion around six central convictions:

- Access to land for self-reliant food growing is a fundamental human right; it cannot be denied to communities or nations by global trade regimes or in the interests of international trade processes.
- Loss of small holders' farmlands to highly concentrated large corporations is a primary cause of poverty and hunger in the world, as well as of environmental devastation.
- Wherever people are still living and working on their traditional lands, incentives and policies should help them remain in place, working for their families and communities, and not for the global market. Where communities have been deprived of their lands, *distributive land reform* is crucial.
- The bias of international bureaucracies like the World Bank, IMF, and WTO toward large-scale, export-oriented monocultural production must be reversed. Invigorating small farms and indigenous agricultural practices that protect local biodiversity and innovation devoted to sustainable use for local populations must be encouraged.
- Solutions must serve to shorten the distance between producer and consumer.
- The ultimate sustainable agriculture solution is transition to noncorporate, small-scale organic farming as practiced for millennia.

### EIGHT KEY CHANGES

Here, then, is a partial list of policies and actions that can help produce the needed changes.

*1. Permit Tariffs and Import Quotas That Favor Subsidiarity*

Most international trade rules now favor export production and the global corporations that dominate it. These must be replaced by rules that emphasize support for local production, local self-reliance, and real food security. This means applying the principle of *subsidiarity:* whenever production can be achieved by local farmers, using local resources for local consumption, all rules and benefits should favor that option, thus shortening the distance between production and consumption. We are not suggesting that there should be no trade at all in food products but only that trade should be confined to whatever commodities cannot be supplied at the local level, rather than export trade being the primary driver of production and distribution—its raison d'être.

New rules must permit the judicious use of selected trade tariffs and import quotas to regulate imports of food that can be produced locally, and to help prevent dumping below actual cost of subsidized commodities from rich countries. For example, a country like South Korea, which can easily be self-sufficient in its staple food, rice, should never be forced to open its market to subsidized U.S. rice exports. Such policies destroy the livelihoods of Korean farmers and their communities while rendering American farmers vulnerable to the volatility of the global pricing system. In both Korea and the United States, the bias should invariably be toward strengthening local production for local consumption and the reduction of long-distance food shipments.

### 2. Reverse the Present Rules on Intellectual Property and Patenting

The World Trade Organization attempts to impose the U.S. model of intellectual property rights protection on all countries of the world. This model strongly favors the rights of global corporations to claim patents on medicinal plants, agricultural seeds, and other aspects of biodiversity, even in cases where the biological material has been under cultivation and development by indigenous people or community farmers for millennia. Most of these communities have traditionally viewed such plants and seeds as part of the community commons, not subject to ownership and fee structures imposed by outside corporations. (For more on this, see chapter 5, "Reclaiming the Commons.")

These new global patent regimes have become important issues in such countries as India, which has always had a patent regime based on sui generis ownership—that is, community patenting of the biodiversity within each community. Other countries have similar systems that protect local commons from outside expropriation. Many countries, led by India, are battling to retain their domestic systems against the enormous pressures of the WTO and global corporations. In Mexico, thousands of peasant farmers protested against an American company that patented an indigenous bean variety that had long been grown by local farmers; the community is now asked to pay the patent holder $69 million annually to grow this traditional local bean!

Some aspects of this issue recently reached the boiling point when poor nations like South Africa, Thailand, and Brazil attempted to circumvent the WTO rules on intellectual property to make inexpensive generic versions of medical treatments for AIDS; each of these countries is in the midst of a medical crisis made worse by the fact that most of the victims are extremely poor. Millions of people have taken to the streets to protest such unjust rules. They have finally succeeded in gaining negotiated reduced rate settlements with global corporations that had been making windfall profits from the disease. The WTO has also adopted a temporary agreement to allow governments to bypass patent barriers when necessary to protect public health. But at this time, the intellectual property rights rules (TRIPs) still remain in the WTO. These rules should be abandoned to permit reassertion of rules that favor the needs of local and domestic communities and the protection of local biodiversity innovations and knowledge developed over centuries, as well as to deal with public health crises. Placing profits of global corporations before local food sustainability and public health defies logic and justice.

### 3. Localize Food Regulations and Standards

In the name of food safety, many international rules, such as the WTO's Agreement on the Application of Sanitary and Phytosanitary Standards (SPS) and the Codex Alimentarius, have enforced a kind of processing of foods that works directly against local and artisanal food producers while favoring the global food giants. Among other things, they require irradiation of certain products, pasteurization, and standardized shrink-wrapping of local cheese products.

Such rules as these tremendously increase costs for small producers and also negatively affect taste and quality. In fact, the greatest threats to food safety and public health do not come from small food producers but from industrial farms and distributors whose practices have accelerated the incidence of salmonella, *e. coli* infection, *listeria,* and other bacteria in foods, as well as Mad Cow disease, hoof-and-mouth disease, and others. Industrial processes make it impossible for food producers to observe food quality closely, whereas small and artisanal food producers can more easily stop disease outbreaks. Ironically, while describing themselves as working for food safety, the SPS agreement and Codex permit even higher levels of pesticide residue (including DDT) in food, and they subject every member nation's health, safety, and environmental standards to being challenged as unfair barriers to trade. Other aspects of the WTO have also effectively prevented governments from introducing labeling of genetically modified foods. These homogenized global standards are exquisitely attuned to the primary goal of benefiting global corporate producers. Food production standards should be localized and every nation permitted to set high standards for food safety.

*4. Allow Farmer Marketing—Supply Management Boards*

Currently disallowed by the WTO and NAFTA, these price and supply regulations let farmers negotiate *collective* prices with domestic and foreign buyers to help ensure that they receive a decent price for their commodities. Less than two years after NAFTA went into effect, Mexican domestic corn prices fell by 48 percent as a flood of cheap U.S. corn exports entered the country. Stable prices for Mexico's domestic corn growers could have been achieved by the government price regulation agencies dismantled by NAFTA. Without these, thousands of farmers have been forced to sell their lands.

*5. Eliminate Direct Export Subsidies and Dumping*

Although the World Bank and IMF have pressured most poor nations to eliminate direct payment to small farmers, rich countries continue to provide significant export subsidies to agribusinesses. For example, the U.S. Overseas Private Investment Corporation, supported by U.S. taxpayers, provides vital insurance to U.S. companies investing overseas. Even loans from the IMF to Third World countries have been channeled into export subsidies for U.S. agribusinesses. Such subsidies help multinational corporations dominate smaller local businesses both domestically and abroad and were a major cause of the breakdown of talks in Cancun. Subsidies also lead to export dumping, a major grievance of poor countries. These export subsidy policies should be eliminated. No country should have the right to dump subsidized commodities. Finally, programs that permit and encourage low-interest loans to small farmers, creation of domestic seed banks, and emergency food supply systems should be allowed.

### 6. Recognize the Failure of WTO Market Access Rules

Many Southern countries were originally persuaded to join the WTO and to open their markets because of the promise that Northern countries would do likewise, in a fair exchange. But while Southern countries *have* opened markets, most Northern countries have maintained barriers on key products for developing country exporters. This, combined with the technological advantages and greater wealth and subsidies already enjoyed by Northern agricultural producers, has led to even greater imbalance in the system. Subsidized Northern imports have destroyed rural communities and self-sufficient livelihoods throughout the South, and many people now working for poverty wages as Nike subcontractors are refugees from self-sufficient farming regions. Many in the South are furious about this turn of events.

Some activists strongly argue that developing countries *must* have market access as promised, to level the playing field. But others believe that the entire export model is doomed because it is destructive to basic self-sufficient traditional farming. These divergent viewpoints have led to a partial rift among activists, depending upon whether one feels the situation is now so desperate that market access can provide the only quick fix or whether one takes a longer view toward a paradigm of community self-sufficiency. Still, most activists who advocate for agricultural self-sufficiency acknowledge that in the short term, many Southern nations remain dependent on agricultural exports to the North. Hence, they recognize that transition strategies are needed to help nations that often feel trapped in colonial trade patterns to shift toward greater food security and self-sufficiency.

The International Forum on Globalization has hosted several debates on this point, and we will continue to do so, although most of our members feel the WTO is probably an unsustainable institution (see chapter 10) and that these issues would be better dealt with by a less corporate-oriented bureaucracy—one that embraces the ten principles for sustainable societies.

### 7. Promote Redistributive Land Reform

History shows that the *redistribution* of land to landless and land-poor rural families is an effective way to improve rural welfare. Dozens of successful land reform programs were carried out after World War II. According to a report by Food First, "When a significant portion of quality land was distributed to a majority of the rural poor, with policies favorable to successful family farming, and when the power of rural elites was broken, there have been measurable poverty reduction and improvement of human welfare. The economic success of Japan, South Korea, Taiwan, and China has partly resulted from such reforms."

According to a report by Miguel Altieri and former Food First codirector Peter Rosset, "Our research shows that small farmers are more productive and more efficient, and contribute more to broad-based regional development than do the larger corporate farmers. Given secure tenure, small farmers can also be much better stewards of natural resources, protecting long-term productivity of their soils and conserving functional biodiversity."

So effective has serious land reform been that even the World Bank has grudgingly accepted the principle that it is a fundamental requirement to help offset the grossly inequitable ownership of reproductive resources in many countries and that this maldistribution of land is negatively affecting meaningful economic development. The bank has now begun to include land reform among the requirements in some policy packages when dealing with Third World countries. Unfortunately, however, as Rosset has written, "What the bank calls land reform is essentially privatization and 'market-led' mechanisms of redistribution. These are a far cry from what Via Campesina, Food First, and others are calling for. But at least the bank is making it legitimate again to call for land reform and to struggle over its definition."

When communal lands are privatized, as has happened among Mexico's *ejidos* and as current World Bank policies promote, systems of individual land titling, registries, and land market schemes can result in mass sell-offs of small holders' plots. This increases landlessness, land ownership concentration, and migration to urban areas. Even when lands are not sold off under these schemes, the privatization of small holdings negatively affects the sense of community management and the construction of community-style agricultural systems like terracing and small-scale irrigation. The usual community approaches give way to a new individual profit motive that undermines collective activity and community welfare.

As for "market-led redistribution"—the current favorite of the World Bank—it is fraught with risks, says Rosset. He notes: "Landowners often choose to sell only the most marginal plots (steep slopes, dense rainforests, desert margins, and so on) often at exorbitant prices." Trying to farm these kinds of lands can often lead to ecologically unsustainable practices to attempt to eke out some productivity. Also, loans offered to purchasers under World Bank financing schemes may leave poor farmers with high debts on marginal lands, thus leading to deeper poverty and land degradation, as with many of the failed reforms of earlier decades. In addition, World Bank loan packages often require a commitment to pesticide and chemical production and to the use of nontraditional export crops.

All of these policies have been prescriptions for failure, as was the case with market-led reforms in Brazil, which the World Bank is still trying to duplicate in the Philippines and elsewhere.

Food First and other activist groups oppose that kind of land reform and are fighting for a truly redistributive land reform that has worked where it has been fully supported by government policies. Food First lists several crucial ingredients that must apply if land reform is to be successful:

- Government grants of land must be debt-free.
- Women must have full rights of title and use.
- Only good quality land should be used (past failures have often resulted when lands were of poor quality).
- There must be a highly supportive policy environment—reasonable credit terms and good infrastructures for sound local environmental technologies.
- There must be easy access to markets.
- The power of rural elites must be broken so they can no longer block and distort policies, subsidies, and profits in their favor.
- Reforms must apply to the majority of the rural poor so they have sufficient strength in numbers to be politically effective.
- Most important, a new farm economy should be the centerpiece of a country's entire economic development model. When land reform is viewed as welfare, failure is inevitable.

## 8. Change at the Grassroots

There are many opportunities for local communities, too, to assist the transition away from globalized agriculture. The International Society for Ecology and Culture lists several of these opportunities, already well under way in some places:

- *Buy-local campaigns.* These campaigns help local food businesses thrive and prevent money from "leaking" from the local economy. This protection of the local is also expressed by hundreds of regional campaigns against the entry of global franchises like McDonald's and Wal-Mart.
- *Farmers' markets.* Thriving in many parts of the world, farmers' markets are now also being rediscovered and supported throughout industrial countries. These markets are ways of directly connecting consumers with local producers, often organic farmers, who can keep prices down by avoiding distribution costs.

---

### BOX R: CUBAN ORGANIC AGRICULTURE

*By Helena Norberg-Hodge, Todd Merrifield, and Steven Gorelick,*
*International Society for Ecology and Culture*

In the past few decades, an important shift has taken place in Cuban agriculture—away from chemical-intensive monoculture for export and toward the production of diverse, organic food for local consumption.

Until 1990, the majority of agricultural land in Cuba was devoted to a vast monoculture of sugarcane for the world market (and after the Cuban revolution in 1959, for the Soviet bloc countries). With earnings from sugar, Cuba imported chemicals and oil needed to support its agriculture, as well as much of its food; before 1990, the country imported an estimated 57 percent of its caloric intake. With the collapse of the Soviet market and the tightening of the U.S. embargo, Cuba experienced an 80 per-

cent drop in pesticide and fertilizer imports and a 50 percent decline in food imports. Remarkably, the government responded by adopting a range of innovative strategies to diversify production, lessen dependence on chemical inputs and fossil fuels, encourage popular participation in farming, and enhance national food security.

These strategies included the breakup of huge state-controlled farms into smaller worker-owned and -managed farm collectives, as well as reorientation of agriculture toward basic food needs. Cuba encouraged diversification of crops, crop rotation, intercropping, manuring, and soil conservation. The country's agricultural research sector also reoriented itself toward low-

CONTINUED

- *Local food co-ops.* These are small retail outlets, similar to farmers' markets but where financial benefits are shared by producers and consumers.
- *Community banks and loan funds.* Run by community boards, these increase capital available for local residents and businesses and allow people to invest in their neighborhoods rather than in distant corporations. Such banks favor small-scale local activity over global corporate activity.
- *Local currencies.* Growing in popularity, these alternative scrips used only in communities enable people to avoid the dominant currencies and keep money inside the local community. Local currency schemes are similar in intent to Local Exchange Trading Systems (LETS), which are large-scale barter systems for local communities, often facilitated by a central credit and debit accounts system. Among the leading examples of a successful LETS program is the Berkeley Regional Exchange and Development (BREAD). (For further information about this movement, see www .breadhours.org.)

---

BOX R: CONTINUED

input ecological methods, giving rise to biofertilizing and biological pest control. Oxen have been bred to replace tractors that cannot be used for lack of fuel. To meet the new demand for agricultural labor, the government improved rural services and incentives for people to remain on the land. It also relaxed price controls and restrictions on the direct sale of produce, which led to new farmers' markets around the country.

Urban gardens have also had an important role. An Urban Agriculture Department oversees these efforts, and by 1998 there were over eight thousand gardens in Havana, cultivated by over thirty thousand people. The Ministry of Agriculture replaced its front lawn in Havana with a garden of lettuce, bananas, and beans, and many of the ministry's employees work in the garden. These urban gardens have reduced the burden on rural areas and led to a reduction in food transport and storage while increasing quality and variety of produce in cities.

Although Cuba made these changes out of necessity and may abandon some of them when the nation is not as isolated, its experience is nonetheless encouraging. It shows the possibilities of a more ecologically and socially sensitive agriculture on a national scale, and demonstrates that, with political will, governments can shift from a focus on global food to local food and implement policies that are good for people, communities, and the environment.

SOURCE: Adapted from Helena Norberg-Hodge, Todd Merrifield, and Steven Gorelick, "Is a Shift in Direction Possible? Lessons from Cuba," in Helena Norberg-Hodge, Steven Gorelick, and Todd Merrifield, eds., *Bringing the Food Economy Home.* West Hartford, CT: Kumarian Press and London: Zed Books, 2002.

- *Urban gardens.* Urban gardens are one of the most original and revitalizing movements among urban dwellers, especially in Northern countries where access to natural sites may be difficult. Making use of empty lots, small patches of private property, and public parks, urban gardens enable city dwellers to grow their own organic foods. Such projects are helpful in educating urban children about where food comes from. Many schools are initiating such gardens on their own property, teaching a survival skill that can bring confidence, self-reliance, and joy.

## Global Media

As we described in part 1, a key goal of economic globalization is that every place on earth should be more or less like every other place on earth: *globalized.* Whether it's the United States or Europe or once-distant places in Asia and South America, all countries are meant to develop the same tastes, values, and lifestyles; such a model serves the marketing needs of global corporations. Diversity, whether cultural, political, or biological, undermines efficiency goals of global corporations that seek to market identical products everywhere to an ever expanding world of consumers.

Free trade agreements like the WTO, NAFTA, and the proposed Free Trade Area of the Americas have the specific mandate to create and enforce rules that accelerate this rush toward global homogenization. They require that all countries operate from the same set of corporate-created standards, preventing nations from regulating corporate activity in order to protect local and national resources, local livelihood or culture, local labor rights, or health standards. *But that is only the external process of homogenization.*

In any truly efficient centralized design, the assignment is also to make over the *internal landscape,* to remake human beings themselves—our minds, our ideas, our values, behaviors, and desires—to create a *monoculture* of humans that is compatible with the redesigned external landscapes. The idea is for our minds and values to match the commercial corporate systems around us, like so many compatible computers.

The assignment for this internal cloning goes to global mass media, particularly television and advertising, though we could surely also add film, radio, the music industry (and education). These are the instruments that speak directly into the minds of people everywhere on earth, imprinting them with patterns of thought, sets of images and ideas, and frameworks for understanding how life should be lived.

We have entered an age of nearly total envelopment by media. As the late mass media critic Neil Postman once put it, "The tremendous power of media is the most crucial subject that we're doing nothing about." Maybe the difficulty most people have in grasping the scale and importance of the subject is that media offers itself as such a benign, friendly package: entertaining, colorful, and to some degree informative, and it is all around us, part of our everyday lives.

Most important, media offers the illusion of transparency; it seems to be just a neutral window through which reality is passed on to us, rather than a set of technologies in the hands of specific people with specific intent who are often deeply engaged in choosing, creating, and defining the realities we experience, which are then "entered" directly into millions of brains around the world.

Far from being a neutral window, media has a central role in influencing political, cultural, economic, social, and environmental issues, and in determining whether people and communities will fully grasp the true situations they face or what to do about them. As such, its proper functioning is fundamental to democratic societies.

In this section of the chapter we look at three major aspects of the situation: the very shocking figures on global concentration of ownership of media, revealing that only a handful of people are actually speaking to the whole world through these powerful instruments; the generally unappreciated reach and political and social impacts of the most important medium, television, and its partner, advertising, as primary instruments that shape global consciousness; and finally alternatives. For the latter we turn to growing resistance movements, including a very impressive recent uprising against the Federal Communications Commission (FCC) in the United States, and the expanding effective uses of the Internet, alternative media systems, and a list of other new ideas.

WHO OWNS THE MEDIA?

The single most alarming fact about global media today is how few firms own and operate it. The degree of concentration in global media ownership rivals that of the oil industry. But the difference between concentration in the oil industry and in the media is that the former deals with tangible things, while the latter deals with *consciousness*. As such it may be the central factor shaping how societies evolve, and whether any shred of democracy can survive.

In his seminal book *Rich Media, Poor Democracy*, leading media authority Robert McChesney of the University of Illinois, has compiled an extremely important set of statistics and analyses on global and domestic (U.S.) media concentration that has ominous implications for the future functioning of democracy.

As of 1999, says McChesney, only eight giant global corporations owned over 70 percent of global media. *All* global media. Not just television but also newspapers, magazines, radio, satellite systems, cable, book publishing, film production and distribution, movie theater chains, major aspects of the Internet, billboards, and theme parks. Since then, the rules of the World Trade Organization and domestic policies within countries have only increased the trend toward concentration.

These eight corporations are already capable of speaking to hundreds of millions of people on every continent on a daily and hourly basis, and they do. The eight largest global giants are: Time Warner, Disney, Fox News, Viacom, Seagram, General Electric, Sony, and Bertelsmann. The first three on that list own more than 50 percent of the combined total of the eight companies. And with the exception of Bertelsmann, these same corporations also dominate the U.S. media market.

There is also a second tier of several dozen media firms that do not operate quite on the scale of the big eight, but tend to concentrate within regions and niche markets. In North America these include, for example, Dow Jones, CBS, Newhouse, Comcast, Clear Channel, Knight Ridder, the New York Times, and others. In Europe, second-tier firms include Kirch, Havas, Mediaset, Hachette, Prisa, Canal Plus, Reuters, Kluwer, Axel Springer, and others.

The oligopolisitic condition of the global media market is also matched inside most countries, and in individual media categories. "The global music industry," says McChesney, "is dominated by five firms, all but one of which (EMI) are part of larger media transnational corporations. These five music giants earn 70 percent of their revenues outside of the United States." Major

U.S. film and TV producers likewise generate about 50 to 60 percent of their revenues outside the United States.

Such a degree of media concentration is not readily apparent to casual observation, since most local and even international affiliates continue to operate under other names. CNN, for example, is actually owned by Time Warner, which also owns HBO, Court TV, Warner Brothers and Cinemax films, *Time* and *Fortune* magazines, among *hundreds* of others. Disney owns ABC television and radio networks, and such global cable TV channels as ESPN, Lifetime, A&E, History, and E! Entertainment, among hundreds of other networks and stations and various other media ventures around the world. Fox News owns twenty-two U.S. TV stations, over 130 daily newspapers around the world, twenty-three magazines, British Sky TV, Asian Star satellite, Latin Sky Broadcasting, and hundreds of other holdings.

*It would be extremely difficult to overstate the importance of these figures, or the influence these few corporations obviously have on government officials and public policies throughout the world.* Given such a situation, one might ask if there can possibly be a free enough flow of information for real democracy to survive. It would also be difficult to overstate the impacts of these few powerful corporations on public opinion when major issues are in play, whether concerns with the environment, social policy, or national elections.

A startling example of the problem became highly visible in the United States in early 2004, about nine months after the U.S. invasion of Iraq. A national survey found that people who received their news and information from Fox News (as much as 40 percent of the population) had an entirely different view of the circumstances that led up to the war than people who read newspapers or watched other networks. Fox News consistently showed a strong right-wing, prowar leaning in its coverage, and the polls showed that 80 percent of its viewers believed at least one of the following: that there was a conspiratorial connection between Saddam Hussein and Al-Qaeda terrorists, that weapons of mass destruction were found in Iraq, and that the majority of the world population supported U.S. activities there. Indeed, 45 percent of Fox viewers believed all three of these statements, even long after all other media and governments had accepted that there were no terrorists, no WMD, and little global support.

This is one of the thousands of examples one could use to demonstrate the degree to which public knowledge is directly derivative of slants taken by popular media. In this case, after an appalling period of unquestioning support for war policies, there developed some divergent voices within media. But in all too many cases there is not. And where there are no countering viewpoints, how can the public believe other than what it is told? Most events covered in the media occur so far away from direct contact with viewers and the public that the public is at great pains to have much of an independently generated perspective. In the modern world, media has become the primary basis of public knowledge. And among the media today, the majority of people in the world get their information from television. As we described in chapter 5, "Reclaiming the Commons," true public television has largely been eliminated in most countries, or drastically diminished, in favor of commercial TV, with its tendency toward entertainment packaging and trivialization of news content.

As the adage goes, "Who controls the media controls the world."

Another consequence of this staggering degree of concentration is the media's ability to influence policies of local governments and global bureaucracies like the World Trade Organization, which works hard to accelerate the trend toward concentration. The rules of the WTO already favor the largest corporations, and with conclusion of the current negotiations within the General Agreement on Trade in Services (GATS), *new* rules of investment may make it nearly impossible for national governments anywhere to keep out global media conglomerates that seek control over local domestic media companies, thus leaving little room for local culture and values, furthering the homogenization we described earlier.

Right now, we are witnessing a fierce new round of global acquisitions and mergers as first-tier and second-tier media companies are racing to buy each other out, leaving fewer and fewer global media giants and themselves becoming ever larger and larger. All of them share common commercial values and worldviews. So we are left with the most powerful and pervasive communications system in history, dominated by a tiny handful of people who believe they know how we all should live and think.

## THE REACH AND POWER OF TELEVISION AND ADVERTISING

To truly grasp the significance of this degree of global corporate media concentration, it is useful to describe the power, scale, and reach of its primary communications instruments: television and advertising.

We begin with some more alarming statistics. Some may have read these numbers before, but they bear repetition in order to fully understand their impact. First, the United States.

According to the A.C. Nielsen Company, as reported in *Advertising Age* in 2002, 99.5 percent of American homes had television sets, and 95 percent of the population watches at least some television every day, an apparent sign of their commitment or addiction to it. The average home has a TV set playing for more than eight hours per day, even when no one is watching. The average adult viewer watches about four and a half hours of TV per day. The average child age eight to thirteen watches about four hours per day. At ages two to four, they watch nearly three hours daily, not counting any television they may see in school. (A lot of advertising is directed at this age group.) A recent report by the Kaiser Family Foundation found that not even infants are free of television, for about 20 percent of U.S. parents leave a TV on next to their baby's crib, finding it has some kind of hypnotic effect, keeping the child quieter. (Many researchers have established this hypnotic effect as functioning to some degree in all age groups among heavy viewers; studies also show that small children, far from being quieted by TV, seem quieter only when watching and then revert to hyperactive behavior, caused by heavy viewing.)

Thinking about such statistics, they mean that roughly half the U.S. population is watching more than four hours per day. How is that possible? By heavy viewing every night, and then all weekend. In the United States, people now watch more television than they do anything else in life besides sleeping, working, or going to school. (Neither have these figures changed since the advent of computers and the Internet; all the latter have done is add to the amount of time during which people are engaged with information machines.) In the United States, television viewing has become the *main thing* people do with their days. It's replaced community life, family life, culture. It has replaced the environment. In fact, it has *become* the environment that people interact with each day, albeit a far more aggressive environment than trees and nature. It has become the culture as well, and by this we do not mean so-called popular culture, which sounds somehow democratic. Television is not democratic. The viewers at home do not make television; they receive it. No one elected those eight giant corporations, or TV's local affiliates either. They occupy that position because of their corporate wealth, and because the airwaves, once considered public property open to all comers, have been nearly totally privatized. (See also chapter 5.) Television expresses *corporate* culture, not popular culture.

Given these statistics, it is fair to say that ours is the first generation in history to have essentially moved its life inside media—to have replaced direct contact with other people, other communities, and nature for simulated, re-created, or edited versions of events, including news, that we can have little means of judging for veracity. Television is the original "virtual reality."

The situation verges on the bizarre, the stuff of science fiction. If an anthropologist was sent from the Andromeda galaxy to earth to study its people and if that individual hovered over the United States, chances are the report back home would read something like this: "They're sitting night after night in dark rooms. They're staring at a light. Their eyes are not moving. They're not thinking. Their brains are in a passive-receptive state (measured as 'alpha' for heavy viewers) and nonstop imagery is pouring into their brains, images from someplace where they are not, thousands of miles away. The images are being sent by a very small number of people, and they are of toothpaste and cars and guns and blood and people running around in bathing suits. The whole thing seems to be some kind of experiment in mind control." And it just may be.

Internationally, the situation is little different from the United States. About 80 percent of the global population has access to television, with most industrialized countries reporting similar viewing habits as in the United States. In Canada, England, France, Germany, Italy, Russia, Greece, Poland, and many other countries in Europe and South America, the average person watches three to four hours per day. In Japan and Mexico, they watch more than in the United States. In many parts of the world, the programming they watch comes from the United States and from other countries in the West, with few local shows.

Even in places on earth where there are no roads—tiny tropical islands, icy tundras of the north, or log cabins—millions of people are sitting, night after night, watching white people in Dallas driving sleek cars, or standing around swimming pools, or drinking martinis while plotting ways to do each other in, or they're looking at "Baywatch," the most popular show in the world. Life in Texas, California, and New York is made to seem the ultimate in achievement, while local culture, even where it's extremely vibrant and alive—which is still true for a fair amount of the earth—is made to seem backward, unworthy, not good.

The act of watching TV is quickly replacing other ways of life and value systems. People everywhere are beginning to carry identical images and craving the same commodities, from cars to hairsprays to Barbie dolls to Palm Pilots. TV is turning everyone into everyone else. It's cloning all cultures to be alike. In his classic novel *Brave New World*, Aldous Huxley envisioned this global cloning process taking place via drugs and genetic engineering. We have those too, but TV does it nearly as well, because of the medium's reach and power.

Another "hidden" or invisible aspect of media power has to do with the role and scale of advertising. Of course, everyone is aware of advertising—we see it routinely every day—but most people tend to be less aware of its power and influence. The more highly educated we are, the more we tend to see it as trivial and believe it does not really affect us, that our intellect will save us. If so, a lot of money is being spent foolishly by corporations that put out tens of millions of dollars believing that the ads surely do have a decisive effect on how people view their choices and satisfactions, whether they went to college or not.

*In the United States, the average viewer of television sees about twenty-eight thousand commercials every year.* That is twenty-eight thousand times that they are hit by extremely invasive imagery saying virtually the same thing. One may be about toothpaste, and another about cars, cosmetics, or drugs. But the intent of each of these commercials is identical: to persuade people to view life as a nonstop stream of commodity satisfactions. Cumulatively, globally, the commercializing effect is immense.

Of course, not every viewer of every ad goes directly out to a store to buy that thing, and advertisers know this. They are playing a numbers game. The more times any viewer ingests an advertising image—repetition of ads is one primary way they become effective—the more it becomes a part of the viewer's consciousness. The image sticks in the brain like a fly to flypaper.

Celebrated advertising executive and media gadfly of the 1960s Howard Gossage frequently spoke to audiences of "the dirty little secret among advertising people that their apparently superficial, silly images are nonetheless an effective kind of brainwashing. It doesn't matter how intelligent you are." In other words, if you are watching television you *will* see and take in the images. Worse, once the image is embedded, it is there permanently. "If you don't think so," said Gossage, "how come if I say 'Jolly Green Giant' most people will instantly get a picture in their heads of this huge green character wearing green leotards selling canned peas? Or if I say, 'Better things for better living through chemistry,' do you think of Du Pont? Of course you do."

Gossage said all this back in the 1960s. More contemporary examples might include the Taco Bell Chihuahua—can you picture him?—or Britney Spears selling Pepsi, or the jingle "Like a rock" for Chevy pickup trucks, or that weird guy with the big white head: Jack in the Box. Did you know those things were living in your head? The point of the exercise is that your intellect can't save you. Advertising imagery goes in, is difficult to erase, and can become a kind of internal billboard, ready to flash at appropriate moments. This is why so much money is spent on it, with most of that money going to television. Unlike print media, where imagery is static, television provides moving imagery that enters cleanly into the minds of millions of people, like riding on a freeway there. Viewer discernment and intelligence have no role. All advertisers understand the potential of this power. Most of the public does not.

According to Robert McChesney, advertisers in the United States spent about $214 billion in 1999, representing over 2.1 percent of the total U.S. GDP for that year. About half of that went to television ads, with the rest divided among newspapers, magazines, billboards, radio, and other media. Of the top twenty corporate advertisers, eleven represented only two industries: automobiles and drugs. Other major categories include cosmetics, communications, fast-food retail, financial services, toiletries, airlines, and so on.

(One little-noted additional category of ad expenditures are those directed toward children under the age of eight. According to psychologists Tim Kasser and Allen D. Kanner, authors of *Psychology and Consumer Culture,* advertising targeted at small children now represents $12 billion per year in the United States, with $95 million of that coming from just Burger King and Quaker's Captain Crunch cereal. This advertising is immensely aided by tens of millions of dollars in psychological research into what gets kids to push their parents into certain buying decisions.)

Advertising in the United States represents about half of the total advertising spent in the world, although European spending is increasing rapidly, by more than 10 percent per year. And advertising in China—the great hope for big new markets—has been growing by 40 to 50 percent per year during the last decade.

Corporate concentration among advertising agencies is nearly what it is for media generally, partly because of the globalization of product markets, thus making it more efficient for global ad agencies to undertake the global message and production and placement coordination. The largest agency is Omnicom ($8.6 billion in 2003 revenues), which owns fourteen other major ad agencies, including BBDO Worldwide and DDB Needham Worldwide. The two other global ad agency giants are WPP Group ($7.3 billion), and Interpublic Group ($5.9 billion). These three agencies have combined income greater than the following ten.

The consolidation trend among ad agencies is increasing because global marketers largely prefer to work with a single agency throughout the world for the sake of efficiency. So it's a small handful of giant corporations, working with a small handful of giant advertising companies, putting out tens of billions of dollars of similar images to every national population and ethnic group, telling them how life can be better with the products of industry.

There is also a direct political dimension to this dreamy relationship between television and advertising; the following are good examples for anyone who doubts the power of that combination to profoundly change thinking and beliefs.

In 2004, the new governor of California, the very popular action movie hero Arnold Schwarzenegger, was trying to promote a $15 billion bond issue to be voted upon in a special election. When first introduced, the public was a strong 70 percent opposed. But Schwarzenegger was able to raise $8 million to spend in TV advertising spots, condensed into a two-week period just before the vote. He starred in the commercials himself, thus bringing celebrity to the cause. The opposition to the bond issue was unable to muster any significant opposing funds, and in the absence of an opposing view Schwarzenegger managed to sway public opinion in only two weeks' time in exactly the opposite direction. The final vote was 70 percent *in favor* of the bond issue. If there had been opposing funds, it might have been possible to point out how the state would be dumping a fantastic debt onto future generations.

Another example comes from the U.S. presidential campaign of that same year. The George Bush for President team deeply understood the power of advertising, and particularly that in the absence of an opposing view, it will usually be believed. They raised about $200 million for advertising, the greatest amount for a candidate in history, and virtually all of it for television. According to the campaign's ad director, much of the money was to be used to "define John Kerry," the Democratic candidate, "for a public that doesn't know him well." By defining him, they essentially meant attacking with half-truths and nontruths about his thirty-year public record while positioning the president as a forceful brave leader of a nation at war. Such is the power of the medium that after only a few days of *unanswered* ad placements, polls showed support for Kerry plummeting. Interviews in *USA Today* revealed a public that mimicked exactly the language of the commercials: "Kerry is a waffler." "Kerry will raise all our taxes." And so on. How could it be otherwise? How could an average person know what is true and what is not, unless the message is directly countered with equal volume and skill? In the absence of an alternative perspective, the public will accept what it sees.

In this case, the Kerry camp recognized the dangers of unanswered charges and made an all-out effort to raise $100 million of its own to at least partly offset Republican expenditures. As we go to press, we do not know the final outcome of this epic media and money battle. But the point is that political campaigns in the United States are now much less about the key issues of the time. Campaigns have essentially been reduced to battles of television and advertising imagery, a war of ad agencies for unimpeded entry to the public mind with information and edited imagery that may or may not be true, a *virtual* campaign in which the made-up has the power of the real.

So where does this leave us? It leaves us with a global communications system in which billions of people sit for long hours night after night in dark rooms in a semiconscious state staring at television imagery, sent to them from very far away by people they do not know, that wavers between meaningless trivia to purposeful messages with the ability to persuade viewers

*yes media — adv imp.*
*but also, how it doesn't report on the act.*
*comps*

that commodity-oriented life is best. The situation is increasingly the same everywhere on earth.

We have the most powerful and pervasive communications system in history, dominated by a tiny handful of corporate people, describing how life should be lived. *Is this good?* Is it OK for billions of people to be receiving nonstop doses of powerful images and information controlled by such few sources, essentially telling them to be unhappy about their own cultures and values—how they live and who they are—to get onto the commodity treadmill, to put their trust in corporations, and to embrace a global homogenization of Western values? Will this bring a sustainable, equitable society? Many think not. The following section is about their ideas for change.

REFORMS AND ALTERNATIVES

Given this situation, it's a wonder that there is not more public outrage. A dominant media model that places hypercommercialism far above the public good has not been a front-burner issue for most groups promoting the progressive reform agenda. Though millions of people have been protesting globalization, there have been no significant protests at the doorways of Disney and Fox or Vivendi and Time Warner. Yet all of these companies are among the leading salespeople avidly hawking globalization. They are in effect the "consciousness glue" that cements the model together across all boundaries on the planet, and they are also among the primary beneficiaries of the expansion of the model.

There may be several reasons for the lack of organized action on this matter. First, there's the daunting scale of the problem; the media is everywhere and, at the same time, all-encompassing and totally dominant, and yet seemingly neutral. One doesn't know where to start. Second, the global corporate media, and the domestic media too, do not report or carry analyses of issues concerning their own powerful role or dictatorial concentration of ownership except back in the business pages, which leaves the subject largely absent from the public mind. And third, some activists and organizers see themselves as dependent on the mainstream media to break out crucial information on their issues, or at least they remain hopeful this can be done. Hopeful enough to continue to see mass media more as an opportunity than a problem. The occasional moment when their efforts succeed is truly the exception that enforces the rule.

However, there is evidence that things are starting to shift. For example, in November 2003 the first National Conference on Media Reform took place in Madison, Wisconsin, sponsored by Free Press, drawing more than two thousand activists. It was an important statement that a new movement had finally begun. The attendees discussed issues ranging from the problem of media ownership and concentration, to public access and public broadcasting policies, to successes of alternative media movements abroad, to negative impacts of the WTO and FCC, to the low quality of journalism by commercial media. Most of all they made a powerful case that all activist groups, whatever their primary issues, need to focus on the problems of media today or their own work would be continually hindered. Media reform needs to move to the front burner of every group working toward democratic outcomes and a free flow of information.

At the Madison conference, several examples were offered of surprising successes by alternative media activists around the world, notably in South America where opposition to neoliberalism is popular and growing. In one speech, Ecuador-based Sally Birch of the Latin America Information Agency insisted that we can no longer assume that alternative media is invariably "marginal," and she gave three examples of South American campaigns greatly aided by media activists.

The first concerned the attempted ouster of the democratically elected President Chavez of Venezuela. That attempted coup was largely led by business interests in close contact with the United States, and their cause was loudly trumpeted by the media conglomerates of Venezuela. Birch indicated that it was the unified voices of the extensive alternative media system in Venezuela that roused the population to prevent Chavez's removal.

A second example occurred in Bolivia, where the mainstream media supported the World Bank's privatization campaigns, including water, despite the immense havoc it brought to the general public. The alternative media in Bolivia was a key factor in keeping the information flowing and the opposition in touch with itself. And in Colombia, the right-wing government of President Juan Uribe recently lost a major referendum, a complete surprise to everyone but the small presses and alternative news sources that had led the "underground" campaign.

Meanwhile, in the United States, during early 2003 a major shift took place: a huge public uprising against new corporate-friendly rules proposed by the U.S. Federal Communications Commission (FCC).

The FCC had proposed startling new deregulatory measures that would have permitted, among other things, extensive newspaper-broadcast cross-ownership mergers, and eliminated most restrictions on the number of TV stations a single company could own locally and nationally. (The prevailing rules now limit one company to only one station per market.) So, in any given city one media giant might have come to own the major newspapers and several television stations and radio stations, a pretty good prescription for nearly total control of public policy.

Global media corporations under the new rules would have also been permitted to own sufficient broadcast outlets nationally to reach 45 percent of the entire U.S. population, an unprecedented degree of access for a single corporation to the public's mind.

The chairman of the FCC, Michael Powell, a right-wing Bush appointee and the son of Secretary of State Colin Powell, imperiously announced that he would not attend public hearings around the country on the new rules. He had already done everything possible to prevent any public discussion of the matter as "unnecessary." In fact, because there was no public benefit from the rules and considerable potential harms to the democratic process, public discussion would make the issue far more difficult to pass. Keeping the media silent was the most prudent path.

Despite the efforts of two Democratic commissioners, and under extreme pressure from Fox News, Clear Channel, Disney, Viacom, and others, the measures passed along party lines by three to two. But not before an unexpected public outcry began in some surprising quarters. A larger number of conservative Republicans joined media activist groups in opposing the rules on the grounds of dangers to democracy and localism of such corporate concentration. The opposition included the likes of the National Rifle Association, many conservative congresspeople, and the *New York Times's* conservative columnist William Safire, who all agreed with the arguments being made by progressive groups like Consumers Union, Free Press, Common Cause, MoveOn (www.MoveOn.org) and elements of organized labor. Combined, they brought forth more than 750,000 responses to the FCC and Congress, an unprecedented outburst, and succeeded in making the issue into a political hot potato in an election season. As of this writing, despite considerable maneuvering in Congress (which has power over the FCC), *none* of the rules have been approved, and the whole matter has moved to the back burner from where it may or may not be revived. Whatever the final outcome, a turning point may have been reached in which a passive public has seen its democratic rights gravely threatened by media conglomerates and learned it can do something about them.

### The Role of the Internet

Such huge resistance as in South America and in the FCC case was partly aided by inventive uses of the Internet. In the United States both liberal and conservative groups spread the word of their opposition via the Internet, and urged responses. Further evidence that the Internet has emerged as a major player in political campaigns was the huge volume of support for Democratic presidential candidate Howard Dean in 2003, even including the ability to raise some $40 million. And of course, one Internet-based activist organization, MoveOn has gathered more than two million members and has had a significant impact on several mainstream political campaigns, including as a creative independent advertising company working against George Bush.

Many progressive elements see the Internet as the ultimate tool to beat back corporations on behalf of more democratic community and individual empowerment. And the instrument has much to recommend it. However, while acknowledging this potential, cautionary notes are appropriate, because the Internet may ultimately be subject to many of the same commercial interventions from powerful corporations as plague the rest of the mass media; furthermore, it does not inevitably perform for the progressive side of the agenda.

In their remarkable pamphlet *It's the Media, Stupid,* the media critic for the *Nation* magazine, John Nichols, joined Robert McChesney in taking a measured approach to the potential of the Internet to reform media. According to the authors, the main argument for the utopian potential of the Internet goes something like this: "Because anyone can start a Web site at relatively nominal expense, and because anyone can access any Web site, the giant media firms are dinosaurs from another age, and their monopoly control surely must be doomed."

Although it is certainly a democratic expression to be able to start a Web site, and people have now done so by the millions, very few Web sites have had sufficient promotional support or effective management to make major impacts on public policy, the prior examples notwithstanding.

Nichols and McChesney argue that the more immediate consequence of the digital revolution may be "convergence, whereby telephone companies like AT&T, and computer companies like Microsoft, become active in digital media, telecommunications, and computer industries." AT&T has become the country's largest cable company and Microsoft has purchased scores of media, cable, and telecommunications companies all over the globe, with potentially ominous future consequences for a "free" Internet.

Another sobering point in any assessment of the political directions of the Internet is that although it surely assists progressive forces in organizing, communicating, and stimulating public response, it has corresponding benefits for the most powerful corporations in the world—banking, natural resources, manufacturing, and communications. *The modern global corporation of today would not exist at its present scale, or operate with the speed and effect it does, without this global telecommunications network to keep its thousand-armed global enterprise smoothly in touch seven days per week, twenty-four hours a day, every day of the year.* Global corporations use these networks not only for communication but concretely to shift immense resources anywhere in the world at the tap of a key; billions of dollars, say, can be transferred from a bank in London to Sarawak, where forests get cut down or local currencies get bought up and sold, destabilizing small governments. It may be the ultimate assessment of the so-called communications revolution that while benefiting opponents of centralized corporate power, in the end it benefits the corporations more.

So as we continue to use the technology, we should be aware it may not be the ultimate utopian solution some think it might be and that other areas of organized activity are also at least as important.

*Steps Toward a More Democratic Media*

Any serious movement toward media reform must include several simultaneous goals: Drastically reduce the powers and concentration of global commercial media—globally and within each country; this means challenging the enabling rules of such bodies as the World Trade Organization and the corresponding domestic bodies such as the FCC in the United States.

Dramatically increase the power and viability of the nonprofit, noncommercial sectors of media, especially in the broadcast system. Do everything possible to create, support, expand, and empower new alternative voices on local, national, and international levels.

These are, of course, daunting tasks, but they may seem less so once we realize that all people and groups can make progress toward the larger goals by activating themselves *locally*, where they may have direct impact, while also seeking national and international connections and opportunities. For activists and other groups, *the primary first step is to put the matter on the front burner* and to realize that all causes are lost causes, whether concerning the environment, or health, or political issues, if the commercial media continues to overwhelm and cloud the public mood and mind on behalf of trivialization, hypercommercialism, and ultimate self-interest.

The following, then, is a list of opportunities, ideas, and activities that can combine in a broad new international campaign toward a democratic media. Of course, the list doesn't begin to be comprehensive, and it must continue to grow as we all become more experienced in this new movement.

*1. Pressure the Global Rulemakers* We have mentioned the powerful role being played by the World Trade Organization's General Agreement on Trade in Services (GATS). We will briefly reemphasize here that if the GATS negotiations succeed, they will give global media giants greatly increased access to domestic markets everywhere and an increased ability to buy up local affiliates, and they will also permit unimpeded entry of foreign media into domestic contexts—print, television, film—on the same terms as local media. The new rules may also label public subsidies for such efforts as public broadcasting, or noncommercial stations, illegal forms of restraint on free trade, banned under WTO rules. This could prove to be the death of public broadcasting in many countries.

Countries eager to protect traditional cultural values, or local programming, or local ownership of information dispersion, or seeking to help commercial-free media, will be prevented by GATS rules from doing so, thus potentially leading to local media being overwhelmed by films, television, and newspapers owned by foreign conglomerates. So far, the countries of Canada and France have been the leaders of opposition to the GATS rules, joined by some other countries that are deeply worried about preserving traditional culture and values. *The fundamental principle we must work to sustain is that no international body should have the power to require that national or local governments permit unimpeded foreign investment and ownership of local media and cultural industries.* The ultimate decisions on these matters must be local. (For more information on this issue see the Web sites of Public Citizen, Council of Canadians, and Institute for Policy Studies, which are listed in the resources section at the back of this volume.)

2. *Pressure Domestic Rulemakers*   Aside from impositions from the WTO that inhibit local and domestic regulations, most rules on ownership and programming are the province of national counterparts of the U.S. Federal Communication Commission, and the domestic legislative bodies that oversee such commissions. We talked earlier about how a large public outcry can challenge these domestic bodies, though regrettably the U.S. public's response to the FCC rules was one of very few cases where Americans were motivated enough and organized enough to be effective.

In other countries there are some far more highly developed movements. As Nichols and McChesney report, in Sweden the very activist Left party has managed to put all aspects of domestic media reform into hot public debate, arguing in their basic platform that "prerequisites for democracy are freedom of speech and press freedom. In a living democracy it is necessary to have a broad and independent choice of media. Everyone should be able to express their opinions in one form or another. All opinions should be able to reach the public." Among the reforms the Swedish Left party advocates are abolition of all advertising on radio and television, and significant subsidies for diverse print media, even those expressing radical and unpopular views.

A similar movement in New Zealand was formed in 1991 by an amazing coalition of Greens, Maoris, and labor movements, which merged into the Alliance party. They have focused campaigns on mass media domination as a "human rights issue" and campaigned for increased noncommercial programming, protections for New Zealand's equivalent of NPR and PBS, a minimum of 30 percent "local content" in all programming, a new youth network, and new radio and TV stations to serve ethnic minorities, as well as elimination of all advertising directed at children, among other ideas.

Other countries where there are major public movements on media issues include Australia, where the mainstream Democratic party has become the leading defender of public broadcasting against privatization and made it into a national issue, with a good chance of success. In South Africa, the Congress of South African Trade Unionists (COSATU) has had considerable success in influencing government policy toward a more open and diverse media system. In Brazil, media activism has become a major influence in the Workers party of President Lula; there have been many demonstrations outside the offices of global media conglomerates demanding a more serious effort in the news to present all viewpoints. Similar effective national campaigning is ongoing also in Britain, India, and Canada, among other countries. (For more information, see the Free Press Web site in the resources section.)

There is no reason why American activists should not make similar demands and campaign on them. Among other good campaign ideas would be to insist on far more stringent public service requirements and standards for issuance of broadcast licenses, revival of the fairness doctrine requiring a balance of information on controversial issues, and a firm limit of ownership by any one owner to one station per market.

*3. Impose Fees on Commercial Broadcasters for Use of the Public's Broadcast Commons* Commercial broadcasters in the United States are now making free use of what is legally the public's property, recognized and encoded into U.S. law as it is in many other countries. As we argued in chapter 5, these airwaves are part of the public commons, protected for public use, participation, and benefit, and must be respected as such. Instead, commercial broadcasters have had seventy-five years to exploit this extremely valuable public property—the broadcast spectrum commons—from which they have made tens of millions of dollars, while *not* serving the public interest and not paying anything for the privilege. There is no logical argument for this pattern to continue, especially because public broadcasting itself, and so many other nonprofit media, are being starved for the funding they deserve.

Public subsidy of commercial broadcasting must stop, or be radically diminished. If commercial broadcasters were required to pay user fees, or pay a percentage of their advertising revenues into a public media fund, the entire face of the broadcast system, and of journalism, would change for the better, diminishing the dominant power of the commercial system and increasing the opportunity for alternative voices.

Aside from supporting expanded public broadcasting, monies formerly used for subsidies to wealthy corporations could be used to assist local and community broadcast outlets, low-power and microradio initiatives, and

print media and to create a balance of information, new access opportunities, and special media targeted to low-income, elderly, and ethnic communities that are now poorly served. These funds could also assist starving cultural and art projects within communities as well as start-up publishing and
cooperative ventures, thus revitalizing democratic participation in information exchange.

   *4. Increase Subsidies for Public Broadcasting*   If present subsidies for commercial broadcasting are diminished even by a small amount, there would be
a new annual fund of tens of millions of dollars that could go toward truly
public broadcasting on the public's airwaves. Right now, as mentioned earlier, public subsidies for noncommercial broadcasting on the public's airwaves have been reduced to little more than 10 percent of annual operating
budgets, and the very existence of the remaining noncommercial broadcast
outlets is threatened. (In certain right-wing corners, public broadcasting's
*right* to exist is questioned as inconsistent with free market ideology—as if
public subsidy for commercial broadcasters *is* somehow consistent with free
markets.) A new fund garnered from reduced commercial subsidies should
go directly toward full funding for public broadcasting—so it is not dependent on corporations—and for an expanded number of public broadcasting
outlets on both television and radio, as well as in print media, to provide
democratic information balance. Of course, commercial broadcasters will
vehemently oppose this, because they have made billions from properties
they obtained for free and do not want any added competition on the airwaves—from noncommercial media—that might take away listeners, reduce
ratings, and affect advertising revenues.

   *5. Set New Limits on Advertising*   Many countries limit the amount, kind,
and target audiences of advertising. This is in recognition of the extreme
power of the medium to influence public consciousness, and to create a society driven by commercial values. Some countries ban all advertising directed
at children; all paid advertising in political campaigns, instead providing free
airtime for candidates to present their views during a limited period close to
the election; and all advertising on public broadcasting channels, among
many other limits on content. Many also strictly limit the amount of time
per hour that ads may run. The United States has none of these restrictions.
In fact, the only present limit on commercial advertising is the rule against
the advertising of cigarettes on television.

Regulation of advertising in the United States has had an extremely rocky road, because courts have declared it a protected form of speech under the First Amendment of the U.S. Constitution, equal to the protection afforded individual speech. It is truly a preposterous situation; commercial advertising speech, a medium available only to the wealthy, is considered the same, legally speaking, as individual speech.

And yet, at the time of the creation of the Constitution, advertising barely existed, corporations did not exist in their present form, and media itself consisted only of one-sheet newspapers, handbills, and soapbox oration. It was surely not the intention of the framers of the Constitution to protect a form of speech that did not yet exist, and that shared few characteristics of individual speech that needed protection to be sure of an information balance in a democratic society. Besides, advertising speech is now capable of utterly overwhelming—because of its sheer volume and power—all individual voices, and the voices of a free press too, thus creating just the kind of information imbalance the Constitution went to great pains to avoid.

The last time a serious effort was made in the United States to regulate advertising was in the 1970s. The Federal Trade Commission (under Jimmy Carter) began hearings on the question of whether the advertising of sugary cereals to children under eight years old was "fair" under legal standards that demand approximate mental equality between buyers and sellers. The FTC thought that having huge staffs of highly paid psychologists, focus group researchers, and advertising writers and artists collaborating with each other and then spending tens of millions of dollars in ads directed at vulnerable young children in order to sell them harmful products, might have constituted an *inherently unfair imbalance* in the exchange.

The media outrage at this FTC initiative was spectacular to behold. It was not only major networks and right-wing media that became righteously indignant. The *New York Times* and the *Washington Post* also ran fierce editorials decrying this challenge to "freedom of speech." Eventually, President Carter was forced to fire the FTC's chairman Michael Petschuk and eliminate the hearings. Very few government agencies have made any similar forays since. (Alas, recent studies on the present epidemic of childhood obesity in the United States by the Kaiser Family Foundation has put a lot of the blame on the heavy television advertising of sugary cereals and fatty foods directly to kids, who then pester their parents to buy these things.)

Nonetheless, there are organizations including Action for Children's Television, Campaign for a New American Dream, TV Free America, Free Press, and Adbusters' Media Foundation that are again campaigning about these matters. (See the resources section.) There is also the possibility of new legal challenges on protected commercial speech targeted at children, or in political campaigns. Here is a place where a strong outpouring from the public could make a difference. A few thousand angry letters directed to Congress, advertisers, the FTC, the FCC, and local representatives and local media, could prove meaningful.

*6. Support and Empower Alternative Media*   The National Conference on Media Reform, mentioned earlier, drew over two thousand activists, many of whom are directly engaged in attempting to build a new media rising up to someday displace, or at least diminish, the dominant model. There is no telling how many such alternative outlets now exist, but MediaChannel (www.MediaChannel.org) lists 1,103 such organizations in the United States alone, focused primarily on media issues. Meanwhile, the Alternative Press Index shows about five hundred groups presenting information from non-mainstream perspectives.

The Media Access Project lists no fewer than thirty-four hundred organizations that have applied to the FCC for approval of low-power FM radio transmission; these are community-based radio projects that can reach within a three- to five-mile radius. It was a struggle to get the FCC to approve these projects because they were opposed by commercial stations, and even, in a burst of shortsightedness, by National Public Radio. Low-power radio transmission has significant potential to serve local communities that have little access to any other media, and can become important players, especially on local issues.

On the antiglobalization front, one organization stands out for having made a major difference: Indymedia. That project began in 1999 during the demonstrations at the WTO ministerial in Seattle. Most of the major media, ignorant of what the protests were about, were engaged in a convulsion of misreporting and distortion, overstating the violence (which was actually minor) and understating the impact of the demonstrations (which was huge). A group of filmmakers, videographers, journalists, Web designers, and others decided to take matters into their own hands and instantly began to make and distribute their own versions of events to the local media in

Seattle and to the world with great effect, bringing a far more balanced and insightful view of what had been going on. (See the resources section.)

Since Seattle, Indymedia has created a grassroots network that has spread to over 130 locations in fifty-one countries and has been a steady force in reporting on major breaking news relevant to the globalization and social justice movements. More of this activity is required. It directly diminishes the ability of the dominant media to get away with unchallenged imagery and news.

7. *Support Local Organizing*   John Nichols and Robert McChesney have written that "local media activism is the foundation of the media reform movement, and much can be done at the local level. As the Christian Coalition recognized a decade ago, an effective national movement has as much to do with school board races as presidential nominations. This is even more true when it comes to media reform." Challenges to local media coverage, or to proposed consolidations of media, or to buyouts of local media by distant corporations, or to offensive advertising, can all be effective if well organized. *All media are inherently responsive to public complaints,* especially if the complaints are significant in number.

Nichols and McChesney cite the work of Denver's Rocky Mountain Media Watch in providing people the tools to be effective campaigners making an impact on local media. Fairness and Accuracy in Reporting (FAIR) has also adopted useful organizing models to stimulate local discussion groups, mass campaigns, and letter writing, as well as Internet responses; these have brought significant responses against media mergers, the sale of newspapers, and coverage of issues of import to local communities. And we have mentioned the role of Indymedia internationally.

Another arm of this activism is the growing "media justice movement," which focuses on issues of race, class, gender content, and structure. Two significant players in this national movement of local activists are San Francisco's Media Alliance and Philadelphia's Media Tank; both are attempting to build new local production and distribution outlets while also working toward regulatory and policy reforms. Influencing the dominant media today will certainly not be easy, but it is crucial. *The first step is the most important*—to recognize that the media must be made a primary part of the program of all groups interested in democratic action—whether on labor issues, children's issues, the environment, public health, safe food, or others.

No victory will be possible on any of these issues without diminishing the oppressive voice of the dominant media and increasing the opposing voices from public broadcasting and alternative media.

## People's Alternative Initiatives

This chapter and chapter 7 have detailed the myriad problems with the major operating systems of society, geared as they are to corporate control and global orientation. Also presented were ideas to radically alter that model in ways that support the ten core principles of sustainable societies offered in chapter 4. Many of these ideas are still at the discussion stage, others have movements pushing for their implementation, and others still have been put into place with success around the world. While the ideas continue to circulate, however, action moves ever forward. In the following paragraphs we provide a snapshot of the tremendous wealth of living, breathing alternative systems that communities around the world are creating right now. From Kentucky to Kenya, from Bangladesh to Bolivia, and from Indonesia to Italy, the communities listed here are only representative of countless others that are directly challenging the "inevitability" of economic globalization by reclaiming their rights to land, healthy food, water, dignity, biodiversity, political autonomy, and a safe and sustainable environment, or simply the right to live in harmony with one another. Each has established meaningful and powerful alternatives that make clear that a better world is not only possible, it is here.

### HORIZONTALISM: ARGENTINA

As described in chapter 3, Argentina was a poster child for the IMF for decades, with corrupt government leaders implementing the IMF's destructive policies with zeal. With the economy crashing, a popular rebellion began in December 2001, with the cry "Que se vayan todos" ("They all must go") leading to the downfall of several successive governments and the rejection of both the IMF and the neoliberal model. Few were surprised when the economy crashed completely in early 2002. With no government and no economy, the people of Argentina organized themselves. The new model that emerged is most often referred to as *horizontalism*. It is not focused on state power but rather on the collective uniting of movements. Horizontalism is not described as an ideology but as a relationship—a way of relating to one another in a directly democratic way while at the same time continually creating through the process of discovery.

The result is the uniting of a complex of movements, each working to provide for basic services, community organizing, collective thought, and imagining the future. Using direct democracy and collective decision making, they range from hundreds of occupied and producing factories, to dozens of neighborhood assemblies, to piquetero groups, many of whom are organized into a network of the Movement of Unemployed Workers, to hundreds of autonomous neighborhood kitchens and centers of popular education. Horizontalism is a break with hierarchical organizing and is focused, like the Zapatistas, from whom they get much inspiration, on dignity, autonomy, and collective organizing.

## CALETA CONSTITUCIÓN: CHILE

Founded in 1997 in Chile, Caleta Constitución is an alternative sustainable fishing community founded by local fisherfolk. Caleta was created by families who wanted to implement their vision of a sustainable local fishing economy. They took their plans to the regional government (which helped in financing) and the United Nations Development Program (which helped in planning). Today, Caleta's seventy-six families use modern but appropriate-to-scale infrastructure for transport, energy, water, and communications. Solar energy powers their homes and small businesses. The fisheries resources are managed as a local commons. The local fishers' union creates a management plan, which the community self-governs using only a limited area at any given time. They only use harvesting equipment and techniques agreed to through the communal decision-making processes. Small boats launch early in the morning from a pier specially designed and located to minimize impacts on the marine habitat and return in the afternoon to deliver their catch to markets. Financial stability comes from serving the sizeable market of nearby Antofagasta City. Community members also hope to begin processing their raw fish into value-added products to retain the maximum value of their resources.

## NAYAKRISHI ANDOLON: BANGLADESH

This Bangladeshi farmers' movement is reviving traditional crops by saving, storing, and sharing seeds as the basis of household food security. In response to the harmful effects of industrial agriculture, farmers gathered together to implement alternative farming methods that are community based and organic. These methods mix traditional knowledge and wisdom with newer ideas and scientific innovations that are suitable for farmers as well as the environment. Approximately sixty-five thousand families across Bangladesh follow a set of ten simple principles for Nayakrishi farming, all focusing on the use of locally available resources to enhance the efficiency of land, water, biodiversity, and energy, as well as the control over seeds in the farming community.

In addition to using chemical-free agricultural practices, the production of biodiversity is built into the Nayakrishi method of food production. As a fundamental principle, Nayakrishi farmers reject monoculture and base their practices on mixed cropping and crop rotation. In Nayakrishi villages, farmers derive more varieties of fish, together with a wide range of uncultivated crops, which either come as accompanying crops due to multiple cropping in the fields or grow on the common land where no herbicides are used. Livestock and poultry also grow more rapidly, thereby enriching the food security of the people. Similarly, the planting of local-variety trees is an integral part of the practice in Nayakrishi villages, which, in turn, attracts birds, butterflies, and other pollinators and predators.

## BENEFICIO MAJOMUT COFFEE GROWERS' UNION OF EJIDOS AND COMMUNITIES: MEXICO

In 1983, small coffee producers (most of them Tzotzil and Tzeltal indigenous people) in San Cristóbal de las Casas, in the highlands of Chiapas, Mexico, organized the Beneficio Majomut Coffee Growers' Union of Ejidos and Communities. A grassroots social organization with 1,450 members in twenty-five communities, the Majomut Union was established to unify farmers in the processing and marketing of their coffee. Members work an average of two hectares and cultivate corn, beans, and coffee. As the coffee is sold, it forms the main source of family income. Gradually, work has expanded to include the entire productive process and has become a means for organizing, managing, and carrying out integral development projects for the communities.

The organization converted to organic agriculture in 1992 and received its first organic certificate in 1995. Organic techniques have been introduced through the training of community promoters who create experimental organic lots in each community as a base for the learning process and research. Activities are based on the exchange of experiences through a farmer-to-farmer approach, including development and evaluation of agro-ecological practices, participatory research through farmer experimentation, and training of community promoters and community participation.

### NAVDANYA: INDIA

In response to growing threats to traditional farmers from economic globalization, Vandana Shiva's Research Foundation for Science, Technology, and Ecology initiated the Navdanya movement in India. Navdanya, or *nine seeds*, signifies a diverse ecological balance. Navdanya facilitates conservation and exchange of traditional seed varieties by local groups and communities through a national network of community seed banks and in situ (on-farm) conservation programs. Navdanya has pioneered community biodiversity registers to document the resources and knowledge of local, regional, and national communities. These registers help rejuvenate the ecological basis of agriculture, while asserting farmers' prior intellectual innovations to set limits on intellectual property rights monopolies.

In late 1996, Navdanya Foods was initiated, with the aim of bringing sustainably grown, chemical- and pesticide-free, healthy and nutritious, diverse organic food to the urban Indian consumer. Navdanya Foods specializes in grains from indigenous crops threatened by extinction. The program bridges the gap between the small-scale farmers who want to continue practicing ecological and sustainable agriculture and urban consumers who want to purchase nutritious and safe food for their families.

Currently, Navdanya is implementing Bija Yatra, a nationwide campaign aimed at creating debate and awareness of the erosion of genetic diversity, the devastating effects of the Green Revolution, the pending threat of a

WTO-promoted intellectual property rights regime, and the links to diminishing food security in India. The Bija Yatra campaign protects farmers' rights to use and conserve their own seeds, strengthens local communities, and creates a real alternative to corporate globalization.

### AUTONOMOUS GOVERNMENT IN CHIAPAS: MEXICO

Facing an unraveling of political, economic, and cultural life, the Zapatista Army of National Liberation (EZLN) emerged from the poorest state in Mexico, which was also the one with the greatest number of indigenous people. After ten years of quiet organizing, on January 1, 1994, the Zapatistas led an uprising in San Cristobal, Ocasingo, and five other municipal seats in Chiapas, Mexico. The uprising was timed to coincide with the signing of NAFTA to demonstrate Zapatista opposition to what they termed a "death certificate for the ethnic people of Mexico."

The Zapatistas have since created a new model of community organization based on civilian, regional, indigenous self-government (autonomy) and collective work for the community. Decisions are based on consensus-oriented horizontal structures. They have created five centers of autonomous, regional civil government known as *caracols* (conch shells) and autonomous, regional governance structures called *juntas de buen gobierno* (good government committees). The committees are composed of representatives from each autonomous county in the region. The counties democratically elect their own county councils to carry out the usual functions of local government: recording births, marriages, and deaths; obtaining development projects; constructing schools and clinics; and so on.

Without the support of government agencies, the Zapatistas have increased medical services with their network of microclinics, significantly lowering the infant mortality rate, and now offer a collaborative, community-directed school system in areas that previously offered virtually no educational opportunities. They have also developed an autonomous justice system for dispute resolution that is in demand as a fair and neutral mediator—adjucative body even in opposition communities. Finally, they have also developed an indigenous economy, rooted in the traditions of peasant farmers, such as the primary importance of community and collective work.

## SARVODAYA SHRAMADANA MOVEMENT: SRI LANKA

Sarvodaya Shramadana is a peoples' participatory democracy movement working in ten thousand villages involved with nearly four million people across Sri Lanka. Founded in 1958, Sarvodaya means *awakening of all.* Shramadana means *sharing of labor or energy.* The message is the awakening of everyone through sharing. As an organization, it is voluntary, non-governmental, nonprofit, nonsectarian, and apolitical. It works to fulfill basic human needs such as a clean and healthy environment, water, clothing, food, health care, housing, energy, education, and spiritual and cultural needs. Sarvodaya is divided into a number of legally independent sub-units that each take responsibility for a range of activities. The units include Village Development Programs; Sarvodaya Legal Services Movement; Human Rights, Conflict Resolution, Legal Education; Peace Education and Peace Work; Sarvodaya Women's Movement Ltd.; and Sarvodaya Economic Enterprises Development Services Bank (SEEDS).

## MOVIMENTO DOS TRABALHADORES RURAIS SEM TERRA (LANDLESS WORKERS MOVEMENT): BRAZIL

Brazil's Landless Workers Movement (MST) emerged in reaction to the evictions, expropriations, and displacements in Brazil during the dictatorial period of 1979 to 1983. MST is made up of diverse landless peasant organizations demanding the right to live and grow their own food on unused lands. Through "occupations" of idle land MST has settled more than a million people on fifteen million acres while forcing agrarian reform to the top of the national political agenda. Brazil's government has formally recognized MST's rights to farm these lands. MST's five hundred independent production cooperatives process, market, and distribute farm products while actively promoting organic farming methods. Their three credit unions have thousands of members.

Typical occupations consist of one thousand to three thousand families who turn idle land into productive farms. They sell their produce in the marketplaces of the local towns and buy their supplies from local merchants. Not surprisingly, those towns with nearby MST settlements are better off economically than other similar towns, and many mayors now actually petition the MST to carry out occupations near their towns. MST has succeeded in reducing malnutrition, joblessness, and poverty in its settlements while increasing literacy rates. The success story of MST in Brazil has been an inspiration to many similar movements in other countries.

## GREEN BELT MOVEMENT: KENYA

In 1977, under the auspices of the National Council of Women of Kenya, the Green Belt Movement (GBM) was founded to avert desertification in Kenya by focusing on environmental conservation, community development, and capacity building. It has since grown to thousands of members, who, among other things, have planted over twenty-five million trees in farms, public lands, and forests. While tree planting has always been the focal activity, GBM programs have expanded to include projects in indigenous tree planting, civic education, advocacy, food security, greenbelt eco-safaris, and "women and change." For example, all group members are trained in methods of organic farming, intensive land management, and values of indigenous food crops for better health.

Advocacy activities in the GBM began in the late 1980s when gross mismanagement and abuse of the environment were tolerated by the government. In response, GBM directed its advocacy efforts toward preventing forest destruction, ending poor governance, and ending human rights atrocities and corruption (especially the illegal allocation of public land). The movement has made significant contributions not only to rehabilitating the physical environment but also to raising environmental consciousness through myriad workshops and seminars on civic and environmental education, which have trained close to ten thousand people to date. The movement's efforts directly led to the preservation of Uhuru Park, Karura Forest, and Jivanjee Gardens, all major green spaces in the city of Nairobi that were threatened by illegal allocation.

## GLOBAL FAIR TRADE MOVEMENT

The Fair Trade Movement (see also the discussion in chapter 11) seeks to operate outside the confines of global free-trade rules by using trade as a grassroots tool to address global inequality, economic instability, malnutrition, and hunger and social and political injustice. Trade is seen not as a goal in itself but rather as a means to achieve these more fundamental goals. Fair trade rules require that producers receive living wages for their products and that they operate in environmentally sustainable ways. Fair trade encourages production cooperatives, small farming, and organic agricultural practices. The fair trade movement in the United States is helping make the trade in goods such as coffee, chocolate, indigenous artisanal products, and other goods a model for promoting justice in trade and sustainable production for every commodity. Products with a fair trade label assure consumers that the products they purchase support the livelihood of producers and the health of the environment.

## EL CEIBO: BOLIVIA

In 1997, four village communities in the Alto Beni region of Bolivia established El Ceibo as an umbrella organization to market cocoa independently. El Ceibo supports farmer-oriented agricultural practices and organic production to ensure the sustained development of the local population and the preservation of the rainforest. El Ceibo improves the living conditions of the members while also increasing crop diversity and productivity. Since 1999, El Ceibo has had 810 members, mostly families of small farmers usually of indigenous descent.

El Ceibo was the first Bolivian cocoa cooperative to convert to organic production, gain organic certification, and process its own cocoa. It has also received fair trade certification. The farmers export their own cocoa butter and cocoa liquor and sell their chocolate domestically. El Ceibo's fair trade premiums are used to support agricultural improvement and community development. For example, the cooperative offers incentives for organic production, has a fund for community projects and activities, and has a Safety Fund for medical emergencies.

## COMMUNITY SUPPORTED AGRICULTURE: U.S.A.

Community Supported Agriculture (CSA), linking small producers directly to consumers, is spreading in the United States. In a typical CSA farm model, local community members purchase a share in a local farm's operation at the start of each growing season and in return receive a fresh, nutritious box of produce directly from their grower on a weekly basis. In this arrangement, members agree to pay the costs of production regardless of the actual harvest. This allows the farmer and consumer to share many of the financial burdens typically borne by the farmer alone and for both to bypass the conventional industrial-agriculture marketing and retail system. CSAs range from small gardens with five to twenty members to large farms serving nearly a thousand families. CSAs create direct and personal relationships with the farmer—and often the land on which the food is grown—offering a positive alternative to systems where consumers have no choice but to purchase days- or weeks-old produce from the supermarket shelf. They also provide farmers with a viable economic alternative, allowing them a greater percentage of the food dollar (close to or at 100 percent) and a stable revenue stream.

## SLOW FOOD MOVEMENT: ITALY

Founded in 1996 in Italy in response to the homogenous, unhealthy, and socially and environmentally destructive processes of industrial agriculture, the Slow Food Movement has generated renewed appreciation of local and regional food specialties and is reviving threatened agricultural varieties. In 1996, Slow Food launched the "Ark of Taste," a project that documents, catalogues, and safeguards small and quality agricultural diversity that is threatened, or potentially threatened, with extinction. Safeguarded products include plant species, varieties, and ecotypes, as well as well-adapted animal populations in a specific territory.

Local producers promote their products, preserve degraded land, and create employment through *presidias*. The presidias set production regulations taking into consideration a product's cultural and historical aspects, biodiversity, environmental problems, and the needs of small-scale economies. Agronomic and livestock practices are proposed that are not aggressive to the natural environment. In some cases, the production regulations are explicitly organic and prohibit synthetic fertilizers and pesticides. Examples include Saraceno grain from Valtellina, Italy, and the Zolfino bean from Pratomagno, Italy. Slow Food went international in Paris in 1998 and now the movement is found in forty-five countries and has eighty thousand members.

## WHITE EARTH LAND RECOVERY PROJECT: U.S.A.

The WELRP was founded in 1989 by White Earth tribal member Winona La Duke. In 2004, WELRP received the prestigious International Slow Food Award at the Fourth International Slow Food Congress in Naples, Italy. The project was recognized for its work to preserve wild rice and biodiversity and to restore local food systems on the White Earth reservation in eastern Wisconsin. The project works to facilitate recovery of the original land base of the White Earth Indian reservation while preserving and restoring traditional practices of sound land stewardship, language fluency, and community development and strengthening their spiritual and cultural heritage.

The White Earth reservation, home to the Anishinaabeg people, is also home to one of the oldest wild rice pollens known today—predating the Anishinaabeg people by a thousand years. According to the oral history of the Anishinaabeg, *manoomin,* or wild rice, was a gift given by the Creator and is a centerpiece of the nutrition and sustenance of the community. The project works to oppose the genetic modification and patenting of wild rice in White Earth but also around the world, working in collaboration with indigenous communities and other peoples' movements to ensure that native rights, natural harvesting, and food security are guaranteed for generations to come.

## ORGANIZATION OF COMMUNAL FOREST PRODUCERS OF THE ZONA MAYA: MEXICO

The OEPFZM in Mexico has been creating its own model of commercial forest production that allows Mayan communities to conserve their native culture and the natural systems on which they depend. OEPFZM has over five thousand families on over one million acres of communally owned and managed tropical forests in the southeastern state of Quintana Roo. These Mayan communities took these steps to increase their say in how local forests are used and who benefits from that use. The land is divided into one hundred plots, with selective harvesting in only one plot per year over the next century. OEPFZM's operations have been certified by the Forest Stewardship Council, an independent ecolabel organization that informs consumers of how wood products were harvested.

## THE ASSOCIATION OF CAMPESINO AND INDIGENOUS FOREST COMMUNITIES: CENTRAL AMERICA

ACICFOC combines small-scale timber-producing and non–timber-producing forest communities from Guatemala, Belize, El Salvador, Nicaragua, Honduras, Costa Rica, and Panama. It provides a networking space for community leaders to identify common challenges and seek solutions on issues of timber production, small-scale fishing, farming, and ecotourism. ACICFOC members work communally to address issues such as access and development of community forest concessions. They develop local systems for financial support, ensuring access by forest communities to possible payments for environmental services such as carbon sequestration, water purification, and biodiversity conservation. They also promote programs to improve practices that increase production while protecting the natural systems upon which forest communities depend.

### FORESTRADE: U.S.A.

The largest U.S. importer of organic spices, ForesTrade helps farmers in Guatemala, Madagascar, Grenada, and throughout Asia enter the global fair trade market. The company helps farmers shift to organic methods and diversify their crops. Its products are the result of a cooperative network that fosters sustainable small farm development, natural resource conservation, and biodiversity. It supports social and economic progress in the farming communities with which it works.

### YAKAMA TRIBE: U.S.A.

The Yakama tribe of Washington supports its nine thousand members using environmentally sustainable harvesting of over $40 million worth of timber per year. The tribe uses traditional techniques, which maintain a high diversity of forest species, ages, and ecosystems. The process is managed by the entire community at the tribal council level. The business they generate supports their town, paying for all education, building, and health care.

## THE ORGANISATION OF AFRICAN UNITY: AFRICA

The Organisation of African Unity (OAU) has produced model national legislation to address the rising threat of biopiracy, the privatization of genetic
resources that traditional peoples have cultivated for millennia. The legislation provides for the recognition of and protection of local communities,
farmers, and breeders from biopiracy, and for the regulation of and access to
genetic resources. This, in turn, has led African trade ministers to form a powerful block of biodiversity-rich nations in the WTO to demand that the intellectual property rights agreement (TRIPs) be rewritten explicitly to "exclude
the patentability of life forms." Going beyond their trade ministers, rural
communities are publicly defying the WTO's patent rights for the "life science" industry by reclaiming local control over the biodiversity that defines
their existence. This rising tide of village-level assertions of rights, together
with the global campaign for "No Patents on Life," is progressing toward
policies that truly respect and protect the global genetic commons.

## PUSSPAINDO: INDONESIA

In response to the near-extinction of many local rice varieties, in 1997
Pusspaindo, a biodiversity organization, launched a project for the recovery
of local rice varieties. The goal was to promote farmers' independence
through the use of local varieties, local wisdom, and traditional production
systems. Farmers each gave one kilogram of a local rice variety that was then
planted, multiplied, and redistributed among other farmers. Pusspaindo promotes the production of rice using organic methods of pest control and has
shown that local rice varieties can achieve higher yields than the new varieties. Yields of ten to fourteen tons per hectare have been achieved. The local
rice has also been found to have excellent qualities: it has a better flavor, is
more nutritious, can be grown continuously throughout the year, is easier to
plant, and is more economical, especially if grown organically. Furthermore,
some local varieties have medicinal properties helpful for common diseases.

## CUBASOLAR: CUBA

With the collapse of the Soviet Union, Cuba lost its access to Soviet oil.
Rather than seek oil from alternative sources, the Cubans turned instead to

renewable energy. The Cuban government established a new program, CubaSolar, to promote renewable energy resources across the country. The focus has been on educating a new generation of professionals, workers, and citizens on design, construction, operation, maintenance, and understanding of renewable energy systems. CubaSolar initiates and supports demonstration projects in renewable energy and environmental conservation. It also helps provide financing for local communities that develop and implement projects themselves. The program has given over seven hundred local organizations legal status to carry it out directly.

## LA COORDINADORA DE DEFENSA DEL AGUA Y DE LA VIDA: BOLIVIA

After the World Bank required that Cochabamba privatize its water systems, and the privatizer—Bechtel Corporation—sent water prices skyrocketing, the people of Cochabamba, Bolivia, organized to reclaim their water. They formed an alliance of workers, farmers, indigenous communities, environmentalists, and human rights and community activists, known as *La Coordinadora de Defensa del Agua y de la Vida* (Coalition in Defense of Water and Life) to coordinate the struggle. After successfully forcing Bechtel to abandon the contract (see also chapter 5), La Coordinadora, the workers of the water company, and other citizens worked with the local government to establish a system of community-controlled and -operated water delivery that has been successfully providing water since April 2000.

A publicly and democratically elected rotating board was established to oversee the company; it consists of two workers, two community members, and two local government officials (although the makeup of the board has not always remained constant). Regular meetings take place in different neighborhoods to assess needs, prices, and overall functioning of the system. Wealthier citizens subsidize those with lower incomes in such a way that the company has stabilized prices while successfully expanding services to the city's poorest neighborhoods that had never received water before. Funding proposals were devised to attract investment to make the company solvent. Despite funding and other problems, the water company continues to provide water more universally, fairly, and reliably than before.

## URUGUAYAN CO-OPERATIVIST CENTRE: URUGUAY

The Uruguayan Co-operativist Centre has been working for thirty years to implement innovative ways to address a persistent housing shortage in Uruguay. Its work has focused on the low-income population, which was hit hardest by the shortage. It has channeled low-cost state loans directly to communities while helping them to work together through cooperatives to solve their housing problems through collective self-organizing.

## BELO HORIZONTE: BRAZIL

In 1993, the newly elected municipal government of Belo Horizonte, Brazil, initiated a series of programs to reduce food insecurity in the city. First, food was declared a right of citizenship. To help guarantee this right, the city provides plots for local farmers to grow their own food using organic practices. The farmers are now able to provide for themselves while the city helps keep prices for locally grown food low for others in the community. School lunches are made with these crops and the entire city is encouraged to purchase these products as part of a healthier, affordable diet.

## GRAMEEN BANK: BANGLADESH

Established two decades ago in Bangladesh, Grameen Bank is a rural credit system based not on property collateral but on small-group mutual responsibility. Grameen's microcredit loan program, made to 2.5 million low-income villagers, mostly women, has since been adopted in over fifty-eight countries.

## MONDRAGÓN COOPERATIVE CORPORATION: BASQUE REGION OF SPAIN

The Basque region of Spain has one of the most advanced networks of alternative businesses financed by worker-owned cooperative banks. In 1955, worker-owned cooperatives decided that to expand in a way they could control, they needed to create and control their own system of credit. By pooling what capital they had, the workers founded the Caja Laboral

Popular credit cooperative, a cooperative bank that was to prove a key element in the future of the Mondragón Cooperative Corporation (MCC). Today, almost half a century after its foundation, the Mondragón Cooperative Corporation is the largest business corporation in the Basque country and the seventh largest in Spain, as measured by both sales and workforce.

The more than two dozen examples provided here are simply ripples on a moving river of alternative systems that are operating, growing, and being imagined around the world. The story of each one could fill a book in itself. Each is a representation of the point made repeatedly in this volume: that economic globalization is not inevitable. It is but one among many competing models that are far superior. The alternatives offered here and throughout this book are meant to be seen as tools, bases of critique and learning, and maybe most importantly, inspiration. We look forward to the many more we are yet to know and that are yet to be.

PART THREE

# GLOBAL GOVERNANCE

*Global systems are now dominated by two power centers: a small number of gigantic global corporations and the Bretton Woods "unholy trinity"—the World Bank, the IMF, and the WTO. Combined, they have achieved de facto global governance. Though none were elected to rule, and none are transparent or democratic, their powers can overwhelm nations. Drastic revisions and replacements are mandatory.*

*We offer a long list of suggestions for reigning in corporate powers. As for global bureaucracies, new institutions must replace most of the functions of failed older ones, new institutions that answer to a different hierarchy of values that are consistent with the ten principles for sustainable societies. We close with a chapter on ways in which you can become directly involved in achieving these changes.*

# CHAPTER NINE

# Corporate Structure and Power

IN DECEMBER 2001, shock waves rippled first through the business world and then through all segments of society. The front-page story of almost every newspaper in every country shifted from the war on terror to another: one of the most dominant and successful energy companies in the world had suddenly filed for bankruptcy. Enron Corp., once celebrated as the leader of a new wave of innovative enterprise, had managed to spearhead the conversion of electricity provision in much of the United States into a privatized speculative commodity, contributing to big energy problems in California while avoiding government oversight. It had also brilliantly contributed toward and then exploited the global deregulation juggernaut that accompanied the new rules of the WTO, the GATS, and other agreements in order to gain entry into foreign countries and gather up tens of billions of dollars in overseas assets, while causing grave social and environmental problems in such countries as India, Bolivia, the Dominican Republic, and over two dozen others.

Enron had also enjoyed windfall benefits from the structural adjustment loan programs of the World Bank and the IMF by steering—with the help of the banks—development loan funds given to foreign governments back to itself through fat contracts built into the loans. It used corporate-friendly U.S. tax laws to hide negative performance and appear profitable despite dangerously overextending itself.

Finally, on the brink of ultimate failure, the company abandoned the interests and loyalty of its own workers by knowingly allowing their stock investments in the company to collapse. At the same time, top executives sold their own stocks at huge profits, even receiving bonuses as they departed.

Once it was exposed, Enron's performance was seen as so shocking, and the public outrage was so great, that even company backers in the White House found themselves too politically vulnerable to assist their former friends and colleagues. They tried to treat Enron as if it were the rare exception to otherwise responsible corporate behavior in the United States—the proverbial "one rotten apple in the barrel."

Unfortunately, the Enron experience actually teaches very different lessons. First, the evidence that has emerged since this scandal first broke shows that although its activities were unconscionable, many were within the bounds of the law—the fruits of corporate cohabitation with government and a deregulated system.

Second, this kind of reprehensible behavior was entirely predictable, considering the nature of corporate structure today and the prevailing rules that guide corporate priorities and institutional investors—short-term profit and hypergrowth with little place for community concerns.

Finally, as has been exquisitely revealed by subsequent examples, from WorldCom to Halliburton, Xerox, Tyco, and other corporate giants, the problems are far from unique to Enron. In fact, they are *systemic.* Enron was only a case in point. The way to fix Enron, like other corporations, is to fundamentally change the system.

At the dawn of the twenty-first century, the global corporation stands as the dominant institutional force at the center of human activity and the planet itself. Indeed, according to a report by Sarah Anderson and John Cavanagh of the Institute for Policy Studies, by the year 2000 the combined sales of the world's top two hundred corporations exceeded a quarter of all countries' measured economic activity. If one listed the top one hundred economic units on the planet, fifty-two would be corporations, and only forty-eight would be countries. These globe-girdling firms have become both the prime beneficiaries of and the driving forces behind the new architecture for global governance and the trade, finance, and investment regimes that now rule people and life on earth.

The immense scale and extreme concentration of the powers of global corporations stifle both democratic expression and market competition. In six key industries, for example—consumer durables, automotive manufacturing, aircraft manufacturing, aerospace, electronic components, and steel—five firms control more than 50 percent of the global market. So, rather than contributing to healthy market competition as envisioned by globalization and capitalist theories, globalization has instead led directly to global oligopolies. In many cases, as in agriculture, the dominant few global corporations (Archer Daniels Midland, Monsanto, Novartis, and others like them) exercise control over multiple aspects of the production cycle—the raw material inputs and distribution, the seeds and chemicals, the farmers, the processors, the distributors, and the retailers—amounting to extensive vertical integration. Global prices and the food supply—and its quality—are thus subject to corporate control. Such staggering corporate concentration utterly overpowers and defies traditional market theories that envision a multitude of healthy small and medium-size enterprises competing with each other over quality, price, and innovation. It also impedes all conditions favorable to democracy, economic justice, and environmental values.

Corporations have become the primary organizing instrument for economic, political, and social activity on the planet. Through their market power, billions of dollars in campaign contributions, public relations, advertising, and sheer scale, corporations create the visions we live by and exert great influence over the political power structures that rule us. It is fair to conclude, as David Korten has written, that corporations have already achieved "corporate rule" to the detriment of democracies, social equity, and nature. It is exactly for such reasons that fierce global protests have brought millions of people onto the streets to demand massive structural change in corporations, the rules they operate by, and their very existence.

In any just and sustainable society, it is unlikely that global corporations would operate as the primary organizing force they are in our world today. Indeed, if we are to achieve such a society, corporate structure will need to be altered—away from the current model that brings with it an intrinsic set of values that have to do only with the narrow successes of the corporation itself and are diametrically opposed to the ten principles for sustainable societies outlined in chapter 4. We must dramatically change the publicly traded, limited liability global corporation, just as previous generations set out to eliminate or control the monarchy. Any citizens' agenda for transforming the global economy must be rooted in plans to solve this problem.

This chapter focuses on the possibilities for such change. It begins with a brief review of certain key features of corporate structure today, because much of the problem of corporate behavior is rooted in the institutional forms and structures themselves.

Next, the chapter reports on the variety of activities already being undertaken by citizen groups around the world, covering a spectrum from reform of corporations to their decommissioning. Finally, it presents some ideas about alternative business structures that are far more consistent with our ten principles.

## Corporate Structure Today

Corporations are generally divided into two categories, those that are *privately owned* by a small number of individuals or families and those that are *publicly owned and traded.* There are important and consequential distinctions between them.

### PUBLIC AND PRIVATE CORPORATIONS

Some privately owned corporations have grown very large, even global (for example, Bechtel, Cargill, and the other highly secretive grain-trading companies). These large private companies have gained many of the benefits that publicly held corporations have: efficiencies of scale, domination of markets and resources, political influence, attractiveness to lending institutions. But large private corporations are relatively few in number, and their overall impact is less than the greater number of large publicly held, limited liability global corporations.

When corporations are said to be *publicly traded,* it means that their ownership shares are freely exchanged in public share markets by large numbers of people who have little involvement with the operations of the firm, other than hoping for a passive financial return. Trading in such public shares is called *investing,* but it also may be likened to a sophisticated form of gambling, rather like betting on a horse race. Most shares of public corporations are not actually held directly by individuals but by professionally managed mutual funds, insurance companies, pension plans, and other investment institutions. When people buy shares in these managed funds, they usually have little knowledge about precisely which companies the funds own, let alone what kinds of activities those companies engage in with their invested money.

To attract investments from the public, there is heavy pressure on most public corporations to make their stocks seem as appealing as possible in terms of growth and profitability, leading many to make decisions based on short-term appearances of health (as with Enron, WorldCom, Halliburton) or to engage in rapid depletion of natural resources, like forests or fisheries, to create short-term profits at the expense of long-term environmental health and a permanent resource base. The intrinsic need of public corporations to drive optimistic impressions of investment opportunity is at the root of considerable social and ecological harm. Publicly held companies must seek continual growth and expansion—ever more markets, labor, and resources—because they must show positive balance sheets, even in their quarterly reports, to impress investors, bankers, and the financial communities on which they depend. The homily "grow or die" is especially apt for public companies as growth and profit become obsessive goals, far outweighing any moral, ethical, or environmental considerations.

On the other hand, although privately held companies often behave exactly as public companies do, they do not have the same built-in systemic imperative to impress the financial community or investment markets because they are partly outside that system. A family or individuals running a private corporation have, at least theoretically, greater freedom to make decisions that are not solely in the interest of maximizing profits but might be thoughtful of the community, workers, and nature. There is room in a private company for a mix of values, and we have seen examples of privately held, usually smaller companies—Patagonia, Ben & Jerry's, and The Body Shop are a few—that were willing to sacrifice some profits to support greater community or environmental goals. Of course, the private corporation sometimes "goes public" through stock offerings or is bought out by a much larger public company. Once that happens, altruism may decline or disappear. None of this is meant to ignore the performance of those private corporations that seem never to have noticed that they have a greater opportunity for responsible behavior. Indeed, some companies remain private for secrecy reasons, because private companies are not required to file financial reports with the SEC and other government agencies. And some private firms, particularly in the textile sector, have abysmal labor records.

As for the term *limited liability,* it refers to the fact that though corporate management is technically accountable to shareholder-owners and acts on their behalf, shareholder-owners have no personal liability besides their investment in the firm for any consequences of corporate management acts. This built-in distance between the technical owners of the corporation and the people who actually operate it insulates them from liability for (and even knowledge of) any harms eventually done by the corporation. It also removes a level of engagement, accountability, and transparency that would more likely exist if investor liability was maintained. (In practice, most CEOs are now paid overwhelmingly through stock options and have become large owners of the companies they also run; in this ownership capacity, they too enjoy limited liability.)

### CORPORATE CHARTERS

Corporations dominate societies and help create the power structures that rule us, yet paradoxically, they remain ephemeral entities. Although such names as ExxonMobil, McDonald's, Shell, Microsoft, Disney, Sony, and Monsanto are emblazoned in our brains, as familiar to us as old friends, in fact these institutions have no real physical existence. They own buildings and stadiums and wield stupendous powers, but corporations themselves have no concrete form. They have people who work in them, but corporations are themselves not alive, so they cannot inherently embody the same range of values and emotions that we expect of responsible people: altruism, shame, community concern, loyalty to one another, and so on. This distinction between corporate structure and the people who work within corporations becomes crucially important in explaining, as former American University professor Ralph Estes puts it, "why corporations make good people do bad things" (from his book *Tyranny of the Bottom Line*).

In the United States, corporations gain their existence through the laws of state governments, augmented by federal regulation. Corporations are direct legal creations of state corporate charters, so theoretically they are expressions of popular sovereignty. State corporate charter rules *could* theoretically set any conditions that popular will might dictate—from who should be on the boards to the values corporations must operate by to whether they may buy up other enterprises, move to other cities and countries, or do anything else that affects the public interest.

Hundreds of years ago, state charters contained significant restrictions and much higher standards of accountability and responsibility than they do today. But as the landmark research of Richard Grossman and Frank Adams of the Program on Corporations, Law and Democracy (POCLAD) has revealed, corporations have managed over the centuries to wear down the kind and quality of state charter rules as well as the state and federal laws that govern their existence. By now, these directives contain relatively few restrictions, and even when corporations violate these restrictions their permanent existence is rarely threatened. Governing bodies today, beholden to corporations for campaign finance support, are loath to enforce any sanctions except in cases of extreme political embarrassment, such as has occurred with Enron, Arthur Andersen, and select others. Even then, effective sanctions may be few and small.

These virtual entities that we call corporations have now advanced to where they enjoy a great many rights similar to those granted human beings. As we explain later in this chapter, U.S. courts have ruled that corporations are "fictitious persons," with the right to buy and sell property as if they were people, to sue in court for injuries, and to express "corporate speech." Advertising, public relations, and campaign funding have all been ruled legitimate, *protected* forms of corporate speech—under the First Amendment of the U.S. Constitution. (See also chapter 8.)

Although corporations enjoy legal "personhood rights," they have not been required, for the most part, to abide by normal human responsibilities. They are strongly protected by limited liability rules, so shareholder-owners of a corporation cannot be prosecuted for acts of the institution. Nor, in any meaningful sense, is the corporation itself vulnerable to prosecution. Corporations are sometimes fined for their acts or ordered to alter their practices, but the life of the corporation, its (virtual) existence, is very rarely threatened—even for great crimes that, if carried out by people in many states of the United States, might invoke the death penalty.

In fact, corporations are likely to outlive the human beings who have been part of their operation, even those who own them, the private or public shareholders. Unlike humans, corporations have the possibility of immortality, at least until some future generation of owners files papers that put them to death.

The central point is this: lacking the sort of physical, organic reality that characterizes the existence of human beings—including the feelings of altruism or, on the other hand, shame—the corporate entity, this concept, this collection of paperwork that has been granted such enormous power, is literally incapable of the social, environmental, or community ideals that we keep hoping it will pursue. Its entire design is to advance only its own self-interest.

Under the distorted system by which corporations are chartered today, it is not in their structure or nature to operate with altruism, idealism, or community or environmental values. When corporations do trumpet such values—as they sometimes do in public relations and advertising or in response to scandal or political pleadings—it is usually precisely because public outrage about a lack of morality has forced them to do so.

Of course, most people will argue that corporations could be more responsible or moral and less self-interested if only the individuals working in them would steer the machine in a more positive direction. (A section following this will make that point.) But the possibilities of that kind of change are ultimately small, at least for publicly held corporations. We have the terrible experiences of the *Exxon Valdez* oil spill off Alaska, for example, and the Union Carbide chemical releases in India. In both cases, when the accidents became known, the heads of each corporation expressed great personal grief and issued apologies for the actions of the corporation. And yet, within a few weeks, they had completely reversed themselves. Where they had first reacted as human beings, they soon had to withdraw from personal feelings that were inapplicable to corporate structure. They began battling mightily against all legal efforts to force them to admit blame or agree to pay damages. This too is built into the corporate form. If corporations officially admit guilt, then stock prices fall, shareholders revolt, bankers withdraw support, lawsuits develop, and investigations and prosecutions sometimes ensue. As for the executives making such admissions, they would certainly be fired for violating the limits of the corporate form, and the next person would be strapped onto the wheel. *When it comes to corporate behavior, form determines function.*

In addition to these unfortunate characteristics, the corporation is also one of the most authoritarian of human institutions. Management authority resides in a chief executive officer, who is accountable to a board of directors charged with assuring that the CEO represents shareholder financial interests. Although the size of a large corporation demands substantial decentralization of actual decision making, formal power resides primarily with the CEO, who has virtually unlimited authority to hire and fire employees, open and close plants, and buy and sell companies. Those whose lives are harmed—even devastated—by these decisions have little recourse.

These limitations of publicly held corporations are particularly evident in U.S. firms. Some Asian and European countries have created checks that allow more space for corporate actions that reflect the broader public good. In Germany, for example, firms larger than a certain size must place worker representatives on their boards of directors. This introduces the direct concerns of a vital segment of society into the corporate boardroom.

Similar rules could, of course, be made in any country about board structure, involvement of stakeholders from the community, restrictions on corporate mobility, worker rights, environmental values, or reinvestment of profits. In the United States, an appropriate mechanism would be to build such new rules into state charters, giving the citizenry a much higher degree of control over corporate behavior and options than at present and confirming citizen sovereignty over the institutions that run society. The Program on Corporations, Law and Democracy is currently attempting to institute initiatives to realize this strategy; we will come back to those later in this chapter. And some years ago, Ralph Nader promoted the idea of a federal charter for corporations, with many new rules to assure responsible behavior by corporations and a shift away from the value system by which corporations currently operate. Shifting the locus from the state to the federal level eliminates the option that corporations might relocate out of any state that adapts tougher chartering language. With the Enron and WorldCom scandals still fresh in our minds, this might be a good time to reintroduce the concept of a federal corporate charter in the United States.

Meanwhile, such possible innovations notwithstanding, corporations as currently structured remain free of any ultimate responsibility to act in moral, altruistic, or any other ways that are beneficial to the community, workers, or the environment. For corporations today, the only principles that have meaning are these:

- The absolute imperative to make a profit
- The imperative to continuously grow and expand territorially and functionally
- The need to control the regulatory, investment, and political climates—locally and globally—to remain as unrestricted as possible in behavior, geographical reach, and access to markets, resources, and labor

## Citizen Actions Against Corporate Power

There is a rich history of citizen and worker movements attempting to resist corporate power around the world. The issues gained a new urgency during the 1990s as corporations accelerated their global consolidation.

Citizen activists have pursued a variety of campaign strategies to resist the corporate advance, ranging from reformist to transformative approaches. Reformist strategies—which include attempts to increase corporate responsibility and accountability and to exclude or remove corporations—assume that although there is a need to fine-tune the existing system to somehow strengthen the role of social and environmental values in corporate decision making, the system is basically sound and corporations are, on balance, playing essential and positive roles. *Reformists* implicitly believe that global corporations are here to stay, have a right to exist in their current form, and have the potential to function as responsible citizens—even to chart humanity's collective course to a just and sustainable world.

Some activists, however, reject the idea that corporations have a natural right to exist. Following the Battle of Seattle, Kalle Lasn and Tom Liacas of *Adbusters* magazine called attention to what they term the *corporate crackdown.*

> The corporation won't come out of this intact. The new activists—and this is what . . . all the keepers of the old order don't get—are no longer protesting against the harms that corporations do, they are protesting against *the corporation itself.* These new activists want to go back to the beginning, back to the laws and legal precedents that gave birth to the corporate "I." They want to tinker with the corporate genetic code, to change the laws under which charters are granted and revoked, the laws that protect investors from even the foulest taint of their investments, and the rules and regulations under which corporations operate from the local to the international level.

We can call this group the *corporate abolitionists* because they believe it is no longer sufficient to single out those corporations that cause harm to people and the environment and try to make them become more socially responsible. They seek the death penalty for corporations with a habitual record of criminal activity. They call for a comprehensive rethinking and redesign of the corporate charter and corporate law to eliminate those characteristics that make public corporations a threat to the well-being of people and the planet, with their concentration of power, absentee ownership, and limited liability.

The underlying premise of the corporate abolitionists is that to end corporate rule, it is necessary not only to eliminate persistent corporate recidivists but also to eliminate those features of the corporation that make corporate rule possible. It will take decades to achieve this end.

In the meantime, there is a place for all of the varied strategies that the different activist groups currently employ. We lay out six options here, starting with the more reformist and going through to the more transformational.

## PROMOTE CORPORATE RESPONSIBILITY

One of the long-standing strategies of corporate activists is to call for corporate responsibility. More than the other reformists, those calling for corporate responsibility accept the existence of corporations but ask them to act in a more socially responsible manner, often in relation to specific environmental, labor, and human rights issues. This call is often backed by consumers and shareholders. Religious organizations that have investments in a corporation, for example, may file a shareholder resolution calling for changes in its operations concerning a concrete case of social or ecological harm and organize other shareholders to support the resolution. This strategy was effectively used during the 1970s and 1980s to press commercial banks and other financial institutions in North America and Europe to withdraw loans from the apartheid regime in South Africa. Eventually, this shareholder call for divestment proved to be an effective tool in weakening the apartheid regime.

New York–based Corporate Campaign, Inc. carries out what it calls a *power analysis* of the main stakeholders of offending corporations in order to develop strategies targeted to those corporations' critical vulnerabilities. The strength of this approach was demonstrated by environmental activists in British Columbia in the mid-1990s, in their successful campaign to stop clear-cut logging in old growth forests. By targeting the customers and suppliers of the big forest corporations, they were able to exert sufficient counterpressures to compel the companies to change their destructive practices.

In recent years, corporate responsibility strategies have taken other forms as well. Litigation continues to be used as a tactic to promote socially responsible behavior on the part of corporations. In the United Kingdom, for example, cases have been brought before the British courts against Rio Tinto for uranium dust exposure, and against Thor Chemicals for mercury exposure affecting workers in other countries. In addition, voluntary codes of conduct have been negotiated with big clothing manufacturers, like The Gap and Levi Strauss, to encourage them to adopt more socially responsible employment practices for workers in the Central American and other factories where they have subcontracting relationships. Yet there is no guarantee of compliance, and lack of enforcement invariably arises as a problem because even the most committed corporation faces constant market pressures to cut corners on social and environmental responsibility.

Many corporate responsibility initiatives center on voluntary codes of conduct. This is the case with the United Nations Global Compact, which was launched in 2000. A number of transnational corporations in various sectors of the global economy were invited to sign nine guidelines for responsible corporate action. Those that joined the compact agreed to send case study reports once a year, showcasing their best practices advancing labor, environmental, and human rights standards, to be posted on a United Nations Web site. For many of the participating corporations—like Nike or Rio Tinto, which have poor track records on human and environmental rights and have been the targets of activist campaigns—the Global Compact turned into little more than a calculated public relations exercise.

Indeed, its sponsorship of the Global Compact dealt a blow to the credibility of the United Nations. By appearing to certify the actions of socially and environmentally destructive corporations, the U.N. became tainted by their actions. The Global Compact delivered an even more direct blow to U.N. credibility when business leader Goran Lindahl, whom Secretary-General Kofi Annan had appointed as a high-level adviser and recruiter for the compact, was forced out of his position in the wake of a pension fund scandal at Asea Brown and Boveri Corporation, where he was CEO until 2001. Lindahl left with a retirement package of some U.S. $53 million in a year when the company lost $691 million, and its stock price plummeted on the announcement of previously undisclosed asbestos liabilities. The Swedish prime minister called on Lindahl to resign; Kofi Annan decided not to renew his contract; and the company he once headed demanded that he return some of the money.

Despite all this, global corporations argue vigorously that they should not be subject to public oversight or regulation. They maintain that voluntary codes of conduct allowing individual corporations to determine the standards to which they will subscribe, monitor their own performance, and choose which results, if any, they will make public are adequate to deal with issues of corporate responsibility.

Former corporate executive, staunch Republican conservative, investment fund manager, and corporate turnaround specialist Robert Monks makes this observation in his book *The Emperor's Nightingale*:

> From the perspective of company management today the decision whether to obey the law is simply a cost-benefit calculation. The corporation in effect asks whether the costs of disobedience—discounted by the probability of being discovered, prosecuted, and fined (there is almost no risk of jail)—equal the costs of compliance. In many cases, the costs of disobedience are lower than the costs of compliance, and so many corporations find it to their economic advantage to break the law. . . . Corporations are not people; they have no conscience. Although corporate acts are carried out by individuals, even individuals with high moral standards often find themselves caught up in a corporate action that is beyond their control—or even, in some cases, their knowledge.

Monks's conclusion is confirmed in the daily reports of criminal corporate conduct in the *Wall Street Journal*. Such disregard of the law poses severe challenges for the effectiveness of voluntary, self-monitored, self-enforced codes of corporate conduct. Besides breaking the law, lying is another logical manifestation of current corporate structures. The Enron scandal is only a more visible example of the practice of corporate lying not only to the public and the government but also to their own shareholders—and with the complicity of their auditors, whose professional function is to certify to shareholders, the government, and the public that the corporations' financial statements accurately present their financial condition. There was much discussion in the business press after the Enron story broke about how lying has become virtually a way of life in the corporate world. It is widely acknowledged that the dot-com stock bonanza of the late 1990s was built largely on marketing hype. As a practical matter, it must be assumed that institutions that habitually lie to their shareholders and treat obeying the law as a cost-benefit calculation may also lie about their compliance to voluntary corporate codes, with the complicity of their auditors.

Although promoting corporate social responsibility may not ultimately solve the problem, such efforts as consumer boycotts and shareholder actions do serve two important functions: they temporarily reduce some of the damage, and they engage citizens in the practice of democracy and raise public consciousness of the realities of corporate wrongdoing.

## ESTABLISH CORPORATE ACCOUNTABILITY

Corporate accountability campaigns seek to establish legally enforceable standards for corporate conduct. These strategies are pursued through legislative initiatives on wages and working conditions, public health and safety, the environment, financial institutions and transactions, political campaign contributions, and lobbying practices. Often such regulations are voted into place only in the wake of serious scandal and public outcry.

Some local communities are leading the way in passing legislation aimed at making corporations more publicly accountable. A referendum passed by local voters in 1994 gave the town council of Arcata, California, a clear directive to ensure democratic control of all corporations conducting business in the city.

At the national and global levels there have been initiatives aimed at making the overseas operations of home-based corporations more publicly accountable. For example, former U.S. representative Cynthia McKinney (D-GA) introduced a bill before Congress that would require U.S. corporations to act in a more publicly accountable manner domestically and internationally. The standards include paying a living wage to workers; banning pregnancy testing, retaliation against whistle-blowers, and mandatory overtime for workers under age eighteen; respecting basic ILO standards, such as the right to unionize and health and safety protections; and adhering to both international and U.S. environmental laws and regulations. The code would be enforced first by giving preference to compliant corporations in granting U.S. government contracts and export assistance, and second by empowering the victims, including non–U.S. citizens, to sue the corporations in U.S. courts. Similarly, there is a U.K. case designed to set a precedent for making the head offices of global corporations accountable for the actions of their overseas subsidiaries through the British courts. At a global level, Friends of the Earth has led a coalition effort calling for a corporate accountability convention that would require firms to disclose information to the public about their environmental, labor, and human rights policies.

Such efforts go far beyond voluntary codes of corporate conduct and reduce the organizing burden on consumers and stockholders. However, they do not change the nature of the corporation itself, and they leave governments saddled with the burden of attempting to enforce the law against institutions that are able to spend millions of dollars on lawyers, lobbyists, and politicians to weaken the rules and thwart enforcement action.

### EXCLUDE OR EXPEL PREDATORY CORPORATIONS

Some activists have acted to bar unwanted transnational corporations from their communities. For example, when the chemical giant Du Pont attempted to relocate a hazardous nylon manufacturing plant from the United States to the Indian state of Goa during the early 1990s, the U.S. trade representative was dispatched to apply pressure at high levels of the Indian government to facilitate the process. As a result, the central government of India not only approved the application but also provided Du Pont with land in a village of Tamil Nadu, without consulting the local government. The villagers rose up and refused to accept the plant, forming an anti–Du Pont committee to lead the resistance. When the villagers organized a blockade, corporate representatives and the local police attacked; one youth was shot while dozens more were injured in the clashes. After the land was repossessed by village squatters, the local government decided to overturn the planning permit, an act later upheld by a ruling of the high court of India. It was a stunning demonstration of the ability of an organized community to block the entry of a powerful corporation backed by the U.S. government.

The Du Pont case is only one of several examples of corporate exclusion campaigns in India. Ever since the Union Carbide plant explosion in Bhopal that resulted in the deaths of thousands of innocent people, there has been a strong resolve on the part of that country's citizens to resist and expel unwanted corporate intruders. In recent years, Coca-Cola, Kentucky Fried Chicken, Monsanto, Cargill, and Enron have all been the targets of popular resistance. For instance, a "Monsanto: Quit India" campaign was launched in 1999 by farmer and consumer organizations after hundreds of suicides in small farm families due to the failure of genetically engineered cotton crops.

Many U.S. communities too have successfully mobilized to exclude Wal-Mart, Rite Aid, and other large retailers. Applying the "three strikes, you're out" principle, Pennsylvania's Wayne Township passed a law stating that any corporation with three or more regulatory violations over seven years is forbidden to establish operations in its jurisdiction.

Although these are basically "not-in-my-backyard" initiatives, they raise public consciousness of the destructive impact of global corporations on people, communities, and the environment. They also prove that corporate domination is not inevitable if citizens organize to take a stand.

## REVOKE OR REVISE CORPORATE CHARTERS

In some countries, notably the United States, citizens are reclaiming their right to participate in government decisions about whether specific corporations should be granted a license to operate. As we already noted, a corporation comes into being only when a government grants it a corporate charter. Without that, the corporation does not exist as a legal entity and therefore cannot own property, borrow money, sign contracts, hire and fire, or accumulate assets or debts. In the early days of the United States, corporations were created to serve the public good and existed at the pleasure of the legislature, which could withdraw a charter at will. Citizens could thus keep corporations on a short leash, spelling out the rules they had to follow and holding their owners liable for harm or injuries caused. This situation began to change after an 1886 Supreme Court ruling recognized corporations as "natural persons" under the U.S. Constitution. Hundreds of state laws were struck down, and new laws were passed granting corporations ever greater rights and protections, including limitations on the liability of their shareholders.

Today, the Program on Corporations, Law and Democracy in the United States is leading the way in assisting citizens in reclaiming their sovereign rights over the chartering and rechartering of corporations. According to POCLAD, citizens have the historic right to insist that state-sanctioned corporate charters be periodically reviewed, renewed, and if necessary, revoked. In Pennsylvania, for example, citizen groups have initiated an amendment to the state's corporation code, calling for corporate charters to be limited to thirty years. A charter can be renewed, but only after successful completion of a review process during which it must prove it is operating in the public interest. In California, a coalition of citizen organizations (including the National Organization for Women, Rainforest Action Network, and National Lawyers Guild) petitioned the attorney general to revoke the charter for Union Oil Corporation. Citing California's own corporation code, which authorizes revocation procedures, the coalition fortified the petition with a battery of evidence documenting Union Oil's responsibility for environmental devastation, exploitation of workers, and gross violation of human rights.

Rewriting corporate charters is a step toward changing the nature of the corporate institution. Revoking a charter—the corporate equivalent of a death sentence—begins to put some teeth into the idea of accountability. Eliot Spitzer, attorney general of New York State, declared in 1998: "When a corporation has been convicted of repeated felonies that harm or endanger the lives of human beings or destroy the environment, the corporation should be put to death, its corporate existence ended, and its assets taken and sold at a public auction." Although Spitzer has not won a death sentence against a habitual corporate criminal, he has taken up battle with several giants, including General Electric.

In 1998 in Alabama, Judge William Wynn went so far as to personally file a legal petition to dissolve six tobacco companies on the grounds that they had broken state child abuse laws. Wynn referred to his actions as a "citizen's arrest," but the ruling judge, after meeting with the tobacco companies' legal team, dismissed the case on a technicality.

Although dechartering a major corporation and selling off its assets at a public auction (discussed in the next section) would not solve the larger structural problem, it would certainly send a strong signal to corporate managers and shareholders that obeying the law may be a financially prudent choice.

## ELIMINATE LIMITED LIABILITY
## AND CORPORATE PERSONHOOD

As already noted, corporations have acquired special rights and exemptions
that place them beyond the reach of many laws and liabilities to which
ordinary mortals are subject. Shareholders enjoy virtual immunity when it
comes to legal responsibility for harms committed against the environment,
workers, or communities. So, for example, when Union Carbide caused the
deaths of thousands of people in Bhopal because of a plant explosion, or
when Exxon destroyed a coastline as a result of the *Valdez* oil spill, the
shareholders who invested in these corporate giants were not held liable.
Changing the rules to make investors liable for harms done to others in their
name would make investing a more serious affair and would greatly change
financial calculations made by corporations when deciding what actions to
take to protect people and nature. Investors would be compelled to evaluate
the environmental, labor, and human rights track record of a corporation
before becoming shareholders. Similarly, the CEO and management would
give such concerns a higher priority. Some activists are developing legal
strategies to challenge and change the laws that grant limited liability to
corporate shareholders. Changed laws would truly transform corporate
accountability.

As amazing as it seems, the 1886 decision that established the legal doctrine of corporate personhood was based on a simple pronouncement by a
single judge. According to the official case record, U.S. Supreme Court
Justice Morrison Remick Waite made this pronouncement before the beginning of argument in the case of *Santa Clara County v. Southern Pacific Railroad:*

> The court does not wish to hear argument on the question of whether the
> provision in the Fourteenth Amendment to the Constitution, which forbids a
> State to deny any person within its jurisdiction the equal protection of the
> laws, applies to these corporations. We are all of the opinion that it does.

Few judicial pronouncements have dealt democracy and human rights a
more bitter blow. This one established a legal doctrine of corporate personhood that has been used ever since, by corporate lawyers in country after
country, to place corporations ever further beyond public accountability for
their actions. The authors of this volume strongly endorse citizen action

working toward legal and legislative action to eliminate the legal fiction of corporate personhood.

## DISMANTLE CORPORATIONS
## AND BUY OUT ABSENTEE OWNERS

Finally, some civil society activists are also calling for breaking up large corporations and spinning off their component businesses for sale to workers, customers, suppliers, and community members. This would at once eliminate harmful concentrations of power that distort markets and political processes and greatly reduce the public scourge of absentee ownership—not to mention making markets more efficient.

The challenge is to put in place regulatory regimes and tax policies that mandate or support the breakup of large corporations into human-scale enterprises owned by local stakeholders. Where appropriate, such firms could join cooperative associations or networks to carry out larger projects or achieve economies of scale. When such associations are entered into by local stakeholder-owned enterprises, activities of virtually any scale can be undertaken while remaining locally rooted and accountable. Fast food and beverage franchises might be reorganized as individually owned units that operate under the umbrella of a branding and marketing cooperative. Specifics would vary by industry and corporation, but society should always work from the principle that smaller and locally owned is preferable, in the absence of a compelling argument to the contrary, with the burden of proof resting with those who argue in favor of concentration.

Antitrust reform can tighten the standards for what constitutes excessive concentration. Graduated taxes on assets and total sales—with larger corporations paying a sharply graduated marginal rate—would make size increasingly costly, thus forcing larger enterprises to be more efficient or break themselves up voluntarily. Banking rules might prohibit a single bank from having more than three branches, for example, forcing the breakup of banking conglomerates to spin off clusters of independent community banks. Or there might be a rule that a single enterprise could not own more than one radio or television station using the public airwaves and that its ownership must be limited to people who live in its service area, thus forcing the breakup of media conglomerates and the sell-off of individual stations to people in their own communities. (For detailed recommendations on policy measures to encourage employee ownership, see Jeff Gates, *The Ownership Solution*.)

## Ending Corporate–State Collusion

A belief that sovereignty resides in people and gives them an inalienable right to self-governance is the sacred foundation of democracy. Governments are the voluntary creation of the people and therefore subject to their will. Corporations are in turn created when governments issue corporate charters. They are therefore properly subject to the will of the people through their governments. Yet people the world over find corporations corrupting the political system and the courts in order to co-opt governmental powers and rewrite the laws to advance their own interests.

This process has been carried out by corporate elites who forge common agendas outside the formal institutions of democracy. They use forums such as the Trilateral Commission, the International Chamber of Commerce, the World Economic Forum, trade associations, and the many national and international business and industrial roundtables. The IMF, the World Bank, and the World Trade Organization have all been used by these elites to replace democratic decision making in economic affairs with processes dominated by corporate interests. Although they pay lip service to democracy, the truth of their politics was well stated in a 1974 report of the Trilateral Commission, titled "The Crisis of Democracy," which set forth the argument that "an excess of democracy" had created "a deficit in governability."

By the 1990s, governmental and corporate elites in most countries had largely recast the state from protector of human rights and interests to protector of corporate rights and property. Public resources directed to securing human welfare were redirected to securing corporate welfare. The underlying principle of democracy was turned on its head.

By the early twenty-first century, the name *Halliburton* became synonymous with this collusion. Halliburton's former CEO, Dick Cheney, came to the firm from the highest echelons of U.S. government and returned to them as George W. Bush's vice president. With Cheney as CEO, Halliburton incorporated dozens of its subsidiaries in offshore tax havens, thereby minimizing the company's contribution to government tax revenues. Cheney continued to draw some compensation from Halliburton while serving as vice president. And no corporation performed more contracts for the U.S. government to "reconstruct" Iraq than Halliburton, even after the company was caught overcharging the U.S. government tens of millions of dollars. (When exposed, Halliburton apologized and promised to return the overcharges.)

Governmental bodies at both global and national levels now function as if sovereignty resided in global corporations. Their function is to serve the corporate interest, using their coercive powers to protect corporate property, guarantee corporate profits, break up unions, sell off public assets at giveaway prices, stifle dissent, and make sure that people fulfill their roles as obedient workers and compliant consumers.

Efforts to transform the corporate institution to eliminate its capacity to rule society must be supported by parallel efforts to restore the integrity of democratic institutions and reclaim the resources that corporations have co-opted. This will require a five-pronged program of action.

## GET CORPORATIONS OUT OF POLITICS

It is the place of corporations to observe the rules and restrictions that people democratically choose to impose through their elected representatives. A corporation has no rightful role in making those rules; its role is to provide the information that governments or citizens request of it. Except in the case of criminal proceedings, such requests and the information provided should be public.

Shareholders, managers, employees, consumers, and others have every right as private citizens to express their political views for or against the corporate interest. They also have the right to form and fund not-for-profit organizations to advance any cause they wish to support privately, using their personal funds. Corporations have no such natural right. Nor do corporations have the right to use shareholder monies for political purposes that may be contrary to individual shareholders' preferences. Appropriate legislation would establish the following:

- *A prohibition on any for-profit corporation providing political funds or in-kind support or services.* This includes giving to a political candidate, public official, political action committee, political party, lobbyist, ballot initiative, political convention, meeting of public officials, issue ad, policy group or institute, or any organization that engages in public education or advocacy on matters of public policy. Corporate officers responsible for the violation of this prohibition would be subject to criminal penalties, including imprisonment.

- *Criminal penalties, including imprisonment, for any person who acts in the capacity of corporate officer to solicit political contributions.* Such penalties would also cover those who request or contract with others to support a political party or candidate, or otherwise seek to influence public policies, regulations, or appointments to positions of public trust.

### END CORPORATE WELFARE

Contrary to their claims of efficiency, most large corporations are massively inefficient, spending an inordinate portion of society's resources on advertising, executive perks and salaries, transportation and communications to far-flung corporate empires, and lobbying expenses. Most depend for their profits and survival on a complex regime of public subsidies, exemptions, and externalized costs, including the indirect subsidies they gain when allowed to pay less than a living wage, maintain substandard working conditions, market hazardous products, dump untreated wastes into the environment, and extract natural resources from public lands at below-market prices. Ralph Estes, CPA and professor-turned-corporate-critic, estimates that, in 1994, corporations like Enron and Halliburton extracted more than $2.6 trillion a year in such subsidies in the United States alone—roughly five times their reported profits. By extrapolation, this suggests that the global public costs of corporate welfare may exceed $10.7 trillion annually. It is one of the basic principles of efficient market function that the full costs of a product or service be borne by the seller and passed on to the buyer. Yet many corporations would be forced to close their doors or restructure if they had to bear the true full costs of their operations. It is time to test the corporate claim of market efficiency by taking legislative action to eliminate all direct cash and in-kind subsidies to corporations, establish and enforce appropriate regulatory standards to compel the full internalization of social and environmental costs, and eliminate special corporate tax exemptions.

## GIVE PREFERENCE TO INDEPENDENT ENTERPRISES

To build sustainable communities, it is imperative that local citizens exercise substantial control over the means of production and distribution on which their livelihoods depend. This requires reforming industrial and tax policies—from the global to the local levels—to favor ownership of enterprises and productive resources by local, nonfinancial stakeholders such as workers, community members, customers, and suppliers. Educational programs should inform citizens about the powers and responsibilities of ownership participation and the dysfunctions of absentee ownership.

As chapter 6 detailed, much can be done to encourage local communities to assume responsibility for their own economic and environmental revitalization. Steps can be taken to strengthen community capacity to understand the issues; set clear local economic priorities favoring local ownership and self-reliance; deal with industrial pollution, housing shortages, land use, and transportation issues; hold corporations with operations in a jurisdiction accountable to local social and environmental priorities; and use industrial, environmental, and tax policy measures to encourage the responsible use and maintenance of local natural resources, including forests, fisheries, and water.

Community boards composed of elected citizen representatives might be established to review, approve, and monitor the local operations and investment plans of domestic and foreign-based corporations. These boards might help to establish community accountability rules and obligations for enterprises in their jurisdiction, including banks and other financial institutions.

### REREGULATE CORPORATE INVESTMENT

As we have seen, governments have been largely stripped of the powers and tools they once had to regulate the investments of global corporations. Yet regulating corporate investment is essential if people are going to take democratic control of the operations of global corporations and banks. A series of new measures needs to be designed for legislative action, such as "site-here-to-sell-here" policies, the chartering of corporations, restrictions on plant closures, and rules against the patenting of life forms. Governments should be challenged to establish new investment requirements for job content, food safety, and environmental standards, as well as to put more emphasis on worker control, community ownership, and related social responsibilities as conditions for investment. Similarly, governments need to be pressed to reassert control over fiscal policies by reregulating financial instruments (such as derivatives) and banking. To move in this direction, steps need to be taken to identify the obstacles to government control that are built into the new free trade agreements and find strategies to repeal them.

### RENEGOTIATE OR ABROGATE TRADE DEALS

As we have seen, the new globalization regimes—for example, the WTO, NAFTA, and the proposed Free Trade Area of the Americas—are, in effect, the constitutions of the new world order, designed primarily to protect the rights and freedoms of global corporations. A program to dismantle this corporate rule, therefore, would have to include strategies either to terminate altogether or to renegotiate specific components of these agreements, keeping in mind that they themselves contain specific clauses and procedures for abrogation that can be exercised by one or more of the partners. The main power tools of NAFTA, such as the investor-state mechanism that allows corporations to sue governments, should be eliminated. Chapter 10 of this volume calls for the decommissioning of the WTO and its replacement with a smaller international trade authority that advances the ten principles for sustainable societies. A variety of social movements actively engaged in campaigns against NAFTA and the FTAA have already shifted their attention to identifying the economic, social, and environmental priorities that need to be addressed as well as other provisions that need to be included in alternative systems based on fair trade. Common platforms can be developed around such campaigns to repeal or renegotiate specific components of free market regimes. Steps could also be taken to organize communities into WTO- and NAFTA-free zones.

## Toward Alternative Business Structures

Modern life is now so dominated by global corporations that it is difficult for many people to imagine how the world might go on without them. But businesses may assume many other forms. Transition to more economically democratic structures becomes easier to visualize once we recognize that many human-scale, locally owned enterprises already exist. They include virtually all of the millions of local, independent businesses now organized as sole proprietorships, partnerships, cooperatives of all types, and worker-owned businesses. They include family-owned businesses, small farms, artisanal producers, independent retail stores, small factories, farmers' markets, community banks, and so on. In fact, though these kinds of businesses get very little government support, they are the primary sources of livelihood for most of the world's people.

There are very few of our daily needs that cannot be met by small and medium-size enterprises operating within a market economy of a kind—but one that is characterized by a multitude of small players rather than a handful of giant, absentee owners. And all of them would operate without the benefits of stock market investing, limited liability, or corporate personhood, so crucial to large corporations.

From the point of view of sustainability and democracy, there is no reason why giant transnational corporations are needed to run hamburger stands, produce clothing and toys, publish books and magazines, grow and process and distribute food, make the goods we need, or provide most of the things that contribute to a satisfying existence. In truth, the largest corporations often contract out many of their actual production processes to networks of smaller, independent producers. The dominant global corporations, however, maintain control of market access to be sure of their own ability to dictate terms and prices—in violation of basic market principles—capturing profits for themselves and shifting risks to smaller producers. This is a gross misuse of power, not a sign of superior efficiency. Change is mandatory.

In this chapter, we have described in detail the spectrum of actions now being taken to attempt to control corporate behavior and change many structural elements. In summary, however, from a macro perspective, there are three key ingredients that will characterize any overall shift away from the domination of global corporations and toward more democratic and socially and ecologically sustainable enterprises:

- *Where globalization has encouraged globe-spanning corporate concentration, the course must be reversed.* This can be done by giving priority to smaller businesses capable of functioning as human-scale communities of interest in which people know each other, are dedicated to a common purpose, and share rewards more equitably. The era of CEOs being compensated at five hundred times the level of office workers or line workers must end.

- *Where global corporations now enjoy complete mobility, businesses must be required to be rooted in a place.* They must be owned by people who have direct involvement in the operation—workers, community representatives, suppliers—rather than by distant investors who buy and sell without personal engagement other than profit, growth, and balance sheet figures.

- *All businesses must be transparent and accountable to all stakeholders in the community.* These people bear the ultimate impact of decisions taken. They may include workers, environmentalists, public health officials, human rights advocates, and the like. All have suffered from local activities controlled by distant owners.

And so we see that size, ownership, and accountability are the main issues. Smaller enterprises, with local roots and equitable ownership of productive assets, combined with democratic regulation are essential for socially just, efficient, and sustainable enterprises.

By their nature, *human-scale* enterprises—of small and medium size—will distribute power and ownership far more equitably and democratically than global corporations could possibly do. Lacking a global corporation's ability (or desire) to "buy" politicians, dictate consumer choice, or manipulate the symbols of personal identity through mass advertising, smaller enterprises are intrinsically more likely to be responsive to community interests.

The European Commission has defined small and medium businesses as those with less than 250 employees, annual sales under $35 million, and total assets under $24 million. Even this may seem too large for some, but not by the standards of megacorporations: total sales of the Forbes Global 500 list of companies for 2003 ranges from a low of $9.4 billion to $258.7 billion—Wal-Mart—to Citigroup's $1.1 trillion in assets. Still, the category of small and medium can include substantial enough enterprises to be able to produce most essential goods and services efficiently.

Where necessary to help deal with new technologies and sophisticated markets, smaller-scale enterprises have shown they can collaborate and network with one another to achieve some efficiencies of scale. Chapter 7 offers some examples of these, but we mention here the case of Denmark, where the entire industrial sector has traditionally been made up of small firms that have sometimes formed consortiums to deal with larger projects. For example, a group of apparel firms jointly employ a designer who has turned once-uncoordinated product lines of clothing into a tailored collection aimed at the larger German market. A consortium of small furniture makers, woodworkers, and interior designers have undertaken joint bidding on the furnishings of convention centers and other projects that are larger in scale than any one company can handle. Similarly, Northern Italy's furniture industry is built on networks of small firms supported by a producers' association that helps provide common services such as warehousing, purchasing, and inventory management.

Although the authors of this report favor *local* procurement and marketing wherever possible, such arrangements as these demonstrate the possibilities of achieving advantages of scale in a system that remains predominantly local.

Of course, the role of *ownership* is also crucial. As discussed earlier, there is an obvious and important distinction between an *engaged stakeholder-owner*—a person who lives within a community and is deeply concerned about its future—and the presently dominant global system of largely *absentee owners*, who have no direct relationship to any community. Global corporate management may be thousands of miles away, across oceans; investors may be anywhere at all, completely unaware of a firm's local activities or impact. This kind of absentee ownership is a perfect precursor for the production of out-of-control harms to the community, just as absentee owners of a house or a building can make life impossible for a local tenant, who has no recourse.

People who live in a place—whether they operate a business or own a home or live on the land—are far more likely to invest well in its maintenance and nurture relationships with their social and environmental context. Ownership adds to their commitment. When businesses are similarly owned by their workers, customers, suppliers, and community members, the owners bear the actual outcomes of their decisions. *Accountability* is built into the fabric of the economic system; *transparency* and openness are impossible to avoid.

In addition to all this, every society also needs enforceable rules, and the marketplace is no exception. The present trend toward deregulation of corporate enterprises, as if they were the one social element that can be counted on to behave responsibly, has been producing disaster after disaster. Enron provides a case in point.

Without comprehensive and firm regulatory mechanisms, even optimum conditions for social and economic efficiency will quickly erode. Size must be regulated, costs internalized (including the environmental and social damages now absorbed by taxpayers), contracts enforced, and health, safety, and environmental standards observed and enforced with great dedication. The earlier chapter on subsidiarity suggests many other rules for optimizing social and environmental benefits by businesses, from site-here-to-sell-here rules, to encouragement of local investors rather than outside sources, to corporate finance and mobility regulations. When ownership and rule making are predominantly rooted in local realities, with community welfare as the primary value, then everything else may fall naturally into place, fairly and effectively balancing the interests of local business enterprises with other community values for the mutual benefit of all.

What we have presented here is only a blueprint, and many practical questions remain. Skeptics may fairly ask if such localized, small arrangements would satisfy people's need to earn a living. Who would provide the food? Who would finance research into new medicines? And if publicly traded corporations were eliminated—and with them the stock market—who would finance retirements? These and other giant issues need to be exhaustively discussed; we hope this chapter serves as a beginning point of such discussions. But we must also begin the discussion with full recognition that the system we have now has utterly failed to solve any of these problems satisfactorily, equitably, and without great harms.

Take the question of jobs. For all their economic power, the number of jobs that global corporations provide relative to the world's workforce is trivial. According to the *Top 200,* a report by Sarah Anderson and John Cavanagh of IPS, although sales of the world's two hundred largest corporations are equivalent to 27.5 percent of world GDP, they employ only 0.78 percent of the world's workers. As we have said, the majority of the world's jobs are provided even today by small and medium-size enterprises—the same enterprises that are also responsible for creating nearly all new jobs. As corporations get ever larger and consolidate, merge, and consume other companies, they convert to production systems and technologies that *reduce* jobs rather than increase them.

Next, food. Before a combination of intentional public policy and corporate monopolization of marketing and distribution forced most independent farmers into bankruptcy, small farms were the backbone of most communities and the primary suppliers of food, even in the Northern industrial countries. Even now they retain central roles in most Southern countries. Smaller, independently managed farms using environmentally sound organic agricultural practices are far more efficient in their use of scarce land than are corporate factory farms, and they provide more jobs. Localizing production to reduce the distance between farm and market means fresher, more nutritional food and big energy savings—a subject that is addressed in more detail in chapter 7.

As for drug research, if development of copycat drugs is excluded, most basic research on new drug treatments is publicly funded and much of it carried out in universities. For all their claims that monopoly pricing is necessary to recover research costs, drug companies spend far more on marketing than on research. These costs are a larger factor in the exorbitant drug prices than research costs. The greatest barrier to the deconcentration of drug production and distribution is not technology but the granting of monopoly patent rights to giant pharmaceutical companies for essential drugs developed with public research money. A reduction in patent protection to allow entry to smaller, more local competitors would be a step toward freeing the market to gain the benefits of greater competition.

Financing retirement? Those who are presently fortunate enough to have the money to participate in the stock market, and lucky enough to pick the right stocks at the right time, can use it to finance an affluent retirement. However, we must not be misled by the fact that although some retirement accounts profited handsomely from the giant stock bubble of the 1990s, many others were decimated. It would be a stretch to assume that society can feed, house, clothe, and provide medical care for an aging population based on stock bubbles. Meeting the needs of the retired necessarily depends on the willingness of those of working age to lend their labor and assets to the task of providing for them as part of an intergenerational social contract. The corporate global economy is actually decapitalizing the human and physical infrastructure needed to support the young and old alike in favor of short-term financial gains, eroding the social contract between generations. To rebuild the social contract—the social and physical infrastructure needed to meet the needs of children, working people, and the elderly—it is essential to restore the concept of community, in part by rebuilding prosperous community economies.

When the full costs are taken into account, most of the real needs of people can be more efficiently met by a local market system, which also has the potential to improve the quality of life of nearly everyone. With proper care and a just distribution of the planet's sustainable bounty, the world's six billion—plus inhabitants can live full and dignified lives. Hardship and material deprivation can be eliminated. This necessarily means less material consumption for the world's favored few. It may, however, prove that "less is more" in terms of achieving sustainable societies.

# CHAPTER TEN

# New International Structures

THOSE OF US who have contributed to this volume have all faced variations on a nagging question from journalists, pundits, and government officials as we debate economic globalization around the world. "Isn't economic globalization, along with the key global institutions that underlie it, inevitable?" That this question persists for institutions that have existed from merely a decade (the World Trade Organization) to a half-century (the World Bank and the IMF) is a tribute to the power of the forces that have backed and benefited from economic globalization during this period.

But as this volume goes to print, the grip of inevitability is loosening. With colossal failures by the Bretton Woods institutions in Asia, Africa, Eastern Europe, and most recently Argentina, coupled with the confidence-shattering collapse of Enron Corp., WorldCom, and others, the notion is spreading that perhaps the guardian institutions of economic globalization are not guarding so well—or are guarding only the few. And perhaps more important, the array of forces rising in opposition to economic globalization have begun making a convincing case for the replacement of the Bretton Woods institutions with alternatives that could better serve humanity and the planet.

It is the subject of this chapter to outline a number of these alternatives. We start by analyzing the need for change, then outline the essential elements of a more just and sustainable international system and its institutions. We go on to make the argument for decommissioning the core multilateral economic institutions and unifying global economic governance under a restructured United Nations system. We end with proposals on what new institutions might do the job better.

## A Review of the Current Situation

The experience of the Southern countries is instructive of the need for alternatives. As earlier chapters described, when the traditional institutions of colonialism were phased out, the newly liberated nations sought a pathway to economic development. Seeking to create a demand for its services, the World Bank stepped forward with a simple formula: Development is synonymous with economic growth. Economic growth depends on investment. Poor countries have little to invest, so foreign borrowing would be their salvation. The more the foreign borrowing, the more rapid the growth and the faster the development.

It is true that foreign borrowing can be a sound choice *if* the borrowed funds are used to buy essential capital goods from abroad that are not available domestically *and* those capital goods are used in ways that generate sufficient export earnings to repay the foreign loans. Unfortunately, such conditions were rarely met. To this day, most foreign borrowing pays for the import of luxury goods and military arms or finds its way into the foreign bank accounts of privileged elites.

Unpayable debts accumulated under the World Bank programs until the IMF stepped in to protect the interests of creditors. Domestic economies were reoriented to produce for export to earn the foreign exchange to repay the debts. Whether from ignorance or malice, the World Bank and the IMF favored policies that stripped governments of their ability to manage the movement of goods and money across their borders. When import controls were relaxed, many countries experienced a dramatic increase in imports but no increase in their ability to pay for them. Firms producing for domestic markets suffered. Concurrent relaxation of foreign exchange controls unleashed waves of foreign borrowing, capital flight, and financial speculation. This added to already high foreign claims (including foreign debt) against the country's current and future foreign exchange earnings and created further pressure to increase exports and attract yet more foreign funds—including speculative portfolio investments that contribute nothing to productive capacity but add significant volatility and instability to the financial system.

Because many countries lacked the capacity to produce manufactured or service exports, they came under strong pressure from the World Bank and the IMF to devote still more of their national resources to producing shrimp, cotton, timber, coffee, and other primary commodities for export. The World Bank and the regional development banks commonly financed such expansion with loans to pay for the infrastructure that subsidized the projects of foreign corporate investors. But because many countries were doing the same thing, a flood of coffee, cocoa, and other commodities onto world markets depressed prices. Foreign debt continued to grow as a result of new borrowing, but falling export earnings reduced capacity to repay. Falling commodity prices also resulted in downward pressure on wages in the commodity-producing sectors. This in turn placed downward pressures on wages in other sectors, including the industrial sector, thus giving foreign corporations greater incentives to export jobs from the North to take advantage of exploited workforces in the South.

The World Bank and IMF are leading advocates of markets unfettered by the distortions of subsidies and government intervention—except when the distortions favor corporate interests. The artificial depression of commodity prices is a market distortion that in turn artificially depresses wages in both the South and the North, creates the illusion that environmental resources are abundant at a time of growing scarcity and encourages their wasteful consumption, undermines the South's terms of trade with the North, and favors returns to investors at the expense of labor and the public treasury. That corporate profits are enhanced at the expense of equity and environmental security is not a random inevitability; like all of today's globalization rules, it is based on a set of subjective policy choices.

The pundits who dismiss antiglobalization protestors as know-nothings and economic illiterates, depriving the poor of an opportunity for a better life, would do better to apply such labels to the World Bank and IMF ideologues who advocate and defend the policies that have had such disastrous consequences. (See also Box S.)

As discussed in chapter 3, the General Agreement on Trade and Tariffs (GATT) and the World Trade Organization (WTO) have exacerbated the imbalances and distortions. A key to understanding the failure of the globalists' free market ideology is that it views economic policies from the perspective of returns to the corporation rather than to the community. Thus,

---

## BOX S: UNEMPLOYMENT:
## THE ROLE OF MONETARY POLICY

*By Martin Khor, Third World Network*

There has been much concern in Northern countries about the impact on domestic employment and wages of the corporate export of jobs to lower-wage countries. Less attention has been given to the extent to which high unemployment and falling wages in the Northern countries themselves are an intentional consequence of the monetary policies of central bankers. Many Northern countries base their monetary policies on a formula known as NAIRU—the nonaccelerating inflation rate of unemployment—on the theory that keeping unemployment above a particular level will maintain sufficient downward pressure on wages to prevent inflation. For those who read the business press, it is public knowledge that in most Northern countries the explicit goal of the central bankers responsible for monetary policy is to keep wages low and stock prices rising, which ensures a steady increase in the economic power of those who hold shares in the financial markets relative to those who live from their labor. A new approach to monetary policy is needed, with the goal of maintaining full employment and living wages everywhere while keeping a lid on speculative bubbles in share prices and land values.

---

there is no conflict between corporate and community interests. By their reckoning, increased profits for corporations mean increased wealth for the community. But as chapter 9 explained, this is a false assumption.

Global corporations are driven by stock markets to maximize short-term financial profits without regard for the health of individuals, the social fabric, or the environment, even though these are all essential to the well-being of people and communities. Global corporations maximize profit by employing the smallest possible number of people at the lowest possible wage; in contrast, the healthy community seeks living-wage jobs for all who need employment. A global corporation can obtain a quick return by clearcutting a forest and then moving on to another; in contrast, communities prosper by sustaining productive yield of their natural resource base.

Markets need rules. Because the purpose of the market is to serve people, these rules should favor community interests. This can happen only if the rules are made by people acting in their capacity as citizens of communities.

When corporations make the rules, corporate interests are inevitably given priority over community interests. Corporations will seek to capture economic gains for themselves while shifting costs to communities. They will seek to increase their own rule-making power while weakening their accountability to people. The legal boundaries that define the corporation's assets will be well protected. The political boundaries that define the assets of communities—the commons—will be weakened or erased. This is exactly what has happened in the global economy as rule-making power shifted from people to corporations.

It is useful to look at the corporate concept of free trade from this perspective. In the name of free trade, corporate globalists call for the virtual elimination of the boundaries that define communities and nations. Local efforts to regulate or manage exchanges with other communities and countries are dismissed as protectionism, an infringement of market freedom. Corporate globalists effectively dismiss the very existence of community interests that might actually merit protection.

These same individuals take a very different position, however, when it comes to matters relating to trade among or within corporations—insisting that it is the right of the individual corporations to regulate and manage the most minute details of their trade relations with other subsidiaries or other corporations as they see fit. They reserve the right to do business only with others of their choice and on terms of their own choosing. Thus, in the world of the corporate globalist, when private interests are at stake, the rules of free trade do not apply: borders are well defended and trade is carefully managed. And because the largest corporations command internal economies larger than those of most countries, this is not a trivial matter.

Yet public interests are real, and it is an essential responsibility of governments to protect them. Just as corporations demand the right to manage trade among themselves in the defense of private interests, communities and nations must manage trade and investment relationships among themselves in defense of the public interest.

One essential reason why a community must manage its trade relations with its neighbors is to keep the value of its imports and exports in balance. If it is paying more for imports than it earns from its exports, it is living beyond its means and building up debt to its neighbor. Usually the beneficiaries are those who hold power while the burden of repayment falls to future generations and the weaker elements of the society. If a country is exporting more than it is importing, then people are not enjoying the benefits of their own labor and resources. Usually the primary burden of producing the export surplus is borne by the poorer members of society while the financial surplus finds its way into the foreign accounts of the rich and powerful. Such imbalances create instability in the international system and do not serve the public interest.

In the press to expand trade for its own sake, a simple but obvious truth has been forgotten: the primary reason for a country to export is to generate foreign exchange to pay for the import of goods it cannot reasonably produce for itself. But as the Bretton Woods institutions have forced Southern countries to open their borders to the free flow of goods across their borders, the result has been a surge in imports with no corresponding increase in the ability to pay for them. Many of the imports are nonessential goods that subsidized producers are able to sell at less than full cost. This creates unfair competition for domestic producers that do not enjoy comparable subsidies, and a growing external debt that can only be repaid by shifting the balance of the domestic economy from import surplus to export surplus—thus diverting resources away from meeting domestic needs and requiring a decrease in domestic consumption. The result is a downward spiral of dependency and impoverishment that contradicts the claim of free market ideology, that trade liberalization leads to accelerated economic growth.

There is a wealth of evidence to document this contradiction. The United Nations Conference on Trade and Development (UNCTAD) *Trade and Development Report, 1999* found that for developing countries, excluding China, the average trade deficit in the 1990s was higher than in the 1970s by 3 percent of GDP, whereas the average growth rate was down by 2 percent. Inappropriate trade liberalization contributed to this negative phenomenon.

A 1994 UNCTAD study of forty-one least developed countries (LDCs) came to a similar conclusion. It found that over a ten-year period there was "no clear and systematic association" between trade liberalization and devaluation, on the one hand, and the growth and diversification of output and growth of output and exports of LDCs, on the other. In fact, it found that in many LDCs, trade liberalization had been accompanied by deindustrialization.

Disturbing evidence of post-1980 liberalization episodes in the African and Latin American regions have also been documented. For example, Senegal experienced large job losses following liberalization in the late

1980s; by the early 1990s, employment cuts had eliminated one-third of all manufacturing jobs. The chemical, textile, shoe, and automobile assembly industries virtually collapsed in the Ivory Coast after tariffs were abruptly lowered by 40 percent in 1986. Similar problems have plagued liberalization attempts in Nigeria. In Sierra Leone, Zambia, Zaire, Uganda, Tanzania, and the Sudan, liberalization in the 1980s brought a tremendous surge in consumer imports and sharp cutbacks in foreign exchange available for purchases of intermediate inputs and capital goods, with devastating effects on industrial output and employment. In Ghana, liberalization caused industrial sector employment to plunge from 78,700 in 1987 to 28,000 in 1993, mainly because "large swaths of the manufacturing sector were devastated by import competition," according to UNCTAD. Adjustment programs introduced in the 1990s have also been difficult for much of the manufacturing sector in Mozambique, Cameroon, Tanzania, Malawi, and Zambia. Import competition precipitated sharp contractions in output and employment in the short run, with many firms closing down operations entirely.

Some developing countries outside Africa have experienced similar problems. According to a 2001 study, "Liberalization in the early nineties seems to have resulted in large job losses in the formal sector and a substantial worsening in underemployment in Peru, Nicaragua, Ecuador, and Brazil. Nor is the evidence from other parts of Latin America particularly encouraging." The regional record suggests that the normal outcome is a sharp deterioration in income distribution, with no clear evidence that this shift is temporary in character.

A responsible national trade policy depends on calibrating national trade rules to achieve a balance between imports and exports. Many Southern countries are unable to increase imports because of production constraints on their ability to increase export earnings. Moreover, the main exports of many developing countries are primarily commodities, the prices of which have declined significantly over time. Also, the products exported by Southern countries face trade barriers imposed by Northern countries. If import liberalization proceeds while the conditions for successful export growth are not yet in place, there can be adverse results—such as increases in the trade deficit and balance-of-payment difficulties—which then add to the level of external debt and greater debt-servicing burden, leading to slowed economic growth and increased unemployment.

Similar problems have arisen in the area of finance. Since 1997, a continuous series of devastating financial and economic crises has hit Mexico, Thailand, Indonesia, South Korea and Malaysia, Russia, Brazil, Turkey, and Argentina. There have been conflicting reasons given for these crises, the dominant one (propagated by the IMF, the World Bank, and the developed countries) is that the affected countries suffered from bad political and economic governance. This is quite remarkable, because most of the affected countries had been lavishly praised just prior to their crises as shining examples of good economic management.

A more accurate and credible explanation is that these crises were caused by the financial liberalization and deregulation that have swept the world since the early 1970s. As a result, there has been an explosive increase in financial speculation as investment funds and speculators move rapidly across borders in search of profits. In recent years, many developing countries were also advised to deregulate and liberalize their financial systems. The controls over the inflow and outflow of funds, which these countries previously had, were significantly relaxed. This led to excessive short-term borrowing by local firms and banks, as well as the entrance of international funds and players that invested, speculated, and manipulated currencies and stock markets.

IMF action to impose financial liberalization is a violation of Article VI of its own articles of agreement, which specifically sanctions the right of a nation to adopt capital controls. This is integral to a nation's right to economic self-determination, and it is inappropriate for outside parties to pressure a national government to abandon them. The crucial question of *when* or *how* a state wishes to liberalize its capital account—or *whether* it wishes to embark on such liberalization at all—is properly left to its sole determination, without outside pressure.

The IMF, the World Bank, and the rich countries involved in these institutions that want access to the emerging markets for their financial institutions have for years promoted the idea that liberalization is beneficial and poses little danger. When the crisis struck, the IMF made it worse by misdiagnosing the cause and promoting even further financial liberalization as part of its loan conditionality, as well as a policy package (high interest rates, tight monetary policies, and closure of local financial institutions) that converted a financial-debt problem into a structural economic recession. The

IMF also denied that hedge funds and other highly leveraged institutions had played a destabilizing role. It took the near-collapse of a giant private hedge fund, Long-Term Capital Management (LTCM), to expose the risks posed by these highly leveraged speculative funds.

# Essential Rules of a Just and Sustainable International Trade and Finance System

The global trade and finance system and its primary rule-making institutions—the Bretton Woods institutions—have come to a crossroads. Decisions made in the next few years will have important effects on which direction the system will take. There is no question of the need for a multilateral system of rules for international trade and finance. A proper system of rules is essential to stability, predictability, and fairness for all participants; the present system is unstable, unpredictable, and extremely unfair.

Rules are essential, but they must be determined democratically to serve the public interest.

In addition to being stable, predictable, and fair, a suitable international system should support the following four goals.

### DEMOCRATIC SELF-DETERMINATION

The democratic right of all people to establish their own economic priorities and policies must be protected as long as their actions do not infringe on the rights and freedoms of those in other localities and nations. This means that people, communities, and nations should own the productive assets on which their livelihoods depend, be free from illegitimate foreign debts, and have the right and ability to manage the flow of goods and money across their borders that is essential to setting their own economic priorities and to maintaining high social and environmental standards consistent with community well-being. In a just and sustainable system, stronger and more affluent countries would not be able to demand access to the markets or resources of weaker and less affluent countries against their will and interests. Nor would any corporation have such rights. If a corporation wishes to do business in a jurisdiction other than the one in which it is chartered, it could be required to apply for a charter in that country subject to its requirements, laws, and taxes. The most pressing restraints on Southern countries are their lack of control over their own economic resources, their inability to determine their own economic priorities, and the limits on their access to essential technologies.

## BALANCED TRADE

Every country, both Northern and Southern, has a responsibility to its international neighbors to maintain a balance between imports and exports. It has been a basic premise of trade theory, going back to David Ricardo, that in a fair and mutually beneficial international system, each country maintains stable, balanced trade relations with its neighbors (imports equal exports), and investment is national. International debts accrue when the value of a country's imports is greater than its exports. When a country's trade is balanced it has no reason to accumulate foreign debts, eliminating a major potential source of economic instability, domination, and exploitation.

## FAIR COMMODITY PRICES

Economic theory has long recognized the inherent instability of commodity markets because of the interplay between short-term price sensitivity and long-investment lead times. As a result, there are periodic swings between an artificial scarcity that drives market prices far above real production costs and an artificial oversupply that depresses market prices below true production costs. As we elaborated earlier, there is a need for international commodity agreements and mechanisms among countries to maintain fair and stable commodity prices that reflect the full costs of production, including a living wage and all environmental costs. There should be institutional mechanisms at the international level through which nations can coordinate their policies to achieve fairness and stability in international market prices. The appropriate international concern here is to insulate international markets from the consequences of domestic subsidies or price supports that may artificially depress international market prices at the expense of efficient producers in other countries.

## OPEN ACCESS TO INFORMATION AND KNOWLEDGE

Intellectual property rights should be limited to measures necessary to stimulate innovation and creativity. Restrictions undermine the public interest when used to enforce corporate monopolies over information and technology. Information and technical knowledge are among the few resources that can be infinitely reproduced and freely shared without negative environmental impacts or depriving anyone of their use. Open access to information and beneficial technology is a key to a just and sustainable human future. Every contemporary human invention necessarily builds on the common knowledge accumulated over countless generations—the information commons. The proper use of intellectual property rights is to ensure acknowledgment and reward for those who contribute to that pool, not to establish publicly defended information monopolies. It is revealing that the same corporate globalists who eagerly promote the free movement of goods and money, which tends to undermine community self-determination and self-reliance, are adamantly opposed to the free movement and sharing of information and knowledge that has the potential to increase self-determination and self-reliance. The international interest, particularly of Southern countries (and the former Soviet Union and Eastern Europe), is best served by international regimes that seek to minimize barriers to the free flow and sharing of information and technology. Indeed, a commitment by Northern countries to share their capital stock of information and technology with Southern countries might be considered partial compensation to the people of the South for the wealth the North has extracted from them over the past five hundred years.

If public policy is to serve community interests, countries of both South and North need adequate policy space and freedom to choose trade and investment policies consistent with the interests of their people and domestic enterprises. This principle should be central to any system of international rules on trade and finance. Its application should accomplish the following:

• Help countries prevent debt and financial crises by implementing measures that regulate and control the type and extent of foreign loans that the public and private sectors are allowed to obtain and that prevent speculation and manipulation in stock and currency markets.

- Enable affected countries to manage financial crisis effectively so that debtors and creditors share the burden equitably, including the option of a debt standstill arrangement and recourse to an international debt arbitration court or panel, which would then arrange for a debt workout.
- Permit countries to establish systems of control over the inflow and outflow of funds, particularly the speculative variety, without fear of attracting penalties.
- Obligate governments of countries that are sources of internationally mobile funds to discipline and regulate their financial institutions and players to prevent them from causing volatility and speculation abroad.
- Provide for international regulation of hedge funds, investment banks, and other highly leveraged institutions, offshore centers, currency markets, and derivatives trade.
- Stabilize currency exchange rates.
- Give poor countries a fair say in the policies and processes of international institutions like the WTO and IMF by increasing the transparency of decision processes and increasing their voting shares.

Essential reforms to restore the integrity of the international financial system are closely related to essential reforms in other areas, such as trade. When a country liberalizes its imports even though its local sectors are not prepared to compete and it has no capacity to increase its export revenue, its trade and balance-of-payment deficits and therefore its international debt burden will inevitably worsen. A nation must have the right and capacity to manage flows of both money and goods across its borders.

Under assault from predatory corporations and financial speculators, developing countries have no choice but to institute domestic measures to protect themselves. In particular, they should have regulations that control the extent of public and private sector foreign loans (for example, restricting them to projects that yield the capacity to repay in foreign currency), prohibit manipulation of their currencies and stock markets, and treat foreign direct investment in a selective way that avoids buildup of foreign debt.

The array of national policy instruments should include capital controls that would allow the country to avoid an excessive buildup of external debt, curb volatility of the flow of funds, and provide scope to adopt macroeconomic policies that can counter recession (such as lower interest rates or budget expansion) while reducing the risks of volatility in the exchange rate and flow of funds.

As a first step toward creating a just and sustainable global system, the processes of liberalization should be halted. All proposals to expand the scope and authority of the IMF and the World Trade Organization should be rejected, including these:

- Proposals to amend the IMF Articles of Agreement to give it jurisdiction over capital account convertibility, which would give the IMF additional authority to force developing countries to remove remaining controls over their capital accounts and markets.
- Efforts by the OECD countries to revive negotiations on a multilateral agreement on investment that would give unfettered freedom of mobility to all types of capital flows.
- Proposals for giving the WTO new authority over international investment, government procurement, ownership of public services, and environmental and social standards that would be used to eliminate capital controls, standards for foreign investments, public ownership of essential services, and the ability of governments to give preference to local procurement and to set social and environmental standards appropriate to local conditions and public interests. (These are not trade issues, and to the extent that there is a need for global rules, there are more appropriate venues in which to address them.)

There is a related need to review and roll back provisions of existing trade agreements that distort development, the environment, public health, and labor and are otherwise contrary to important public interests. Particular attention should go to the following:

- The existing WTO TRIMs and specialized financial services agreement that open domestic finance to foreign corporate control, and the TRIPs agreement on intellectual property rights that supports corporate monopolization of essential information and technology. Serious consideration should be given to transferring responsibility for these agreements from the WTO to more suitable forums.

- IMF and World Bank structural adjustment provisions that impose harmful liberalization policies on Southern countries.

- United Nations Conference on Trade and Development could take a lead role in these reviews and in calling for a moratorium on proposals to expand the authority and mandates of the Bretton Woods institutions.

## Restructuring the Institutional Framework

In addition to these immediate interim measures to prevent further damage and begin to reframe the problem, there is a need for a basic restructuring of the institutions of international economic governance to create a system that is accountable to the needs and preferences of people, communities, and nature. Our recommendations follow.

### UNIFY GLOBAL GOVERNANCE UNDER A RESTRUCTURED UNITED NATIONS

Global governance functions today are divided between the United Nations system—including the U.N. secretariat; its specialized agencies, such as the World Health Organization, the International Labor Organization, the Food and Agriculture Organization; and its various development assistance funds, such as UNDP, UNFPA, UNICEF, and UNIFEM—and the Bretton Woods system. (Although the Bretton Woods institutions are commonly included in lists of United Nations organizations and may, when it is to their advantage, claim themselves to be part of the United Nations system, the relationship actually has no substance. The Bretton Woods institutions have their own governing boards and budgets and acknowledge no accountability or subordination to the United Nations or its governing bodies.) The U.N. system has by far the broader mandate, and despite its considerable flaws, is more open and democratic. In practice, it has given much greater weight to human, social, and environmental priorities than have the more secretive Bretton Woods institutions.

Erskine Childers and Brian Urquhart, in their 1994 report *Renewing the United Nations System,* point out that the founders of the United Nations intended that the responsibility for global economic affairs—including the overall supervision and policy direction of the Bretton Woods institutions—

would fall under the jurisdiction of the Economic and Social Council of the U.N. General Assembly. The scope of its intended role in this regard is spelled out in Article 55 of its charter, which provides that the United Nations shall promote the following:

- Higher standards of living, full employment, and conditions of economic and social progress and development
- Solutions for international economic, social, health, and related problems
- International cultural and educational cooperation
- Universal respect for, and observance of, human rights and fundamental freedoms for all without distinction as to race, sex, language, or religion

But the United States and other corporate-dominated Western governments—the same ones that took the lead in creating both the United Nations and the Bretton Woods systems after World War II—allowed and even encouraged the latter to act as a global government with the ability to impose their will on nation-states in disregard of U.N. conventions and treaties.

Also, throughout most of the 1980s and 1990s, the U.S. Congress refused to pay the full dues owed by the United States to the United Nations, starving it of the financial resources necessary to carry out its mandate and creating a permanent crisis atmosphere in what should be the most important, influential, and stable international body. In contrast, the World Bank, the IMF, the WTO, and the global corporations they faithfully serve have been flush with resources. Underfunded, understaffed, and bypassed by the United States and other Northern governments in most economic matters, the United Nations largely ceded to the Bretton Woods institutions the power to shape global economic policies and relationships.

Dividing governance of the global affairs of one world between two competing governmental systems is not wise policy. The complexity of labor, health, food, human rights, environmental, trade, and investment issues is now much greater than in 1945, and the need for coherent global-level policies is far more urgent.

A choice must now be made either to expand the power and mandate of the Bretton Woods system to provide the leadership at the global level or to reaffirm the mandate of the United Nations and build its capacity to fulfill its intended function. Expanding the mandate of the Bretton Woods system appears to be a grave error from both a human and a planetary perspective.

It is true that these institutions have been far more effective in implementing well-defined agendas than has the United Nations. Yet although the United Nations has been less effective, its more open and democratic decision processes and greater responsiveness to the will of the people have often resulted in more consensual agendas aligned with human and planetary interests.

True democracy rests not on application of brute force but on consent of the governed. Force is the instrument of the self-interested tyrant. The poor and the weak are generally better served by less coercive regimes. As the coercive power of the corporate-dominated Bretton Woods institutions has grown, they have increasingly chosen to impose rules that serve the strong at the expense of the weak.

Clearly, there is a need for international rules. To serve the whole of humanity, however, they must be based on the consent of the governed, and enforcement must be left primarily to democratically elected local and national governments. The decision processes of the United Nations largely align with these principles. Limiting the powers and mandates of the IMF, the World Bank, and the WTO will create a greater space for a reformed United Nations to fulfill its intended functions and for people to act through their national and local governments to establish a policy framework consistent with the healthy, authentic development of people and communities.

We are the first to acknowledge that the United Nations has been greatly weakened and compromised over the past two decades. From the time Ronald Reagan became president of the United States in 1981, the U.S. government has actively undermined those U.N. agencies it viewed as interfering with market freedom. The United States has continued to use its great power status in the wake of the Cold War to manipulate the United Nations to serve a number of narrow U.S. political and economic interests. In addition, the United Nations inevitably suffers from the democratic deficits of many of its member states. The fact that many governments poorly represent the will of their people is likewise reflected in flawed decision making.

A related threat to the capacity of the United Nations to perform its intended functions on behalf of humanity is the increasingly successful effort by corporate interests—led by the International Chamber of Commerce and the World Business Council on Sustainable Development—to establish a presence in the United Nations to ensure that its resources and policies align with the corporate agenda and that there is no meaningful and enforceable call for corporate accountability in U.N. forums. Starved of financial resources and bullied by the U.S. government, the United Nations has been actively solicitous of corporate engagement. The July 2000 Global Compact that the United Nations launched with forty-four global corporations increases the corporate influence, placing at risk the U.N.'s legitimacy and credibility with the civil society groups that have launched increasingly effective campaigns to immobilize and eventually close the Bretton Woods institutions. Civil society generally has been highly supportive of the United Nations, but a corporate-dominated United Nations would not be immune to similar attacks.

The United Nations is an institution of governments and people. There is no legitimate place in its deliberations and decision processes for corporations that represent only the narrow financial self-interests of a small, wealthy elite. If the United Nations takes on a larger role in reforming and democratizing economic relations among and within nations, it will be more important than ever that it is freed of corporate influence and serve as a fully open and democratic body, solely accountable to its member governments and the people these governments presume to represent.

We believe that the time has come to reshape the system of global economic governance under the auspices of the United Nations, providing it with the human and financial resources to fulfill its original mandate and introducing reforms intended to strengthen its function as a democratic governing body.

## DECOMMISSION THE BRETTON WOODS INSTITUTIONS

The larger goal is to replace a governing system that serves the needs of global financiers and transnational corporations with one that serves the needs of people and communities. The Bretton Woods institutions, the cornerstones of the former system, thus need to be dismantled.

As this volume has explained, these institutions have persistently advanced the economic interests of powerful corporations and the economic advantages of the rich countries. They embrace an ideology that denigrates the right of a country to pursue policies consistent with the interests of its own people and radically dilutes the right of low-income countries to special and differential treatment. They have raised inequality to a principle of decision making. Finally, they are staffed by economists so indoctrinated in free market ideology that they are unable to accept even the possibility of more equitable and sustainable alternatives. It would be unrealistic to turn to these institutions for leadership in resolving the crisis that they have played such a major role in creating.

A number of Southern countries achieved important social and economic progress between 1950 and 1980, before centralized power was institutionalized in a set of all-encompassing and powerful multilateral organizations. Much of the momentum was lost between 1980 and 2000 as the World Bank and the IMF consolidated their power and began imposing their ideological policy prescriptions. Many of the poorest countries suffered reversals.

It is a tragic truth that much of the work ahead centers on repairing the enormous damage caused by the Bretton Woods institutions. Debts must be canceled, commodity prices stabilized, control established over the goods and money flowing across borders, antitrust measures implemented to break up concentrations of corporate power, corporations with repeat criminal convictions dechartered, national economies rebuilt and redirected with proper regulatory regimes to meet local needs, the environment healed, the power of corporations curbed, financial speculation brought under control, wealth redistributed to create a semblance of equity, and the democratic accountability of governments established.

An ongoing debate in civil society concerns whether the triumvirate of Bretton Woods institutions can be reformed or should be closed. Institutional reform is a viable strategy when the institutions in question are fundamentally fair and aligned with a legitimate purpose but have simply been corrupted, as is the case with many national governments. It is not a viable strategy when a system is in its structure, mandate, purposes, principles, and processes so fundamentally at odds with the human interest as is the case with the Bretton Woods institutions.

To borrow a phrase applied to aging nuclear power plants, it is time to begin a decommissioning process. Developing countries' governments and international civil society ought not allow their energies to be hijacked into reforming these institutions. The best they could hope for would be to administer a facelift to fundamentally flawed institutions.

### The World Trade Organization

The WTO is often promoted as a "rules-based" trading framework that protects the weaker and poorer countries from unilateral actions by the stronger states. But the opposite is true. The WTO, like many other multilateral institutions and agreements, institutionalizes and legitimizes inequality. It serves as an instrument by which stronger countries can impose a discipline of their own choosing on weaker countries at less cost than would be possible in a more fluid, less structured international system.

The GATT had limited power and was more flexible and sympathetic to the special status of developing countries. Furthermore, what power the GATT did have was counterbalanced by a variety of other international actors, including UNCTAD, the International Labor Organization (ILO), evolving trade blocs such as Mercosur in Latin America, SAARC in South Asia, SADCC in Southern Africa, and ASEAN in Southeast Asia, many of which actively sided with Southern interests. This flexibility and active support allowed countries in East and Southeast Asia to craft successful development strategies of their own design in which activist states promoted exports on the one hand and protected domestic industries on the other.

The claim made that the only alternative to a powerful WTO is chaos constitutes pure fear-mongering by those who profit from the current situation. If anything, the international system has become less stable and has suffered more serious trade imbalances and disputes since the WTO was established in 1995. The return to a more fluid, less structured, more pluralistic world with multiple checks and balances will again allow developing nations and poor communities worldwide the opportunity to carve out the space they need to put themselves on a positive path based on their values, their rhythms, and the strategies of their choice.

Any plan for a new round of WTO negotiations or an expansion of the WTO mandate or membership should be firmly rejected. So too should attempts to shift the WTO expansion agenda to regional negotiations, such as the Free Trade Area of the Americas. The focus of the WTO member countries should instead be on negotiating an orderly rollback of many of the rules put in place by and following the GATT Uruguay Round and the orderly phaseout of WTO operations, including its staff and assets. After such a rollback, what remains of the original GATT framework would need to be updated to ensure transparency and accountability. Some aspects of the original International Trade Organization, first proposed after World War II, should be reexamined. This rollback will clear the way for the many other actions required to repair the damage of the Bretton Woods era.

### The IMF and the World Bank

As for the IMF and the World Bank, we recommend the appointment of an international "decommissioning commission" for each institution, to oversee phasing out its operations and disposing of its assets and liabilities. Certainly, half the members of these bodies should come from the civil society organizations that have been instrumental in bringing to light their destructive impact.

This decommissioning commission would mandate an immediate rollback of all structural adjustment programs in the Third World and the former socialist world. It would implement a concurrent reduction in the IMF professional staff from over a thousand to a few hundred, with commensurate cuts in IMF capital expenditures and operational expenses. Most of the group's economists are today employed in micromanaging adjustment programs. Because their functions will be eliminated along with these programs, their services will no longer be needed. The commission would coordinate with the International Insolvency Court (described in the next section) to determine the proper disposition of outstanding debts owed to the IMF. The decommissioning should be completed within a few years. At the end of this time, the remaining staff would be released. All buildings and facilities would be turned over to the United Nations as they become available for use by the new institutions to be created under the U.N. jurisdiction. We recommend that the commission model the termination benefits that will be provided to IMF staff on the benefits typically offered to persons terminated from public employment under IMF structural adjustment programs.

The World Bank decommissioning commission would take similar steps with regard to its staff and assets, with the goal of releasing all World Bank staff and turning over all remaining assets to the United Nations within a few years of its appointment.

International civil society will need to act quickly and forcefully. With their credibility and legitimacy in tatters, the IMF and the World Bank are in severe crisis. We may expect, however, that rather than taking decisive action, the powers that be will attempt to wait for the storm to blow over while talking about reform. With the IMF and the World Bank sidelined and ultimately removed, the way will be open to move ahead with putting in place an international financial system that favors long-term productive investment over short-term speculation, stability over volatility, and local over foreign investment and ownership.

## Strengthening the Countervailing Powers of the U.N. System

As the Bretton Woods institutions are dismantled, the countervailing institutional power required to reform the global trade and financial systems and end global corporate rule can come from strengthened states and a reformed United Nations. We hasten to note that though we believe the United Nations should be strengthened in its mandate and resources, we continue to believe that international institutions should have responsibility and authority for only those functions that cannot be reasonably carried out at national and local levels. Wherever possible, the primary responsibility of international institutions should be to support effective and responsive democratic local governance.

There are strong arguments for upgrading the capacity of the World Health Organization, the International Labor Office, and the United Nations Environment Program to address trade-related health, labor, and environmental issues. Trade-related standards should come under the jurisdiction of the U.N. agencies, with the primary responsibility and expertise on the related standards. Good health is an end. Worker rights, dignified wages, and safe working conditions are ends. A healthy environment is an end. In contrast, international trade and investment are merely means and should be dealt with accordingly. Appropriate programs will need to be worked out for each relevant U.N. agency. This next section of the chapter takes UNCTAD as an example of the kind of strengthened roles these agencies might play in global economic governance under a new regime.

## THE ROLE OF UNCTAD

The United Nations Conference on Trade and Development (UNCTAD) was created in 1964. Over the next decade, it became the principal vehicle used by Third World governments to restructure the global economy to support their national development efforts. Subsequently, as the Bretton Woods institutions gained power, UNCTAD became increasingly marginalized along with the concerns of Southern countries.

If trade is to serve a process of just and sustainable development, with a bias toward the needs of the poor and workers as well as low-income countries, there is a strong argument for making a strengthened UNCTAD the primary United Nations rule-making body for international trade. The failing credibility of the Bretton Woods institutions has created a moment of opportunity for UNCTAD to position itself as a contender. An appropriate first step would be to raise a serious challenge to the premise that the full integration of developing countries into the world economy is the way to prosperity, and to position itself as chief advocate in the international system for a true alternative based on the principles outlined in this volume.

UNCTAD's former influence came primarily from serving as a voice of Southern governments and an advocate for their development interests. Debt relief and a rollback of structural adjustment are two of the most immediate and widely recognized needs of Southern countries. They are also issues high on the civil society agenda. There is the basis here for a natural alliance between Southern governments and civil society groups working on these issues that would strengthen the hands of both. UNCTAD is well positioned to be a broker of this alliance.

It should also be of interest to Southern governments that civil society's call for debt relief and a rollback of structural adjustment is part of a much larger agenda that seeks to dismantle a global system that is arguably little more than a re-creation of the institutions of colonialism with a more friendly face, and to put in its place a system designed to strengthen the role of national governments in facilitating national development based on democratic self-reliance and self-determination in a supportive global framework. This agenda is strongly aligned with the interests of Southern countries. Again, UNCTAD can take the lead in brokering dialogue on such possibilities in the U.N. system.

We urge UNCTAD also to take a lead role in challenging the hegemony of the WTO as the ultimate arbiter of trade and development issues. It should propose an arrangement whereby the relevant expertise of organizations such as UNCTAD, the ILO, the WTO, the United Nations Environment Program (UNEP), and the implementing bodies of multilateral environmental agreements and regional economic blocs is brought to bear on these issues, participating as equals to clarify, define, and implement international economic policies in service to people and planet.

It took five hundred years of colonialism and fifty years of Bretton Woods to put the existing system in place. The need for an alternative is urgent, but realistically it will take several decades to establish it fully and bring global economic relationships into an equitable and sustainable balance. In the meantime, there is an urgent need for new international agreements that begin the process of transition to a new economy. UNCTAD can and should initiate the transition. Here are three transitional international agreements that UNCTAD might initiate to begin to move the world toward a more just, sustainable, and democratic system:

- *An agreement on economic self-determination.* Such an agreement would accord Southern countries "special and differential treatment" in global trade, investment, and finance. It would acknowledge the perils posed for Southern countries from indiscriminate liberalization and guarantee their right to give priority to their domestic development needs in their economic relationships with the North, including their right to establish controls over financial flows across their borders, set the terms of foreign investment, give preference to domestic finance and ownership, place limits on resource extraction, and favor local value-added processing of export commodities. It would also establish a framework for creating an international system of commodity price supports and for securing preferential access to Northern markets to the extent required to generate the foreign exchange to repay international debts and pay for imports from Northern nations.
- *An agreement on trade claims.* UNCTAD could also play a key role in addressing the critical nexus of trade and the environment. Together with the U.N. Environment Program and UNDP, UNCTAD could lead in drafting an agreement specifying broad but binding guidelines and a

pluralistic mechanism involving civil society actors that would resolve the conflicting claims of trade bodies, multilateral environmental agreements, governments, and NGOs.

• A *"New Deal" for agriculture in developing countries and for small farmers in developed countries.* UNCTAD could lead in forging such a program. The emphasis would not be the integration of agriculture into world trade but the integration of trade into a development strategy that puts the emphasis on raising incomes and employment in the agricultural sector, achieving food security through a significant degree of food self-sufficiency, and promoting ecologically sustainable production.

It is wholly appropriate for UNCTAD, as the U.N. voice of the South, to assume a leadership role as we move to a new economy. Southern countries know best the reality and consequences of the present unjust, unsustainable, and undemocratic system and have the most immediate stake in achieving rapid progress toward an alternative.

These proposals would also put Southern countries on the leading edge of bringing the new economy into being. For example, the agreement on economic self-determination would address the particular needs of Southern countries. It would also create a prototype for a new approach to international economic relationships ultimately as appropriate to the North as to the South.

UNCTAD does not have the material resources of the Bretton Woods institutions, but it has something that their economic power cannot buy—legitimacy among Southern countries and their governments.

## Creating New Global Institutions

In addition to reforming and strengthening existing U.N. bodies, a small number of new institutions at the global level need to be created under U.N. authority and oversight. Here are ideas on five such bodies.

### U.N. INTERNATIONAL INSOLVENCY COURT

Debt relief is the appropriate response to the continuing debt crisis of poor countries. People cannot be both free and in debt. We therefore endorse recommendations to create an International Insolvency Court (IIC) that have already come from UNCTAD, the Jubilee 2000 Coalition, and the Canadian government. The IIC would comprise a conciliation panel and an arbitration panel. The former would facilitate negotiated settlements between debtors and creditors. Where parties failed to reach a settlement, the arbitration panel would make a legally binding final ruling. Debtor countries might be supported in the preparation and presentation of their cases by UNCTAD and by the International Finance Organization, proposed in the next section. We envisage the following essential elements of the IIC:

- It must be an independent body insulated from the influence of the IMF and the World Bank—so long as they exist—and have balanced representation from debtor and creditor nations.
- Privately incurred debts, unless originally guaranteed by a government in an open democratic process consistent with established law, should remain private. Where repayment of a private debt is in dispute, it should be a matter between the private contracting parties to be settled in the appropriate civil courts.
- Its work must be fully transparent and open to public observation and review.
- A debtor government that determines that its debt obligations have reached a critical level and cannot be repaid without impairing the well-being of its citizens would voluntarily initiate the procedure by presenting its case to the court.
- After a preliminary assessment, the debtor country would be granted a stay on its repayments for a period sufficient to complete the court's review and decision process. In the meantime, it would also agree to incur no new debt.
- An assessment process would determine how much a country owes and is able to pay over time without compromising its ability to perform essential governmental functions, including the delivery of necessary social services. The court would also review the debt portfolio to identify odious debts subject to legal repudiation, including debts to the World Bank and the IMF that were not legitimately contracted or were used for purposes that yielded no public benefit. The latter would include

debts incurred for bank-designed projects that failed as a result of faulty design and negligent bank oversight.

- On the basis of the assessment, a debt-relief plan would be negotiated to cover any amounts a country owes after repudiation of odious debts, with adequate allowance for necessary government functions and the delivery of essential services. The plan would provide for necessary debt rescheduling, reduction, and cancellation—taking into account the implicit debt owed to debtor countries in the South by creditor countries in the North for wealth extracted without proper compensation.

- Debt-relief plans would seek to leave a country with its international accounts balanced and free of international debt. Debt-relief agreements should include strict limits on incurring new international debts and provide guidelines for financial regulation and trade management intended to keep current accounts in balance.

The IIC can become operational as the World Bank and the regional development banks are decommissioned, with any remaining assets of the decommissioned institutions applied to debt relief.

## U.N. INTERNATIONAL FINANCE ORGANIZATION

The proposed International Finance Organization (IFO) would work with U.N. member countries to achieve and maintain balance and stability in international financial relationships, free national and global finance from the distortions of international debt and debt-based money, promote productive domestic investment and domestic ownership of productive resources, and take necessary actions at the international level to support nations and localities in creating equitable, productive, sustainable livelihoods for all. The IFO would replace the IMF but with full accountability to the United Nations. Lacking either lending capacity or enforcement powers, its functions would be to maintain a central database on international accounts, flag problem situations, and facilitate negotiations among countries to correct imbalances. It would also provide advisory services on request. Its charter would mandate that it favor human, community, and environmental interests over the interests of global corporations and financiers in all its activities. More specifically, IFO functions would include the following:

- Monitor and publish regular statistical compilations on national trade and current account balances and facilitate negotiations toward agreement on corrective action where a country's import and export accounts are in consequential and persistent imbalance.
- Maintain a central information facility on practices and experiences of different governments relating to capital controls, foreign borrowing, and the management of trade balances. In cooperation with UNDP, provide advisory services, on request, to assist national governments in establishing appropriate and adequate capital controls that strengthen domestic employment, investment, ownership, and technical capability; discourage financial speculation; and keep international accounts balanced.
- Facilitate the negotiation and implementation of international agreements by which national governments will take coordinated action to prevent the use of offshore banks and tax havens for money laundering and tax evasion.
- Carry out policy studies relating to measures intended to dampen speculative financial movements, facilitate the negotiation of appropriate agreements, and provide support as requested for implementing actions.
- Carry out policy studies on the feasibility of shifting money creation from banks to governments, develop implementing proposals, and provide advisory support to interested governments.

The International Financial Organization and the regional monetary funds recommended in the following paragraph may be phased in as the IMF is decommissioned. Any remaining IMF assets could be applied to debt relief and to capitalizing the regional funds.

### REGIONAL MONETARY FUNDS

Recognizing the legitimate need for access to short-term emergency foreign exchange loans, while also recognizing that finance should be local to the extent possible, we endorse the creation of regional monetary funds accountable to the member countries of their region. These regional funds would provide quick-response, short-term emergency loans in the event of an unanticipated foreign exchange shortfall. Accountable to their region's governments, these funds would reflect regional sensibilities and interests. Although all countries would be welcome to send representatives to their meetings as observers, no country should be allowed to be a voting member of more than one regional fund.

## U.N. TRADE DISPUTES COURT

Steps toward the localization of production and consumption recommended in this volume would lead to a reduction in the movement of goods between countries. Even so, the world will continue to need a system of rules to maintain the stability and fairness of the international trading system, because so long as there is trade among nations there will be disputes and the potential for abuse and coercion of the weak by the strong. The world has no need, however, for a World Trade Organization that regulates democratic governments to prevent them from setting and enforcing rules and standards to protect the public interest.

Trade is a means, not an end; the expansion of trade per se is not a goal; and responsibility for negotiating and enforcing trade rules should rest with agencies that understand this distinction. Thus, we are inclined to the view that the jurisdiction for trade issues should be distributed among the U.N. agencies concerned with such matters as development, health, food, labor, and the environment. The responsibility should rest with the same agencies responsible for the outcomes that trade should support.

As suggested earlier, UNCTAD might have a lead in the rule-setting process. The U.N. International Finance Organization would track current account balances and raise a warning when international intervention is required.

There remains the need for a body to mediate and arbitrate trade disputes. To meet this need, we propose the creation of a U.N. Trade Disputes Court. It would have a structure similar to that of the U.N. International Insolvency Court, with a conciliation panel to facilitate negotiated settlements between trading partners and an arbitration panel to make legally binding rulings based on the provisions of relevant international agreements—including treaties and declarations on human rights, labor, health and safety, and the environment—where parties fail to reach a voluntary settlement.

What might require the intervention of a trade disputes court? Say, for example, a country's trade accounts are seriously and persistently out of balance. Here is an important case in point. The United States has a massive and persistent import surplus, which suggests it is living beyond its means, supporting wasteful and environmentally destructive lifestyles by expropriating the labor and resources of others with far greater need. China, in contrast, has a large and persistent export surplus based on a large supply of exploited labor. The losers in this instance include other low-wage countries that are unable to compete in world markets against China's low wages and marginal working conditions. The debt of the United States to the rest of the system is cumulative so long as the imbalance exists. To bring itself back into balance with the rest of the system, the United States must export more or import less. China must import more or export less. Ideally, the United States would embrace the challenge of learning to live within its means. China should direct more of its productive capacity to meeting the needs of its own people. In both cases, there will be a long and difficult process of adjustment with impacts on the trade relations of both China and the United States with many countries. These are not simple matters and appropriately involve complex dialogue and negotiations with all consequential trading partners.

Another example would be a country that believes a trading partner has taken a precipitous trade action for purely political reasons to extort some concession, such as access to oil or a particular vote in the United Nations. In general, a country should have the right to reorient its social, environmental, and economic priorities from time to time and to adjust its trade relationships as appropriate. But this should be done in an orderly, phased manner, undertaken in agreement with trading partners and giving all parties time to adjust to the change. Member countries could turn to the U.N. Trade Disputes Court if bilateral negotiations to resolve the situation fail.

### U.N. ENVIRONMENT ORGANIZATION

Citizens' networks like Friends of the Earth International are calling on the UNEP's Global Ministerial Environment Forum (GMEF) to strengthen international environmental governance. Beginning with the large number of legally binding agreements already created, strengthened global governance should first be targeted at improved compliance with existing multilateral environmental agreements (MEAs), ensuring that transnational corporations and the WTO comply with MEAs. The GMEF should provide a clear mandate to ensure sufficient and reliable financial support to UNEP and reform it into a U.N. Environment Organization (UNEO) so that it is able to fulfill its role as the bedrock of international environmental governance.

In particular, a UNEO should do the following:

- Provide effective support, including financial, technical, and political support, to implement existing international agreements in the field of environmental sustainability.
- Ensure effective compliance and dispute settlement with legally binding agreements in the field of sustainable development, including compliance by transnational corporations.
- Reaffirm that MEAs, and not the WTO, have primary competence to determine environmental objectives and the necessity of MEA-related trade measures.
- Promote and participate in a joint U.N. review of the impact on the environment of the implementation of existing trade agreements.
- Promote and actively participate in the establishment of a World Commission on Trade and Agriculture, which should review the impact of existing trade agreements on environmentally sustainable agriculture and explore the modalities of an international legally binding instrument in the field of environmentally sustainable agriculture, food security, and sovereignty.

## U.N. ORGANIZATION FOR CORPORATE ACCOUNTABILITY

Second only to financial speculation, the greatest economic threat to the well-being of people and planet is the growth and abuse of unchecked corporate power. There are virtually no mechanisms in place at the international level for dealing with this threat, and the Bretton Woods institutions regularly seek to block corrective actions at national levels. Giant corporations move freely around the world, buying off politicians and playing states, communities, and people against one another in competition for the jobs, finance, and access to technology that corporations control. Eliminating the Bretton Woods institutions, rescinding structural adjustment programs, and canceling provisions in international trade agreements that place the interests of global corporations and financiers ahead of human interests would be important steps toward restoring the right and responsibility of governments to hold corporations accountable to public interests.

The primary function of the proposed U.N. Organization for Corporate Accountability would be to support national initiatives on corporate accountability through the provision of information and advisory services, facilitating negotiation of relevant bilateral and multilateral agreements and coordinated bilateral and multilateral implementing actions. Although enforcement authority would lie entirely at the national and local levels, the OCA would provide both governments and the general public with comprehensive and authoritative information on corporate practices as a basis for legal action and for investor and consumer action. More specifically, the OCA would do the following:

- Compile and publicize periodic reports on corporate concentration in major sectors and produce special studies on monopolistic practices, including strategic alliances and cartels contrary to sound market principles. Focus international attention on the implications of corporate concentration in key sectors such as banking, media, and agribusiness to encourage appropriate antitrust actions by national governments.
- Monitor pricing practices in international trade to document and publicize unfair competitive practices, such as export subsidies or pricing goods below cost to unfairly drive competitors from the market.
- Maintain comprehensive and readily accessible public records of regulatory infractions and civil and criminal prosecutions and convictions for all corporations with consequential transnational operations. Publish an international watch list of corporations that exhibit persistent patterns of illegal activity, which might serve as a trigger for consumer boycotts or legal actions at the national level to decharter or decertify.
- Maintain comprehensive and readily accessible public records for the one thousand largest global corporations, listing by corporation all identified direct and indirect subsidies, including special tax concessions and the public costs of substandard wages and working conditions, the sale of harmful products, the discharge of harmful wastes, and other externalized costs.
- Coordinate the negotiation and implementation of international agree-

ments ensuring the right of those harmed by the actions of a reckless corporate subsidiary in one country to sue and recover damages from the parent corporations, wherever they may be located.

- Coordinate the negotiation of a recommended uniform code of standards for corporations operating in more than one country. This code would serve as a recommended model for use by governments in framing national and local laws regulating the activities of global corporations operating within their jurisdiction. Such standards should ensure a consistent bias in favor of smaller, locally owned enterprises. For example, corporations with operations in more than one country should be expected to adhere to the highest of international, local, or home country standards on human rights, labor, environment, health, and safety wherever they operate; decline any special concessions, subsidies, or tax breaks not generally available on equal or more attractive terms to local businesses; obey all national and international laws; provide no payments or gifts to public officials or politicians and refrain from any attempt to influence elections and public policies; deal in good faith with unions; provide at least a living wage to all employees; provide full and accurate labeling of products; and publicly disclose all toxic releases. Global corporations commonly claim that they adhere to the highest international standards wherever they operate. Those corporations that in fact live by this principle have no reason to object to the public being informed about their actual records. Although the OCA would have no actual enforcement powers, it would monitor and publicize compliance or noncompliance with these standards as guides to governmental and public action.
- Assist U.N. member countries in establishing and enforcing antitrust legislation and other legislation related to setting and enforcing standards for corporate accountability.
- Convene an international panel to recommend national legislation to limit the political influence of global corporations on government policymaking, including limits or prohibitions on corporate financial contributions to political parties and candidates, and corporate spending on advertising and public relations campaigns related to legislation and public issues.

CHAPTER ELEVEN

# Global to Local

*What You Can Do*

AS THE TWENTY-ONE AUTHORS OF THIS BOOK have met with hundreds of thousands of other individuals over the past decade in protests, social experiments, local house meetings, national hearings, global teach-ins, and the World Social Forums, we have experienced the transformation of anger about economic globalization into a politics of hope for the future. Hope lies in many promising events, from the declining legitimacy of the key institutions of corporate globalization to the flowering of citizen groups and peoples' movements to the emergence of new governments that reject the old models. Most fundamentally, hope lies in the remarkable spectrum of alternatives work that spans piecemeal reform to visionary proposals and local economic experiments to national transformations in countries like Brazil.

After decades of Margaret Thatcher and other globalization cheerleaders telling us there were no alternatives, that fiction has been exposed. There are alternatives—tens of thousands of them. The failing legitimacy of the institutions of global corporate rule combined with the political force of an enlivened civil society have created an unprecedented moment of opportunity to rethink and transform the institutions of economic life, advance the democratic project, and realize the ageless human dream of liberty, justice, and prosperity for all.

Thus far, we have attempted to empower readers by offering new ways to think about alternatives to economic globalization, by laying out the principles that citizen groups have offered as a basis for alternatives, and by describing what others are doing to create a better world. Although most positive change takes place through collective action, there is also a great deal that you, our readers, can do as individuals.

Transforming the global economic system is an enormous task that will require many hands and considerable time. But you, as individuals, can start tomorrow to take actions that will help create a more equitable and sustainable world.

Of course, the corporate globalists would like you to think otherwise. It is in their interest to have you believe that your identity in the economy is limited to that of a passive consumer. They bombard you with slick images and slogans, hoping to persuade you that bigger vehicles mean more freedom, the latest deodorant will lead to dates with supermodels, and everyday low prices are the ultimate human conquest.

For these profiteers of a consumer culture, it is good news that the most popular gathering spaces in many communities are now shopping malls while funding is shrinking for public parks, libraries, and other spaces where individuals can come together to meet, read, play, and act collectively.

We all need to buy things. But as human beings, in all our complexity, we need much more than material goods to lead fulfilling lives. And it is important to remind ourselves that we can take action on many levels to shape a better world. We can be active rather than passive consumers, and many of us can make better use of the powers we have as workers, investors, students, and members of faith-based and other organizations. Moreover, as communities and nations have become more interconnected, we often have opportunities to act not only as local and national citizens but also as citizens of the globe. And as citizens, we need to exercise rights that go far beyond the right to buy more stuff.

In this concluding chapter we offer just a few ideas on how you can act in each of your multifaceted capacities. In addition, we encourage you to use the resources at the end of this book to find contact information on organizations working on globalization issues; they will be able to give you more details on how to get involved.

## Steps You Can Take as a Consumer

Global firms can only make their billions of dollars selling deadly cigarettes, gas-guzzling Hummers, hormone-filled beef, butter from the other side of the planet, underwear made in sweatshops, and genetically engineered corn if people buy them. There are several ways that individual consumers can strive to ensure that their spending reflects their values.

## BE AN INFORMED CONSUMER

A central tenet of the market economy is that consumers have full information. A market can only operate efficiently if consumers know every detail about how a good is produced, who produced it, how it is disposed of, and under what conditions and at what environmental or human cost these actions take place. As production becomes more globalized and under corporate control, this information is increasingly difficult to come by. However, the more we become informed consumers—either by forcing corporations to reveal this information, or finding it out ourselves—the more successful we will be in choosing products that benefit, rather than harm, our world. There are dozens of organizations (examples are provided in the resources section) around the world that provide lists of "green" or environmentally sound products, "blue" products produced with sound workers rights, and other social indicators to help consumers make informed decisions. There are also hundreds of examples of corporate campaigns in which consumers and community activists join together to force businesses to either meet their demands on the environment, worker rights and safety, consumer health and the rights of communities, or close up shop.

## BUY LOCAL

In many parts of the world, farm systems are being transformed as consumers increasingly head for local farmers' markets and demand organically produced fruit and vegetables. Organic food sales in the United States have been growing at the spectacular rate of 10 percent a year. A simple act such as buying a locally grown organic tomato has ripple effects throughout the global food assembly line by reducing food miles and the environmental havoc wreaked by too many refrigerated containers on too many oceangoing vessels. In general, steering money toward local businesses and services has a positive multiplier effect on local communities, whereas spending money in large chains typically funnels it back to headquarters—and often into the pockets of overpaid CEOs.

## JOIN A COMMUNITY-SUPPORTED AGRICULTURE (CSA) PROGRAM

You may wish to join a CSA program and also support local farmers' markets and urban gardens. (For more information, see "Agriculture and Food Systems" in chapter 8.) Most cities offer CSAs that allow urban consumers to make direct relationships with organic farmers, thus bypassing the conventional retail and marketing systems. By joining for a reasonable fixed amount per month, city dwellers receive boxes of fresh produce delivered personally from the farms. This supports local organic farms, as well as providing extremely fresh produce. Similarly, local farmers' markets offer direct contact with farmers bringing fresh produce. And a growing urban garden movement is enabling urban dwellers to use vacant land to grow their own produce.

## SUPPORT FAIR TRADE

Some things we consume can't be produced just down the road, such as coffee and cocoa for the billions who live in colder climes. For these and other products, a vibrant fair trade or alternative trading market has emerged around the world. (See again chapter 8.) Whereas most corporations treat the producer as a faceless factor of production whose costs are to be minimized, fair trade organizations strive for the opposite—living wages and safe and dignified working conditions for developing-country artisans and farmers.

One reason why fair trade organizations can afford to pay well is that they reduce the number of middlemen and minimize overhead costs. They often work with producer cooperatives that ensure safe and dignified working conditions and allow producers a say in how their products are created and sold. Cooperatives are also encouraged to provide benefits such as health care, child care, and access to loans and to reinvest profits into their communities—for example, to build clinics or other community projects. Some fair trade organizations work to shift processing and packaging activities to the developing world so that as much value-added work as possible remains in the producer country.

Fair trade commodities, including coffee, chocolate, handicrafts, tea, bananas, honey, and other products, are certified by nonprofit organizations in seventeen different countries, all of which are affiliated with Fairtrade Labeling Organizations International. The fair trade coffee system alone benefits over 350,000 farmers organized into over three hundred cooperatives in twenty-two countries. More than 40,000 cocoa farmers are organized into eight cooperatives in eight different countries. The business generated by fair trade organizations in Europe and the United States accounts for about $400 million per year. Although this is still only about one-tenth of one percent of all global trade, the market is growing rapidly. The fair trade industry in North America and the Pacific Rim grew an impressive 37 percent in 2003, according to the Fair Trade Federation and the International Federation for Alternative Trade. Total fair trade sales in the United States, Canada, and the Pacific Rim now surpass $250 million a year.

Some argue that fair trade encourages Southern farmers and entrepreneurs to become dependent on fickle global markets over which they have no control. In so doing, it could undermine the local economies that stand at the center of the alternatives posed in this book. However, supporting fair trade is one way to combat the dire problem of poverty, at least in the medium term, while we work to promote policies that will help strengthen domestic demand in poor nations in the long term.

In addition to fair trade, consumers can favor ecofriendly products and services. More and more products now carry ecolabels, which certify some degree of ecological consciousness in the production of the goods. Some services, like ecotourism, likewise may be given such ecolabels. Consumers can purchase fruits, vegetables, meat, and fish that are produced in ecofriendly ways and avoid companies with unfair labor standards and environmentally damaging policies.

## Steps You Can Take as a Worker

Most people have an influence on the economy through their roles as workers and could do more to utilize this power to reinforce the alternatives spelled out in this book. Over the past hundred-plus years, trade unions have represented the most powerful way for workers to gain a voice and win basic rights in the workplace. Joining a union, organizing a union, supporting those who do, and helping other kinds of worker organizations all can help you as a worker and others in the workplace.

## EXERCISE YOUR PENSION POWER

Hundreds of millions of workers now belong to unions and similar institutions that fight for basic rights and better working conditions. Many of these unions have won pension benefits for their members, and as pensions have grown, so too has the collective economic clout of workers. In the United States, for example, workers' savings account for $6 trillion and make up the largest pool of investment capital in the country. Union federations like the AFL-CIO in the United States are working on strategies to harness the power of these pensions to support firms that respect basic worker rights. Because the pension system is so varied and complex (the type of pension, the structure of the pension system, the decision structure within unions), there is currently less room for individual workers to influence overall decisions about their pensions. Still, in many workplaces, individuals do have choices over what sort of funds their retirement accounts should invest in, opening the door to socially and environmentally responsible choices.

## FORM AND SUPPORT WORKER-OWNED CO-OPS

As an alternative to hierarchical business structures, people around the world have formed worker-owned cooperatives, in which, as the name implies, the workers own and operate the enterprise themselves. Thus, workers are not working for other people who take their earnings and give them a small portion back. Decisions are generally made democratically, on a one-person, one-vote basis. The labor involved in running the enterprise, and the wages and other benefits that result, are shared. For example, earnings are generally divided equally, or according to hours worked, skill level, or some other method determined by the group. Decisions about how work is to be done, by whom, on what schedule, and under what conditions are also decided democratically by the group rather than by managers selected by distant owners.

Workers can also push at their workplace to adopt policies that reflect social and environmental values. For example, you can encourage your workplace to do the following:

- Support public transportation or carpooling through financial incentives and take advantage of any tax breaks offered by the local government for firms that offer them.
- Stock the employee kitchen with fair trade coffee, favor unionized vendors, and buy recycled, reusable, and other ecofriendly office supplies.
- Cut down on waste by upgrading computers instead of junking them and recycling cell phones, pagers, printer cartridges, office paper, newspapers, and cans and bottles.
- Take full responsibility for its products from the point of production to the point of disposal, acting in full transparency to ensure that consumers, workers, and community members have free and easy access to all information about the product as it affects their lives.
- Invest a set proportion of its profits in the communities in which it operates as well as share new safety and greener technologies with those communities.
- Apply the same standards for its operations abroad as domestically.

## Steps You Can Take as a Depositor and Investor

Whether you have $50 in a savings account or $500,000 in the stock market, your financial decisions can make a difference.

Decades ago, most financial institutions were local, and deposited savings were lent back out to the local community. Today, most local banks are part of giant national banks that relend the money on international markets where it contributes to the highly volatile global casino economy. It doesn't have to be that way. You can do the following:

- Open an account with a socially responsible bank or a credit union. In the United States, you can determine a bank's community involvement by asking any branch for a copy of their bank's Community Reinvestment Act Performance Evaluation. This evaluation rates how well the bank meets the needs of low- and middle-income people locally.
- Investigate how your bank invests in local community development. For example, some banks invest their deposits in development projects such

as lending programs for affordable housing, conservation, education, and development of inner cities. Other financial institutions work toward strengthening Native American communities.

- Check into whether you qualify for a credit union. These not-for-profit institutions often offer better customer service than the megabanks, as well as low interest rates on loans and lower fees.
- Donate to important causes as you use your credit card. Many organizations now offer credit cards that allow a percentage of your purchase dollars to be invested into the organization itself. This allows you to contribute to organizations while promoting your values.

In another vein, you can support the local currency movement in your community. Alternative money schemes, located in many cities, represent a partial alternative to engaging in the dominant economy. Communities of people agree to use a local scrip rather than dollars for some of their needs and to exchange services at agreed rates. The effect is to recycle funds and services inside a community, keeping resources local.

Many people have extra income that they choose to invest. In the United States, a growing variety of mutual funds allow individuals to pool small savings amounts with others in a fund that then collectively invests the totals. For over a decade, the numbers of funds that specialize in socially or environmentally responsible corporations has been growing. These funds use a variety of screens, some focusing on environmental and labor rights criteria, others steering clear of alcohol, tobacco, or weapons-related companies.

## Steps You Can Take as a Citizen

Most people identify themselves as citizens of a country; some are citizens of two countries. Yet, in an increasingly interdependent world, we are all part of several worlds simultaneously. We are local citizens, and there is a great deal we can do to strengthen our local communities. As national citizens too we can be part of an alternative discourse. And we are all global citizens, and there is much we can do to oppose economic globalization while inhibiting its negative effects. Here are a few ideas as starting points.

## AS A LOCAL CITIZEN

- Seize control of your local operating systems—transport, energy, waste—where global policies most directly play out. Insist that your local government support initiatives in each of these areas that reduce impacts on environment and encourage local solutions that avoid global corporate involvement.
- Create your own minialternatives summit in your community. Bring together civil society organizations, religious groups, activists, community members, students, scholars, elected officials, and so on, to present, discuss, and implement alternatives to economic globalization in your community.
- Learn about the myriad community organizing efforts taking place where you live. Participate in these or join with others in your community to create your own movement to see real alternatives implemented at home. If you already participate in several community groups, such as your place of worship, your school, or your food co-op, try to bring these communities together to work on issues of shared concern. You can also participate in online organizing communities. The Internet provides many avenues for activists to learn new ways of organizing and to bring attention to alternatives to globalization.
- Attend your city council meetings and learn about and participate in issues affecting the community. Get involved in political campaigns in support of progressive candidates, and consider running for office yourself. Participate actively in local public hearings.
- Organize ecoinitiatives in your neighborhood to promote urban agriculture and community development, such as cooperatives.
- Work against urban sprawl by voicing your concerns at county and state meetings and organizing community leaders.
- Organize cleanups in your neighborhood and city through community activism.
- Find out if your local community offers tax credits to revitalize or preserve your property. Some offer tax credits for home and business owners. These incentives not only help create sustainable, revitalized local communities but also create new jobs and can promote historic tourism.

- Support voter education and registration efforts in your community. Low levels of political participation and voter turnout, especially among low-income and younger people, only increase the excessive influence of global corporations on our political system.
- Become a media activist. Support alternative media that reflect noncommercial values, but also make yourself heard by the major media: call talk shows and raise alternative viewpoints; write to editors, producers, and especially advertisers when their content is objectionable. Such letters and e-mails *are* read and change can result. Get your colleagues and neighbors to join you in protests in such matters.

### AS A NATIONAL CITIZEN

As citizens of countries whose governments make daily choices about how to interact with the global economy, there is a great deal we all can do to influence the paths our nations take. Countries vary widely on the democratic space that exists. In some countries, citizens have taken the bold step of electing governments that reject the path of corporate globalization in favor of alternatives; in the past half-decade, majorities have brought in new governments espousing critical views in Brazil, Argentina, Bolivia, Ecuador, and Venezuela. In the United States and other G-8 countries it is crucial that movements grow and pressure the most powerful countries to change policy. Deep political change requires more than simply voting more progressive politicians into office. It requires an active and mobilized citizenry engaged in every aspect of public life. Become active in a political party. Organize local issues forums. Get to know your political representatives and let them know your opinions. Run for office.

In developing countries where governments remain closely aligned with corporate globalization, such as the Philippines, strong national campaigns have nonetheless put effective pressure on governments to reject market-opening policies of the World Bank, the IMF, and the World Trade Organization. Get active in campaigns on these and related issues in your own country.

The energy of citizen engagement is growing nearly everywhere around a vast array of issues that in the end come down to justice, environmental sustainability, and democracy. All are in the end integrally related to one another and to the institutions and culture of corporate globalization. The growing power of global civil society rests in part on its progress in building alliances across conventional divisions of nationality, issue, religion, race, and gender. Be part of the alliance-building process. Reach out in solidarity.

An enormously helpful resource outlining ideas on what you can do is the new book *MoveOn's 50 Ways to Love Your Country: How to Find Your Political Voice and Become a Catalyst for Change,* a how-to book that details specific actions people can take to "turn inspiration into action." The titles of the chapters read like a catalogue of political activities, including these:

- Create an Effective Online Petition
- Mobilize Underrepresented Voters
- Register Voters in Unlikely Places
- Organize an Issue-Specific Voter Registration Drive
- Get Your Office to Vote
- Participate in a Phone Bank
- Respond to Biased Reporting
- Write Letters to Congress That Work
- Talk to the Officials You Didn't Elect
- Respond Locally to National Issues
- Host a Political Salon
- Express Your Political Views through Art

## AS A GLOBAL CITIZEN

Perhaps the most striking shift in the consciousness of many people over the past two decades has been the rise in global awareness and the avenues open for people to act globally. You can participate on the global stage in many ways:

- Participate in international exchanges. Travel globally with organizations to learn about how economic and social issues are affecting a region. Global Exchange and Witness for Peace are two of a growing number of international organizations working to increase public awareness of international problems by organizing international travel programs that bring people into direct contact with the issues and people they rarely hear about in the news. Participants learn firsthand of the consequences of U.S. policies in places like Venezuela, Mexico, El Salvador, Argentina, Palestine, and Iraq. If you are thinking about taking an international tour on your next vacation, consider signing up for one of these.

• Learn about how the World Bank, IMF, WTO, and other global institutions function and how their policies affect your country and other areas of the world. Organize public forums in your community to educate people about the consequences of their policies. Make clear to the people who manage your pension fund that you don't want your money invested in World Bank bonds.

• Follow the outcomes of regional alternative summits to see how they connect with the people and groups working to implement alternative ideas. Get involved with an international gathering like the World Social Forum or one of the growing number of regional and national social forums.

• Join the growing movement of people around the world who converge on every gathering of the leaders of corporate globalization to protest the current model and demand alternatives while simultaneously embodying those alternatives through community empowerment, democratic decision making, and equality in organizing. Then, when you return home, continue the connections made with other people, movements, and organizations locally and around the world to continue to work together to implement alternatives.

• Join organizations working for social justice, environmental sustainability, human rights, and local control. You will find an extensive list in the resources section of this book. If you don't find an organization doing what you think needs to be done, start your own organization or organize your community and start creating the change you want to see right now.

What we write here should lay to rest the claim by corporate globalists that the goal of those of us who resist is the elimination of all institutions of global governance. This has always been a serious misrepresentation. The goal of civil society is to replace the autocratic institutions of corporate rule with democratic institutions, as earlier generations replaced the institutions of monarchy with those of political democracy.

Over the past decade, to make this point, Public Citizen's Lori Wallach has developed her upper-body strength by lugging around copies of the thousands of pages that constitute the agreements establishing the World Trade Organization and NAFTA. By crashing them down on podiums around the world, she reminds audiences that these institutions are the creations of men and a few women whose vision of governance begins and ends with the short-term needs of companies like Enron, ExxonMobil, and Monsanto. As the creations of humans, these institutions can be replaced.

The time has come to create democratic institutions of global governance that will end corporate rule, secure the human rights and democratic sovereignty of people everywhere, and restore control of national economies and resources to their own governments. (See also chapter 10.) All of this can be achieved through a framework of international agreements that support economic justice, food security, full employment, environmental sustainability, and financial stability. Consistent with the ten principles for sustainable societies that we outlined in this volume, such a system would support national and local jurisdictions in controlling and using their own resources to meet their own needs in ways that are appropriate to their own circumstances and cultures. Rule making, standard setting, and enforcement functions would be predominantly local and national. Global-level rule making and intervention would be reserved primarily for matters of compelling international interest, such as maintaining stable, balanced economic relationships among nations or stopping climate change. Trade and investment agreements would embody a strong bias for the poor in all countries and would seek to secure weak nations against predatory actions by strong nations and global corporations.

Now is the time to join the growing political struggle that will embrace new pathways such as those we describe here. The International Forum on Globalization will continue to work with hundreds of other civil society organizations on every continent to discuss, refine, and introduce into public policy many of these and other ideas. We hope you will join in this crucial process.

# Resources

*Groups Working Toward Alternatives to Economic Globalization*

50 YEARS IS ENOUGH
*United States*
http://www.50years.org
Coalition of citizens groups working to reform the World Bank (WB) and International Monetary Fund (IMF). It calls for debt cancellation, ending WB and IMF structural adjustment policies, and transparency and accountability within international financial institutions.

ACTION, RESEARCH & EDUCATION NETWORK OF AOTEAROA (ARENA)
*New Zealand*
http://www.arena.org.nz
An Aotearoa/New Zealand network of individuals and organizations committed to resisting corporate globalization in all its forms. Promotes an alternative development model based on self-determination, social justice, genuine people-centered development, and environmental sustainability.

ACTION FOR SOLIDARITY, EQUALITY, ENVIRONMENT, AND DEVELOPMENT (A SEED)
*The Netherlands*
http://www.aseed.net
A network that initiates actions and campaigns on environmental and social justice issues, promoting small, local organic farms instead of agribusiness, biotechnology, and supermarkets selling genetically modified food; helps coordinate the World Bank boycott in Europe.

ALLIANCE FOR RESPONSIBLE TRADE
*United States*
http://www.art-us.org
A U.S. network of labor, family-farm, religious, women's, environmental, development, and research organiza-

tions that promotes equitable and
sustainable trade and development.

ALTERNATIVE INFORMATION AND
DEVELOPMENT CENTRE
*South Africa*
http://www.aidc.org.za
Works together with popular organizations and social movements in South
and southern Africa for economic
justice and social transformation.

AMAZON ALLIANCE
*United States*
http://www.amazonalliance.org
Works to defend the rights, territories,
and environment of indigenous and
traditional peoples of the Amazon
Basin.

AMAZON WATCH
*United States*
http://www.amazonwatch.org
Works with indigenous and environmental organizations in South
America to defend the environment
and advance indigenous peoples'
rights in the face of large-scale
industrial development, including
oil and gas pipelines, power lines,
roads, and other megaprojects.

AMERICAN FARMLAND TRUST
*United States*
http://www.farmland.org
A nationwide organization dedicated
to protecting agricultural resources
by working to stop the loss of
productive farmland and promote
farming practices that lead to a
healthy environment.

ANTI-PRIVATISATION FORUM
*South Africa*
http://www.apf.org.za
Unites struggles against privatization
in the workplace and community.
Links workers' struggles for a living
wage and jobs with community struggles for housing, water, electricity, and
fair rates and taxes.

APPALACHIAN SUSTAINABLE
DEVELOPMENT
*United States*
http://appsusdev.org
Works to develop healthy, diverse, and
ecologically sound economic opportunities through education and training;
also develops cooperative networks
and marketing systems that focus on
sustainable forestry and wood products
and sustainable agriculture.

ASSOCIATION FOR THE TAXATION OF
FINANCIAL TRANSACTIONS FOR THE
AID OF CITIZENS (ATTAC)
*France*
http://www.attac.org
An international movement for
democratic control of financial
markets and their institutions;
major advocate of the Tobin tax
on financial transactions.

AUSTRALIAN FAIR TRADE AND
INVESTMENT NETWORK
*Australia*
http://www.aftinet.org.au
A national network of fifty-nine
community and union organizations,
including environmental groups,
unions, church groups, low-income

groups, and human rights groups conducting community education and debates to develop an alternative fair trade framework.

### BANK INFORMATION CENTER
*United States*
http://www.bicusa.org
A research, publishing, and activist organization that empowers citizens in developing countries to influence multilateral development bank-financed operations and policies in a manner that fosters social justice and ecological sustainability.

### CAMPAIGN FOR LABOR RIGHTS
*United States*
http://www.campaignforlaborrights.org
Mobilizes grassroots support throughout the United States to promote economic and social justice by campaigning to end labor rights violations around the world.

### CANADIAN CENTRE FOR POLICY ALTERNATIVES
*Canada*
http://www.policyalternatives.ca
Offers an alternative to the message that people have no choice about the policies that affect their lives. Undertakes and promotes research on issues of social and economic justice.

### CENTER FOR ALTERNATIVE DEVELOPMENT INITIATIVES
*Philippines*
http://www.cadi.ph
Dedicated to the study, encouragement, and implementation of sustainable development in the Philippines and the world.

### CENTER FOR A NEW AMERICAN DREAM
*United States*
http://www.newdream.org
Advocates "responsible consumption" to protect the environment, enhance quality of life, and promote social justice.

### CENTER FOR ECOLITERACY
*United States*
http://www.ecoliteracy.org/
Dedicated to fostering educational systems that offer a profound understanding of the natural world, grounded in direct experience, that leads to sustainable patterns of living.

### CENTER FOR ECONOMIC AND POLICY RESEARCH
*United States*
http://www.cepr.net
Provides analysis of globalization issues, educates the public, and promotes democratic debate on economic and social issues affecting peoples' lives, in particular globalization, the World Trade Organization, and intellectual property rights.

### CENTER FOR ECONOMIC JUSTICE
*United States*
http://www.econjustice.net
Aids in strengthening international grassroots movements to counter corporate-driven globalization and promote just alternatives.

CENTER FOR FOOD SAFETY
*United States*
http://www.centerforfoodsafety.org
Works to protect human health and
the environment by curbing the proliferation of harmful food production
technologies and promoting organic
and other forms of sustainable
agriculture.

CENTER OF CONCERN
*United States*
http://www.coc.org
Catholic research and educational
organization promoting just and
sustainable international finance
and trade systems.

CHEFS COLLABORATIVE
*United States*
http://www.chefscollaborative.org
A network of chefs, restaurateurs,
and other culinary professionals
who promote sustainable cuisine
by teaching children, supporting
local farmers, educating each other,
and inspiring their customers to
choose healthy foods. One of the
group's main principles is that
good, safe, wholesome food is
a basic human right.

CHILEAN ALLIANCE FOR JUST
AND RESPONSIBLE TRADE
*Chile*
http://www.comerciojusto.cl
Chilean coalition of environmental,
labor, and other groups on economic
integration.

CHILE SUSTENTABLE
*Chile*
http://www.chilesustentable.net
Promotes the environmental sustainability of Chile through economic,
political, and social transformation
and opposition to the neoliberal
model of development in force
toward sustainable development.

CITIZENS TRADE CAMPAIGN
*United States*
http://www.citizenstrade.org
Coalition of environmental, labor,
consumer, family farm, religious, and
other civil society groups promoting
environmental and social justice in
trade policy.

COALITION FOR JUSTICE
IN THE MAQUILADORAS
*United States*
http://www.coalitionforjustice.net
Coalition of religious, environmental,
labor, Latino, and women's organizations that pressure U.S. transnational
corporations to adopt socially responsible practices in the maquiladora
industries.

COMMON FRONTIERS
*Canada*
http://www.web.net/comfront
Multisectoral working group that
proposes an alternative (through
research, analysis, and action) to
the social, environmental, and
economic effects of economic
integration in the Americas.

COMMUNITY ALLIANCE
WITH FAMILY FARMERS
*United States*
http://www.caff.org
Building a movement of rural and
urban people to foster family-scale
agriculture that cares for the land,
sustains local economies, and
promotes social justice.

COMMUNITY FOOD SECURITY
COALITION
*United States*
http://www.foodsecurity.org
Works to bring about lasting social
change by promoting community-
based solutions to hunger, poor
nutrition, and the globalization
of the food system.

CONFEDERATION OF INDIGENOUS
NATIONALITIES OF ECUADOR
*Ecuador*
http://www.conaie.org
A representative body that guarantees
indigenous peoples a political voice
by defending their rights against
mounting threats to their livelihoods
and cultures.

CONSUMERS CHOICE COUNCIL
*United States*
http://www.consumerscouncil.org
An association of environmental,
consumer, and human rights organizations from twenty-five different
countries dedicated to protecting the
environment and promoting human
rights and basic labor standards

through ecolabeling. Strives to
ensure that consumers have the
information they need to purchase
products that are produced in more
environmentally sustainable and
socially just ways.

CONSUMERS INTERNATIONAL
*United Kingdom*
http://www.consumersinternational.org
Runs campaigns and programs on
world trade, environmental issues,
consumer education, and corporate
social responsibility. Strives to
promote a fairer society by defending the rights of all consumers,
especially the poor, marginalized,
and disadvantaged.

CONVERGENCE OF MOVEMENTS OF
PEOPLES OF THE AMERICAS (COMPA)
*Haiti*
http://www.compasite.org/compa/
index.php
Strives to bring together groups from
throughout the Americas to construct
alternatives to neoliberal globalization;
covers issues of indigenous peoples and
lands, free trade agreements, rural development, peace and militarization, and
foreign debt and structural adjustment.

CO-OP AMERICA
*United States*
http://www.coopamerica.org
Focuses on economic and business
strategies to create a socially just
and environmentally sustainable
society.

CORDILLERA PEOPLES ALLIANCE
*Philippines*
A federation of indigenous peoples'
grassroots organizations at the forefront
of indigenous peoples' struggle for the
defense of land, life, and resources.

CORPORATE EUROPE OBSERVATORY
*The Netherlands*
http://www.corporateeurope.org
European-based research and campaign
group targeting the threats to democracy, equity, social justice, and the environment posed by the economic and
political power of corporations and
their lobby groups.

CORPWATCH
*United States*
http://www.corpwatch.org
Counters corporate-led globalization
through education, network building,
and activism.

COUNCIL OF CANADIANS
*Canada*
http://www.canadians.org
Citizens' watchdog organization that
works to promote economic justice,
advance alternatives to corporate-style
free trade, and preserve the environment. Currently has campaigns on
trade, water, health, biotech, and
sustainable agriculture.

CUBASOLAR
*Cuba*
http://www.cubasolar.cu
Educates professionals, workers, and
citizens on design, construction, operation, maintenance, and understanding

of renewable energy systems; initiates
and supports demonstration projects in
renewable energy and environmental
conservation.

CULTURAL CONSERVANCY
*United States*
http://www.nativeland.org
An indigenous rights organization
dedicated to the preservation and
revitalization of native communities
and their ancestral lands.

CULTURAL SURVIVAL
*United States*
http://www.cs.org
Promotes the rights, voices, and
visions of indigenous peoples.
Publishes *Cultural Survival Quarterly,*
the leading journal of indigenous
affairs in the United States.

DEVELOPMENT ALTERNATIVES
*India*
http://www.devalt.org
A development and consultancy
organization established in 1983
that fosters new relationships in the
people, technology, and environment
interactions needed to attain the goal
of sustainable development.

DEVELOPMENT ALTERNATIVES WITH
WOMEN FOR A NEW ERA
*Fiji*
http://www.dawn.org.fj
A network of women scholars and
activists from the South who engage
in feminist research and analysis of
the global environment and are committed to working for development

alternatives that are equitable, just, and sustainable.

DEVELOPMENT GAP

*United States*

http://www.developmentgap.org

Collaborates with citizens' organizations overseas to demonstrate practical alternatives to prevailing policies and programs.

EARTH ISLAND INSTITUTE

*United States*

http://www.earthisland.org

Develops and supports projects that promote the conservation, preservation, and restoration of the earth. Currently has projects on safe energy, protecting Lake Baikal, promoting ecological justice, and protecting the rights of indigenous people in Borneo.

EARTHJUSTICE

*United States*

http://www.earthjustice.org

Addresses trade and the environment, and human rights and the environment, and helps build environmental law in other countries. Works through the courts to safeguard public lands, national forests, parks, and wilderness areas; to reduce air and water pollution; to prevent toxic contamination; and to preserve endangered species and wildlife habitat.

ECONOMIC POLICY INSTITUTE

*United States*

http://www.epinet.org

Seeks to broaden the public debate about strategies to achieve a prosper-

ous and fair economy. Research areas include trade and globalization, labor markets, and government and the economy.

E. F. SCHUMACHER SOCIETY

*United States*

http://www.schumachersociety.org

Implements and promotes a vision of ecologically based economics and is developing models for local economic institutions.

ENVIRONMENTAL MONITORING GROUP

*South Africa*

http://www.emg.org.za

Encourages the development of policies and practices that promote civil society participation, environmental justice, and sustainable development. It focuses on trade, environmental governance, rural livelihoods, and water justice.

EQUAL EXCHANGE

*United States*

http://www.equalexchange.com

Worker-owned co-op dedicated to fair trade with small-scale coffee farmers in the developing world.

ETC GROUP

*Canada*

http://www.etcgroup.org

Works with civil society organizations for cooperative and sustainable self-reliance in disadvantaged societies by providing information and analysis of socioeconomic and technological trends and alternatives.

THE EUROPEAN FAIR TRADE
ASSOCIATION (EFTA)
*The Netherlands*
http://www.eftafairtrade.org
A network of eleven fair trade organizations in nine European countries that import fair trade products from some four hundred economically disadvantaged producer groups in Africa, Asia, and Latin America. The objectives are to make fair trade importing more efficient and effective and to promote fair trade products to commercial and political decision makers.

FOCUS ON THE GLOBAL SOUTH
*Thailand*
http://www.focusweb.org
Research and advocacy related to international finance and other global issues. Provides analysis and information on trade and finance, militarization, environment, global governance, multilateral institutions, and security issues in the Asia-Pacific region.

FORESTRADE
*United States*
http://www.forestrade.com
The largest U.S. importer of organic spices; helps farmers in Guatemala, Madagascar, Grenada, and throughout Asia to enter the global fair trade market. Also helps farmers shift to organic methods and diversify their crops. The products that ForesTrade markets are the result of a cooperative network that fosters sustainable small farm development, natural resource conservation, and biodiversity. The group supports social and economic progress in the farming communities with which it works.

FOREST STEWARDSHIP COUNCIL
*Germany*
http://www.fsc.org
An international body that supports environmentally appropriate, socially beneficial, and economically viable management of the world's forests through a product certification program.

THE FOUNDATION
ON ECONOMIC TRENDS
*United States*
http://www.foet.org
Examines new trends in science and technology and their impacts on the environment, the economy, culture, and society. The foundation currently has a campaign on the hydrogen economy, an anticloning campaign, and a treaty initiative to establish the earth's gene pool as a global commons to be jointly shared by all peoples.

FRIENDS OF THE EARTH
*The Netherlands*
http://www.foe.org
International environmental organization that focuses on greening trade agreements, reforming international institutions, making corporations accountable, and stopping international financial institutions from financing environmentally and socially harmful oil, mining, and gas projects.

GLOBAL EXCHANGE
*United States*
http://www.globalexchange.org
An international human rights organization dedicated to promoting

environmental, political, and social justice. It advocates democratizing the global economy by raising public awareness on free trade agreements, global institutions, fair trade, and sweatshop labor.

GRAMEEN BANK

*Bangladesh*

http://www.grameen-info.org

Provides credit to the poor in rural Bangladesh, without any collateral, through its microcredit program. Uses credit as a cost-effective weapon to fight poverty; serves as a catalyst in the overall development of socioeconomic conditions of the poor who have been kept outside the banking system on the grounds that they are not bankable.

GREEN BELT MOVEMENT

*Kenya*

http://www.greenbeltmovement.org

Founded more than twenty years ago to avert desertification in Kenya, the Green Belt movement has grown to thousands of members who have planted more than twenty million trees. It has become a motivating model of locally based development; Green Belt women empowered by tree planting have gone on to stand up for democracy in Kenya and promote village food security.

GREENPEACE

*The Netherlands*

http://www.greenpeace.org

Exposes the most crucial worldwide threats to the planet's biodiversity and environment. Campaigns to stop climate change, eliminate toxic chemi-

cals, protect ancient forests, save the oceans, encourage sustainable trade.

GROUNDWORK

*South Africa*

http://www.groundwork.org.za

A nonprofit environmental justice service and developmental organization working to improve the quality of life of vulnerable people in South Africa, and increasingly in southern Africa, by helping civil society to have a greater impact on environmental governance.

IBASE

*Brazil*

http://www.ibase.br

Brazilian institute for socioeconomic analysis; leading player in the World Social Forum convenings.

IBON FOUNDATION

*Philippines*

http://www.ibon.org

Undertakes the study of socioeconomic issues confronting Philippine society and the world today; explores alternatives and promotes a new understanding of socioeconomic issues in order to serve the interests and aspirations of the Filipino people.

INDIGENOUS ENVIRONMENTAL NETWORK

*United States*

http://www.ienearth.org

Helps indigenous communities and tribal governments to develop mechanisms to protect their sacred sites, land, water, air, natural resources, and the health of both their people and all living things and to build economically sustainable communities.

INDIGENOUS PEOPLES COUNCIL
ON BIOCOLONIALISM
*United States*
http://www.ipcb.org
Assists indigenous peoples in the protection of their genetic resources, knowledge, and cultural and human rights from the negative effects of biotechnology.

INDIGENOUS PEOPLES' INTER-
NATIONAL CENTER FOR POLICY
RESEARCH AND EDUCATION
NETWORK/TEBTEBBA
*Philippines*
http://www.tebtebba.org
An indigenous people's organization that seeks the recognition, promotion, and protection of indigenous peoples' rights and aspirations while building unity to uphold social and environmental justice and sustainability. Has programs on indigenous peoples' rights, sustainable development, biodiversity and indigenous knowledge, and finance and trade.

INFACT
*United States*
http://www.infact.org
Exposes abuses by transnational corporations and organizes grassroots campaigns to hold corporations accountable to consumers and society at large.

INSTITUTE FOR AGRICULTURE
AND TRADE POLICY
*United States*
http://www.iatp.org

Promotes family farms, rural communities, and ecosystems worldwide through research, education, science and technology, and advocacy; is a leader in campaigns against global trade bureaucracies.

INSTITUTE FOR FOOD
AND DEVELOPMENT POLICY
(FOOD FIRST)
*United States*
http://www.foodfirst.org
Highlights root causes of and value-based solutions to hunger and poverty around the world; its commitment is to establish food as a fundamental human right.

INSTITUTE FOR LOCAL SELF-RELIANCE
*United States*
http://www.ilsr.org
Provides technical assistance and information on environmentally sound economic strategies based on local control of resources and development.

INSTITUTE FOR POLICY STUDIES
*United States*
http://www.ips-dc.org
Independent center of ideas for action on peace, justice, and the environment, including projects on global economy, peace, and security, sustainable energy and economies, and campaigns for migrant workers' rights.

INSTITUTE FOR SUSTAINABLE
DEVELOPMENT
*Ethiopia*
Provides a focal point for discussion and debate on environment and devel-

opment in Ethiopia. One project directly involving farmers deals with better management of the overall ecological systems in the farming community to maximize production and improve environmental conditions.

INTERFAITH CENTER
ON CORPORATE RESPONSIBILITY
*United States*
http://www.iccr.org
Puts pressure on companies to be socially and environmentally responsible. Issue areas include environmental justice, global warming, and water and food.

INTERHEMISPHERIC RESOURCE CENTER
*United States*
http://www.irc-online.org
Works to make the United States a more responsible member of the global community by promoting progressive strategic dialogues that lead to new citizen-based agendas. Provides independent analysis of U.S. foreign policy through its global affairs program and its Americas program.

INTERNATIONAL CENTER
FOR TECHNOLOGY ASSESSMENT
*United States*
http://www.icta.org
Provides the public with full assessments and analyses of technological impacts on society of issues ranging from sustainable agriculture and bio-technology to transportation, globalization, and intellectual property.

INTERNATIONAL COALITION TO
PROTECT THE POLISH COUNTRYSIDE
*Poland*
http://www.icppc.pl
Works to protect Poland's one and half million family farms from being converted to large-scale agribusinesses by promoting traditional family farms as a model for Europe; challenges the Polish government to support its small farms rather than accept the EU system of subsidies for large-scale factory farms.

INTERNATIONAL DEVELOPMENT
EXCHANGE
*United States*
http://www.idex.org
Works for economic justice among low-income communities in Asia, Africa, and Latin America by partnering with grassroots organizations whose programs promote economic development and rights for women, indigenous peoples, and youth.

INTERNATIONAL FAIR TRADE
ASSOCIATION (IFAT)
*United Kingdom*
http://www.ifat.org
Composed of over two hundred members in fifty-five countries, its mission is to improve the livelihoods and well-being of disadvantaged producers by linking and promoting fair trade organizations and speaking out for greater justice in world trade.

INTERNATIONAL INDIAN TREATY
COUNCIL
*United States*
http://www.treatycouncil.org

Organization of indigenous peoples from the American continent and the Pacific; works for their sovereignty and self-determination and the recognition and protection of indigenous rights, traditional cultures, and sacred lands.

INTERNATIONAL LABOR RIGHTS FUND
*United States*
http://www.laborrights.org
Advocacy organization dedicated to achieving just and humane treatment for workers worldwide.

INTERNATIONAL RIVERS NETWORK
*United States*
http://www.irn.org
Works to halt the construction of destructive river development projects and promote sound river management worldwide. Supports local communities, working to protect their rivers and watersheds, and encourages equitable and sustainable methods of meeting needs for water, energy, and flood management.

INTERNATIONAL SOCIETY FOR
ECOLOGY AND CULTURE
*United Kingdom*
http://www.isec.org.uk
Promotes locally based alternatives to the global consumer culture in order to protect both biological and cultural diversity. Its main programs focus on bringing the food economy home and shifting away from dependence on a global economy dominated by huge corporations and institutions toward economic structures that are more decentralized, diversified, and ecological.

JUBILEE SOUTH
*No official headquarters*
http://www.jubileesouth.org
A network of social movements, people's organizations, communities, NGOs, and political formations working to cancel the debt owed by countries of the South to global finance and trade institutions.

JUBILEE USA NETWORK
*United States*
http://www.jubileeusa.org
Coalition of labor, churches, religious organizations, AIDS activists, and trade campaigners working to cancel developing-country debt.

JUST TRANSITION ALLIANCE
*United States*
http://www.jtalliance.org
A coalition of labor, economic, and environmental justice activists, indigenous people, and working-class people of color working for the just transition of communities and workers from unsafe workplaces and environments to healthy, viable communities with a sustainable economy.

KOREAN PEOPLE'S ACTION
AGAINST FTA & WTO
*Korea*
A coalition of more than fifty organizations in Korea, ranging from trade unions, peasants, women, environmental and student mass movements, political parties, and NGOs fighting liberalization of trade and investment.

LATIN AMERICAN WORKING GROUP

*United States*

http://www.lawg.org

A coalition that works to encourage U.S. policies in Latin America that promote human rights, justice, peace, and sustainable development.

MAJOMUT COFFEE GROWERS UNION

*Mexico*

http://www.majomut.org/liks/liks.html

An organization of indigenous small-scale farmers in Chiapas that has focused on farming organic coffee as a way of improving yields, quality, and the income of its cooperative.

MEXICAN ACTION NETWORK
ON FREE TRADE

*Mexico*

http://www.rmalc.org.mx

Coalition of labor, environmental, and human rights groups promoting an alternative to free trade.

MOVIMENTO DOS TRABALHADORES
RURAIS SEM TERRA (LANDLESS
WORKERS MOVEMENT; MST)

*Brazil*

http://www.mstbrazil.org

A land reform movement that emerged in the mid-1980s, the MST has helped settle more than 250,000 families on fifteen million acres of formerly idle land in almost every state of Brazil and has reduced malnutrition and joblessness and increased literacy in its settlements. The MST is reembedding the market in community and actively promoting cooperative enterprises and organic farms.

NATIONAL CAMPAIGN FOR
SUSTAINABLE AGRICULTURE

*United States*

http://www.sustainableagriculture.net

A nationwide coalition of farmers, environmentalists, and consumer advocates focusing on educating the public on the importance of a sustainable food and agriculture system that is economically viable, environmentally sound, socially just, and humane.

NATIONAL FAMILY FARM COALITION

*United States*

http://www.nffc.net

Brings together farmers and others to organize national projects focused on preserving and strengthening family farms; serves as a network for groups opposing corporate agriculture.

NATIONAL NETWORK FOR IMMIGRANT
AND REFUGEE RIGHTS

*United States*

http://www.nnirr.org

A coalition of immigrant, refugee, community, religious, civil rights, and labor organizations and activists that educates communities and the general public and develops plans of action on immigrant and refugee issues.

NAVDANYA

*India*

http://www.navdanya.org

Helps to preserve indigenous Indian knowledge in the face of growing corporate monopolization of seeds and intellectual property rights. The Navdanya project has helped a hundred thousand Indian farmers return to traditional, organic farming methods in villages now dubbed "freedom zones."

NEW ECONOMICS FOUNDATION
*United Kingdom*
http://www.jubilee2000uk.org
Promotes innovative solutions that challenge mainstream thinking on economic, environmental, and social issues. Projects include international economics and markets, democracy; and local economic renewal.

ORGANIC CONSUMERS ASSOCIATION
*United States*
http://www.organicconsumers.org
Grassroots organization that campaigns for food safety, organic agriculture, fair trade, and sustainability. Advocates a global moratorium on genetically engineered foods and crops.

OUR WORLD IS NOT FOR SALE
*No official headquarters*
http://www.ourworldisnotforsale.org
A network of organizations, activists, and social movements worldwide fighting against the current model of corporate globalization embodied in global trading systems. Committed to a sustainable, socially just, democratic, and accountable multilateral trading system.

OXFAM INTERNATIONAL
*United Kingdom*
http://www.oxfam.org
Dedicated to finding long-term solutions to poverty, hunger, and social injustice around the world. Works to eliminate the root causes of social and economic inequities by challenging the structural barriers that foster conflict and human suffering and limit people from gaining the skills, resources, and power to become self-sufficient.

PACIFIC ENVIRONMENT
*United States*
http://www.pacificenvironment.org
Works to protect the living environment of the Pacific Rim by strengthening democracy, supporting grassroots activism, empowering communities, and redefining international policies. Provides direct support to over one hundred grassroots organizations throughout Siberia, the Russian Far East, China, and Japan.

PEOPLE-CENTERED
DEVELOPMENT FORUM
*United States*
http://www.pcdf.org
Envisions human societies in which justice, inclusiveness, and sustainability serve as organizing principles of public policy.

PEOPLE'S FOOD SOVEREIGNTY
*No official headquarters*
http://www.peoplesfoodsovereignty.org
A global coalition of peasant-farmer organizations and NGOs working on food and agriculture issues.

PESTICIDE ACTION NETWORK
*United States*
http://www.panna.org
Links local and international consumer, labor, health, environment, and agricul-

ture groups into an international network to challenge the global proliferation of pesticides; defends basic rights to health and environmental quality.

POLARIS INSTITUTE

*Canada*

http://www.polarisinstitute.org

Works with citizen movements to fight for democratic social change in an age of corporate-driven globalization. Has programs on biojustice, water rights, and militarization.

PROGRAM ON CORPORATIONS,

LAW AND DEMOCRACY (POCLAD)

*United States*

http://www.poclad.org

Produces publications and conducts workshops that challenge the excessive power of corporations.

PUBLIC CITIZEN

*United States*

http://www.tradewatch.org

Public Citizen's Global Trade Watch division fights for better international trade and investment policies. Campaigns focus on the current mechanisms of globalization, such as the World Trade Organization, the North American Free Trade Agreement, the proposed Free Trade Area of the Americas, and the General Agreement on Trade in Services and the procedures by which such policies are designed and implemented.

RAINFOREST ACTION NETWORK

*United States*

http://www.ran.org

Works in alliance with environmental and human rights groups around the world to protect the earth's rainforests and support the rights of their inhabitants through education, grassroots organizing, and nonviolent direct action. Programs include a campaign to stop old-growth logging and a campaign on global finance (business accountability).

RAINFOREST ALLIANCE

*United States*

http://www.rainforest-alliance.org

Works to protect ecosystems and the people and wildlife that live within them by implementing better business practices for biodiversity conservation and sustainability. It is a member of the Sustainable Agriculture Network, a coalition dedicated to promoting tropical conservation that recognizes that the well-being of societies and ecosystems is dependent on environmentally sound, socially equitable, and economically viable agriculture.

REDEFINING PROGRESS

*United States*

http://www.rprogress.org

Works with a broad array of partners to shift the economy and public policy toward sustainability. Measures the real state of the economy, environment, and social justice with tools like the genuine progress indicator (GPI) and the Ecological Footprint, and designs policies such as environmental tax reform.

RED NACIONAL DE ACCIÓN
ECOLÓGICA (RENACE)
*Chile*
http://www.renace.cl
Chilean grassroots organization work-
ing on Chilean environmental issues.

RESEARCH FOUNDATION
FOR SCIENCE, TECHNOLOGY,
AND ECOLOGY
*India*
http://www.vshiva.net
Works on biodiversity conservation and
protecting people's rights to their livelihoods and environment threatened by
centralized systems of monoculture in
forestry, agriculture, and fisheries. Has
projects on seed saving, impacts of
trade liberalization on agriculture,
and no patents of life.

RESOURCE CENTER OF THE AMERICAS
*United States*
http://www.americas.org
Educates and organizes to promote
human rights, democratic participation,
economic justice, and cross-cultural
understanding in the context of globalization in the Americas.

RURAL DEVELOPMENT
SERVICES NETWORK
*South Africa*
http://www.rdsn.org.za
A network of independent rural development organizations that aims to contribute to the eradication of poverty
and the empowerment of rural people
through campaigning, networking, collaborating, and building a wider and
stronger membership base.

SIERRA CLUB
*United States*
http://www.sierraclub.org
The leading U.S. grassroots conservation organization working for
the protection of the earth's wild
places; includes programs on trade
and globalization.

SLOW FOOD MOVEMENT
*Italy*
http://www.slowfood.com
With eighty thousand members in
forty-five countries, this movement is
successfully reviving threatened seed
varieties and generating renewed
appreciation of local and regional
food specialities.

SOUTHWEST NETWORK
FOR ENVIRONMENTAL
AND ECONOMIC JUSTICE
*United States*
http://www.sneej.org
A coalition of activists and
grassroots organizations that
works to develop and broaden
collective regional strategies and
perspectives on environmental
degradation and other social,
racial, economic, and gender
injustices.

SURVIVAL INTERNATIONAL
*United Kingdom*
http://www.survival-international.org
An international organization
supporting tribal peoples and their
right to decide their own future;
works to protect indigenous lives,
lands, and human rights.

## THE SUZUKI FOUNDATION

*Canada*

http://www.davidsuzuki.org

Works to find ways for society to live in balance with the natural world that sustains us. Focuses on four program areas: oceans and sustainable fishing, forests and wild lands, climate change and clean energy, and the web of life.

## SWEATSHOP WATCH

*United States*

http://www.sweatshopwatch.org

A coalition of labor, community, civil rights, immigrant rights, and women's, religious, and student organizations working to eliminate sweatshop conditions in the global garment industry.

## THIRD WORLD NETWORK

*Malaysia*

http://www.twnside.org.sg

A network of developing-country NGOs that articulates a Southern perspective on economic, social, and environmental issues pertaining to the South. Includes trade issues and developments, global financial institutions, biotechnology, biodiversity and indigenous rights, biopiracy, tourism, and women's rights and gender issues.

## TRADE JUSTICE MOVEMENT

*United Kingdom*

http://www.tradejusticemovement.org .uk

A coalition of aid agencies, environment and human rights campaigns, fair trade organizations, and faith and consumer groups that campaigns for fundamental change to the unjust rules

and institutions governing international trade, so that trade is made to work for all.

## TRANSFAIR USA

*United States*

http://www.transfairusa.org

The only independent, third-party certifier of fair trade practices in the United States. Through regular visits to fair trade farmer cooperatives conducted by Fairtrade Labeling Organizations International (FLO) and partnerships with U.S. companies, TransFair verifies that the farmers who produce fair trade certified products are paid a fair price.

## TRANSNATIONAL INSTITUTE

*The Netherlands*

http://www.tni.org

International network of activist-scholars providing critical analyses of global problems with a view to providing intellectual support to those movements concerned with steering the world in a democratic, equitable, and environmentally sustainable direction. Programs include alternative economic governance and sustainability and alternatives to water privatization.

## UNION OF CONCERNED SCIENTISTS

*United States*

http://www.ucsusa.org

An alliance of scientists and citizens who aim to augment rigorous scientific research with public education and citizen advocacy to help build a cleaner, healthier environment and a safer world. Offers programs on clean energy, global environment, clean vehicles, food and environment, and global security.

U.S. LABOR EDUCATION
IN THE AMERICAS PROJECT
*United States*
http://www.usleap.org
Supports economic justice and rights for workers in Latin America. Focuses especially on the struggles of those who are employed directly or indirectly by U.S. companies, working to secure global rules for the global economy that ensure respect for the basic rights of workers.

VIA CAMPESINA
*Honduras*
http://www.viacampesina.org
An international movement that coordinates peasant organizations of small- and middle-scale producers, agricultural workers, rural women, and indigenous communities from Asia, Africa, America, and Europe.

WHITE EARTH LAND
RECOVERY PROJECT
*United States*
http://www.welrp.org
Facilitates recovery of the original land base of the White Earth Indian reservation while preserving and restoring traditional practices of sound land stewardship, language fluency, and community development and strengthening spiritual and cultural heritage.

WOMEN'S EDGE
*United States*
http://www.womensedge.org
Advocates for international economic policies and human rights to help women worldwide end poverty in their lives, communities, and nations.

WORLD DEVELOPMENT MOVEMENT
*United Kingdom*
http://www.wdm.org.uk/index.htm
Works to change the policies of governments and business that keep people poor. Researches and promotes positive alternatives.

WORLD FEDERALIST ASSOCIATION
*United States*
http://www.wfa.org
Works to democratize the institutions of globalization, achieve U.S. support for prosecuting war criminals through the International Criminal Court, improve global environmental governance, and reform U.N. peacekeeping to allow intervention before a conflict escalates into genocide.

WORLD FORUM
OF FISHER PEOPLES
*India*
http://www.wffp.org
Strives to protect livelihoods, uphold fishing rights, human rights, fundamental rights, social justice, and community responsibilities, and preserve and promote the fisher peoples' culture; is committed to sustaining fisheries and aquatic resources.

WORLD RAINFOREST MOVEMENT
*Uruguay*
http://www.wrm.org.uy
An international network of Northern
and Southern citizens' groups involved
in efforts to defend the world's rain-
forests. It works to secure the lands
and livelihoods of forest peoples and
supports their efforts to defend the
forests from commercial logging, dams,
mining, plantations, shrimp farms,
colonization, and settlement.

WORLDWATCH INSTITUTE
*United States*
http://www.worldwatch.org
Dedicated to fostering the evolution
of an environmentally sustainable
society, one in which human needs
are met in ways that do not threaten

the health of the natural environment
or the prospects of future generations.
Publishes the annual flagship books
*State of the World* and *Vital Signs*.

WUPPERTAL INSTITUTE FOR CLIMATE,
ENVIRONMENT, AND ENERGY
*Germany*
http://www.wupperinst.org
Explores and develops environmental
policy guidelines, strategies, and instruments in order to promote sustainability at the regional, national,
and international levels. The main
focus is on ecology and its interrela-
tion with the economy and society.
Publishes Wuppertal papers on issues
such as responsible corporate governance, balancing trade and environment, and ecoefficiency.

# Resources

*Useful Tools and Indicators*

THE COMPASS OF SUSTAINABILITY
http://www.iisd.org/cgsdi/compass
.htm
Provides a Sustainable Development
Index.

THE DASHBOARD OF SUSTAINABILITY
http://www.iisd.org/cgsdi/intro_dash
board.htm
Provides a Policy Performance
Index.

THE ECOLOGICAL FOOTPRINT
http://www.redefiningprogress.org
/programs/sustainabilityindicators/ef
Estimates consumption of natural
resources.

THE ENVIRONMENTAL
SUSTAINABILITY INDEX
http://www.ciesin.org/indicators/ESI/
Includes twenty indicators on environmental sustainability.

THE LIVING PLANET INDEX
http://www.panda.org/news_facts
/publications/general/livingplanet
/lpro2.cfm
Includes indexes on animal species
and ecosystem change.

UNITED NATIONS DEVELOPMENT
PROGRAM HUMAN DEVELOPMENT
REPORTS
http://hdr.undp.org
Annual global, regional, and
national reports that include a
Human Development Index, a
Gender-Related Index, a Gender
Empowerment Measure, and a
Human Poverty Index.

THE WELLBEING ASSESSMENT/
BAROMETER OF SUSTAINABILITY
http://www.iucn.org/info_and_news/
press/wonback.doc
Measures human and ecosystem
well-being together.

# Sources

Ahn, Christine, ed. *Shafted: Free Trade and America's Working Poor.* Oakland: Food First Books, 2003.

Allen, Will, Eddie DeAnda, and Kate Duesterberg. *Cotton Subsidies: Who Needs Them? Who Gets Them?* www.organicconsumers.org/clothes/willallen011504 .cfm. December 2003.

Altieri, Miguel. *Genetic Engineering in Agriculture: The Myths, Environmental Risks, and Alternatives.* Oakland: Food First Books, 2001.

Altieri, Miguel, and Peter Rosset. *Ten Reasons Why Biotechnology Will Not Ensure Food Security, Protect the Environment, and Reduce Poverty in the Developing World.* Oakland, CA: Food First Books, 1999.

Anderson, Ray. *Mid-Course Correction.* Atlanta: Peregrinzilla Press, 1998.

Anderson, Sarah, ed. *Views from the South: The Effects of Globalization and the WTO on Third World Countries.* San Francisco: International Forum on Globalization, 2000.

Anderson, Sarah, and John Cavanagh. *Top 200: The Rise of Corporate Global Power.* Washington, DC: Institute for Policy Studies, December 2000.

Anderson, Sarah, John Cavanagh, Chris Hartman, and Betsy Leondar-Wright. *Executive Excess 2001: Layoffs, Tax Rebates, and the Gender Gap.* Washington, DC: Institute for Policy Studies and United for a Fair Economy, May 2001.

Anderson, Sarah, John Cavanagh, and Thea Lee. *A Field Guide to the Global Economy.* New York: New Press, 2000.

Barker, Debi, and Jerry Mander. *Invisible Government: The World Trade Organization, Global Government for the New Millennium?* San Francisco: International Forum on Globalization, 1999.

Barlow, Maude. *Blue Gold: The Global Water Crisis and the Commodification of the World's Water Supply.* San Francisco: International Forum on Globalization, 2001.

SOURCES

————. *The Free Trade Area of the Americas: The Threat to Social Programs, Environmental Sustainability, and Social Justice.* San Francisco: International Forum on Globalization, 2001.

————. *Profit Is Not the Cure.* Toronto: McClelland & Stewart, 2002.

Barlow, Maude, and Tony Clarke. *Blue Gold: The Battle Against Corporate Theft of the World's Water.* New York: New Press, 2002.

————. *Global Showdown: How the New Activists Are Fighting Global Corporate Rule.* Toronto: Stoddart, 2002.

Barnes, Peter. *Who Owns the Sky?* Washington, DC: Island Press, 2001.

————. "Capitalism, the Commons, and Divine Right." Speech delivered at the E. F. Schumacher Society, October 25, 2003.

Barnes, Peter, Jonathan Rowe, and David Bollier. *The State of the Commons 2003–04.* Point Reyes Station, CA: Friends of the Commons. http://www.friendsof thecommons.org.

Barnet, Richard J., and John Cavanagh. *Global Dreams: Imperial Corporations and the New World Order.* New York: Simon & Schuster, 1994.

Barshefsky, Charlene. "Barshefsky on U.S. Trade Agenda for 2000." Presentation to the United States Mission to the European Union, Brussels, Belgium, February 8, 2000. http://www.useu.be/Issues/barsho208.html.

*A Basic Call to Consciousness: The Hau de no sau nee Address to the Western World.* Akwesasne Notes. Rooseveltown, NY: Mohawk Nation, 1978.

Bello, Walden. *The Future in the Balance: Essays on Globalization and Resistance.* San Francisco: Food First and Focus on the Global South, 2001.

————. *Pax Romana Versus Pax Americana: Contrasting Strategies of Imperial Management.* Bangkok: Focus on the Global South, April 23, 2003. http://www.focusweb.org/popups/articleswindow.php?id=311.

————. "The Crisis of the Globalist Project and the New Economics of George W. Bush." Address given at the McPlanet Conference, Berlin, July 10, 2003. http://www.focusweb.org/popups/articleswindow.php?id=334.

————. "Diplomacy by Vendetta." *Newsweek International,* November 24, 2003. www.msnbc.com/news/994164.asp?cp1=1#BODY.

Bello, Walden, Nicola Bullard, and Kamal Malhotra, eds. *Global Finance: New Thinking on Regulating Speculative Capital Markets.* London: Zed Books, 2000.

Bello, Walden, Shea Cunningham, and Li Keng Poh. *A Siamese Tragedy: Development & Disintegration in Modern Thailand.* London: Zed Books, 1998.

Bello, Walden, Shea Cunningham, and Bill Rau. *Dark Victory: The United States, Structural Adjustment, and Global Poverty.* London: Pluto Press, 1994.

Bello, Walden, with David Kinley, and Elaine Elison. *Development Debacle: The World Bank in the Philippines.* San Francisco: Institute for Food and Development Policy, 1982.

Bello, Walden, and Stephanie Rosefeld. *Dragons in Distress: Asia's Miracle Economies in Crisis.* San Francisco: Institute for Food and Development Policy, 1990.

*Book of Knowledge: Investing in the Growing Education and Training Industry.* New

York: Merrill Lynch, Global Securities Research & Economics Group, Global Fundamental Equity Research Department, 1999.

Braun, Henry. *The Phoenix Project: An Energy Transition to Renewable Resources.* Phoenix: Research Analysts, 1990.

Brecher, Jeremy, Tim Costello, and Brendan Smith. *Globalization from Below: The Power of Solidarity.* Cambridge, MA: South End Press, 2000.

Broad, Robin, ed. *Global Backlash: Citizen Initiatives for a Just World Economy.* Lanham, MD: Rowman & Littlefield, 2002.

Brown, Lester. *Building a Sustainable Society.* New York: W. W. Norton, 1981.

———. *Eco-Economy: Building an Economy for the Earth.* New York: W. W. Norton, 2001.

Brown, Lester, Christopher Flavin, Hilary French, and others. *State of the World 2001.* Washington, DC: Worldwatch Institute, 2001.

Brown, Lester R., and others. *State of the World 1988.* Washington, DC: Worldwatch Institute, 1988.

Bruno, Kenny, Joshua Karliner, and China Brotsky. *Greenhouse Gangsters Versus Climate Justice.* San Francisco: Transnational Resource and Action Center, 1999.

Bunyard, Peter. "Industrial Agriculture: Driving Climate Change." *The Ecologist,* 26(6), November–December 1996.

———. "A Hungrier World." *The Ecologist: Special Issue, Climate Crisis, 29*(2), 1998.

Capra, Fritjof. *The Hidden Connections: A Science for Sustainable Living.* London: HarperCollins, 2002.

———. *The Hidden Connections: Integrating the Biological, Cognitive, and Social Dimensions of Life into a Science of Sustainability.* New York: Doubleday, 2002.

Carstensen, Michelle, and David Morris. *Biochemicals for the Automobile Industry.* Washington, DC: Institute for Local Self-Reliance, 1997.

Cashman, Ty. "Fuel from Water." *Whole Earth Review,* Spring 1994, pp. 50–53.

———. "Hydrogen Energy." *Whole Earth Review,* Winter 2001, p. 46.

———. "Jump-Starting Renewables: What It Takes to Enter the Hydrogen Era." *Whole Earth Review,* Winter 2001, p. 57.

Cavanagh, John, ed. *South-North: Citizen Strategies to Transform a Divided World* (pamphlet). San Francisco: International Forum on Globalization, November 1995.

Central Intelligence Agency. *Global Trends, 2015.* Langley, VA: Central Intelligence Agency, 2000.

Childers, Erskine, and Brian Urquhart. *Renewing the United Nations System: Special Issue of Development Dialogue.* Uppsala, Sweden: Dag Hammarskjøld Foundation, 1994.

Chomsky, Noam. *World Orders Old and New.* New York: Columbia University Press, 1994.

———. "Confronting the Empire." *Dissident Voice,* February 4, 2003. www.dissidentvoice.org/Articles/Chomsky_ConfrontingEmpire.htm.

———. "Dominance and Its Dilemmas: The Bush Administration's Imperial Grand

Strategy." *Boston Review,* October–November 2003. http://bostonreview.net/
BR28.5/chomsky.html.

Chossudovsky, Michel. *The Globalisation of Poverty: Impacts of IMF and World Bank
Reforms.* Penang, Malaysia: Third World Network, 1997.

Clarke, Tony. *Silent Coup: Confronting the Big Business Takeover of Canada.* Ottawa:
Canadian Centre for Policy Alternatives, 1997.

———. *By What Authority!* San Francisco: International Forum on Globalization,
1999.

Clarke, Tony, and Maude Barlow. *MAI: The Multilateral Agreement on Investment and
the Threat to Canadian Sovereignty.* Toronto: Stoddart, 1997.

Cobb, Clifford, and Ted Halstead. "The Need for New Measurements of
Progress." In Jerry Mander and Edward Goldsmith, eds., *The Case Against the
Global Economy: And for a Turn Toward the Local.* San Francisco: Sierra Club
Books, 1996.

Commoner, Barry. *Making Peace with the Planet.* New York: New Press, 1992.

Daly, Herman E. *Beyond Growth: The Economics of Sustainable Development.* Boston:
Beacon Press, 1996.

Daly, Herman E., and John B. Cobb, Jr. *For the Common Good: Redirecting the
Economy Toward Community, the Environment, and a Sustainable Future.* Boston:
Beacon Press, 1989.

Danaher, Kevin. *10 Reasons to Abolish the IMF & World Bank.* New York: Seven
Stories Press, 2001.

———, ed. *Democratizing the Global Economy: The Battle Against the World Bank and the
IMF.* Monroe, ME: Common Courage, 2001.

Das, Bhagirath Lal. *The WTO and the Multilateral Trading System.* London: Zed
Books, 2003.

Doniger, David, David Friedman, Roland Hwang, Daniel Lashof, and Jason Mark.
*Dangerous Addiction: Ending America's Oil Dependence.* New York: Natural
Resources Defense Council and the Union of Concerned Scientists, 2002.

Douthwaite, Richard. *The Growth Illusion.* Dublin: Lilliput Press, 1992.

———. *Short Circuit: Strengthening Local Economies for Security in an Unstable World.*
Dublin: Lilliput Press, 1996.

Dowie, Mark. "In Law We Trust." *Orion,* July–August 2003, pp. 19–25.

*Draft Convention on Cultural Diversity.* Ottawa, Canada: International Network for
Cultural Diversity, March 2002.

Dunn, Seth. "Micropower: The Next Electrical Era." Worldwatch Paper No. 151.
Washington, DC: Worldwatch Institute, 2000.

———. "Decarbonizing the Energy Economy." In Lester Brown, Christopher
Flavin, Hilary French, and others, eds., *State of the World 2001.* Washington,
DC: Worldwatch Institute, 2001.

———. "Hydrogen Futures: Toward a Sustainable Energy System." Worldwatch
Paper No. 157. Washington, DC: Worldwatch Institute, 2001.

"Eight Benefits of Micropower." *Whole Earth Review,* Winter 2001, p. 20.

*Energy Innovations: A Prosperous Path to a Clean Environment.* Cambridge, MA: Union of Concerned Scientists, 1997. www.ucsusa.org/energy/find.ei.html.

Estes, Ralph. *Tyranny of the Bottom Line: Why Corporations Make Good People Do Bad Things.* San Francisco: Berrett-Koehler, 1996.

*A Fair Globalization: Creating Opportunities for All.* Geneva: International Labor Organization/World Commission on the Social Dimensions of Globalization, February 2004.

Faux, Jeff, and Lawrence Mishel. "Inequality and the Global Economy." In Will Hutton and Anthony Giddens, eds., *Global Capitalism.* New York: New Press, 2000.

Finnegan, William. "The Economics of Empire: Notes on the Washington Consensus." *Harper's Magazine,* May 2003, pp. 41–54.

Fisher, William F., and Thomas Ponniah. *Another World Is Possible: Popular Alternatives to Globalization at the World Social Forum.* London: Zed Books, 2003.

*For a Sustainable Chile: A Citizen's Agenda for Change.* Santiago: Sustainable Chile Program, 1999.

Gabel, Medard, and Henry Bruner. *Globalinc: An Atlas of the Multinational Corporation.* New York: New Press, 2003.

Gardner, Gary, and Payal Sampat. "Mind Over Matter: Recasting the Role of Materials in Our Lives." Worldwatch Paper No. 144. Washington, DC: Worldwatch Institute, 1998.

Garrett, Laurie. *The Coming Plague: Newly Emerging Diseases in a World Out of Balance.* New York: Farrar, Straus and Giroux, 1994.

Gates, Jeff. *The Ownership Solution: Toward a Shared Capitalism for the Twenty-First Century.* Cambridge, MA: Perseus, 1999.

George, Susan. *A Fate Worse Than Debt.* London: Penguin Books, 1988.

———. *The Debt Boomerang: How Third World Debt Harms Us All.* London: Pluto Press, 1992.

George, Susan, and Fabrizio Sabelli. *Faith and Credit: The World Bank's Secular Empire.* London: Penguin Books, 1994.

*Global Energy Technology Strategy. Addressing Climate Change.* Washington, DC: Battelle, 2000.

"Globalization, Inc. Concentration in Corporate Power: The Unmentioned Agenda." *ETC Group Communique, 71,* July–August 2001.

Global Resource Action Center for the Environment. "Model Sustainable Energy Statute Summary." www.gracelinks.org/nuke/sustainable_energysummary2 .html, 2002.

Goldsmith, Edward. *The Way.* Athens: University of Georgia Press, 1998.

———. "How to Feed People Under a Regime of Climate Change." *The Ecologist, Asia edition,* January 2004.

Goldsmith, James. *The Trap.* New York: Carroll & Graf, 1993.

Gorelick, Steven. *Small Is Beautiful, Big Is Subsidized.* Berkeley, CA, and Devon, UK: International Society for Ecology and Culture, 2002.

Gray, John. *False Dawn*. New York: New Press, 1998.

Greider, William. *One World, Ready or Not: The Manic Logic of Global Capitalism*. New York: Touchstone, 1998.

———. *The Soul of Capitalism: Opening Paths to a Moral Economy*. New York: Simon & Schuster, 2003.

Grossman, Richard L., and Frank T. Adams. *Taking Care of Business: Citizenship and the Charter of Incorporation*. Cambridge, MA: Charter, Inc., 1993.

Hancock, Graham. *Lords of Poverty: The Power, Prestige, and Corruption of the International Aid Business*. New York: Atlantic Monthly Press, 1989.

Hartman, Thom. *Unequal Protection*. Emmaus, PA: Rodale Press, 2002.

Hawken, Paul. *The Ecology of Commerce: A Declaration of Sustainability*. New York: HarperBusiness, 1993.

Hawken, Paul, Amory Lovins, and L. Hunter Lovins. *Natural Capitalism: The Next Industrial Revolution*. Boston: Back Bay Books, 2000.

Hemispheric Social Alliance. "Alternatives for the Americas." www.asc-hsa.org, 2001.

Henderson, Hazel. *Paradigms in Progress: Life Beyond Economics*. Indianapolis: Knowledge Systems, 1991.

———. *Creating Alternative Futures: The End of Economics*. West Hartford, CT: Kumarian Press, 1996.

———. *Beyond Globalization: Shaping a Sustainable Global Economy*. West Hartford, CT: Kumarian Press, 1999.

Hertsgaard, Mark. *Earth Odyssey*. New York: Broadway Books, 1998.

Hickey, Ellen, and Anuradha Mittal, eds. *Voices from the South: The Third World Debunks Corporate Myths on Genetically Engineered Crops*. San Francisco: Food First, June 2003.

Hines, Colin. *Localization: A Global Manifesto*. London: Earthscan Publications, 2000.

Hines, Colin, and Vandana Shiva. *A Better Agriculture Is Possible: Local Food, Global Solution*. A report for the U.N. Food and Agriculture Organization Food Summit, Rome, Italy, June 2002.

Hoffman, Peter. *Tomorrow's Energy: Hydrogen Fuel Cells and the Prospects for a Cleaner Planet*. Cambridge: MIT Press, 2001.

Independent Science Panel. *The Case for a GM-Free Sustainable World*. London: Institute of Science in Society, 2003.

International Forum on Globalization. *Does Globalization Help the Poor?* San Francisco: International Forum on Globalization, 2001.

Juhasz, Antonia. "Capitalism Gone Wild." *Tikkun*, January–February 2004, pp. 19–22.

———. "Ambitions of Empire: The Bush Administration's Economic Plan for Iraq (and Beyond)." *LeftTurn Magazine*, *12*, February–March 2004.

Karliner, Joshua. *The Corporate Planet*. San Francisco: Sierra Club Books, 1997.

Kasser, Tim, and Allen D. Kanner, eds. *Psychology and Consumer Culture: The Struggle for a Good Life in a Materialistic World.* Washington, DC: American Psychological Association, 2004.

Kaul, Inge, Isabelle Grunberg, and Marc A. Stern. *Global Public Goods: International Cooperation in the 21st Century.* New York: United Nations Development Program and Oxford University Press, 1999.

Kelly, Marjorie. *The Divine Right of Capital: Dethroning the Corporate Aristocracy.* San Francisco: Berrett-Koehler, 2001.

Khor, Martin. "The Revolt of Developing Nations." *The Seattle Debacle: Special Issue of Third World Resurgence,* December 1999–January 2000.

———. *Globalization and the South: Some Critical Issues.* Penang, Malaysia: Third World Network, 2000.

———. *Globalization and the Crisis of Sustainable Development.* Penang, Malaysia: Third World Network, 2001.

———. "The WTO, the Post-Doha Agenda, and the Future of the Trade System: A Development Perspective." Special paper from Third World Network. http://www.twnside.org.sg. 2002.

Khor, Martin, and Lim Li Lin. *Good Practices and Innovative Experiences in the South: Vol. 1: Economic, Environmental, and Sustainable Livelihood Initiatives.* London: Zed Books, 2001.

———. *Good Practices and Innovative Experiences in the South: Vol. 2: Social Policies, Indigenous Knowledge, and Appropriate Technology.* London: Zed Books, 2001.

———. *Good Practices and Innovative Experiences in the South: Vol. 3: Citizen Initiatives in Social Services, Popular Education, and Human Rights.* London: Zed Books, 2001.

Kimbrell, Andrew. *The Human Body Shop: The Engineering and Marketing of Life.* San Francisco: HarperSanFrancisco, 1993.

———. "Defending the Genetic Commons." *UTNE Reader,* January–February 2002, p. 44.

———, ed. *Fatal Harvest: The Tragedy of Industrial Agriculture.* Washington, DC: Island Press, 2002.

Klein, Naomi. *No Logo: Taking Aim at the Brand Bullies.* New York: Picador, 1999.

Korten, David C. *The Post-Corporate World: Life After Capitalism.* San Francisco: Berrett-Koehler and West Hartford, CT: Kumarian Press, 1999.

———. *When Corporations Rule the World* (2nd ed.). West Hartford, CT: Kumarian Press and San Francisco: Berrett-Koehler, 2001.

———. "From Empire to Earth Community." Keynote address at the Earth Charter Community Summit, September 2002. *YES! A Journal of Positive Futures.* http://www.yesmagazine.org/iraq/kortenempire.htm.

Korten, David, Nicanor Perlas, and Vandana Shiva. *Global Civil Society: The Path Ahead.* Discussion paper. Bainbridge Island, WA: People-Centered Development Forum, November 20, 2002. http://www.pcdf.org/civilsociety/path.htm.

Kriebel, David, Joel Tickner, Paul Epstein, and others. *The Precautionary Principle in*

*Environmental Science.* Boston: Alliance for a Healthy Tomorrow. http://healthy-tomorrow.org/pdf/kriebel_et_al.pdf.

La Duke, Winona. *Indigenous Peoples, Power, and Politics: A Renewable Future for the Seventh Generation.* Minneapolis: Honor the Earth Publications, 2004.

Lang, Tim, and Colin Hines. *The New Protectionism: Protecting the Future Against Free Trade.* London: Earthscan Publications, 1993.

Lappé, Frances Moore. "Meet the P7." *Guerrilla News Network,* December 18, 2001. www.guerrillanews.com/globalization/doc243.html.

Lappé, Frances Moore, Joseph Collins, and Peter Rosset. *World Hunger: Twelve Myths.* New York: Grove Press, 1998.

Lappé, Frances Moore, and Anna Lappé. *Hope's Edge: The Next Diet for a Small Planet.* New York: Jeremy P. Tarcher/Putnam, 2002.

Lasn, Kalle, and Tom Liacas. "Corporate Crackdown." *Adbusters,* August–September 2000, pp. 36–48.

Lovins, Amory B., Michael Brylawski, David Cramer, and Timothy Moore. *Hypercars: Materials, Manufacturing, and Policy Implications.* Snowmass, CO: Rocky Mountain Institute, 1996.

Lovins, Amory B., and L. Hunter Lovins. "Frozen Assets?" *RMI Solutions: Newsletter of the Rocky Mountain Institute,* Spring 2001, pp. 1–3, 20–21.

Lovins, Amory B., L. Hunter Lovins, and Paul Hawken. "A Road Map for Natural Capitalism." *Harvard Business Review,* May–June 1999, pp. 145–158.

Lucas, Caroline, Michael Hart, and Colin Hines. *Look to the Local: A Better Agriculture Is Possible!* Discussion paper. The Greens/European Free Alliance, European Parliament, December 2002.

Luttwak, Edward. *Turbo Capitalism: Winners and Losers in the Global Economy.* New York: HarperCollins, 1999.

MacArther, John R. *The Selling of "Free Trade": NAFTA, Washington, and the Subversion of American Democracy.* New York: Hill & Wang, 2000.

Madeley, John. *Big Business, Poor Peoples: The Impact of Transnational Corporations on the World's Poor.* London: Zed Books, 1999.

Mander, Jerry. *In the Absence of the Sacred: The Failure of Technology and the Survival of the Indian Nations.* San Francisco: Sierra Club Books, 1991.

———. "Alternatives to Globalization: A Better World Is Possible." Speech given at the World Affairs Council, San Francisco, April 2, 2003.

Mander, Jerry, and Edward Goldsmith, eds. *The Case Against the Global Economy: And for a Turn Toward the Local.* San Francisco: Sierra Club Books, 1996.

*Manifesto on the Future of Food.* San Rossore, Italy: International Commission on the Future of Food and Agriculture, 2003.

McChesney, Robert W. *Rich Media, Poor Democracy: Communication Politics in Dubious Times.* Urbana/Chicago: University of Illinois Press, 1999.

———. *The Problem of the Media: U.S. Communication Politics in the 21st Century.* New York: Monthly Review Press, 2004.

McDonough, William, and Michael Braungart. "The Next Industrial Revolution."
    *Atlantic Monthly*, October 1998, pp. 82–92.
McLaren, Deborah. *Rethinking Tourism and Ecotravel: The Paving of Paradise and What
    You Can Do to Stop It.* West Hartford, CT: Kumarian Press, 1998.
Meacher, Michael. "Natural Governance." *Resurgence*, January–February 2004, pp.
    28–31.
Meadows, Donella, Dennis L. Meadows, and Jorgen Randers. *Beyond the Limits.*
    Post Mills, VT: Chelsea Green, 1992.
Menotti, Victor. *Free Trade, Free Logging: How the World Trade Organization
    Undermines Global Forest Conservation.* San Francisco: International Forum on
    Globalization, 1999.
Mishel, Lawrence, Jared Bernstein, and John Schmitt. *The State of Working America,
    1998–99.* Washington, DC: Economic Policy Institute, 1999.
Monks, Robert A. G. *The Emperor's Nightingale: Restoring the Integrity of the
    Corporation in the Age of Shareholder Activism.* Reading, MA: Addison-Wesley,
    1998.
Morris, David. *Getting from Here to There: Building a Rational Transportation System.*
    Washington, DC: Institute for Local Self-Reliance, 1992.
———. *Seeing the Light: Regaining Control of Our Electricity System.* Washington, DC:
    Institute for Local Self-Reliance, 2001.
Motavalli, Jim. "The Reckoning: Global Warming Is Likely to Cause Huge
    Climatic Changes—and Possibly a New Ice Age." Reprinted by *E/The
    Environmental Magazine*, November–December 2003.
*MoveOn's 50 Ways to Love Your Country: How to Find Your Political Voice and Become a
    Catalyst for Change.* Maui, HI: Inner Ocean Publishing, 2004.
Nader, Ralph, William Greider, Margaret Atwood, David Philips, and Pat Choate.
    *The Case Against Free Trade: GATT, NAFTA, and the Globalization of Corporate
    Power.* San Francisco: Earth Island Press, 1993.
"National Security Strategy of the United States." Washington, DC: The White
    House, September 2002.
Nichols, John, and Robert W. McChesney. *It's the Media, Stupid.* New York: Seven
    Stories Press, 2000.
Norberg-Hodge, Helena. *Ancient Futures: Learning from Ladakh.* San Francisco:
    Sierra Club Books, 1991.
Norberg-Hodge, Helena, Peter Goering, and John Page. *From the Ground Up:
    Rethinking Industrial Agriculture.* London: Zed Books, 2001.
Norberg-Hodge, Helena, Steven Gorelick, and Todd Merrifield. *Bringing the Food
    Economy Home.* West Hartford, CT: Kumarian Press and London: Zed Books,
    2002. (Originally published as a report by International Society for Ecology
    and Culture.)
Northrop, Michael. "Addressing Global Warming: A Way Forward." *Environmental
    Grantmakers Association: News and Updates, VI*(I), Winter 2002, pp. 1, 21–22.

————. *Leading by Example: Successful Strategies for Cutting Greenhouse Gas Emissions.* Unpublished report, 2003. Originally presented at the first Conference of the Reducers, convened by the Center for Clean Air Policy, National Institutes for Public Health and the Environment, the German Marshall Fund, and the Rockefeller Brothers Fund, the Netherlands, May 11–13, 2003.

————. "Fears Are Overblown: Reducing Emissions Is Possible and Profitable." *National Academy Review: Climate Change Edition,* May 2004.

Parr, Douglas. "Right to Decide." *Resurgence,* January–February 2004, pp. 18–19.

Pauli, Gunter. "Industrial Clustering and the Second Green Revolution." Lecture presented at Schumacher College, Devon, United Kingdom, May 1996.

Payer, Cheryl. *Lent and Lost: Foreign Credit and Third World Development.* London: Zed Books, 1991.

Perkins, Logan R. R. "Why Reduce Automobile Dependence?" *Livable Cities, 1,* November 1997.

Perlas, Nicanor. *Shaping Globalization: Civil Society, Cultural Power, and Threefolding.* Quezon City, Philippines: CADI and GlobeNet3, 2000.

————. *Decoding the BU.S.H Doctrine: The U.S. as Empire.* Ortigas, Pasig City, Philippines: The Global Network for Social Threefolding, August 2003. www.globenet3.org/Essays/Essay_Bush_Doctrine.shtml.

Posey, Darrell Addison, ed. *Cultural and Spiritual Values of Biodiversity.* London: Intermediate Technology Publications, 1999.

Pretty, Jules. "Agricultural Alternatives." *Resurgence,* January–February 2004, p. 23.

————. *Regenerating Agriculture Policies and Practice for Sustainability and Self-Reliance.* London: Earthscan Publications, 1995.

Program on Corporations, Law & Democracy. "By What Authority?" *Challenging Empire's Story, 4*(2), Spring 2002, pp. 1–7.

Raghavan, Chakravarthi. *Recolonization: GATT, the Uruguay Round, and the Third World.* Penang, Malaysia: Third World Network, 1990.

*Real Price of Gasoline.* Washington, DC: International Center for Technology Assessment, 2002.

Register, Richard. *Ecocity Berkeley: Building Cities for a Healthy Future.* Berkeley: North Atlantic Books, 1987.

————. *Ecocities: Building Cities in Balance with Nature.* Berkeley: Berkeley Hills Books, 2002.

Retallack, Simon. *Climate Crisis: A Briefing for Funders.* London: Think Publishing, 2001.

Rich, Bruce. *Mortgaging the Earth: The World Bank, Environmental Impoverishment, and the Crisis of Development.* Boston: Beacon Press, 1994.

Rifkin, Jeremy. *Biosphere Politics: A New Consciousness for a New Century.* New York: Crown, 1991.

————. *The Hydrogen Economy.* New York: Tarcher/Putnam, 2002.

Ritz, Dean, ed. *Defying Corporations, Defining Democracy: A Book of History and Strategies*. New York: Apex Press, 2001.

Robertson, James. *Future Wealth: A New Economics for the 21st Century*. London: Mansell Publishing, 1989.

Roddick, Anita. *Take It Personally*. London: HarperCollins, 2001.

Rodrik, Dani. *Has Globalization Gone Too Far?* Washington, DC: Institute for International Economics, 1997.

Rosset, Peter. "Access to Land: Land Reform and Security of Tenure." *World Food Summit/Five Years Later, Civil Society Input/Case Studies*. Oakland: Institute for Food and Development Policy, October 2001.

Rowe, Jonathan. "The Hidden Commons." *Yes! A Journal of Positive Futures*, 18, Summer 2001, pp. 12–17.

———. "Fanfare for the Commons," *UTNE Reader*, January–February 2002, pp. 40–44.

Roy, Arundhati. "Confronting Empire." Presentation to the World Social Forum, Porto Alegre, Brazil. January 28, 2003. www.peacewomen.org/resources/voices/declar/arundhati.html.

Sachs, Wolfgang, ed. *The Development Dictionary: A Guide to Knowledge as Power*. London: Zed Books, 1992.

Sale, Kirkpatrick. *Dwellers in the Land: The Bioregional Vision*. San Francisco: Sierra Club Books, 1985.

Sands, Phillipe, ed. *Greening International Law*. Law and Sustainable Development Series. Sterling, VA: Stylus, 1996.

Sassen, Saskia. *Globalization and Its Discontents: Essays on the New Mobility of People and Money*. New York: New Press, 1998.

Seabrook, Jeremy. *The Myth of the Market: Promises and Illusions*. Devon, UK: Green Books, 1990.

Shiva, Vandana. *The Violence of the Green Revolution: Third World Agriculture, Ecology, and Politics*. Mapusa, Goa, India: The Other India Press, 1991.

———. *Biopiracy: The Plunder of Nature and Knowledge*. Boston: South End Press, 1997.

———. *Stolen Harvest: The Hijacking of the Global Food Supply*. Boston: South End Press, 1999.

———. "U.S. Patent System Legalizes Theft and Biopiracy." *The Hindu*, July 28, 1999.

———. *Water Wars: Privatization, Pollution, and Profit*. Boston: South End Press, 2002.

———. Presentation given to the Poverty, Human Rights, and Equity Panel at the People and the Planet: Changing Values for a Sustainable Future Conference, Kingston, Ontario, Canada, June 6, 2002.

———. "The Jaiv Panchayat–Living Democracy Movement." Presentation given at the Living Democracy Convention (Jaiv Panchayat Adhiveshan), New Delhi, November 17, 2003.

———. *Towards a People-Centered Fair Trade Agreement on Agriculture.* Sandnes, Norway: Transcend: A Peace and Development Network, December 2003. http://www.transcend.org/t_database/articles.php?ida=147.

Shiva, Vandana, Afsar H. Jafri, Gitanjali Bedi, and Radha Holla-Bhar. *The Enclosure and Recovery of the Commons.* New Delhi: Research Foundation for Science, Technology and Ecology, 1997.

Shuman, Michael. *Towards a Global Village: International Community Development Initiatives.* London: Pluto Press, 1994.

———. *Going Local: Creating Self-Reliant Communities in a Global Age.* New York: Routledge, 2000.

Simms, Andrew. *The Environmental War Economy.* London: New Economics Foundation, 2001.

Simms, Andrew, Caroline Lucas, and Mike Woodin. "People's Economics." *Resurgence,* January–February 2004, pp. 10–13.

Singer, Peter. *One World: The Ethics of Globalization.* New Haven: Yale University Press, 2002.

Sitrin, Marina A. "Horizontalism in Argentina." *Left Turn,* August–September 2003, pp. 43–47.

Soros, George. *Open Society: Reforming Global Capitalism.* New York: Public Affairs, 2000.

———. *On Globalization.* New York: Public Affairs, 2002.

Speth, James Gustave. *Red Sky at Morning: America and the Crisis of the Global Environment.* New Haven: Yale University Press, 2004.

Stiglitz, Joseph E. *Globalization and Its Discontents.* New York: W. W. Norton, 2002.

Stone, Michael K. "The Hypercar." *Whole Earth Review,* Winter 2001, p. 53.

Strong, Maurice. *Where on Earth Are We Going?* New York: Thomson Texere, 2001.

Sustainable Energy and Economy Network. *The World Bank and the G-7: Still Changing the Earth's Climate for Business, 1997–98.* Washington, DC: Institute for Policy Studies and the International Trade Information Service, December 1998. www.seen.org.

Suzuki, David, and Holly Dressel. *Good News for a Change: Hope for a Troubled Planet.* Toronto: Stoddart, 2002.

Tellus Institute. *Halfway to the Future: Reflections on the Global Condition.* Boston: Tellus Institute, 2001.

Tickner, Joel. "Precaution Is Common Sense." *Cape Cod Times,* August 27, 2000.

———. "A Map Towards Precautionary Decision Making." In C. Raffensperger and J. Tickner, eds., *Protecting Public Health and the Environment: Implementing the Precautionary Principle.* Washington, DC: Island Press, forthcoming. http://www.cpa.most.org.pl/map.html.

Tickner, Joel, and Carolyn Raffensperger. *The Precautionary Principle in Action: A Handbook*. Ag BioTech InfoNet. www.biotech-info.net/handbook.pdf.

Townsend, Mark, and Paul Harris. "Now the Pentagon Tells Bush: Climate Change Will Destroy Us." *The Observer*, February 22, 2004.

Transnational Resource and Action Center. *Tangled Up in Blue: Corporate Partnerships at the United Nations*. San Francisco: Transnational Resource and Action Center, September 2000. www.corpwatch.org.

United Nations Conference on Trade and Development. *International Monetary and Financial Issues of the Nineties*. Geneva: United Nations, 1992.

———. *Trade and Development Report, 1997*. Geneva: United Nations, 1997.

———. *Trade and Development Report, 1999*. Geneva: United Nations, 1999.

United Nations Department of Economic and Social Affairs. *World Economic and Social Survey, 2001*. New York: United Nations, 2001.

United Nations Development Program. *Human Development Report, 1999*. New York: United Nations Development Program and Oxford University Press, 1999.

———. *Human Development Report, 2001*. New York: United Nations Development Program and Oxford University Press, 2001.

Vallette, Jim, and Daphne Wysham. *Enron's Pawns: How Public Institutions Bankrolled Enron's Globalization Game*. Washington, DC: Institute for Policy Studies, 2002.

Wallach, Lori. "Trade Secrets." *Foreign Policy,* January–February 2004.

Wallach, Lori, and Michelle Sforza. *Whose Trade Organization? Corporate Globalization and the Erosion of Democracy*. Washington, DC: Public Citizen, 1999.

Wallach, Lori, and Patrick Woodall. *Whose Trade Organization? A Comprehensive Guide to the World Trade Organization* (2nd ed.). New York: New Press, 2004.

Wallach, Lori, Michelle Sforza, and Ralph Nader. *The WTO: Five Years of Reasons to Resist Corporate Globalization*. New York: Seven Stories Press, 2000.

Walljasper, Jay, and Jon Spayde, eds. *Visionaries: People and Ideas to Change Your Life*. Gabriola Island, British Columbia: New Society Publishers, 2001.

Warshall, Peter. "An Electric Dragon Mantles the North American Continent." *Whole Earth Review*, Winter 2001, pp. 12–19.

Wasserman, Harvey. *The Last Energy War: The Battle Over Utility Deregulation*. New York: Open Media/Seven Stories Press, 1999.

Welton, Neva, and Linda Wolf. *Global Uprising: Confronting the Tyrannies of the 21st Century*. Gabriola Island, British Columbia: New Society Publishers, 2001.

"Whole Systems Thinking." *Annual Report, 2000–01*. Snowmass, CO: Rocky Mountain Institute.

Williamson, Thad, David Imbroscio, and Gar Alperovitz. *Making a Place for Community: Local Politics in a Globalized World*. New York: Routledge, 2002.

*Wingspread Statement: A Common Sense Way to Protect Health & the Environment*. Paper prepared by the Science & Environmental Health Network, January 25, 1998. www.healthytomorrow.org/pdf/wingspread.pdf.

Woodin, Mike, and Caroline Lucas. *Green Globalisation: A Manifesto*. London: Pluto Press, 2004.

World Bank. *World Development Report, 2000–01*. Washington, DC: World Bank and Oxford University Press, 2001.

———. *Global Development Finance: Financing the Poorest Countries, 2002*. Washington, DC: World Bank, 2002.

World Resources Institute. *A Guide to the Global Environment: The Urban Environment*. New York: Oxford University Press, 1996.

Worldwatch Institute. *Vital Signs 2003: The Trends That are Shaping Our Future*. New York: W. W. Norton, 2003.

# Index

# About the Authors

JOHN CAVANAGH is director of the Washington-based Institute for Policy Studies, vice president of the IFG, and coauthor of eleven books on the global economy, including *Global Dreams: Imperial Corporations and the New World Order.*

JERRY MANDER is president of the IFG, senior fellow at the Public Media Center, and author or coeditor of the best-selling books *In the Absence of the Sacred, The Case Against the Global Economy and for a Turn Toward the Local,* and *Four Arguments for the Elimination of Television.*

SARAH ANDERSON is director of the Global Economy Project at the Institute for Policy Studies and coauthor of *A Field Guide to the Global Economy.*

DEBI BARKER is executive director of the IFG and coauthor of *Invisible Government: The World Trade Organization, Global Government for the New Millennium?*

MAUDE BARLOW is national chair of the Council of Canadians, an IFG board member, and author or coauthor of fourteen books, including *Blue Gold: The Battle Against Corporate Theft of the World's Water*—which has been published in ten countries—and *Profit Is Not the Cure.*

WALDEN BELLO is executive director of the Bangkok-based Focus on the Global South, an IFG board member, and author or coauthor of eleven books, including *The Future in the Balance: Essays on Globalization and Resistance.*

ROBIN BROAD is a professor at the School of International Service at the American University and author of *Global Backlash: Citizen Initiatives for a Just World Economy*.

TONY CLARKE is the director of the Polaris Institute of Canada, vice chair of the Council of Canadians, an IFG board member, and author or coauthor of six books, including *Blue Gold: The Battle Against Corporate Theft of the World's Water*.

EDWARD GOLDSMITH is the founding editor of *The Ecologist*, an IFG board member, author of twenty books including *The Way: An Ecological World View*, and coeditor of *The Case Against the Global Economy and for a Turn Toward the Local*. He was awarded the Right Livelihood Award in 1991.

RANDALL HAYES is president of Rainforest Action Network, U.S. director of Destination Conservation, director of the city of Oakland's Commission on the Environment, an IFG board member, and producer of the award-winning documentary film *The Four Corners: A National Sacrifice Area?*

COLIN HINES is founder and coordinator of the Middlesex-based Protect the Local, Globally, and an IFG associate. He is coauthor of *The New Protectionism: Protecting the Future Against Free Trade* and *Localization: A Global Manifesto*.

ANTONIA JUHASZ is a project director for IFG, directs IFG's media relations, and was coordinator of IFG's report *Does Globalization Help the Poor?* Her writing has appeared in the *New York Times, Cambridge University Review of International Relations, The Star* (South Africa), *Tikkun* magazine, and elsewhere.

ANDREW KIMBRELL is founder and director of the Center for Food Safety, an IFG board member, author of numerous books and articles, editor of and contributing writer to *Fatal Harvest: The Tragedy of Industrial Agriculture*, and a featured guest on such television programs as the *Today Show*, the *Early Show, Good Morning America*, and *Crossfire*.

DAVID KORTEN is founder of the People-Centered Development Forum, an IFG associate, and author of numerous publications, including the now-classic *When Corporations Rule the World* and its sequel, *The Post-Corporate World*.

SARA LARRAIN is cofounder of the Chilean national political party, the Partido Alternative de Cambio, coordinates the Chilean Ecological Action

Network, founded the Chilean office of Greenpeace International, and is an IFG board member. She was the leading independent candidate in the 1999 Chilean presidential election.

VICTOR MENOTTI is the director of IFG's Environment Program, the author of IFG's publications *Free Trade, Free Logging: How the WTO Undermines Global Forest Conservation* and *The WTO and Sustainable Fisheries,* and is a contributing author to *Environmental Impacts of Globalization.*

HELENA NORBERG-HODGE is founder and director of the International Society for Ecology and Culture, an IFG board member, and winner of the Right Livelihood Award. She is the author of numerous publications, including the international classic *Ancient Futures: Learning from Ladakh,* which has been translated into more than thirty languages.

SIMON RETALLACK is managing editor of *The Ecologist* magazine's special issues, codirector of the Climate Initiatives Fund, and an IFG associate. He has written or edited many publications and is a contributing editor and writer for the IFG publication *Environmental Impacts of Globalization.*

VANDANA SHIVA is founder and director of the Research Foundation for Science, Technology, and Natural Resource Policy and an IFG board member. She received the Right Livelihood Award in 1993, and in 2001 was named among the top five "Most Important People in Asia" by *AsiaWeek* magazine. She is author of more than three hundred papers in leading journals and numerous books, including *Monocultures of the Mind: Biodiversity, Biotechnology, and the Third World.*

VICTORIA TAULI-CORPUZ is an indigenous activist of the Kankanaey peoples of the Cordillera region in the Philippines. She is director of the Philippines-based Indigenous Peoples' International Centre for Policy Research and Education and an IFG associate. She is also a member of the World Commission on the Social Dimensions of Globalization and chairperson of the United Nations Voluntary Fund for Indigenous Populations.

LORI WALLACH is director of Public Citizen's Global Trade Watch and an IFG board member. Dubbed the "Trade Debate's Guerrilla Warrior" by the *National Journal,* she is coauthor of *Whose Trade Organization? Corporate Globalization and the Erosion of Democracy.*

# About the International Forum on Globalization (IFG)

The International Forum on Globalization (IFG) is a North-South research and educational institution composed of leading activists, economists, scholars, and researchers who provide analyses and critiques on the cultural, social, political, and environmental impacts of economic globalization. Formed in 1994, the IFG came together out of shared concern that the world's corporate and political leadership was rapidly restructuring global politics and economics on a level that was as historically significant as any period since the Industrial Revolution. Yet there was almost no discussion or even recognition of this new neoliberal model or of the institutions and agreements—the World Trade Organization, the International Monetary Fund, the World Bank, the North American Free Trade Agreement, and other such bureaucracies—enforcing this system. In response, the IFG began to stimulate new thinking, joint activity, and public education about this rapidly rising economic paradigm.

Unique in its diversity, depth, and breadth, the IFG works through an active international board of key citizen movement leaders, a small dedicated staff, and a network of hundreds of associates representing regions throughout the world and a broad spectrum of issues. Our work is closely linked to social justice and environmental movements, providing them with critical thinking and frameworks that inform campaigns and activities on the ground.

The IFG produces numerous publications, from books to background papers for the media; it organizes high-profile, large public events; it hosts many issue-specific seminars around the world; and it participates in many other activities that focus on the myriad consequences of globalization. During the last few years, the IFG has launched a pioneering program that focuses on alternative visions and policies to globalization that are more just, equitable, democratic, accountable, and sustainable for people and the planet.

INTERNATIONAL FORUM ON GLOBALIZATION
1009 General Kennedy Avenue #2
San Francisco, California 94129
United States
(415) 561-7650 (tel.), (415) 561-7651 (fax), www.ifg.org